The Road to the White House 1996

The Politics of Presidential Elections

The Road
to the
White House
1996

The Politics of
Presidential Elections

Stephen J. Wayne
Georgetown University

St. Martin's Press
New York

Editor: Beth A. Gillett
Manager, publishing services: Emily Berleth
Editor, publishing services: Douglas Bell
Project management: York Production Services
Production supervisor: Dennis Para
Text design: Leon Bolognese and Associates
Cover design: Rod Hernandez
Cover photo: COMSTOCK INC./HARTMAN-DEWITT
Back cover: Campaign buttons (Alexander, Clinton/Gore, Dole, Dornan, Gramm, Lugar) courtesy of Bold Concepts Unlimited, New York City; (Buchanan, Powell, Specter) courtesy of The G.O.P. Shoppe/Political Americana.
Interior display buttons: Private collection. Photography by Preston Lyon.

Library of Congress Catalog Card Number: 94-74791

0 9 8 7 6
f e d c b a

For information, write:
St. Martin's Press, Inc.
175 Fifth Avenue
New York, NY 10010

ISBN: 0-312-10593-2

Acknowledgments
   Figure 1–1: "State Size According to Population: The 1992 Electoral Vote," *New York Times*, (December 28, 1990): A9. Copyright © 1990 by The New York Times Company. Reprinted with the permission of the *New York Times*.
   Table 2–1: "Costs of Presidential General Elections, Major Party Candidates, 1860–1972" from Herbert E. Alexander, *Financing Politics: Money, Elections, and Political Reform*, 3rd ed. (Washington, DC: CQ Press, 1984), page 7. Copyright © 1984 by Congressional Quarterly, Inc. Reprinted with the permission of the publishers.
   Table 2–2: "Costs of Presidential Nominations , 1964–1992." Data from 1964–1972 is based on Herbert E. Alexander, *Financing Politics: Money, Elections, and Political Reform*, 3rd ed. 45–47. Copyright © 1984 by Congressional Quarterly, Inc. Reprinted with the permission of the publishers. 1992 estimates based on Herbert E. Alexander and Anthony Corrado, *Financing the 1992 Election* (Armouk, New York: M. E. Sharpe, 1995), tables 2–1 and 2–4. Copyright © 1995 by M. E. Sharpe, Inc. Reprinted with the permission of the publishers.

Acknowledgments and copyrights are continued at the back of the book on pages 329–330, which constitute an extension of the copyright page.

To my mother and father,
Mr. and Mrs. Arthur G. Wayne,
and to the memory of my grandmother,
Mrs. Hattie Marks

Contents

V Appendixes   319

Preface

It is easier to follow a political campaign than to understand it. We read about it in the press, view it on television, and occasionally even see or hear a candidate in person. We observe only what others—the candidates, their advisers, reporters, or a host of other self-interested participants—want us to see, and we are expected to use their views to make a judgment on election day.

There is more, however, to presidential elections than meets the eye. Campaign planners work hard to design a strategy to maximize their vote. They understand the intricacies of the process. They know how the system works, who are its beneficiaries, and where they should concentrate their campaign resources. They understand the requirements of finance legislation—how to comply with it, get around it, and take advantage of it. They appreciate the psychological and social motivations of voters and have a feel for which appeals are likely to be most effective most of the time. They are aware of party rules and the ways to build a winning coalition during the nomination period. They can sense the rhythm of conventions and know when events should be scheduled and how various interests can be placated and orchestrated. They know how to organize and plan a general election campaign and how best to present their candidate to the voters. They can usually predict what will happen in the election and interpret the results so as to enhance their political position and governing potential. They may not need to read this book.

On the other hand, people who want to get behind the scenes of presidential campaigns, who want to know why particular strategies were adopted, certain tactics utilized, which of these strategies and tactics had the desired results, how the candidates dealt with the mass media, why the election turned out the way it did, and what implications the vote has for the new presidents and their ability to govern, should benefit from the information contained in this book.

The Road to the White House, 1996: The Politics of Presidential Elections is a straightforward "nuts-and-bolts" discussion of how the system is designed and works. It is primarily concerned with facts, not opinions; with practice, not theory; with implications, not speculations. It summarizes the state of the art and science of presidential electoral politics.

The book is organized into four main parts. The first discusses the arena in which the election occurs. Its three chapters examine the electoral system, campaign finance, and the political environment. Chapter 1 provides a historical overview of nominations as well as elections; Chapters 2 and 3 examine recent developments. Highlighted are the political considerations that candidates need to consider as they plan and structure their presidential campaigns.

Parts II and III are structured sequentially. They describe distinct yet related stages of the presidential campaign: delegate selection, nominating conventions, and the general election. Chapter 4 examines reforms in the selection of convention delegates and their impact on voters, candidates, and the parties. Chapter 5 carries this discussion to the nominating convention, describing its purposes, procedures, policies, and politics. In Chapter 6, the organization, strategy, and tactics of the general election are discussed. Chapter 7 examines media politics, focusing on how the news media cover the campaign, how the candidates try to affect that coverage, how they circumvented some of it in 1992, and how all of this influences the electorate on election day. Detailed illustrations from the most recent elections are used throughout these chapters.

The fourth part looks at the election and beyond by exploring its implications for the government and for the political system. Chapter 8 discusses and evaluates the presidential vote by asking such questions as: Does it provide a mandate? Does it influence the president's ability to govern? Chapter 9 considers problems in the electoral system and possible reforms. It examines some of the major difficulties that have affected the political system and proposals advanced for dealing with them: how the electoral process can be made more equitable; how it can be made more responsive to popular choice; and how that choice can be conveyed more effectively to elected and appointed officials.

These questions are not easy to answer. Members of Congress, academicians, and other students of the American political system have been debating them for some time, and that debate is likely to continue. Without information on how the system works, we cannot intelligently participate in it or improve on it. In the case of presidential politics, ignorance is definitely not bliss.

The road to the White House is long and arduous. In fact, it has become more difficult to travel than in the past. Yet, surprisingly, there are many travelers. Evaluating their journey is essential to rendering an intelligent judgment on election day. However, more is at stake than simply choosing the occupant of the Oval Office. The system itself is on trial in every presidential election. That is why it is so important to understand and appreciate the intricacies of the process. Only an informed citizenry can determine whether the nation is being well served by the way we go about choosing our president.

Few books are written alone, and this one was no exception. For this edition, I was fortunate to have the wise counsel of my Georgetown colleagues and friends, John Bruce, James Lengle, Diana Owen, and Michael Robinson; and of Anthony Corrado of Colby College and two anonymous reviewers who read parts of the manuscript and made extremely valuable comments and suggestions which greatly improved it. Their knowledge of the presidential electoral system helped me broaden my understanding of it and saved me from a few serious errors and many more careless mistakes. Fengyan Shi, a Ph.D. candidate at Georgetown, served as my research assistant. In countless trips to the library, she reviewed and synthesized the new literature, compiled data on the 1992 elections, and aided me in numerous other ways in revising the manuscript.

Richard Bond, former chairman of the Republican National Committee, made numerous 1992 election memos and studies available to me as well as generously shared his astute political observations. I am also indebted to Rick Boylan and Hemal Vaidya of the Democratic National Committee who also kept me abreast of party rules and scheduling changes in the delegate selection process.

I would also like to express my thanks to other political scientists who reviewed previous editions of this book: Richard L. Cole, University of Texas at Arlington; James W. Davis, Washington University; Gordon Friedman, Southwest Missouri State University; Jay S. Goodman, Wheaton College; Anne Griffin, The Cooper Union; Margorie Randon Hershey, Indiana University; Hugh L. LeBlanc, George Washington University; Kuo-Wei Lee, Pan-American University; Robert T. Nakamura, State University of New York at Albany; Richard G. Niemi, University of Rochester; Charles Prysby, The University of North Carolina at Greensboro; Lester Seligman, University of Illinois; Earl Shaw, Northern Arizona University; John W. Sloan, University of Houston; William H. Steward, University of Alabama; Edward J. Weissman, Washington College; and Clyde Wilcox, Georgetown University. My sincere appreciation is extended to the reviewers of this edition: John Bruce, Georgetown University; Anthony Corrado Jr., Colby College; Stephen C. Craig, University of Florida at Gainesville; Diana Owen, Georgetown University; Michael Robinson, Ph.D.; and Priscilla Southwell, University of Oregon at Eugene.

I also wish to acknowledge with gratitude and thanks the many people at St. Martin's Press, especially Don Reisman, former executive editor, Doug Bell, project editor, and Beth Gillett, former marketing manager and current political science editor, who have contributed in numerous ways to the editing, production, and marketing of this book. I also thank

Dolores Wolfe and others at York Production Services, for their work in production.

Finally, everyone makes personal sacrifices in writing a book. My wife, Cheryl Beil, and my sons, Jared and Jeremy, were no exceptions. As always, they gave me lots of encouragement and put up with long days at the office. Jared, especially, helped me keep my political views in check with his own, very different perspective. I wish to thank my family for being so accommodating and especially so understanding.

Stephen J. Wayne
Georgetown University

About the Author

STEPHEN J. WAYNE (Ph.D., Columbia University) is a professor and the head of the American government program at Georgetown University. Besides being a veteran instructor of American government, he has been a Washington insider specializing in presidential politics for over twenty-five years. He has authored numerous articles and published several books about American government and the presidency, including *The Politics of American Government* (St. Martin's Press, 1995) and *Presidential Leadership* (with George C. Edwards III). Invited frequently to testify before Congress and to lecture to senior federal and corporate executives, Wayne also has shaped public opinion about the presidency and electoral politics as a commentator for radio, television, and newspapers.

The Road to the White House 1996

The Politics of Presidential Elections

PART I

The Electoral Arena

Campaign labels of the forerunners of today's two major parties: left, a 1790 symbol of the Democratic-Republican Party, which became the Democratic Party; right, a symbol used by the Whig Party, forerunner of the Republican Party, in the 1840 election. Their candidates, William Henry Harrison and John Tyler, ran on the slogan "Log Cabin and Hard Cider."

Chapter 1

Presidential Selection: A Historical Overview

INTRODUCTION

The road to the White House is circuitous and bumpy. It contains numerous hazards and potential dead ends. Those who choose to traverse it need considerable skill, perseverance, and luck if they are to be successful. They also need substantial amounts of time and money. For most candidates there is no such thing as a free ride or an easy one to the presidency.

The framers of the Constitution worked for several months on the presidential selection system, and their plan has since undergone a number of constitutional, statutory, and precedent-setting changes. Modified by the development of parties, the expansion of suffrage, the growth of the media, and the revolution in modern communications technology, the system has become more open and participatory but also more contentious, more complex, and more expensive.

This chapter is about that system: why it was created; what it was supposed to do; what compromises were incorporated in the original plan; how it initially operated; what changes subsequently affected that operation; whom these changes have benefited; and what effect all of this has had for the parties, the electorate, and American democracy.

In addressing these questions, I have organized the chapter into four sections. The first discusses the creation of the presidential election process. It explores the motives and intentions of the delegates at Philadelphia and describes the procedures for selecting the president within the context of the constitutional and political issues of that day.

The second section examines the development of nominating systems. It explores the three principal methods that have been used—partisan congressional caucuses, brokered national conventions, and state primaries and caucuses—and describes the political forces that helped to shape them and, in the case of the first two, destroyed them.

The third section discusses presidential elections. It focuses on the most controversial ones: those decided by the House of Representatives (1800 and 1824), those influenced by Congress (1876), and those unreflective of popular choice (1888) or in which a relatively small number of votes could have changed the outcome (1960, 1968, and 1976). In doing so, the section highlights the evolution of the Electoral College.

The final section of the chapter examines the current system. It describes its geographic and demographic biases, whom it benefits, and whom it hurts. The section also discusses the system's major party orientation and its effect on third party candidacies.

THE CREATION OF THE ELECTORAL COLLEGE

Among the many issues facing the delegates at the Constitutional Convention of 1787 in Philadelphia, the selection of the president was one of the toughest. Seven times during the course of the convention the method for choosing the executive was altered.

The framers' difficulty in designing electoral provisions for the president stemmed from the need to guarantee the institution's independence and, at the same time, create a technically sound, politically effective mechanism that would be consistent with a republican form of government. They were sympathetic with a government based on consent, a representative government, but not with direct democracy, a government in which every citizen has an opportunity to participate in the formulation of public policy. They wanted a system that would choose the most qualified person but not necessarily the most popular. There seemed to be no precise model to follow.

Three methods had been proposed. The Virginia plan, a series of resolutions designed by James Madison and introduced by Governor Edmund Randolph of Virginia, provided for legislative selection. Eight states chose their governors in this fashion at the time. Having Congress choose the president would be practical and politically expedient. Moreover, members of Congress could have been expected to exercise a considered judgment. Exercising a rational judgment was important to the delegates at Philadelphia, since many of them did not consider the average citizen capable of making a reasoned, unemotional choice.

The difficulty with legislative selection was the threat it posed to the institution of the presidency. How could the executive's independence be preserved if the election of the president hinged on popularity with Congress and reelection on the legislature's appraisal of the president's performance in office? Only if the president were to serve a long term and not be eligible for reelection, it was thought, could the institution's independence be protected so long as Congress was the electoral body. But ineligibility also posed problems, as it provided little incentive for the president to perform well and denied the country the possibility of reelecting a person whose experience and success in office demonstrated qualifications that were superior to others.

Reflecting on these concerns, Gouverneur Morris urged the removal of the ineligibility clause on the grounds that it tended to destroy the great motive to good behavior, the hope of being rewarded by a reappointment.[1] A majority of the states agreed. Once the ineligibility clause was deleted, however, the terms of office had to be shortened to prevent what the framers feared might become almost indefinite tenure. With a shorter term of office and permanent reeligibility, legislative selection was not nearly as desirable, since it could make the president beholden to the legislature.

Popular election was another alternative, although one that did not generate a great deal of enthusiasm. It was twice rejected in the convention by overwhelming votes. Most of the delegates felt that a direct vote by the people was neither desirable nor feasible.[2] Lacking confidence in the public's ability to choose the best-qualified candidate, many delegates also believed that the size of the country and the poor state of its communications and transportation precluded a national campaign and election. The geographic expanse was simply too large to permit proper supervision and control of the election. Sectional distrust and rivalry also contributed to the difficulty of holding a national election.

A third alternative was some type of indirect election in which popular sentiment could be expressed but would not dictate the selection. James Wilson first proposed this idea after he failed to generate support for a direct popular vote. Luther Martin, Gouverneur Morris, and Alexander Hamilton also suggested an indirect popular election through intermediaries. It was not until the debate over legislative selection divided and eventually deadlocked the delegates, however, that election by electors was seriously considered. Proposed initially as a compromise toward the end of the convention, the Electoral College system was accepted after a short debate. Viewed as a safe, workable solution to the selection problem, it was deemed consistent with the constitutional and political features of the new government. Popular election of the electors was not precluded, but neither was it encouraged by the compromise.

According to the proposal, presidential electors were to be chosen by the states in a manner designated by their legislatures. To ensure their independence, the electors could not simultaneously hold a federal government position. The number of electors was to equal the number of senators and representatives from each state. At a designated time the electors would vote and send the results to Congress, where they would be announced to a joint session by the president of the Senate—the vice-president. The only limitation on the voting was that the electors could not cast *both* their ballots for inhabitants of their own states.[3]

Under the original plan, the person who received a majority of votes cast by the Electoral College was elected president, and the one with the second highest total was vice-president. There was no separate ballot for each office. In the event that no one received a majority, the House of Representatives would choose from among the five candidates with the most electoral votes, with each state delegation casting one vote. If two or more individuals were tied for second, then the Senate would select the vice-president from among them. Both of these provisions were subsequently modified by the Twelfth Amendment to the Constitution.

The electoral system was a dual compromise. Allowing state legislatures to establish the procedures for choosing electors was a concession to the proponents of a federal system; having the House of Representatives decide if there was no Electoral College majority, was designed to please those who favored a stronger national government. Designating the number of electors to be equal to a state's congressional delegation gave the larger states an advantage in the initial voting for president; balloting by states in the House if the Electoral College was not decisive benefited the smaller states.

The large-small state compromise was critical to the acceptance of the Electoral College plan. It was argued during the convention debates that in practice the large states would nominate the candidates for president and the small states would exercise the final choice.[4] So great were sectional rivalry and distrust at the time, that the prospect of a majority of the college agreeing on anyone other than George Washington seemed remote.

THE DEVELOPMENT OF NOMINATING SYSTEMS

Although the Constitution prescribed a system for electing a president, it made no reference to the nomination of candidates. Political parties had not emerged prior to the Constitutional Convention. Factions existed, and the framers of the Constitution were concerned about them, but the development of a party system was not anticipated. Rather, it was assumed that electors, whose interests were not tied to the national government, would make an independent judgment in choosing the best possible person as president.

In the first two elections the system worked as intended. George Washington was the unanimous choice of the electors. There was, however, no consensus on who the vice-president should be. The eventual winner, John Adams, benefited from some discussion and informal lobbying by prominent individuals prior to the vote.[5]

A more organized effort to agree on candidates for the presidency and vice-presidency was undertaken in 1796. Partisan alliances were beginning to develop in Congress. Members of the two principal groups, the Federalists and the Anti-Federalists, met separately to recommend individuals. The Federalists chose Vice-President Adams; the Anti-Federalists picked Governor George Clinton of New York.

With political parties evolving during the 1790s, the selection of the electors quickly became a partisan contest. In 1792 and 1796 a majority of the state legislatures chose them directly. Thus, the political group that controlled the legislature also controlled the selection. Appointed for their political views, electors were expected to exercise a partisan judgment. When in 1796 a Pennsylvania elector did not, he was accused of faithless behavior. Wrote one critic in a Philadelphia newspaper: "What, do I chuse Samuel Miles to determine for me whether John Adams or Thomas Jefferson shall be President? No! I chuse him to act, not to think."[6]

Washington's decision not to serve a third term forced Federalist and Anti-Federalist members of Congress to recommend the candidates in 1796. Meeting separately, party leaders agreed among themselves on the tickets. The Federalists urged their electors to vote for John Adams and Thomas Pinckney, while the Anti-Federalists (or Republicans, as they began to be called) suggested Thomas Jefferson and Aaron Burr.

Since it was not possible to indicate the presidential and vice-presidential choices on the ballot, Federalist electors, primarily from New England, decided to withhold votes from Pinckney (of South Carolina) to make certain that he did not receive the same number as Adams (of Massachusetts). This strategy enabled Jefferson to finish ahead of Pinckney with 68 votes compared with the latter's 59, but behind Adams, who had 71. Four years of partisan differences followed between a president who, though he disclaimed a political affiliation, clearly favored the Federalists in appointments, ideology, and policy, and a vice-president who was the acknowledged leader of the opposition party.

Beginning in 1800, partisan caucuses composed of members of Congress met for the purpose of recommending their party's nominees. The Republicans continued to choose candidates in this manner until 1824; the Federalists did so only until 1808. In the final two presidential elections in which the Federalists ran candidates, 1812 and 1816, top party leaders, meeting in secret, decided on the nominees.[7]

"King caucus" violated the spirit of the Constitution. It effectively provided for Congress to pick the nominees. After the decline of the Federalists, the nominees were, in fact, assured of victory—a product of the dominance of the Jeffersonian Republican party as well as the success of the caucus in obtaining support for its candidates.

Opposition arose within the caucuses. In 1808, Madison prevailed over James Monroe and George Clinton. In 1816, Monroe overcame a strong challenge from William Crawford. In both cases, however, the electors united behind the successful nominee. In 1820, they did not. Disparate elements within the party selected their own candidates.

Although the caucus was the principal mode of candidate selection during the first part of the nineteenth century, it was never formally institutionalized as a nominating body. How meetings were called, by whom, and when varied from election to election. So did attendance. A sizable number of representatives chose not to participate at all. Some stayed away on principle; others did so because of the choices they would have to make. In 1816, less than half of the Republican members of Congress were at their party's caucus. In 1820, only 20 percent attended, and the caucus had to adjourn without formally supporting President Monroe and Vice-President Daniel D. Tompkins for reelection. In 1824, almost three-fourths of the members boycotted the session.

The 1824 caucus did nominate candidates. But with representatives from only four states constituting two-thirds of those attending, the nominee, William Crawford, failed to receive unified party support. Other candidates were nominated by state legislatures and conventions, and the electoral vote was divided. Since no candidate obtained a majority, the House of Representatives had to make the final decision. John Quincy Adams was selected on the first ballot. He received the votes of thirteen of the twenty-four state delegations.

The caucus was never resumed. In the end it fell victim to the decline of one of the major parties, the decentralization of political power, and Andrew Jackson's stern opposition. The Federalists had collapsed as a viable political force. As the Republican party grew from being the majority party to the only one, factions developed within it, the two principal ones being the National Republicans and the Democratic Republicans. In the absence of a strong opposition there was little to hold these factions together. By 1830, they had split into two separate groups, one supporting and one opposing President Jackson.

Political leadership was changing as well. A relatively small group of individuals had dominated national politics for the first three decades after the writing of the Constitution. Their common experience in the Revolutionary War, the Constitutional Convention, and the early government produced personal contacts, political influence, and public respect that contributed to their ability to agree on candidates and to generate public support for them.[8]

Those who followed them in office had neither the tradition nor the national orientation in which to frame their presidential selection. Most of this new generation of political leaders owed their prominence and political influence to state and regional areas. Their loyalties reflected these bases of support. The growth of party organizations at the state and local level affected the nomination system. In 1820 and 1824, it produced a decentralized mode of selection. State legislatures, caucuses, and conventions nominated their own candidates. Support was also mobilized on regional levels.

Whereas the congressional caucus had become unrepresentative, state-based nominations suffered from precisely the opposite problem. They were too sensitive to sectional interests and produced too many candidates. Unifying diverse elements behind a national ticket proved extremely difficult, although Jackson was successful in 1824 and again in 1828. Nonetheless, a system that was more broadly based than the old caucus and could provide a decisive and mobilizing mechanism was needed. National nominating conventions filled the void.

The first such convention was held in 1831 by the Anti-Masons. A small but relatively active third party, it had virtually no congressional representation. Unable to utilize a caucus, the party turned instead to a general meeting, which was held in a saloon in Baltimore, with 116 delegates from thirteen states attending. These delegates decided on the nominees as well as on an address to the people that contained the party's position on the dominant issues of the day.

Three months later a second convention was held in the same saloon by opponents of President Jackson. The National Republicans (or Whigs, as they later became known) also nominated candidates and agreed on a platform critical of the Jackson administration.

The following year the Democratic Republicans (or Democrats, as they were later called) also met in Baltimore. The impetus for their convention was Jackson's desire to demonstrate popular support for his presidency as well as to ensure the selection of Martin Van Buren as his running mate. In 1836, Jackson resorted to another convention—this time to handpick Van Buren as his successor.

The Whigs did not hold a convention in 1836. Believing that they would have more success in the House of Representatives than in the nation as a whole, they ran three regional candidates, nominated by the states, who competed against Van Buren in areas of their strength. The plan, however, failed to deny Van Buren an electoral majority. He ended up with 170 votes compared with a total of 124 for the other principal contenders.

Thereafter, the Democrats and their opponents, first the Whigs and then their Republican successors, held nominating conventions to select their candidates. The early conventions were informal and rowdy by contemporary standards, but they also set the precedents for later meetings.

The delegates decided on the procedures for conducting the convention, policy statements (addresses to the people), and the nominees. Rules for apportioning the delegates were established before the meetings were held. Generally speaking, states were accorded as many votes as their congressional representation merited, regardless of the number of actual participants. The way in which the delegates were chosen, however, was left up to the states. Local and state conventions, caucuses, or even committees chose the delegates.

Public participation was minimal. Even the party's rank and file had a small role. It was the party leaders who designated the delegates and made the deals. In time it became clear that successful candidates owed their selection to the heads of the powerful state organizations and not to their own political prominence and organizational support. The price they had to pay, however, when calculated in terms of patronage and other types of political payoffs, was often quite high.

Nineteenth-century conventions served a number of purposes. They provided a forum for party leaders, particularly at the state level. They constituted a mechanism by which agreements could be negotiated and support mobilized. By brokering interests, conventions helped unite the disparate elements within the party, thereby converting an organization of state parties into a national coalition for the purpose of conducting a presidential campaign.

Much of the bartering was conducted behind closed doors. Actions on the convention floor often had little to do with the wheeling and dealing that occurred in the smaller "smoke-filled rooms." Since there was little public preconvention activity, many ballots were often necessary before the required number, usually two-thirds of the delegates, was reached.

The nominating system buttressed the position of individual state party leaders, but it did so at the expense of rank-and-file participation. The influence of the state leaders depended on their ability to deliver votes, which in turn required that the delegates not exercise an independent judgment. To guarantee their loyalty, the bosses controlled their selection.

Demands for reform began to be heard at the beginning of the twentieth century. The Progressive movement, led by Robert La Follette of Wisconsin and Hiram Johnson of California, desired to break the power of state bosses and their machines through the direct election of convention delegates or, alternatively, through the expression of a popular choice by the electorate.

Florida became the first state to provide its political parties with such an option. In 1904, the Democrats took advantage of it and held a statewide vote for convention delegates. One year later, Wisconsin enacted a law for the direct election of delegates to nominating conventions. Others followed suit. By 1912, fifteen states provided for some type of primary election. Oregon was the first to permit a preference vote for the candidates themselves.

The year 1912 was also the first in which a candidate sought to use primaries as a way to obtain the nomination. With almost 42 percent of the Republican delegates selected in primaries, former President Theodore Roosevelt challenged incumbent William Howard Taft. Roosevelt won nine primaries to Taft's one, yet lost the nomination. (See Table 1–1.) Taft's support among regular party leaders who delivered their delegations and controlled the convention was sufficient to retain the nomination. He received one-third of his support from southern delegations, although the Republican party had won only a small percentage of the southern vote in the previous election.

TABLE 1–1

Number of Presidential Primaries and Percentage of Convention Delegates from Primary States, by Party, 1912–1996

	Democratic[†]		Republican	
Year	Number of Primaries	Percentage of Delegates from Primary States*	Number of Primaries	Percentage of Delegates
1912	12	32.9%	13	41.7%
1916	20	53.5	20	58.9
1920	16	44.6	20	57.8
1924	14	35.5	17	45.3
1928	17	42.2	16	44.9
1932	16	40.0	14	37.7
1936	14	36.5	12	37.5
1940	13	35.8	13	38.8
1944	14	36.7	13	38.7
1948	14	36.3	12	36.0
1952	15	38.7	13	39.0
1956	19	42.7	19	44.8
1960	16	38.3	15	38.6
1964	17	45.7	17	45.6
1968	17	37.5	16	34.3
1972	23	60.5	22	52.7
1976	29*	72.6	28*	67.9
1980	31*	74.7	35*	74.3
1984	26	62.9	30	68.2
1988	34	66.6	35	76.9
1992	39	78.8	38	80.4
1996[a]	37	83.5	41	85.9

* Does not include Vermont, which holds nonbinding presidential preference votes but chooses delegates in state caucuses and conventions.

[†] Includes party leaders and elected officials chosen from primary states.

[a] Based on preliminary primary and caucus schedules as of April 1995.

Sources: 1912–1964, F. Christopher Arterton, "Campaign Organizations Face the Mass Media in the 1976 Presidential Nomination Process" (paper delivered at the Annual Meeting of the American Political Science Association, Washington, D.C., September 1–4, 1977); 1968–1976, Austin Ranney, *Participation in American Presidential Nominations, 1976* (Washington, D.C.: American Enterprise Institute, 1977), table 1, p. 6. The figures for 1980 were compiled by Austin Ranney from materials distributed by the Democratic National Committee and the Republican National Committee; figures for elections since 1980 were compiled by the author from data supplied by the Democratic and Republican National Committees.

Partially in reaction to the unrepresentative, "boss-dominated" convention of 1912, additional states adopted primaries. By 1916, more than half of them held a Republican or Democratic contest. Although a majority of the delegates in that year were chosen by some type of primary, many of them were not bound to specific candidates. As a consequence, the primary vote did not control the outcome of the conventions.

The movement toward popular participation was short-lived, however. Following World War I the number of primaries declined. State party leaders, who saw these elections as a threat to their own influence, argued against them on three grounds: they were expensive; they did not attract many voters; and major candidates tended to avoid them. Moreover, primaries frequently encouraged factionalism, thereby weakening the party's organizational structure.

In response to this criticism the reformers, who supported primaries, could not claim that their principal goal—rank-and-file control over the party's nominees—had been achieved. Public involvement was disappointing. Primaries rarely attracted more than 50 percent of those who voted in the general election, and usually much less. The minority party, in particular, suffered from low turnout. In some states rank-and-file influence was further diluted by the participation of independents.

As a consequence of these factors, some states that had enacted new primary laws reverted to their former method of selection. Others made the primaries advisory rather than mandatory. Fewer delegates were selected in them. By 1936, only fourteen states held Democratic primaries, and twelve held Republican ones. Less than 40 percent of the delegates to each convention that year were chosen in this manner. For the next twenty years the number of primaries and the percentage of delegates hovered around this level.

Theodore Roosevelt's failure in 1912 and the decline in primaries thereafter made them at best an auxiliary route to the nomination. Although some presidential aspirants became embroiled in them, none who depended on them won. In 1920, a spirited contest between three Republicans (General Leonard Wood, Governor Frank Lowden of Illinois, and Senator Hiram Johnson) failed to produce a convention majority and resulted in party leaders' choosing Warren Harding as the standard-bearer. Similarly, in 1952, Senator Estes Kefauver, who chaired the highly publicized Senate hearings on organized crime, entered thirteen of seventeen presidential primaries, won twelve of them, became the most popular Democratic contender, but failed to win his party's nomination. The reason Kefauver could not parlay his primary victories into a convention victory was that a majority of the delegates were not selected in this manner. Of those who were, many were chosen separately from the presidential preference vote. Kefauver did not contest these separate delegate elections. As a consequence, he obtained only 50 percent of the delegates in states where he actually won the presidential preference vote. Moreover, the fact that most of his wins occurred against little or no opposition undercut Kefauver's claim to being the most popular and most electable Democrat. He had avoided primaries in four states where he feared that he might either lose or do poorly.

Not only were primaries not considered to be an essential road to the nomination, but running in too many of them was interpreted as a sign of weakness, not strength. It indicated a lack of national recognition or a failure to obtain the support of party leaders or both. For these reasons, leading candidates tended to choose their primaries carefully, and the primaries, in turn, tended to reinforce the position of the leading candidates.

Those who did enter primaries did so mainly to test their popularity rather than to win convention votes. Dwight D. Eisenhower in 1952, John F. Kennedy in 1960, and Richard M. Nixon in 1968 had to demonstrate that being a general, a Catholic, or a once-defeated presidential candidate would not be fatal to their chances. In other words, they needed to prove they could win the general election.

With the possible exception of John Kennedy's victories in West Virginia and Wisconsin, primaries were neither crucial nor decisive for winning the nomination until the 1970s. When there was a provisional consensus within the party, primaries helped confirm it; when there was not, primaries could not produce it.[9] In short, they had little to do with whether the party was unified or divided at the time of the convention.

Primary results tended to be self-fulfilling in the sense that they confirmed the front-runner's status. Between 1936 and 1968, the preconvention leader, the candidate who was ahead in the Gallup Poll before the first primary, won the nomination seventeen out of nineteen times. The only exceptions were Thomas E. Dewey in 1940, who was defeated by Wendell Willkie, and Kefauver in 1952, who lost to Adlai Stevenson. Willkie, however, had become the leader in public opinion by the time the Republican convention met. Even when leading candidates lost a primary, they had time to recoup. Dewey and Stevenson, defeated in early primaries in 1948 and 1956, respectively, went on to reestablish their credibility as front-runners by winning later primaries.

This situation in which the primaries were not the essential route to the nomination changed dramatically after 1968. Largely as a consequence of the tumultuous Democratic convention of that year, in which the party's nominee and platform were allegedly dictated by party "bosses," demands for a larger voice for rank-and-file partisans increased. In reaction to these demands, the Democratic party began to look into the matter of delegate selection. It enacted a series of reforms designed to ensure broader representation at its convention. To avoid challenges to their delegations, a number of states that had used caucus and convention systems changed to primaries. As Table 1–1 indicates, the number of primaries began to increase as did the percentage of convention delegates chosen from them.

New finance laws, which provided for government subsidies of preconvention campaigning, and increased media coverage, particularly by television, also added to the incentive to enter primaries. By 1972, primaries became decisive. In that year, Senator Edmund Muskie, the leading Democratic contender at the beginning of the process, was forced to withdraw after doing poorly in the early contests; in 1976, President Gerald Ford came close to being the first incumbent president since Chester A. Arthur in 1884 to be formally denied his party's nomination because of a primary challenge by Ronald Reagan. In 1980, President Jimmy Carter was also challenged for renomination by Senator Edward Kennedy as was George Bush by Pat Buchanan in 1992.

Since the 1970s, primaries have revolutionized the presidential nomination process. They are used to build popularity rather than simply reflect it. Challengers can no longer hope to succeed without entering them; incumbents can no longer ignore them.

Their impact has been significant, affecting the strategies and tactics of the candidates, the composition and behavior of the convention delegates, and the decision-making process at the national conventions. These nomination contests have shifted power within the party. They have enlarged the selection zone of potential nominees. They have also made governing more difficult. Each of these developments will be discussed in the chapters that follow.

THE EVOLUTION OF THE GENERAL ELECTION

The general election has changed as well. The Electoral College no longer operates in the manner in which it was designed. It now has a partisan coloration. There is greater public participation, but it is still not direct. Although the system bears a resemblance to its past, it has become more democratic. However, it continues to contain electoral biases.

The electoral system for president and vice-president was one of the few innovative features of the Constitution. It had no immediate precedent, although it bore some relationship to the way the state of Maryland selected its senators. In essence, it was invented by the framers, not synthesized from British and American experience, and it is one aspect of the system that has rarely worked as intended.

Initially, the method by which the states chose their electors varied. Some provided for direct election in a statewide vote. Others had the legislatures do the choosing. Two states used a combination of popular and legislative selection.

As political parties emerged around the turn of the nineteenth century, state legislatures maneuvered the selection process to benefit the party in power. This maneuvering resulted in the election of more cohesive groups of electors who shared similar partisan views. Gradually, the trend evolved into a winner-take-all system, with electors chosen on a statewide basis by popular vote. South Carolina was the last state to move to popular selection, doing so only after the Civil War.

The development of the party system changed the character of the Electoral College. Only in the first two elections, when Washington was the unanimous choice, did the electors exercise a nonpartisan and presumably independent judgment. Within ten years from the time the federal government began to operate, they quickly became the captives of their party and were expected to vote for its candidates. The outcome of the election of 1800 vividly illustrates this new pattern of partisan voting.

The Federalist party supported President John Adams of Massachusetts and Charles C. Pinckney of South Carolina. The Republicans, who had emerged to oppose the Federalists' policies, backed Thomas Jefferson of Virginia and Aaron Burr of New York. The Republican candidates won, but, unexpectedly, Jefferson and Burr received the same number of votes. All electors who had cast ballots for Jefferson also cast them for Burr. Since it was not possible in those days to differentiate the candidates for the presidency and vice-presidency on the ballot, the results had to be considered a tie, though Jefferson was clearly his party's choice for president. Under the terms of the Constitution, the House of Representatives, voting by state, had to choose the winner.

On February 11, 1801, after the results of the Electoral College vote were announced by the vice-president, who happened to be Jefferson, the House convened to resolve the dilemma. It was a Federalist-controlled House. Since the winners of the 1800 election were not to take office until March 4, 1801, a "lame-duck" Congress would have to choose the next president.[10] A majority of Federalists supported Burr, whom they regarded as the more pragmatic politician. Jefferson, on the other hand, was perceived as a dangerous, uncompromising radical by many Federalists. Alexander Hamilton, however, was outspoken in his opposition to Burr, a political rival from New York, whom Hamilton regarded as "the most unfit man in the United States for the office of President."[11]

On the first ballot taken on February 11, Burr received a majority of the total votes, but Jefferson won the support of more state delegations.[12] Eight states voted for Jefferson, six backed Burr, and two were evenly divided. This left Jefferson one short of the needed majority. The House took nineteen ballots on its first day of deliberations, and a total of thirty-six before it finally elected Jefferson. Had Burr promised to be a Federalist president, it is conceivable that he would have won.

The first amendment to reform voting procedures in the Electoral College was enacted by the new Congress, controlled by Jefferson's party, in 1803. It was accepted by three-fourths of the states in 1804. This amendment to the Constitution, the twelfth, provided for separate voting for president and vice-president. It also refined the selection procedures in the event that the president or vice-president did not receive a majority of the electoral vote. The House of Representatives, still voting by states, was to choose from among the three presidential candidates with the most electoral votes, and the Senate, voting by individuals, was to choose from the top two vice-presidential candidates. If the House could not make a decision by March 4, the amendment provided for the new vice-president to assume the presidency until such time as the House could render a decision.

The next nondecisive presidential vote did not occur until 1824. That year, four people received electoral votes for president: Andrew Jackson (99 votes), John Quincy Adams (84), William Crawford (41), and Henry Clay (37). According to the Twelfth Amendment, the House of Representatives had to decide from among the top three, since none had a majority. Eliminated from the contest was Henry Clay, who happened to be Speaker of the House. Clay threw his support to Adams, who won. It was alleged that he did so in exchange for appointment as secretary of state, a charge that Clay vigorously denied. After Adams became president, however, he did appoint Clay secretary of state.

Jackson was the winner of the popular vote. In the eighteen states that chose electors by popular vote that year out of a total of twenty-four, he received 192,933 votes compared with 115,696 for Adams, 47,136 for Clay, and 46,979 for Crawford. Adams of Massachusetts, however, had the backing of more state delegations. He enjoyed the support of the six New England states, and with Clay's help, the representatives of six others backed his candidacy. The votes of thirteen states, however, were needed for a majority. New York seemed to be the pivotal state and Stephen Van Rensselaer, a Revolutionary War general, the swing representative. On the morning of the vote, Speaker Clay and Representative Daniel Webster tried to persuade Van Rensselaer to vote for Adams. It was said that they were unsuccessful.[13] When the voting began, Van Rensselaer bowed his head as if in prayer. On the floor he saw a piece of paper with "Adams" written on it. Interpreting this as a sign from the Almighty, he dropped the paper in the box. New York went for Adams by one vote, providing him with a bare majority.[14]

Jackson, outraged at the turn of events, urged the abolition of the Electoral College. His claim of a popular mandate, however, was open to question. The most populous state at the time, New York, did not permit its electorate to participate in the selection of electors. Rather, the New York legislature made the decision. Moreover, in three of the states in which Jackson won the electoral vote but lost in the House of Representatives, he had fewer popular votes than Adams.[15]

Opposition to the system mounted, however, and a gradual democratization of the process occurred. More states began to elect their electors directly by popular vote. In 1800, ten of the fifteen used legislative selection. By 1832, only South Carolina retained this practice.

The trend was also toward statewide election of an *entire* slate of electors. Those states that had chosen their electors within legislative districts converted to a winner-take-all system in order to maximize their voting power in the Electoral College. This change, in turn, created the possibility that there could be a disparity between the popular and electoral vote. A candidate could be elected by winning the popular vote in the big states by small margins and losing the smaller states by large margins.

The next disputed election did not occur until 1876. In that election Democrat Samuel J. Tilden received the most votes. He had 250,000 more popular votes and 19 more electoral votes than his Republican rival, Rutherford B. Hayes. Nonetheless, Tilden fell one vote short of a majority in the Electoral College. Twenty electoral votes were in dispute. Dual election returns were received from Florida (4), Louisiana (8), and South Carolina (7). Charges of fraud and voting irregularities were made by both parties. The Republicans, who controlled the three state legislatures, contended that Democrats had forcibly prevented newly freed blacks from voting. The Democrats, on the other hand, alleged that many nonresidents and nonregistered people had participated. The other disputed electoral vote occurred in the state of Oregon. One Republican elector was challenged on the grounds that he held another federal position (postmaster) at the time he was chosen and thus was ineligible to be an elector.

Three days before the Electoral College vote was to be officially counted, Congress established a commission to examine and try to resolve the dispute. The electoral commission was to consist of fifteen members: ten from Congress (five Republicans and five Democrats) and five from the Supreme Court. Four of the Supreme Court justices were designated by the act (two Republicans and two Democrats), and they were to choose a fifth justice. David Davis, a political independent, was expected to be selected, but on the day the commission was created, Davis was appointed by the Illinois legislature to the United States Senate. The Supreme Court justices then picked Joseph Bradley, an independent Republican. Bradley sided with his party on every issue. By a strictly partisan vote, the commission validated all the Republican electors, thereby giving Hayes a one-vote margin of victory.[16]

The only other election in which the winner of the popular vote was beaten in the Electoral College occurred in 1888. Democrat Grover Cleveland had a plurality of 95,096 popular votes but only 168 electoral votes compared with 233 for the Republican, Benjamin Harrison. Cleveland's loss of Indiana by about 3,000 votes and New York by about 15,000 led to his defeat.

Although all other leaders in the popular vote have won a majority of electoral votes, shifts of just a few thousand popular votes in a few states could have altered the results of other elections. In 1860, a shift of 25,000 in New York from Abraham Lincoln to Stephen A. Douglas would have denied Lincoln a majority in the Electoral College. A change of less than 30,000 in three states in 1892 would have given Harrison another victory over Cleveland. In 1916, Charles Evans Hughes needed only 3,807 more votes in California to have beaten Woodrow Wilson. Similarly, Thomas E. Dewey could have denied Harry S. Truman a majority in the Electoral College with 12,487 more California votes in 1948. In 1960, a change of less than 9,000 in Illinois and Missouri would have meant that John F. Kennedy lacked an Electoral College majority. In 1968, a shift of only 55,000 votes from Richard M. Nixon to Hubert H. Humphrey in three states (New Jersey, Missouri, and New Hampshire) would have thrown the election into the House—a House controlled by Democrats. In 1976, a shift of only 3,687 in Hawaii and 5,559 in Ohio would have cost Jimmy Carter the election.[17]

Not only could the results of these elections have been affected by very small voter shifts in a few states, but in 1948, 1960, 1968, and 1992, there was the further possibility that the Electoral College itself would not be able to choose a winner. In each of these elections, third party candidates or independent electoral slates threatened to secure enough votes to prevent either of the major candidates from obtaining a majority. In 1948, Henry Wallace (Progressive party) and Strom Thurmond (States' Rights party) received almost 5 percent of the total popular vote, and Thurmond won 39 electoral votes. In 1960, fourteen unpledged electors were chosen in Alabama and Mississippi.[18] In 1968, Governor George Wallace of Alabama, running on the American Independent party ticket, received almost 10 million popular votes, 13.5 percent of the total, and 46 electoral votes. In 1992, independent H. Ross Perot received 19.7 million popular votes but none in the Electoral College.[19] Nonetheless, it is clear that close competition between the major parties, combined with a strong third party movement, provides the Electoral College with its most difficult test.

THE POLITICS OF ELECTORAL COLLEGE VOTING

The Electoral College is not neutral. No system of election can be. The way votes are aggregated does make a difference. It benefits some of the electorate and adversely affects others.

The Electoral College usually works to the advantage of the majority; more often than not, it has exaggerated the margin of the popular vote leader. Bill Clinton received only 43 percent of the popular vote in 1992 but 69 percent of the electoral vote. Similarly in 1968, Richard Nixon won only 43.4 percent of the popular vote but 56 percent of the electoral vote. Jimmy Carter's election in 1976 resulted in a smaller disparity. He won 50.1 percent of the popular vote and 55 percent of the electoral vote. In 1980, Ronald Reagan received 51 percent of the popular vote but a whopping 91 percent of the electoral vote.

Although the Electoral College has usually expanded the margin of the popular vote winner, it has also from time to time led to the defeat of

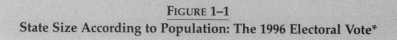

FIGURE 1–1
State Size According to Population: The 1996 Electoral Vote*

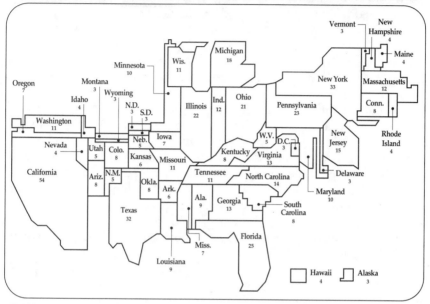

* Each state has a vote in the Electoral College equal to the number of its representatives plus two.

Source: *New York Times*, December 28, 1990, p. A9.

the candidate with the most popular votes. On three occasions—1824, 1876, and 1888—the plurality winner was a loser in the Electoral College. Even though such an electoral loss would be less likely today because the parties are competitive in more states, it is still possible.

The Electoral College contains a number of built-in biases. One of them has already been mentioned—it tends to enhance the victory of the candidate with the largest popular vote. The reason for this "majority bias" is the winner-take-all system of voting that has developed. In almost every instance the presidential and vice-presidential candidates who receive a plurality of the popular vote within the state get all its electoral votes.

In addition to benefiting the candidate with the most votes, this arrangement increases the influence of the largest states, not only because of the number of electoral votes they cast but because the votes are almost always cast in a bloc.[20] Moreover, the advantage that the citizens of the largest states receive increases in proportion to their population. (See Figure 1–1 for the relative advantage large populations confer on the states.)

This large-state advantage is why a greater share of campaign time and resources is spent in these states.

By giving an edge to the larger and more competitive states, the Electoral College also works to benefit groups that are geographically concentrated within those states and have cohesive voting patterns. Those who live in urban areas have a particular advantage. Jewish and Hispanic voters and immigrant populations fall into this category. Rural voters do not. In general African-Americans are disadvantaged by the Electoral College because of their high concentration in small and medium-sized southern states.[21]

There is a slight offsetting gain for the very smallest states. That each receives a minimum of three electoral votes regardless of size increases the voting power of the sparsely populated states. For example, if Wyoming's 1992 population of approximately 466,000 were divided by its three electoral votes, there would be one elector for every 155,333 people. Dividing California's population of 30,867,000 by the 54 electoral votes yields one elector for every 571,778 people. Medium-sized states are comparatively disadvantaged.[22]

Additionally, the Electoral College works to benefit the two major parties. Despite the fact that Republicans have won five of the last seven presidential elections, two political scientists, James C. Garand and T. Wayne Parent, found that it has favored the Democratic candidates more than Republican candidates over the years although the authors could not explain this partisan bias.[23]

The advantage given to the majority parties results in a disadvantage for minority parties. The winner-take-all system within states, when combined with the need for a majority within the college, makes it difficult for third parties to accumulate enough votes to win an election. To have any effect, third party support must be geographically concentrated, as George Wallace's was in 1968 and Strom Thurmond's was in 1948, rather than more broadly distributed across the country, as Henry Wallace's was in 1948 and H. Ross Perot's was in 1992.

Given the limitations on third parties, their most realistic electoral objectives would seem to be to defeat one of the major contenders rather than to elect their own candidate. In 1912, Theodore Roosevelt's Bull Moose campaign split the Republican party, thereby aiding the candidate of the Democratic party, Woodrow Wilson. In more recent elections, third party and independent candidates have cost the major parties votes but do not appear to have changed the outcome of the elections. Truman's loss of Michigan and New York in 1948 apparently was a consequence of Henry Wallace's Progressive party candidacy, and George Wallace in 1968 probably denied Nixon 46 more electoral votes from the South. However, George Wallace's 11.4 percent of the Missouri vote and his 11.8 percent in Ohio probably hurt Humphrey more than Nixon and may explain the loss of these two states by the Democratic candidate. Ford's narrow victory in

Iowa in 1976 (632,863 to 619,931) may be partially attributed to the 20,051 votes Eugene McCarthy received as an independent candidate, votes that very likely would have gone to Carter had McCarthy not run. Surveys of voters in 1992 indicate that Perot drew slightly more support from Republicans than Democrats.

The impact on third parties is more than simply a question of numbers. It affects the psychology of voting for a candidate who has little chance of winning a majority of the electoral vote and may have had little experience in government. In 1980, the Carter and Reagan campaigns appealed to voters sympathetic to John Anderson on the first of these grounds. They urged them not to waste their vote on a candidate who could not win. This "wasted vote" appeal undercut Anderson's ability to raise money and garner political support. In 1992, however, the perception that independent Ross Perot could not win may have had the opposite effect, encouraging those who wished to cast a protest vote to do so without fear of electing their protest candidate president.[24]

SUMMARY

The quest for the presidency has been and continues to be influenced by the system designed in Philadelphia in 1787. The objectives of that system were to protect the independence of the institution, to ensure the selection of a well-qualified candidate, and to do so in a way that was politically expedient. It was intended to be consistent with the tenets of a republican form of government.

Although many of the objectives are still the same, the system has changed significantly over the years. Of all the factors that have influenced these changes, none has been more important than the advent of political parties. This development created an additional first step in the process—the nomination—which has influenced the selection and behavior of the electors and has affected the operation and the beneficiaries of the Electoral College itself.

The nomination process is necessary to the parties, whose principal interest is to get their candidates elected. At first, members of Congress, meeting in partisan caucuses, decided on the nominees. On the basis of common friendships and shared perspectives, they reached a consensus and then used their influence to mobilize support for it. In effect, the system provided for legislative selection of the president in violation of the letter and spirit of the Constitution.

The caucus method broke down with the weakening of the parties, the demise of the Federalists, and the factionalization of the Republicans. It was never restored. In its place developed a more decentralized mode of selection reflective of the increasing sectional composition of the parties.

The new nomination process, controlled by state leaders, operated within the framework of a brokered national convention. There was little rank-and-file participation. The wheeling and dealing were done for the party's electorate, not by them. Demands for greater public involvement eventually opened the system, thereby reducing the influence of state leaders and decreasing the dependence of candidates on them. Power eventually shifted from the political leaders to the candidates themselves, with the people making the final judgment.

Similar trends, rooted in the development of parties and the expansion of suffrage, affected the way in which the electors were selected and how they voted. Instead of being chosen on the basis of their qualifications, electors were selected on the basis of their politics; instead of being elected as individuals, entire slates of electors were chosen; instead of exercising independent judgment, the electors became partisan agents who were morally and politically obligated to support their party's choice. The predictable soon happened: bloc voting by electors in states.

The desire of the populace for greater participation also had an effect. It accelerated the movement to choose the electors directly by the people, which resulted in an increased likelihood of the electoral vote's reflecting, even exaggerating, the popular vote. Only three times in U.S. history has the plurality winner not been elected; however, the shift of a very small number of votes in a few states could have altered the results of other elections, most recently in 1960, 1968, and 1976. This situation raises doubts about the adequacy of the system.

The equity of the Electoral College itself has also come into question. The way it works benefits the larger, more competitive states with the most electoral votes. Within those states, the groups that are better organized, more geographically concentrated, and more cohesive in their voting behavior seem to enjoy the greatest advantage. Their vote is maximized by the winner's taking all the state's electoral votes and the state's having a larger share of the total Electoral College. Candidates keep this size factor in mind when planning and conducting their campaigns.

In summary, the electoral system has been decisive and efficient, but questions about its equity remain. It does not jeopardize the president's independence. In fact, it may do just the opposite; it may isolate the selection of president and vice-president too much from that of other officials for national office. It permits a partisan choice but recently has not contributed to the strength of the party inside or outside the government. It facilitates participation in the nomination process but has not until recently raised the level of public involvement in the general election. The winning candidate often obtains only a bare majority or plurality of the voters, who, in recent elections, have constituted barely half the voting age population. Only 23.7 percent of the eligible population voted for Bill Clinton in 1992, hardly the mandate we might expect in a democracy nor one that is sufficient for governing effectively.

NOTES

1. Gouverneur Morris, *Records of the Federal Convention,* ed. Max Farrand (New Haven, Conn.: Yale University Press, 1921), pp. 2; 33.
2. The first proposal for direct election was introduced in a very timid fashion by James Wilson, delegate from Pennsylvania. James Madison's *Journal* describes Wilson's presentation as follows: "Mr. Wilson said he was almost unwilling to declare the mode which he wished to take place, being apprehensive that it might appear chimerical. He would say however at least that in theory he was for an election by the people; Experience, particularly in N. York & Massts, shewed that an election of the first magistrate by the people at large, was both convenient & successful mode." Farrand, *Records of the Federal Convention,* pp. 1; 68.
3. So great was the sectional rivalry, so parochial the country, so limited the number of people with national reputations, that it was feared that electors would tend to vote primarily for those from their own states. To prevent the same states, particularly the largest ones, from exercising undue influence in the selection of both the president and vice-president, this provision was included. It remains in effect today.
4. George Mason declared, "Nineteen times out of twenty, the President would be chosen by the Senate." Farrand, *Records of the Federal Convention,* pp. 2; 500. The original proposal of the Committee on Unfinished Business was that the Senate should select the president. The delegates substituted the House of Representatives, fearing that the Senate was too powerful with its appointment and treaty-making powers. The principle of equal state representation was retained. Choosing the president is the only occasion on which the House votes by states.
5. Thomas R. Marshall, *Presidential Nominations in a Reform Age* (New York: Praeger, 1981), p. 19.
6. Quoted in Neal R. Peirce and Lawrence D. Longley, *The People's President* (New Haven, Conn.: Yale University Press, 1981), p. 36.
7. Marshall, *Presidential Nominations,* p. 20.
8. Ibid., p. 21.
9. Louis Maisel and Gerald J. Lieberman, "The Impact of Electoral Rules on Primary Elections: The Democratic Presidential Primaries in 1976," in *The Impact of the Electoral Process,* ed. Louis Maisel and Joseph Cooper (Beverly Hills, Calif.: Sage Publications, 1977), p. 68.
10. Until the passage of the Twentieth Amendment, which made January 3 the date when members of Congress took their oath of office and convened, it was the second session of the preelection Congress that convened *after* the election. This made it a lame-duck session.
11. Quoted in Lucius Wilmerding, *The Electoral College* (New Brunswick, N.J.: Rutgers University Press, 1953), p. 32.
12. There were 106 members of the House (58 Federalists and 48 Republicans). On the first ballot, the vote of those present was for Burr, 53–51.
13. Peirce and Longley, *People's President,* p. 51.
14. Marquis James, *The Life of Andrew Jackson* (Indianapolis: Bobbs-Merrill, 1938), p. 439.
15. He captured the majority of electoral votes in two of these states because the electors were chosen on a district rather than statewide basis. William R. Keech, "Background Paper," in *Winner Take All: Report of the Twentieth Century*

Fund Task Force on Reform of the Presidential Election Process (New York: Holmes and Meier, 1978), p. 50.

16. The act that created the commission specified that its decision would be final unless overturned by both houses of Congress. The House of Representatives, controlled by the Democrats, opposed every one of the commission's findings. The Republican Senate, however, concurred. A Democratic filibuster in the Senate was averted by Hayes's promise of concessions to the South, including the withdrawal of federal troops. Tilden could have challenged the findings in court but chose not to do so.

17. Richard M. Scammon and Alice V. McGillivray, *America Votes* 12 (Washington, D.C.: Congressional Quarterly, 1977), p. 15.

18. In Alabama, slates of electors ran against one another without the names of the presidential candidates appearing on the ballot. The Democratic slate included six unpledged electors and five loyalists. All were elected. The unpledged electors voted for Senator Harry Byrd of Virginia, while the loyalists stayed with the Kennedy-Johnson ticket. In Mississippi, all eight Democratic electors voted for Byrd.

19. He came in second in two states, Maine and Utah.

20. Theoretically, two states, Maine and Nebraska, will not always vote as a bloc because they do not select all their electors on an at-large basis. Two are chosen at-large and the remaining ones are elected in each of the states' congressional districts. Since these states have enacted their electoral laws, however, they have cast all their electoral votes for the same candidate.

21. Lawrence D. Longley and James D. Dana, Jr., "The Biases of the Electoral College in the 1990s," *Polity* 25 (Fall 1992): 140–145.

22. Ibid., p. 134.
    There are two other, less obvious, biases in the electoral college. The distribution of electoral votes is calculated on the basis of the census, which occurs every ten years. Thus, the college does not mirror population shifts within this period. Nor does it take into account the number of people who actually cast ballots. It is a state's population, not its turnout, that determines the number of electoral votes it receives, over and above the automatic three.

23. James C. Garand and T. Wayne Parent, "Representation, Swing, and Bias in U. S. Presidential Elections, 1872–1988," *American Journal of Political Science,* 35 (November 1991): 1024, 1029.

24. For a discussion of motivations for voting for independent and third party candidates see Steven J. Rosenstone, Roy L. Behr, and Edward H. Lazarus, *Third Parties in America: Citizen Response to Major Party Failure* (Princeton, N.J.: Princeton University Press, 1984.)

SELECTED READINGS

Abbot, David W., and James P. Levine. *Wrong Winner: The Coming Debacle in the Electoral College.* New York: Praeger, 1991.

Banzhaf, John F. III. "One Man, 3312 Votes: A Mathematical Analysis of the Electoral College," *Villanova Law Review,* 13 (Winter 1968): 303–346.

Best, Judith. *The Case Against Direct Election of the President: A Defense of the Electoral College.* Ithaca, N.Y.: Cornell University Press, 1975.

Bickel, Alexander M. *Reform and Continuity: The Electoral College, the Convention, and the Party System.* New York: Harper & Row, 1971.

Chase, James S. *Emergence of the Presidential Nominating Convention, 1789–1832.*

Urbana, Ill.: University of Illinois Press, 1973.

Congressional Quarterly. *Presidential Elections Since 1789*. Washington, D.C.: Congressional Quarterly, 1995.

Farrand, Max. *The Records of the Federal Convention of 1787*. Vol. 1–5. New Haven, Conn.: Yale University Press, 1911.

Glennon, Michael J. *When No Majority Rules: The Electoral College and Presidential Succession*. Washington D.C.: Congressional Quarterly, 1993.

Longley, Lawrence D., and James D. Dana, Jr. "The Biases of the Electoral College in the 1990s," *Polity* 25 (Fall 1992): 123–145.

Marshall, Thomas R. *Presidential Nominations in a Reform Age*. New York: Praeger, 1981.

Nelson, Michael. "Constitutional Aspects of the Elections," in Michael Nelson (ed.) *The Elections of 1988*. Washington, D.C.: Congressional Quarterly, 1989, pp. 181–209.

Peirce, Neal R., and Lawrence D. Longley. *The People's President*. New Haven, Conn.: Yale University Press, 1981.

Rabinowitz, George, and Stuart Elaine MacDonald," The Power of the States in U. S. Presidential Elections," *American Political Science Review* 80 (March 1986): 65–87.

Roseboom, Eugene H. *A History of Presidential Elections*. New York: Macmillan, 1957.

Smith, Eric R.A.N., and Peverill Squire. "Direct Election of the President and the Power of the States," *Western Political Quarterly* 40 (March 1987): 29–44.

Sundquist, James. *Constitutional Reform and Effective Government*. Washington, D.C.: Brookings Institution, 1986.

United States Senate, Committee on the Judiciary. *The Electoral College and Direct Election*. Hearings, 95th Cong., 1st sess. Washington, D.C.: Government Printing Office, 1977.

____, Committee on the Judiciary. *Hearings on Direct Popular Election of the President and Vice President of the United States*. 96th Cong., 1st sess. Washington, D.C.: Government Printing Office, 1979.

Chapter 2

Campaign Finance

INTRODUCTION

Running for president is very expensive. In 1988, $500 million was spent by major party candidates in their quest for the nomination and election.[1] In 1992, with a major nomination contest in only one party, that amount still increased by 10 percent to $550 million. Of this, $153.2 million was spent on the preconvention nomination, $59.6 million on the conventions, and $310.5 million during the general election with an additional $26.7 as miscellaneous expenses.[2]

The magnitude of these expenditures poses serious problems for presidential candidates, who must raise considerable sums during the preconvention struggle, monitor their expenses closely, make important allocation decisions, and conform to the intricacies of finance laws during both the nomination and general election campaigns. Moreover, such large expenditures raise important issues for a democratic selection process. This chapter explores some of these problems and issues.

The chapter is organized into five sections. The first details the costs of presidential campaigns, paying particular attention to the increase in expenditures since 1960. The next section looks briefly at the contributors, the size of their gifts, and the implications of large donations for a democratic selection process. What happens when the individual's right to give conflicts with government's desire to set limits and level the playing field? Who prevails? Congressional attempts to control spending and subsidize elections are discussed in the third section. The fourth section examines the impact of campaign finance laws on revenues and expenditures in presidential campaigns and on the party system. In the final section, the relationship between campaign spending and electoral success is explored. Can money buy elections? Have the big spenders been the big winners?

THE COSTS OF CAMPAIGNING

Candidates have always spent money in their quest for the presidency, but it was not until they began to campaign personally across the country that these costs rose sharply. In 1860, Abraham Lincoln spent an estimated $100,000. One hundred years later, John Kennedy and Richard Nixon were each spending one hundred times that amount. In the twelve years following the 1960 general election, expenditures increased from about $20 million to over $90 million, an increase that far outstripped the inflation rate during that period. Table 2–1 lists the costs of the major party candidates in presidential elections from 1860 to 1972, the last general election in which campaign spending by major party candidates was unrestricted.

Prenomination costs have risen even more rapidly than those in the general election. Until the 1960s, large expenditures were the exception, not the rule, for gaining the party's nomination. General Leonard Wood spent an estimated $2 million in an unsuccessful quest to head the Republican ticket in 1920. The contest between General Dwight D. Eisenhower and Senator Robert A. Taft in 1952 cost about $5 million, a total that was not exceeded until 1964, when Nelson Rockefeller and Barry Goldwater together spent approximately twice that amount.

In recent elections preconvention expenditures have skyrocketed. The increasing number of primaries, caucuses, and candidates has been largely responsible for the rise. In the 1950s, these preconvention contests were optional; since the 1970s, they have been mandatory. Even incumbent presidents have to enter, and they spend money even when they are not challenged. In 1984, the Reagan campaign committee spent almost $28 million during the nomination period, much of it on voter registration drives for the general election; in 1992, George Bush spent over $27 million in defeating Pat Buchanan, a conservative newspaper columnist who had not previously sought public office. In total, the major party candidates spent over $117.6 million and minor party candidates spent $5.7 million in 1992.[3]

The expenditures for the 1996 nominations will be even greater, approximating $33 million plus fund-raising, legal and accounting expenses for several of the Republican candidates and for President Clinton. To campaign simultaneously in several states requires considerable money to pay for professional services, large organizations, and direct and indirect voter contact. Identifying potential supporters, contacting

TABLE 2-1
Costs of Presidential General Elections, Major Party Candidates, 1860–1972

Year	Democrats		Republicans	
1860	Stephen Douglas	$50,000	Abraham Lincoln*	$100,000
1864	George McClellan	50,000	Abraham Lincoln*	125,000
1868	Horatio Seymour	75,000	Ulysses Grant*	150,000
1872	Horace Greeley	50,000	Ulysses Grant*	250,000
1876	Samuel Tilden	900,000	Rutherford Hayes*	950,000
1880	Winfield Hancock	335,000	James Garfield*	1,100,000
1884	Grover Cleveland*	1,400,000	James Blaine	1,300,000
1888	Grover Cleveland	855,000	Benjamin Harrison*	1,350,000
1892	Grover Cleveland*	2,350,000	Benjamin Harrison	1,700,000
1896	William Jennings Bryan	675,000	William McKinley*	3,350,000
1900	William Jennings Bryan	425,000	William McKinley*	3,000,000
1904	Alton Parker	700,000	Theodore Roosevelt*	2,096,000
1908	William Jennings Bryan	629,341	William Taft*	1,655,518
1912	Woodrow Wilson*	1,134,848	William Taft	1,071,549
1916	Woodrow Wilson*	2,284,950	Charles Evans Hughes	2,441,565
1920	James Cox	1,470,371	Warren Harding*	5,417,501
1924	John Davis	1,108,836	Calvin Coolidge*	4,020,478
1928	Alfred Smith	5,342,350	Herbert Hoover*	6,256,111
1932	Franklin Roosevelt*	2,245,975	Herbert Hoover	2,900,052
1936	Franklin Roosevelt*	5,194,751	Alfred Landon	8,892,972
1940	Franklin Roosevelt*	2,783,654	Wendell Willkie	3,451,310
1944	Franklin Roosevelt*	2,169,077	Thomas Dewey	2,828,652
1948	Harry Truman*	2,736,334	Thomas Dewey	2,127,296
1952	Adlai Stevenson	5,032,926	Dwight Eisenhower*	6,608,623
1956	Adlai Stevenson	5,106,651	Dwight Eisenhower*	7,778,702
1960	John Kennedy*	9,797,000	Richard Nixon	10,128,000
1964	Lyndon Johnson*	8,757,000	Barry Goldwater	16,026,000
1968†	Hubert Humphrey	11,594,000	Richard Nixon*	25,042,000
1972	George McGovern	30,000,000	Richard Nixon*	61,400,000

* Indicates winner.

† George Wallace spent an estimated $7 million as the candidate of the American Independent party in 1968.

Source: Herbert E. Alexander, *Financing Politics* (Washington, D.C.: Congressional Quarterly, 1984), p. 7. Copyrighted material printed with permission of Congressional Quarterly Inc.

them, and getting them to the polls are expensive. The need for television advertising and the price of purchasing it have increased significantly. As a consequence, preconvention expenditures since 1968 have usually exceeded those in the general elections although in 1992, Ross Perot's independent presidential campaign swelled general election expenditures. Table 2–2 lists the totals spent in the last eight campaigns for the major party nominations.

The news media—newspapers, radio, and particularly television—account for much of the spending. This was not always so. When campaigns were conducted in the press, expenses were relatively low. Electioneering, as carried on by a highly partisan press before the Civil War, had few costs other than for the occasional biography and campaign pamphlet printed by the party and sold to the public at less than cost.

With the advent of more active public campaigning toward the middle of the nineteenth century, candidate organizations turned to buttons, billboards, banners, and pictures to symbolize and illustrate their campaigns. By the beginning of the twentieth century, the cost of this type of advertising in each election exceeded $150,000, a lot of money then but a minuscule amount by contemporary standards.[4]

In 1924, radio was employed for the first time in presidential campaigns. The Republicans spent approximately $120,000 that year, whereas the Democrats spent only $40,000.[5] Four years later, however, the two parties together spent more than $1 million. Radio expenses continued to equal or exceed a million dollars per election for the next twenty years.[6]

TABLE 2–2

Costs of Presidential Nominations, 1964–1992 (in millions of dollars)

Year	Democrats	Republicans
1964	(uncontested)	$10
1968	$25	20
1972	33.1	*
1976	40.7	26.1
1980	41.7	86.1
1984	107.7	28.0
1988	94.0	114.6
1992	66.0[†]	51.0

* During a primary in which Richard M. Nixon's renomination was virtually assured, Representative John M. Ashbrook spent $740,000 and Representative Paul N. McCloskey spent $550,000 in challenging Nixon.

[†] Estimates based on Alexander and Corrado, *Financing the 1992 Elections*, Tables 2–1 and 2–4.

Sources: 1964–1972, Herbert E. Alexander, *Financing Politics* (Washington, D.C.: Congressional Quarterly, 1976), pp. 45–47; 1976–84, Federal Election Commission, "Reports on Financial Activity, 1987–88, *Presidential Pre-Nomination Campaigns*," (August 1989), Table A–7, p. 10; Herbert E. Alexander, "Financing the Presidential Elections" (Paper presented at the Institute for Political Studies in Japan, Tokyo, Japan, September 8–10, 1989), pp. 4. 10; Herbert E. Alexander and Anthony Corrado, *Financing the 1992 Elections* (Armonk, N. Y.: M. E. Sharpe, 1995.)

Television emerged as a vehicle for presidential campaigning in 1952. Both national party conventions were broadcast by television as well as radio. Although there were only 19 million television sets in the United States, almost one-third of the people were regular television viewers. The number of households with television sets rose dramatically over the next four years. By 1956 an estimated 71 percent had television, and by 1968 the figure was close to 95 percent; today it exceeds 98 percent, with most homes having two or more sets. Cable subscribers have increased to 60 percent of American households.[7]

The first commercials for presidential candidates appeared in 1952. They became regular fare thereafter, contributing substantially to campaign costs. Film biographies, interview shows, political rallies, and election-eve telethons were all seen with increasing frequency.

In 1948, no money was spent on television by either party's candidate. Twenty years later, expenses exceeded $18 million for radio and television combined, approximately one-third of the total cost of the campaign. By 1992, television expenses exceeded $92 million. This amount, although significant, pales by comparison with what major corporations such as General Motors, Ford, and Procter and Gamble spend promoting their products.

The use of other modern technology has also increased expenditures. In 1968, Democrats Hubert Humphrey and George McGovern spent $650,000 between them on polling, whereas in 1972 the Nixon campaign alone spent more than $1.6 million.[8] In 1992, these expenses approximated $3.5 million for the presidential nomination and election.[9]

Finally, the costs of fund raising have increased. In the past, candidates depended on a relatively small number of large contributors and could personally solicit the funds they needed. Today, most of them depend on a relatively large number of smaller contributors. Although the average size of the contribution has increased in recent years, the proportion of the adult population giving money to candidates has declined. In 1992, only about four percent of the population contributed.[10] The need for private funds combined with the declining proportion of givers has forced candidates to devote considerable time, money, and effort to fundraising activities.

Dwight Eisenhower was the first presidential candidate to make use of the direct mail technique to raise money. His letter to *Reader's Digest* subscribers promising to go to Korea to end the war generated a substantial financial return for his campaign. Unable to obtain support from their parties' regular contributors, Barry Goldwater in 1964 and George McGovern in 1972 targeted appeals to partisans and other sympathizers. Their success, even though they had been well behind in the preelection polls, combined with changes in the law that prohibited large gifts yet ultimately required more spending, has made direct mail solicitation essential for parties and candidates alike. In 1992, Pat Buchanan depended on it to raise $4 million. Robert Dole hopes to raise at least 30 percent of his funds from direct mail in 1996.[11]

Three major issues arise from the problems of large expenditures. One pertains to the donors. Who pays, how much can they give, and what do they get for their money? A second relates to the costs. Are they too high, and can they be controlled without impinging on First Amendment freedoms? The third concerns the impact of spending on the election itself. To what extent does it improve a candidate's chances to win? The next section turns to the first of these questions—the private sources of financial support—and attempts to regulate them. Later in the chapter the other questions are addressed.

THE SOURCES OF SUPPORT

Throughout most of U. S. electoral history, parties and candidates have depended on large contributions. In the midst of the industrial boom at the end of the nineteenth century, the Republicans were able to count on the support of the Astors, Harrimans, and Vanderbilts; while the Democrats looked to financier August Belmont and inventor-industrialist Cyrus McCormick. Corporations, banks, and life insurance companies soon became prime targets of party fund raisers. The most notorious and probably the most adroit fund raiser of this period was Mark Hanna. A leading official of the Republican party, Hanna owed most of his influence to his ability to obtain substantial political contributions. He set quotas, personally assessing the amount that businesses and corporations should give. In 1896, and again in 1900, he was able to obtain contributions of $250,000 from Standard Oil. Theodore Roosevelt personally ordered the return of some of the Standard Oil money in 1904 but accepted large gifts from magnates E. H. Harriman and Henry C. Frick.[12] Roosevelt's trust-busting activities during his presidency led Frick to remark, "We bought the son of a bitch and then he did not stay bought."[13]

Sizable private gifts remained the principal source of party and candidate support until the mid-1970s. In 1972, Richard Nixon and George McGovern raised an estimated $27 million from fewer than 200 individual contributors.[14] In general, the Republicans benefited more than the Democrats from wealthy contributors, known in the campaign vernacular as "fat cats." Only in 1964 was a Democrat—incumbent Lyndon B. Johnson, who enjoyed a large lead in the preelection polls—able to raise more money from large donors than his Republican opponent, Barry Goldwater.

The reluctance of regular Republican contributors to support the Goldwater candidacy forced his organization to appeal to thousands of potential supporters through a direct mailing. The success of this effort in raising $5.8 million from approximately 651,000 people showed the potential of the mails as a fund-raising technique and shattered an unwritten "rule" of politics that money could not be raised by mail. In 1968, Alabama Governor George Wallace, running as a third party candidate, solicited the bulk of his funds in this fashion as did Pat Buchanan in 1992.

Despite the use of mass mailings and party telethons to broaden the base of political contributors in the 1960s, dependence on large donors continued to grow. In 1964, more than $2 million was raised in contributions of $10,000 or more. Eight years later, approximately $51 million was collected in gifts of this size or larger. Some gifts were in the million-dollar range.

The magnitude of these contributions, combined with the heavy-handed tactics of the Nixon fund raisers in 1971–72, brought into sharp focus the difficulty of maintaining a democratic selection process that was dependent on private funding.[15] Reliance on large contributors, who often did not wish their gifts to be made public, the inequality of funding between parties and candidates, and the high cost of campaigning, especially in the media, all raised serious issues. Were there assumptions implicit in giving and receiving? Could elected officials be responsive to individual benefactors and to the general public at the same time? Put another way, did the need to obtain and keep large contributors affect decision making in a manner that was inconsistent with the tenets of a democratic society that all people have equal influence on the selection of and access to public officials? Did the high cost of campaigning, in and of itself, eliminate otherwise qualified candidates from running? Were certain political parties, interest groups, or individuals consistently advantaged or disadvantaged by the distribution of funding? Had the presidency become an office that only the wealthy could afford—or that only those with wealthy support could seek?

FINANCE LEGISLATION

Reacting to these issues, Congress in the 1970s enacted far-reaching legislation designed to reduce dependence on large donors, discourage illegal contributions, broaden the base of public support, and control escalating costs at the presidential level. Additionally, the Democratically-controlled Congress that passed these laws wanted to equalize the funds available to the Republican and Democratic nominees. Finally, the legislation was designed to buttress the two-party system, making it more difficult for minor candidates to challenge major party nominees for elective office successfully.

One law, the Federal Election Campaign Act of 1971 (FECA), set ceilings on the amount of money presidential and vice-presidential candidates and their families could contribute to their own campaigns and the amount that could be spent on media advertising; it also established procedures for the public disclosure of all contributions over a certain amount.

A second statute, the Revenue Act of 1971, created tax credits and deductions to encourage private contributions. It also provided the basis for public funding by creating a presidential election fund. Financed by an income tax checkoff provision, the fund allowed a taxpayer, beginning in 1973, to designate $1 of federal income taxes to a special presidential election account.

These laws began a period of federal government involvement in the presidential electoral process. The history of that involvement is a history of good intentions built on political compromise but marred by unintended consequences of the legislation and its implementation.

Partisan compromises in the enactment of campaign finance legislation were evident from the outset. Although the original funding provision was enacted in 1971, it did not go into effect until the 1976 presidential election. Most Republicans had opposed the policy of government support and regulation. In addition to conflicting with their general ideological position that the national government's role in the conduct of elections be limited, it offset their party's traditional fund-raising advantage. President Nixon was persuaded to sign the bill but only after the Democratic leadership agreed to delay the year in which the law became effective until after Nixon ran for reelection in 1972.

There was also a short but critical delay in the effective date for the disclosure provision of the other 1971 campaign finance act. Signed by the president on February 14, 1972, it was scheduled to take effect in sixty days. This delay precipitated a frantic attempt by both parties to tap large donors who wished to remain anonymous. It is estimated that the Republicans collected $20 million, much of it pledged beforehand, during this period. Of this money, approximately $1.5 million came in forms that could not be easily traced.

Even after the disclosure provision went into effect, violations were numerous. Moreover, pressure on corporate executives by Nixon campaign officials, resulted in a long list of "gifts" that seemed to be in violation of the ban on contributions by corporations and labor unions. The spending of funds on "dirty tricks" and other unethical and illegal activities, such as the burglary of the Democratic National Committee's headquarters, further aroused public ire and eventually resulted in new and more stringent legislation.

Congress responded by amending the Federal Election Campaign Act of 1971. The new provisions, passed in 1974, included public disclosure provisions, contribution ceilings, spending limits, and federal subsidies for major party candidates in the nomination process and complete funding for them in the general election. A six-person commission was established to enforce the law. Two members of the Federal Election

Commission (FEC) were to be appointed by the president and four by Congress.

The amendments were highly controversial. Critics immediately charged a federal giveaway, a robbery of the treasury. Opponents of the legislation also argued that the limits on contributions and spending violated the constitutionally guaranteed right to freedom of speech, that the funding provisions unfairly discriminated against third party and independent candidates, and that appointment of four of the commissioners by Congress violated the principle of separation of powers. One year after the amendments were enacted, the Supreme Court declared some of these portions of the law unconstitutional.

In the landmark decision of *Buckley* v. *Valeo* (424 U.S. 1, 1976), the Court upheld the right of Congress to regulate campaign expenditures but negated two principal parts of the law: the overall limits on spending, and the appointment by Congress of four of the six election commissioners. The majority opinion contended that by placing restrictions on the amount of money an individual or group could spend during a campaign, the law directly and substantially restrained freedom of speech, a freedom protected by the First Amendment to the Constitution. The Supreme Court did allow limits on contributions to candidates' campaigns, however, and limits on expenditures of those candidates who accepted public funds. In doing so, the Court acknowledged that large, often secret, contributions and rapidly increasingly expenditures did pose problems for a democracy, problems that Congress could address.

The Court's decision required that the election law be amended once again. It took Congress several months to do so. In the spring of 1976, during the presidential primaries, amendments were enacted that continued public funding of the presidential nomination and election, based on a figure of $10 million in 1974 adjusted for inflation, but did so on a voluntary basis. Candidates did not have to accept government funds; however, if they did, they were limited in how much they could spend. The amount that could be contributed by individuals and groups to a candidate was also limited. The Federal Election Commission was reconstituted with all six members to be nominated by the president and appointed subject to the advice and consent of the Senate. The law required that three commissioners be Democrats and three Republican.

In 1979, additional amendments to the Federal Election Campaign Act were passed. Designed to reduce the reporting requirements of the law, these amendments raised the minimum contribution and expenditure that had to be filed. To encourage voluntary activities and higher turnout, they also permitted state and local party committees to raise and spend an unlimited and unreported amount of money on get-out-the-vote activities.

Known as the *soft money* provision, this amendment created a gigantic loophole in the law. It permitted, even encouraged, parties to solicit large contributions and distribute the money to state and local parties as they saw fit. It was not until 1992 that the FEC imposed reporting requirements on all soft-money contributions over $200, the total amount of money that the national party allocated to the states, and the individual expenses they spent on soft-money operations.

The amendments to the FECA enacted in 1979 also increased the base grant for nominating conventions of the major parties to $3 million. In 1984, this was subsequently increased to $4 million. This amount is also adjusted for inflation.

The last change in finance legislation occurred in 1993. In that year the Democratically-controlled Congress raised the amount that individual

---

Box 2–1

Key Provisions of
Campaign Finance Legislation

Public disclosure: All contributions of $200 or more must be identified. All expenditures of $200 or more must be reported. Campaign committees are also required to file periodic reports before the election and a final report after it.

Contribution limits: In any election, including a primary, contributions from an individual cannot exceed $1,000 to a single candidate, $20,000 to a national political party committee, and $5,000 to other political committees, with the total not to exceed $25,000 in any one year.

Personal contributions from candidates or their immediate families are limited to $50,000 at the prenomination stage and to $50,000 in the general election if a candidate accepts federal funds. Candidates who do not accept federal funds are not limited to what they can contribute to their own campaign. Individuals and political action committees can spend an unlimited amount on their own for candidates of their choice, provided they do not consult or communicate in any way with the candidate's campaign organization.

Campaign expenses: Candidates who accept public funding cannot spend more than $10 million in their quest for the nomination and $20 million in the general election plus a cost-of-living increment calculated from the base year of 1974. In 1992, the limits were $27.6 million in the postconvention period plus a 20 percent increment for fund raising ($5.5 million), for a total of $32.1 million. In the general election candidates could spend $55.2; however, they could also raise additional money from private donors to pay for accounting and legal costs to comply with the law.

taxpayers could designate to the presidential election fund from $1 to $3. The increase, approximately equal to the inflation that had occurred over the 20-year period, was necessitated by an expected shortfall in the fund in 1996, a shortfall resulting from increasing disbursements to candidates but decreasing checkoffs by taxpayers, unadjusted for inflation. In 1980, 28.7 percent of the returns (in which people owed taxes to the government) designated that $1 or $2 dollars (depending whether the return was individual or joint) go to the election fund; by 1992, that percentage had declined to 17.7.[16] In 1995, legislation was introduced in the Republican Congress to reconsider the issue of public funding. (For a summary of the key provisions of the law, see Box 2–1, "Key Provisions of Campaign Finance Legislation.")

There are also specific spending limits in the states for nomination expenditures. These limits are based on the size of the voting-age population in the state. Candidates who do not accept federal funds have no limit on their expenditures. Additionally, the national parties can spend two cents per citizen of voting age in support of their presidential and vice-presidential candidates. State and local parties can, however, spend unlimited amounts on voluntary efforts to get out the vote.

Matching funds: Major party contenders who raise $5,000 in twenty states in contributions of $250 or less, a total of $100,000, are eligible to receive matching grants during the prenomination period, which begins January 1 of the year in which the election occurs. Only the first $250 of each contribution is matched. In 1992, the government provided $42.9 million in matching funds.

Communication notices: All authorized advertisements by candidates' organizations must state the name of the candidate or agent who authorized them. All nonauthorized advertisements must identify the person who made or financed the ad and his or her organizational affiliation, if any.

Compliance procedures: The Federal Election Commission has authority to investigate possible violations, hold hearings, and assess certain civil penalties. Its decision may be appealed to U. S. District Courts. The Justice Department retains the authority for criminal investigation and prosecution.

THE IMPACT OF THE LAW

Campaign finance legislation has had a significant impact on presidential elections. It has affected the base of contributors, the modes of solicitation, and the objects of spending. It has changed the role of the government, modifying the relationship between the party and its nominees, and influencing the strategies and tactics of the campaign.

Revenue

Individual contributors. One of the most important objectives of the law was to reduce the influence that a small number of large contributors had on the presidential nomination and election. To some extent it has succeeded, particularly in the nomination phase of the process. No longer can candidates depend on a few wealthy friends to finance the quests for their party's nomination. The $1,000 limit on individual donors, which is not subject to a cost-of-living adjustment, the $250 ceiling on matching grants, and the eligibility requirements for federal funds have made the solicitation of a large number of contributors absolutely essential.

There have, however, been variations in the fund-raising tactics of the candidates and their emphasis on relatively larger or smaller contributors. In 1988 and again in 1992, Republican George Bush received the bulk of his contributions during the primary period from those giving between $700 and $1,000. Bill Clinton did not; most of his contributions were $500 or less. Similarly, Republican candidates Pat Robertson (1988) and Pat Buchanan (1992) and Democrats Jesse Jackson (1984 and 1988) and Jerry Brown (1992) obtained most of their money from smaller contributors, defined as those who gave $500 or less. Brown, in fact, refused to accept any donation over $100. (Figure 2–1 lists the proportion of contributions in 1976 and 1992.)

In addition to gifts from individuals, which are the largest single source of revenues, candidates have found other ways to supplement their campaign funds. They can provide some of their own money. There is no restriction on the amount of their personal funds that can be spent in the years prior to the election, until their candidacy is formally established. At the point of candidacy, a $50,000 personal contribution limit is imposed if a candidate accepts federal funds.[17] There is no personal limit for the candidate who does not accept federal funds. Thus, in 1992, H. Ross Perot was able to spend over $60 million of his own money on his campaign in lieu of accepting government funds.

Borrowing money from financial institutions is also possible. The law permits candidates to obtain loans (if they can), provided that the terms of payment are clear and that the money is lent in accordance with regular business practices. Most major party candidates borrow money. They have to do so. The increasing number of early primaries and caucuses

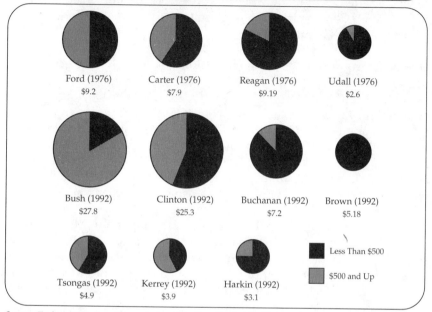

FIGURE 2–1

Size of Individual Contributions to Presidential Primary
Campaigns, 1976 and 1992 (in millions of dollars)

Ford (1976)
$9.2

Carter (1976)
$7.9

Reagan (1976)
$9.19

Udall (1976)
$2.6

Bush (1992)
$27.8

Clinton (1992)
$25.3

Buchanan (1992)
$7.2

Brown (1992)
$5.18

Tsongas (1992)
$4.9

Kerrey (1992)
$3.9

Harkin (1992)
$3.1

Less Than $500

$500 and Up

Source: Federal Election Commission, *The Presidential Public Funding Program* (April 1993),
p. 10.

have forced candidates to borrow early, often using the matching funds
that they expect to receive from the government as collateral.[18] For example, in March 1992 the Clinton campaign borrowed $1.4 million from an
Arkansas bank to have sufficient funds for the southern regional primaries that occurred in early March on Super Tuesday.

Funds raised but not spent by candidates in their campaigns for other
offices, such as for the Senate, House of Representatives, or a state gover-
norship, can be used in their quest for the presidential nomination. Senator Phil Gramm moved $5 million from his previous senate campaigns
into his presidential election fund for 1996. Senator Robert Dole used
$200,000, accumulated from his senate campaigns, as seed money for his
presidential effort in 1996, and he has access to considerably more
unspent election monies.

Although $1,000 is the maximum individual gift, voluntary goods
and services are unrestricted. Artists and musicians, in particular, can
generate considerable revenue for candidates by offering their time and
talent. Concerts, and to a lesser extent art sales, have become excellent
sources of revenue. Bill Clinton and George Bush had considerable

success at $1,000 a plate dinners that their campaigns organized in 1991 and 1992. So have Republicans Phil Gramm, Lamar Alexander, and Robert Dole in 1995. Gramm launched his presidential bid with a Texas barbecue that raised $4.1 million; Alexander's announcement party in Nashville, Tennessee netted $2.2 million whereas a New York gala for Dole brought in $1.5 million.[19] Clinton raised almost $6 million in one week of fund-raising dinners and galas in June 1995.

Nonparty groups and other organizations. Although the election law prohibits corporations and labor unions from making direct contributions to political campaigns, it does allow their employees, stockholders, or members to form political action committees (PACs) and fund them through voluntary contributions. These groups can directly affect the presidential selection process in four ways: by endorsing a candidate, by giving up to $5,000 to a single candidate, by spending an unlimited amount of money independently for or against a candidate, and by communicating to their members and then using their organization to turn out voters.

Surprisingly, direct donations are the least important. Money given directly to candidates by PACs in presidential campaigns rarely exceeds a small percentage of the total amount raised during the election year. In 1992, it constituted only $800,000, the least amount contributed directly by PACs since 1976.[20] Independent expenditures for PACs as well as those spent by an organization communicating with its members about the candidates, parties, and issues or engaging in political activities can be significant, however. In 1992, labor unions spent almost $650,000 in so-called communication costs.[21]

Additionally, PACs can contribute money to state and local political parties in their efforts to turn out a large vote in the general election. Corporations and labor unions may also fund these activities unless prohibited by state law from doing so.

PACs have proven to be so important that presidential candidates now regularly form their own. Known as *leadership* PACs, they have been used primarily to fund organizational activities, build support, and defray travel and other expenses of the candidate in the years preceding the presidential election. In addition, money is often given to other can-didates for their campaigns in the midterm elections. This money is intended to generate reciprocal support for the presidential nominee later on.

One of the earliest and most successful of these leadership PACs was Citizens for the Republic. Started in 1977, this organization had within a year raised $2.5 million and spent $1.9 million on operations. Most of this money was used for fund raising, travel, and other expenses of the PAC's principal speaker, Ronald Reagan. In the process of raising money, the organization developed a list of more than 300,000

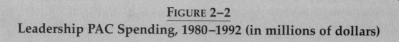

FIGURE 2–2
Leadership PAC Spending, 1980–1992 (in millions of dollars)

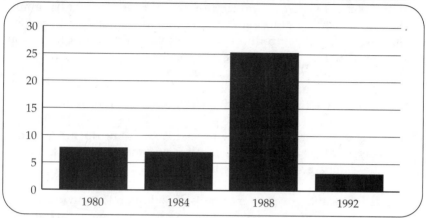

Source: Federal Election Commission, *The Presidential Public Funding Program* (April 1993), p. 10.

contributors. This list was purchased for a nominal fee by the Reagan campaign committee. The Reagan PAC became the prototype for other presidential candidates.

Leadership PACs have become a critical fund-raising instrument. They allow candidates to tap potential donors several times, once during each year of the PACs' existence, and then again after their formal candidacy has been declared. The advent of this type of PAC has effectively elongated the presidential selection process by encouraging candidates to create their own PACs and involve themselves in campaign activities in the year or two before the election cycle begins.[22] Senator Robert Dole is a good example of a presidential candidate who benefited from the pre-presidential activities of his PAC, Campaign America. Not only did Dole receive endorsements from many of the Republican officials to whom his PAC had contributed in their previous campaigns, but his presidential organization began its own fund-raising efforts with a list 500,000 contributors to his PAC. Figure 2–2 depicts spending by leadership PACs since 1980.[23]

Dole also founded an educational foundation, entitled *Better America*, to develop and promulgate policy on a broad range of national issues. The foundation, which raised millions of dollars from individual and corporate donors, was not subject to contribution limits and reporting requirements. Nor did its tax-exempt status permit it to promote a particular candidate. Critics, however, alleged that the Dole presidential campaign used funds from the foundation to raise money and broadcast advertisements that featured Senator Dole. The criticism, voiced by Dole's opponents, prompted the senator to close the foundation in June 1995 and return $4.6 million of remaining funds to contributors.[23]

Lamar Alexander created still another mechanism for extending his visibility and developing a contributor base for his presidential ambitions. He established a non profit corporation, the Republican Exchange Satellite Network, that produced and distributed monthly television shows about public policy, starring Alexander. Funding for the network, raised from private donors, was not subject to reporting requirements nor contribution limits of the Federal Election Campaign Act. Thus Alexander was able to obtain relatively large sums of money from a few wealthy individuals. He received 13 gifts of $100,000 and 200 of $10,000 or more. Additionally, he was able to go back to these same donors for more limited contributions and for help in soliciting other donations once his presidential campaign officially began.[24]

Matching funds and government grants. In addition to individuals and nonparty groups, a third source of money is the government itself. Presidential candidates can receive government matching grants for the nomination process and outright support for the general election. In 1992, these

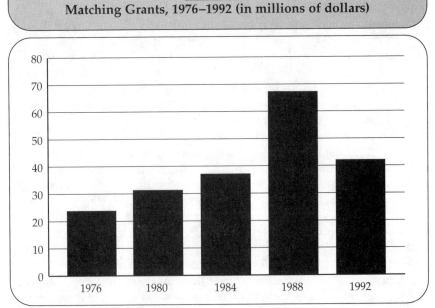

FIGURE 2–3
Matching Grants, 1976–1992 (in millions of dollars)

Source: Federal Election Commission, *The Presidential Public Funding Program* (April 1993), p. 9.

federal subsidies and grants amounted to approximately $175 million. Of this amount $42.7 million went to the candidates running for their party's nomination. Figure 2–3 shows matching fund grants since 1972.

Since the provision for government matching grants went into effect, Democratic candidates have received almost $106 million compared with almost $92 million for the Republicans. George Bush, however, was the largest single beneficiary, receiving almost $25 million for his three nomination campaigns in 1980, 1988, and 1992. Bill Clinton actually received almost $2 million more than George Bush in 1992. He got $12.5 million.

Here's how matching grants work. Eligible federal candidates who receive individual contributions up to $250 can match those contributions by an equal amount from the federal election fund in the calendar year of the election.[25] To be eligible candidates must raise $5,000 in 20 states in contributions of $250 or less.

Raising $100,000 in this matter is not difficult for most national candidates. Phil Gramm was the first of the 1996 Republican candidates to do so. The Federal Election Commission ruled him eligible on March 20, 1995 to receive matching funds in 1996.

Remaining eligible for matching funds is somewhat harder, however, because of the *10 percent rule,* a requirement that candidates receive at least 10 percent of the vote in two consecutive primaries in which they are entered. If they are entered in more than one primary on a given day, they need to win 10 percent in only one of them. Failing to receive 10 percent, however, negates their eligibility until such time as they receive at least 20 percent of the vote in a subsequent primary.[26] This rule helps front-runner candidates and adversely affects those who are lesser known or may be minority candidates. Twice during the 1984 campaign Jesse Jackson lost his eligibility for matching funds, only to regain it later. To ensure their continued eligibility, candidates have tended to avoid nonessential contests.[27]

Minor party candidates are also eligible for matching funds if they seek their party's nomination. Lenora Fulani, New Alliance party, and John Hagelin, Natural Law party, qualified in 1992 and received government grants. Fulani got almost $2 million. The eligibility of minor party candidates has led to the criticism that this provision encourages candidates to run who have no chance of winning, wasting taxpayers' money in the process.

In general, the matching-fund provision does provide greater opportunities for lesser-known aspirants to seek their party's nomination, but it has not substantially reduced the financial advantage that nationally recognized candidates have. Moreover, it encourages all candidates to begin their fund raising well before the election in order to qualify as soon as possible. When Robert Dole announced his candidacy for the 1996 Republican nomination, his organization mailed 1.5 million letters to potential donors asking for contributions.

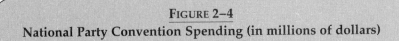

FIGURE 2–4
National Party Convention Spending (in millions of dollars)

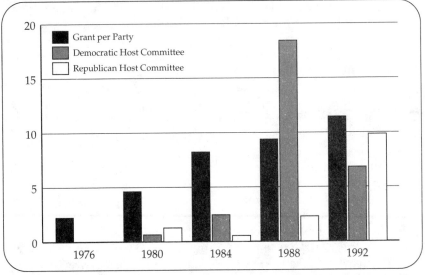

Source: Federal Election Commission, *The Presidential Public Funding Program* (April 1993), p. 25.

Convention and election grants. Federal funding is also extended to the major parties for their national nominating conventions. The convention grant in 1992 was $11,048,000 for each party. In 1996, it is expected to be about $12,400,000. Parties may also seek convention funding from the cities and states in which the event occurs. These state and local supplements can be substantial as Figure 2–4 demonstrates.

Once the major party candidates have been officially chosen, they are eligible for a direct grant for the general election. In 1992 $55.24 million was given to the Republican and Democratic candidates; in 1996 this amount is expected to be approximately $62.2 million.[28] The actual dollar figure is calculated in the election year by the FEC on the basis of inflation. Table 2–3 lists presidential spending limits and the cost-of-living adjustments (COLAs) from 1976 to 1996.

To be eligible for federal funds, major party candidates must agree to limit their campaign expenditures to the amount of the grant. To comply with the law, they cannot accept private contributions except for those designated for accounting and legal fees. Minor party candidates, who may receive private contributions, are also eligible for federal funds in amounts equal to the proportion of the vote they receive, provided it is at least 5 percent of the total. Had Perot accepted federal funds, he would

TABLE 2–3

Presidential Spending Limits and COLAs, 1976–1996
(in millions of dollars)

	Unadjusted Limit 1974 Base Year	1976	1980	1984	1988	1992	1996
COLA*	—	9.1%	47.2%	102%	123%	128%	131%
Primary election limit†	$10	$10.9	$14.7	$20.2	$23.1	$27.6	$31.0
General election limit‡	$20	$21.8	$29.4	$40.4	$46.1	$55.2	$62.2
Party convention limit§	$2	$2.2	$4.4	$8.1	$9.2	$11.0	$12.4
Party general election limit (2 cents x voting-age population adjusted by COLA)	—	$3.2	$4.6	$6.9	$8.3	$10.3	$11.6

* COLA is the cost-of-living adjustment, which the Department of Labor annually calculates using 1974 as the base year.

† Primary candidates receiving matching funds must comply with two types of spending limits: a national limit (listed in this table) and a separate limit for each state. The state limit is $200,000 or 16 cents multiplied by the state's voting-age population, whichever is greater. (Both amounts are adjusted for increases in the cost of living.) The maximum amount of primary matching funds a candidate may receive is half of the national spending limit. In addition, candidates may spend up to 20 percent of their primary election limit on fund raising

‡ Legal and accounting expenses to comply with the law are exempt from this limit. These funds may be raised through private contributions.

§ This limit has been raised twice by legislation: once in 1979 and once in 1984.

1996 figures are author's estimates based on forecasts by the FEC published in Federal Election Commission, *Record*, May 1995, p. 2.

Source: Federal Election Commission, *Annual Report, 1984* (June 1, 1985), pp. 8–9, updated by the author with data supplied by the Federal Election Commission.

have received $25.96 million, 47 percent of the amount the major party candidates were given; however, he would have received it after the election was over.

Perot decided not to accept federal funds. This decision exempted him from the $50,000 limit on personal contributions. It also exempted his campaign from the overall spending limits to which the major party candidates were subject. Perot's campaign expenditures totaled $68.4 million compared to $55.2 for Clinton and Bush (plus their legal and accounting expenses which are not subject to this limit). Most of Perot's campaign revenue, $63.3 million, came from his own fortune.[29] For other independent and third party candidates who do not have the personal wealth or organizational support to finance their presidential efforts, who need federal funds, and who are still constrained by the placed limits on personal ($50,000), individual ($1,000), and nonparty group ($5,000) contributions, the law makes it very difficult for them to raise sufficient money to mount an effective campaign. In other words, the Federal Election Campaign Act works to the advantage of those who enacted it, the two major parties.

Soft money. Direct federal grants to the candidates are not their only sources of funds. They can also benefit from the money political parties raise and spend. The largest source of funds comes from soft money, money that is raised from private contributors to get out the vote. There are no ceilings on these contributions as there are on contributions to federal campaigns. As a consequence both major parties have depended on a small number of large contributors for their soft money. In 1992, the Republicans received contributions of $100,000 or more from 198 people, and Democrats accepted maximum contributions of $100,000 from 375 individuals.[30] The national parties solicit most of the soft money but distribute a substantial portion of it to their state and local affiliates.

Soft money is used to operate telephone banks, to print and distribute campaign literature, and to recruit field organizers and other political operatives. In 1992, both parties' presidential candidates depended on the state parties for these activities and to pay for staff who were based in the states. This arrangement enabled Bush and Clinton to operate with relatively small national staffs, reducing their administrative overhead and their need to fund large grassroots organizations and permitting them to devote much of the public funds to media advertising.

The soft money raised by committees of the national parties for the 1992 presidential election was estimated to be over $60 million, a sum that was greater than the government grants given to their candidates.[31] According to the FEC, ". . . if all of the soft money spent by the national party committees in 1992 had been spent to support Bush and Clinton, it would have represented 23 percent of the total funding available to the

---

TABLE 2–4

**Estimated Soft Money Expenditures, 1980–1992
(in millions of dollars)**

Election	Republican	Democrat
1980	15.1	4.0
1984	15.6	6.0
1988	22.0	23.0
1992	18.9	23.6

Note: Figures indicate the amount of soft money spent on the presidential contest. Other soft money expenditures were made by the national and state parties for other elections.

Source: Herbert E. Alexander and Anthony Corrado, *Financing the 1992 Election* (Armonk, N. Y.: M. E. Sharpe, 1995.), Table 5–1.

TABLE 2–5

Funding Sources for Major Party Nominees, 1988–1992
(in millions of dollars)

	1988		1992	
	Bush	*Dukakis*	*Bush*	*Clinton*
Primary Elections				
Contributions from individuals				
less than $500	$4.9	$7.2	$5.3	$14.0
$500–$749	2.7	4.2	2.6	3.8
$750–$1,000	15.0	8.2	19.8	7.6
Contributions from PACs	0.7	—	—	—
Matching funds	8.4	9.0	10.1	12.5
General Elections				
Grant	46.1	46.1	55.2	55.2
Compliance fund	6.0	3.7	4.3	6.0
Coordinated party expenditures	8.3	8.3	10.2	10.2
Independent expenditures*	12.8	0.7	3.4	0.5
Partisan communications†	0.1	2.0	—	2.4

Other Funding Sources (in millions of dollars)

	1988		1992	
	Bush	*Dukakis*	*Bush*	*Clinton*
Leadership PACs‡	11.2	—	—	—
National party soft money§	22.7	25.0	36.2	31.6

* Includes both the expenditures made in support of a candidate and those made against his opponent.

† Partisan communications are reportable only if the communication is primarily devoted to "the election or defeat of a clearly identified candidate" and the "costs exceed $2,000 for any election." 2 U.S. C §431(9)(B)(iii).

‡ Some have argued that this otherwise lawful spending by leadership PACs indirectly influences presidential elections. (See Chapter 1.)

§ The 1988 figures are estimates. This chart does not include the soft money spent by state party committees. (It should be noted that soft money cannot legally be spent to influence federal elections.)

Source: Federal Election Commission, *The Presidential Public Funding Program* (April 1993), p. 31.

two candidates during the entire election cycle or 32 percent of the funding available in the general election period."[32]

In the first two presidential elections after the soft money amendment was enacted, the Republicans enjoyed a large advantage. In 1988 and 1992, however, they did not. The parties raised close to the same amount.

According to Herbert E. Alexander and Anthony Corrado, Republican committees raised more than Democratic committees, but Democrats spent more on the presidential contest than did the Republicans. Both parties targeted their soft money expenditures to key states.[33] (See Table 2–4.)

In short, a variety of funding sources are available for major party presidential aspirants. These sources, necessitated by the low limits on individual and group contributions, which have not been adjusted for inflation, permit political parties, nonparty groups, and wealthy individuals to use their resources to promote the candidate of their choice. The availability of and need for this money has forced those seeking the presidency to spend an increasing amount of time raising money, particularly in the year preceding the nomination. Despite the intent of the federal legislation to reduce the burdens of this activity and give candidates more time to campaign, much of their initial effort must be devoted to fund raising. Table 2–5 summarizes revenue sources of the major party candidates in the last two presidential elections.

Expenditures

The additional sources of revenue are necessary because campaign costs keep rising with more candidates seeking their party's nomination and with greater use of the mass media to reach voters. Moreover, in most elections these increases have exceeded the rate of inflation. Table 2–6 contrasts campaign costs between 1988 and 1992.

The crunch in expenditures represents the greatest problem at the initial stages of the nomination process. The need to gain recognition, get a boost, or maintain a lead has prompted candidates of both parties to spend much of their money early, well before the first contest is held, and to focus their attention on the states that have these first caucuses and primaries. Lamar Alexander spent $300,000 on television advertising in these two states in the summer of 1995, over 6 months before their delegates were to be chosen. As small states, Iowa and New Hampshire have low spending limits. In 1992, they were $914,332 and $552,400 respectively. The desire to be free of these spending ceilings led one Republican aspirant, John Connally, to reject matching funds in 1980 and another, Pat Robertson, to seriously consider doing so in 1988.

Most campaigns, however, have taken government money and then used their ingenuity to circumvent the limits. They have employed a variety of "legal" tactics to do so. It has become common practice for campaign workers to commute to the early small states from neighboring ones, thus allowing the campaign to allocate only a portion of its expenses between states rather than all in one of them. Another technique is to use national phone banks to canvas voters within these states. Television ads, particularly those directed at New Hampshire, are aired on Boston television, where 85 percent of the cost can be applied to the Massachusetts limit.

Table 2–6
Campaign Costs, 1988 and 1992

	1988	1992	Change
A guaranteed 30-second commercial slot during prime-time on WAGA-TV, a CBS affiliate in Atlanta	$1,500–7,500	$1,800–10,000	+20.0–33.3%
Double room, one night, Atlanta Ritz Carlton	$170	$200	+17.6%
Purchase of an AT&T phone system with two incoming lines and six phones	$3,500	$2,000	-42.8%
One bumper sticker (bought in lots of 1,000)	11¢	20¢	+81.8%
One ream of copy machine paper	$3.67	$5	+36.2%
One campaign flier (one page, three-fold, bought in lots of 1,000)	11½¢	15¢	+30.4%
First-class postage stamp	22¢	29¢	+31.8%
One campaign button (bought in lots of 1,000)	25¢	30¢	+20.0%
Computer list of Georgia's Democratic voters from state Democratic Party	$5,000	$500+	*
Overall limit on prenomination spending, if federal matching funds are accepted	$23.0 million	$33.1 million	+43.9%
Overall limit on individual contributions to campaign	$1,000	$1,000	No change

* In 1988, the state party charged campaigns $5,000 for access to a voting list and all other services, including mailing labels. This year, the party charges a basic $500 access fee, with additional charges depending on the types of services the campaigns request.

Source: New York Times, March 3, 1992, p. A-20.

Beginning with the 1992 nomination process, the FEC took these practices into account by liberalizing its cost allocation policy. It permitted candidates to allocate expenses if they pertained to media, mailings, telephoning, polling, and overhead. Moreover, the commission allowed up to 50 percent of the expenses to be considered fund raising and thus entirely exempt from the state spending limits.

In addition to the expenditure ceilings in states based on voting-age population, there is an overall prenomination spending limit. In 1992, it was $27.62 million plus an additional 20 percent ($5.5 million) for fund raising. In 1996 it is expected to be around $31 million (plus $6.2 million

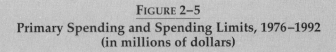

FIGURE 2–5
Primary Spending and Spending Limits, 1976–1992
(in millions of dollars)

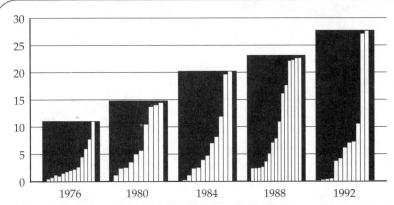

Figure shows what each publicly funded candidate spent in relation to the over-all primary election spending limit. Each large black bar represents the spending limit for the given primary election. The white bars depict the spending by the candidates. (The spending totals reported by the candidates do not necessarily reflect final commission determinations regarding expenditures subject to the limits.) In most election cycles, the two major party nominees made expenditures approaching the national limit.

Source: Federal Election Commission, *The Presidential Public Funding Program* (April 1993), p. 9.

for fund raising). As the campaign progresses candidates do bump up on the total spending ceiling, but since the contests have been effectively set-tled fairly early in the calendar, the overall limits have not been as much of a problem as the limits in Iowa and New Hampshire. Candidate spend-ing for presidential nominations since 1976 are shown in Figure 2–5.

Despite the more liberalized spending policy which was imple-mented by the FEC in 1992, violations continued. The Clinton campaign was forced to repay the United States Treasury $1.34 million for improper primary expenditures in 1992. The Bush primary campaign of that same year also had to make a reimbursement to the Treasury although the amount was much smaller, $200,000. During and after the election, the Federal Election Commission audits campaign expenses and holds cam-paign organizations accountable for them.

Another financial problem, evident in recent presidential nomina-tions and a real one for 1996, has been the concentration of primaries and caucuses on the same days at the beginning of the nomination process. The only way for candidates to reach voters in a number of states during the same time period is through the mass media. Television advertising, in particular, is one of the most expensive forms of communication. Its use

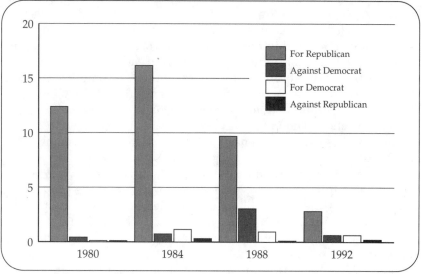

FIGURE 2–6
Independent Spending in Presidential Campaigns, 1980–1992
(in millions of dollars)

Legend:
- For Republican
- Against Democrat
- For Democrat
- Against Republican

Source: Federal Election Commission, *The Presidential Public Funding Program* (April 1993), p. 17.

increases the costs of running for the major contenders, who will need to raise large sums of money *before* the first 1996 primary or caucus is held.

Independent expenditures have also played a role in the nomination and general election process although their impact appear to be declining. In 1980, $13.7 million was reported to the FEC as being spent independently on the presidential campaign. In 1984, this figure reached a high point of $17.5 million, with ideological groups spending the bulk of this money.[34] Since 1984, independent spending has declined. In 1992, it was only $4.4 million for the presidential contest, only about 1 percent of the total funding for the major party candidates during the election cycle.[35] (See Figure 2–6.)

Independent expenditures have benefited Republicans more than Democrats. The largest differential was in 1984 when $16.3 million was spent on behalf of Reagan or against Mondale compared with $1.2 expended for Mondale or against Reagan.[36] In 1992, total spending decreased, but the proportions benefiting the Republicans were still lopsided. Approximately $3.5 million was spent for Bush or against Clinton, whereas slightly more than $567,000 was expended in support of Clinton or in opposition to Bush.[37]

Competition between Parties and Candidates

The FECA created competition within and between the major parties and their nominees. This competition was not the intent of the law, but it has been a consequence of it. By providing funds directly to individuals who seek major party nominations, the law facilitates candidacies and candidate organizations within the national parties, thereby fractionalizing those parties. The organization of the successful candidate is not dismantled after the nomination; it is expanded and often competes with the regular party organization. On the other hand, the 1979 amendments have encouraged the national parties to mount extensive soft money, fund-raising efforts and made their state affiliates increasingly dependent on them for these funds. This has contributed to the strengthening of the national parties.

As previously noted, the law adversely affects minor parties by requiring their candidates to obtain at least 5 percent of the presidential vote to be eligible for public funds. Independent candidate John Anderson qualified in 1980, and eventually received $4.2 million, enough to pay off his debts, but not enough to allow him to mount a vigorous campaign.

Since Anderson was not assured of federal funds during the campaign, he had difficulty borrowing money. Unable to secure large bank loans, he had to depend on private contributions and loans. He raised $12.1 million, mainly through mass mailings. Ironically, having qualified in 1980, Anderson was automatically eligible for funds in 1984 had he chosen to run. Similarly, Ross Perot could receive federal funds in 1996 if he were a candidate and chose to accept them. Thus, the law, despite its intent to bolster the candidates of the major parties, provides an incentive for the continuation of a third party candidacy once that candidacy has been successfully launched in the previous election.

THE CONSEQUENCES OF SPENDING

Is spending related to electoral success? Have candidates with the largest bankrolls generally been victorious? In the general elections at the presidential level, the answers seem to be yes, but it is difficult to determine precisely the extent to which money contributed to victory or simply flowed to the likely winner.

Between 1860 and 1972, the winner outspent the loser twenty-one out of twenty-nine times. Republican candidates have spent more than their Democratic opponents in twenty-five out of twenty-nine elections. The four times they did not, the Democrats won. The trend has continued if independent expenditures, partisan communications, and soft money are considered. In the 1980s, considerably more was spent on behalf of Republican nominees than for their Democratic opponents. In 1992, the Democrats benefited from substantial expenditures from organized labor to mobilize their members. Professors Alexander and Corrado estimate that $35 million was expended in this manner, giving the Democrats an overall financial advantage.[38]

What do all these figures suggest? The pattern of greater spending and electoral victories indicates that *money contributes to success, but potential success also attracts money.* Having more funds is an advantage, but it does not guarantee victory. The fact that heavily favored incumbent Richard Nixon outspent rival George McGovern more than 2 to 1 in 1972 does not explain McGovern's huge defeat, although it probably portended it. On the other hand, Hubert Humphrey's much narrower defeat by Nixon four years earlier was partially influenced by Humphrey's having spent less than $12 million, compared with more than $25 million spent by Nixon. The closer the election, the more the disparity in funds can be a factor.

Theoretically, campaign spending should have a greater impact on the nomination process than on the general election and at the beginning of the process than at the end. The first need, to gain visibility, mobilize support, and develop an effective organization, requires a large outlay of funds. On the Democratic side, the big spender in 1992, Bill Clinton, did well in the early contests and especially on Super Tuesday. Bush's financial resources also worked to his advantage in 1992 but probably was not as critical to his success. He would have won renomination even with less money.

What do the pattern of spending and the results of recent nomination contests suggest about the relationship between money and electoral success? *When* does money matter? According to political scientist Clyde Wilcox, it matters most when the candidates are least known to the voters, when they do not receive a lot of news coverage, and when paid advertising, which, of course, is expensive, can bring recognition and enhance images.[39] Money tends to matter most at the early stages of the campaign, when the candidates are not as well known. As the campaign progresses, as candidates become more easily recognized by the public, the expenditure of funds are not as critical to electoral success. Money buys recognition, but it may not buy much more.

Nor does the expenditure of funds by the candidates seem to be a major factor in the general election. In an examination of campaign advertising spending by Bush in 1988, a group of political scientists found an *inverse* relationship between advertising costs and public support for the candidates. They write, "When Bush spent more in one week than he had in the previous week, the size of his lead actually grew smaller."[40] In contrast, Perot's popularity increased as he was able to generate a public appeal in the debates and with his television advertising.

SUMMARY

Campaign finance became an important aspect of presidential elections by the end of the nineteenth and the beginning of the twentieth centuries. In recent years, however, it has become even more important as costs have escalated. Expanded use of communications, particularly television, to reach the voters has been primarily responsible for the increase, although other methods of contacting voters and assessing their opinions have also added to the sharp rise in expenditures.

With few exceptions, candidates of both major parties turned to the large contributors, the so-called fat cats, for financial support in the early and midtwentieth century. Their dependence on a relatively small number of large donors, combined with spiraling costs, created serious problems for the democratic selection process. The 1972 presidential election, with its high expenditures, "dirty tricks," and illegal campaign contributions, vividly illustrated some of these problems and generated public and congressional support for rectifying them.

In the 1970s, Congress enacted and amended the Federal Election Campaign Act. Its purpose in doing so was to bring donors into the open and to prevent their exercising undue influence on elected officials. By placing limits on contributions, controlling expenditures, and subsidizing the election, Congress hoped to make the selection process less costly and more equitable. It established the Federal Election Commission to oversee compliance and prosecute offenders.

The legislation has been only partially successful. It has increased the importance of having a large base of contributors during the preconvention period but has not eliminated the impact of large donors on the parties' efforts in the general election. It has limited the expenditures of candidates in both the nomination and general election but has not reduced the amount of money spent on presidential campaigns. It has produced greater equity by its limits on contributions and expenditures and by its federal subsidies but has not completely achieved equity among candidates or between parties in either phase of the electoral process. It has provided greater opportunities for those candidates who lack national recognition, but it has not lessened the advantages that national recognition can bring to those who seek their party's nomination. It has benefited major party candidates in the general election but has fractionalized the major parties during the nomination. It has weakened the party leadership's control over their nomination process and over their conduct of the general election campaign, but it has also enhanced the strategic value of the national parties' fund-raising abilities. It has encouraged the formation and involvement of nonparty groups, but it has also increased the importance of state and local party organizations on the campaigns of their candidates.

Finally, the law has contributed to knowledge about the conduct of campaigns. Gifts and expenditures of candidates are now part of the public record. This information is used by candidates to develop strategy, by the news media to cover the election, and by academicians and other analysts to explain the outcome. The publicizing of actions that violate the letter and spirit of the law has served to discourage such actions. In general, compliance has not been a major problem, but there have been persistent, generally minor violations.

NOTES

1. Herbert E. Alexander and Anthony Corrado, *Financing the 1992 Election* (Armonk, N.Y.: M. E. Sharpe, 1995), Table 2–1.
2. Ibid.
3. Ibid., Tables 2–1 and 2–4.
4. Herbert E. Alexander, "Making Sense about Dollars in the 1980 Presidential Campaigns,"in *Money and Politics in the United States,* ed. Michael J. Malbin (Washington, D.C.: American Enterprise Institute/Chatham House, 1984), p. 24.
5. Edward W. Chester, *Radio, Television and American Politics* (New York: Sheed & Ward, 1969), p. 21.
6. Herbert E. Alexander, *Financing Politics*, 3rd ed. (Washington, D.C.: Congressional Quarterly, 1984), pp. 11–12.
7. U. S. Bureau of the Census, *Statistical Abstract of the United States: 1993*, 113th ed. (Washington, D.C.: U.S. Government Printing Office, 1993), p. 561.
8. Herbert E. Alexander, "Spending on Presidential Campaigns" in *Electing the President: A Program for Reform,* ed. Robert E. Hunter (Washington, D.C.: Center for Strategic and International Studies), p. 61.
9. Alexander and Corrado, *Financing the 1992 Election,* Tables 5–3, 5–4, and 5–5.
10. National Election Studies, Inter-University Consortium for Political and Social Research, Center for Political Studies, University of Michigan, 1992.
11. Jason DeParle, "The First Primary," *New York Times Magazine,* April 16, 1995, p. 48.
12. This brief discussion of the sources of political contributions is based primarily on Alexander, *Financing Politics,* pp. 55–59.
13. Quoted in Jasper B. Shannon, *Money and Politics* (New York: Random House, 1959), p. 35.
14. Herbert E. Alexander and Brian Haggerty, *Financing the 1984 Election* (Lexington, Mass.: Lexington Books, 1987), p. 148.
15. In 1972, the chief fund raiser for the Nixon campaign, Maurice Stans, and Richard Nixon's private attorney, Herbert Kalmbach, collected contributions, some of them illegal, on behalf of the president. They exerted strong pressure on corporate executives, despite the prohibition on corporate giving. Secret contributions totaling millions of dollars were received, and three special secured funds were established to give the White House and the Committee to Reelect the President (known as CREEP) maximum discretion in campaign expenditures. It was from these funds that the "dirty tricks" of the 1972 campaign and the Watergate burglary were financed.
16. Anthony Corrado, *Paying for Presidents: Public Financing in National Elections* (New York: Twentieth Century Fund Press, 1993), p. 20. This percentage has continued to decline.

17. The personal lending limit is also $50,000 for candidates who accept federal funds.
18. Those who do not do well and are forced out early are often saddled with sizable debts. Frequently, for the sake of party unity and to obtain the backing of their opponents, party nominees promise to try to help pay off their rivals' debts.
19. Dinners and other galas are less expensive fund-raising techniques than is direct mail. They also generate money more quickly.
20. Federal Election Commission, *Record*, (July 1993), p. 4.
21. Alexander and Corrado, *Financing the 1992 Election.*
22. It costs more to engage in prospective fund raising, going to people who have not contributed for donations, than to go back to those who have. Sometimes, in fact, the costs of prospective fund raising can exceed the dollar return. This is one of the reasons that prospective candidates wish to shift these costs to a leadership PAC rather than have them come out of the campaign fund-raising budget and thus detract from the total amount that can be spent prior to the convention. Having the list in hand also helps obtain money for the critical start-up costs of the campaign.
23. R.H. Melton, "Dole's Tax-Exempt Group Plans to Refund Millions," *Washington Post*, June 21, 1995, pp. 1, 12.
24. Jason DeParle, "The First Primary," p. 33.
25. Contributions received in the previous year are also eligible for matching in the election year, provided they were given to the candidate's official campaign committee.
26. The FEC sought to impose still another eligibility rule—how matching funds had been spent in the past. The commission denied matching funds to Lyndon LaRouche in 1992 on the grounds that his campaign had misused such funds in a previous election. LaRouche, who had been convicted and jailed for engaging in fraudulent fund-raising practices, appealed the FEC's decision and won. On July 2, 1993, the U. S. Court of Appeals ruled that the law did not give the FEC authority to prejudge how a candidate would use his government funds—that was up to the voters.
27. Major party candidates can also notify the FEC that they wish to exclude certain primaries from the 10 percent rule and not campaign in those states even though their names appear on the ballot.
28. Federal Election Commission, "Press Release," August 20, 1993, p. 1.
29. Alexander and Corrado, *Financing the 1992 Election*, Table 5–6.
30. Ibid.
31. Federal Election Commission, *The Presidential Public Funding Program*, April 1993, p. 32.
32. Ibid.
33. Alexander and Corrado, *Financing the 1992 Election.*
34. Federal Election Commission, *Record*, October 1985, p. 5.
35. Federal Election Commission, *Presidential Public Funding*, p. 32.
36. Federal Election Commission, *Record*, August 1989, p. 8.
37. Ibid.
38. Alexander and Corrado, *Financing the 1992 Election.*
39. Michael Robinson, Clyde Wilcox, and Paul Marshall, "The Presidency: Not for Sale," *Public Opinion*, II (March\April 1989): 51.
40. Ibid., p. 50.

SELECTED READINGS

Alexander, Herbert E. "Campaign Finance Reform," *Proceedings of the Academy of Political Science* 37 (March 1989): 123–40.

Alexander, Herbert E. and Anthony Corrado. *Financing the 1992 Election.* Armonk, N. Y.: M. E. Sharpe, 1995.

Corrado, Anthony. *Paying for Presidents: Public Financing in National Elections.* New York: Twentieth Century Fund Press, 1993.

Magleby, David B. and Candice J. Nelson. *The Money Chase: Congressional Campaign Finance Reform.* Washington, D.C.: Brookings Institution, 1990.

Robinson, Michael, Clyde Wilcox, and Paul Marshall. "The Presidency: Not for Sale." *Public Opinion* II (March\April 1989): 49–53.

Sabato, Larry J. *PAC Power.* New York: W. W. Norton, 1985.

Sorauf, Frank J. *Money in American Elections.* Glenview, Ill.: Scott Foresman, 1988.

Stephenson-Horne, Marilee. "The Road to Hell: Unintended Consequences of Unwise Federal Campaign Finance Reforms." *Northern Kentucky Law Review,* 17 (Spring 1990): 547–570.

Wilcox, Clyde. "Financing the 1988 Prenomination Campaigns," in Emmett H. Buell, Jr. and Lee Sigelman (eds.), *Nominating the President.* Knoxville, Tenn.: University of Tennessee Press, 1991: 91–118.

The symbol of the Political Action Committee of the CIO, 1940.

Chapter 3

The Political Environment

INTRODUCTION

The nature of the electorate influences the content, images, and strategies of the campaign and affects the outcome of the election—an obvious conclusion to be sure, but one that is not always appreciated. Campaigns are not conducted in ignorance of the voters. Rather, they are calculated to appeal to the needs and desires, attitudes and opinions, and associations and interactions of the electorate.

Voters do not come to the election with completely open minds. They come with preexisting views. They do not see and hear the campaign in isolation. They observe it and absorb it as part of their daily lives. In other words, their attitudes and associations affect their perceptions and influence their behavior. Preexisting views make it important for students of presidential elections to examine the formation of political attitudes and the patterns of social interaction.

Who votes and who does not? Why do people vote for certain candidates and not others? Do campaign appeals affect voting behavior? Are the responses of the electorate predictable? Political scientists have been interested in these questions for some time. Politicians have been interested for even longer.

A great deal of social science research and political savvy have gone into finding the answers. Spurred by the development of sophisticated survey techniques and methods of data analysis, political scientists, sociologists, and social psychologists have uncovered a wealth of information on how the public reacts and the electorate behaves during a campaign.

They have examined correlations between demographic characteristics and voter turnout. They have explored psychological motivations, social influences, and political pressures that contribute to voting behavior. This chapter examines some of their findings.

It is organized into three sections. The first discusses who votes. Describing the expansion of suffrage in the nineteenth and twentieth centuries, the section then turns to recent trends. Turnout is influenced by partisan, economic, and social factors. It is also affected by laws that govern elections and by circumstances of the vote itself, such as the interest in the election, the closeness of the contest, the effectiveness of the campaign, and even the weather on election day. The impact of these variables on the decision of whether or not to cast a ballot at all is the principal focus of this section.

The second and third sections of the chapter study influences on the vote. First, the *partisan* basis of politics is examined. How do political attitudes affect the ways people evaluate the campaign and shape their actual voting decision? Models of voting behavior are presented and then used to help explain contemporary voting patterns.

Next, the *social* basis of politics is analyzed. Dividing the electorate into distinct and overlapping socioeconomic, ethnic, and religious groupings, this section deals with the relationship of these groupings to voting behavior. It places primary emphasis on the formation of party coalitions during the 1930s and their evolution into the 1990s.

The final part of this section looks to the future. What is happening to the electoral coalitions of the two major parties? Are they going through a period of realignment or dealignment? Are voters becoming more independent in their allegiances and their voting decisions? Recent research provides some answers to these questions.

TURNOUT

Who votes? In one sense, this is a simple question to resolve. Official election returns indicate the number of voters and the states, even the precincts, in which the votes were cast. By easy calculation, the percentage of those eligible who actually voted can be determined. In 1992, 55.2 percent of the voting-age population cast ballots in the presidential election.[1] (See Table 3–1 for turnout in other presidential elections.) Among the states, turnout also varied, ranging from a high of 72 percent in Maine and Minnesota to a low of 42 percent in Hawaii.[2] It was lower in the South (46.5 percent) than outside of it (58.7 percent).[3]

For campaign strategists and political analysts, however, more information than simple percentages of the proportion of the population that voted is needed. In planning a campaign, it is necessary to design and target appeals to attract specific groups of voters. In assessing the results, it is

TABLE 3–1

Suffrage and Turnout

Year	Total Adult Population (including aliens)*	Total Presidential Vote	Percentage of Adult Population Voting
1824	3,964,000	363,017	9%
1840	7,381,000	2,412,698	33
1860	14,676,000	4,692,710	32
1880	25,012,000	9,219,467	37
1900	40,753,000	13,974,188	35
1920	60,581,000	26,768,613	44
1932	75,768,000	39,732,000	52.4
1940	84,728,000	49,900,000	58.9
1952	99,929,000	61,551,000	61.6
1960	109,672,000	68,838,000	62.8
1964	114,090,000	70,645,000	61.9
1968	120,285,000	73,212,000	60.9
1972	140,777,000	77,719,000	55.5
1976	152,308,000	81,556,000	53.5
1980	164,595,000	86,515,000	52.6
1984	174,447,000	92,653,000	53.1
1988	182,600,000	91,602,291	50.2
1992	189,044,000	104,426,659	55.2

* Restrictions based on sex, age, race, religion, and property ownership prevented a significant portion of the adult population from voting in the nineteenth and early twentieth centuries. Of those who were eligible, however, the percentage casting ballots was often quite high, particularly during the last half of the nineteenth century.

Source: Population figures for 1824 to 1920 are based on estimates and early census figures that appear in Neal R. Pierce, *The People's President* (New York: Simon and Schuster, 1968), p. 206. Population figures from 1932 to 1984 are from the U.S. Department of Commerce, Bureau of the Census, *Statistical Abstract of the United States* (Washington, D.C.: Government Printing Office, 1987), p. 250. Figures for 1988 and 1992 were compiled from official election returns supplied by the Federal Election Commission.

also essential to understand how particular segments of the electorate responded. By evaluating turnout on the basis of demographic characteristics and partisan attitudes, strategists and analysts alike obtain the information they need to make sophisticated judgments.

Voting turnout has varied widely over the years. In the first national election, only about 11 percent of the potentially eligible population participated. The presidential vote was even smaller, since most of the electors were designated by the state legislatures and not chosen directly by the people.

In the early period from the end of the eighteenth century until 1824, voters constituted only about 20 to 25 percent of those who were eligible to vote in most states. Without parties or a tradition of participation in politics, the public deferred to the more political prominent members of the society.[4]

Turnout increased in the 1820s, however, spurred by a political reform movement. Known as Jacksonian democracy, this movement advocated greater public participation in the electoral process. By the 1830s, 50 to 60 percent of the electorate voted. With the rise of competitive, mass-based parties in the 1840s, turnout increased to 80 percent and remained within the 70 to 80 percent range for the next fifty years in all regions except the South.[5] There, the rise of one-party politics following the Civil War and the disfranchisement of African Americans after the withdrawal of federal troops substantially reduced the proportion of those who voted.

At the turn of the century, turnout began to decline in the nation as a whole, although the number of voters continued to increase. Thousands of immigrants, who initially spoke little English, enlarged the eligible electorate but reduced the proportion of it who voted. Similarly, the enfranchisement of women in 1920 had much the same effect.

Although voter turnout grew moderately during Franklin Roosevelt's presidency and the post-World War II era, it began to decline following the 1960 presidential election and continued to do so for almost 30 years. By 1988, turnout in presidential elections reached a low point with only one-half of the adult population voting. It rose 5 percent in 1992.

In nonpresidential elections the proportion of eligible voters participating is even lower, in the range of 40 percent or less for midterm elections. In the 1994 congressional elections it was only about 38 percent.

Why do so many people choose not to vote? Does low turnout indicate voter satisfaction or alienation? Does it contribute to stability or create conditions for instability within the political system? What party and which programs benefit and which groups suffer when so many people do not vote? These questions are addressed in an examination of turnout and its implications for the political system.

The Expansion of Suffrage

The Constitution empowers the state legislatures to determine the time, place, and manner of holding elections for national office. Although it also gives Congress the authority to alter such regulations, Congress did not do so until the Civil War. Thus, the states were free to restrict suffrage, and most did. In some, property ownership was a requirement for exercising the franchise; in others, a particular religious belief was necessary. In most, it was essential to be white, male, and over twenty-one.[6]

By the 1830s, most states had eliminated property and religious restrictions, thereby extending suffrage to approximately 80 percent of the adult white male population.[7] The Fifteenth Amendment, ratified in 1870, removed race and color as qualifications for voting. In theory, it enabled all nonwhite males to vote. In practice, it enfranchised those in the North and border states but not those in the South. A series of institutional devices, such as the poll tax, literacy tests, and restrictive primaries in which only Caucasians could participate (known as "white primaries"), combined effectively with social pressure to prevent African Americans from voting in large numbers in the South for another hundred years. In every southern state, a majority of eligible African Americans were *not* registered to vote until the mid- to late 1960s.[8]

Following the Civil War, both the number of eligible voters and the percentage of actual voters increased. Close competition between the parties contributed to this higher level of participation, as did the absence of registration procedures and the use of secret ballots in some states.

In the twentieth century, the passage of the Nineteenth, Twenty-third, Twenty-fourth, and Twenty-sixth Amendments continued to expand the voting-age population. In 1920, women received the right to vote at the national level although some states and territories had granted women suffrage earlier.[9] In 1961, the District of Columbia was granted electoral votes, thereby extending the franchise to its residents in presidential elections; in 1964, the collection of a poll tax was prohibited in national elections; in 1971, suffrage was extended to all citizens eighteen years of age and older.

Moreover, the Supreme Court and Congress began to eliminate the legal and institutional barriers to voting. In 1944, the Court outlawed the white primary.[10] In the mid-1960s, Congress, by its passage of the Civil Rights Act (1964) and the Voting Rights Act (1965), banned literacy tests in federal elections for all citizens who had at least a sixth-grade education in a U.S. school. Where less than 50 percent of the population was registered to vote, federal officials were sent to facilitate registration. No longer was long and costly litigation necessary to ensure the right to vote. Amendments to the Voting Rights Act have also reduced the residence requirement for presidential elections to a maximum of thirty days.

The expansion of suffrage has produced more voters. It has enlarged the electorate, but initially that enlargement also contributed to the smaller percentage of that electorate who voted. The reason for this is that newly enfranchised voters tend to cast ballots less regularly than those who have previously enjoyed the right to vote.

It takes time to develop the practice of voting. Take women, for example. Although they received the right to vote in 1920, the proportion of women who voted was less than the proportion of men who cast ballots for another fifty-six years. By 1980, however, the rate at which women and men turned out to vote was approximately the same. Since 1988, women have been slightly more likely to vote than men.[11]

Concern has been voiced about the relatively low turnout of voters in the United States compared with other democratic countries. Contemporary voting statistics demonstrate that this concern is justified. If the percentage of *eligible* voters in the United States who actually vote are compared with that of twenty other democratic countries located primarily in Western Europe, the United States ranked nineteenth in the 1980s;[12] however, if the percentage of *registered* voters who actually vote is the basis for comparison, the United States fared better, ranking eleventh out of twenty-four.[13] Unlike many other countries, the United States does not impose penalties on those who fail to register and vote; nor does it have a national system for automatic registration as do most other democracies.

It seems clear that registration procedures have impeded voting.[14] For a mobile society, such as that of the United States, with one-third of the population moving on average every two years, the need to reregister decreases the size of the vote. In general, the harder states have made it to register, the smaller the percentage of its citizens who vote. Several political scientists have estimated that turnout could be increased anywhere from 4 to 15 percent (with most predicting a gain of between 8 and 9 percent) by making modest adjustments in the laws to ease registration procedures.[15]

In 1993, Congress responded to this problem. It enacted legislation, known as the motor-voter bill, that requires states that do not already do so to allow people to register by mail or at the time they obtain or renew their driver's license.[16] The law also states that registration materials should be available at certain agencies that provide social services such as welfare offices and those that serve the disabled. The law, which took effect in 1995, was expected to have an impact on the 1996 presidential election; however, several states delayed or refused to implement it ostensibly on the grounds that Congress did not provide the states with money to do so. In 1995, the Justice Department instituted legal action to compel the recalcitrant states to comply.

The implementation of the motor-voter bill has partisan implications as well. Republicans believe that the Democrats will benefit disproportionately from the larger turnout the law was intended to facilitate and thus have been less supportive of it. It is no coincidence that the states that have delayed implementation all have Republican governors.

In addition to registration procedures, there is another reason that turnout in the United States trails that of many other democratic countries. Most elections are conducted in single-member districts in the United States. In these elections the candidate with the most votes wins. This winner-take-all system does not provide much encouragement for those in the minority to get out and vote if they have little or no chance of winning. In contrast, elections conducted in multimember districts and decided on the basis of a proportional vote provide more incentive to do so.

Psychological and Social Influences on Turnout

The electoral system is not the only factor that affects the vote. Other influences on turnout include public interest in the election, concern over the outcome, feelings of civic responsibility, and sense of political efficacy (the belief that one's vote really counts).[17] Naturally, people who feel more strongly about the election are more likely to get involved. Those with more intense partisan feelings are more likely to have this interest, more likely to participate in the campaign, and more likely to vote on election day. Voting, in fact, becomes a habit. The more people have done it in the past, the more likely they will do it in the future. Table 3–2 provides empirical support for the proposition that the newly eligible vote with less regularity than those who have previously exercised their franchise. In 1992, only 38.5 percent of those in the youngest cohort (eighteen to twenty years old) voted. Each subsequent age group in that election voted

TABLE 3–2

Voting Turnout by Population Characteristics, 1968–1992 (in percentages)

	1968	1972	1976	1980	1984	1988	1992
SEX							
Male	69.8%	64.1%	59.6%	59.1%	59.0%	56.4%	60.2%
Female	66.0	62.0	58.8	59.4	60.8	58.3	62.3
AGE							
18–20	—	48.3	38.0	35.7	36.7	33.2	38.5
21–24	51.0	50.7	45.6	43.1	43.5	38.3	45.7
25–34	62.5	59.7	55.4	54.6	54.5	48.0	53.2
35–44	70.8	66.3	63.3	64.4	63.5	61.3	63.6
45–64	74.9	70.8	68.7	69.3	69.8	67.9	70.0
65 & over	65.8	63.5	62.2	65.1	67.7	68.8	70.1
EDUCATION							
8 years or less	54.5	47.4	44.1	42.6	42.9	36.7	35.1
HIGH SCHOOL							
1–3 years	61.3	52.0	47.2	45.6	44.4	41.3	41.2
4 years	—	—	59.4	58.9	58.7	54.7	57.5
COLLEGE							
1–3 years	72.5*	65.4*	68.1	67.2	67.5	64.5	68.7
4 years or more	81.2*	78.8*	79.8	79.9	79.1	77.6	81.0
RACE							
White	69.1	64.5	60.9	60.9	61.4	59.1	63.6
Black	57.6	52.1	48.7	50.5	55.8	51.5	54.0
Hispanic	NA	37.4	31.8	29.9	32.6	28.8	28.9

* Indicates percentage who had completed more than twelve years of schooling.

Source: U.S. Department of Commerce, Bureau of the Census, *Statistical Abstract of the United States* (Washington, D.C.: Government Printing Office, 1993), p. 283.

with greater frequency. Although Table 3–2 does not show it, turnout does decrease after age seventy-five.

Other characteristics related to turnout are education, income, and occupational status. As people become more educated, as they move up the socioeconomic ladder, as their jobs gain in status, they are more likely to vote. Education is the most important of these variables. It has a larger impact than any other single social characteristic.[18] As Table 3–2 demonstrates, the higher the level of education, the greater the percentage voting.

The reason education is so important is that it provides the skills for processing and evaluating information; for perceiving differences among the parties, candidates, and issues; and for relating these differences to personal values and behavior. Education also affects personal success. It increases a person's stake in the system, interest in the election, and concern over the outcome. Since the lesson that voting is a civic responsibility is usually learned in the classroom, schooling may also contribute to a more highly developed sense of responsibility about voting. Finally, education provides the knowledge and confidence to overcome voting hurdles—to register on time, to file absentee ballots properly, and to mark the ballot or use the voting machine correctly on election day.[19]

Given the relationship of education to turnout, why should the rate of turnout have declined from 1960 to 1988 when the general level of education in the United States was rising during this period? One explanation for this trend was the increasing number of younger voters who entered the electorate and their lack of "social connectedness";[20] another is the weakening of partisan attitudes; a third is the growth of political cynicism and apathy among the electorate, particularly among those in the lower socioeconomic groups, and their tendency to withdraw from politics. Before examining each of these factors, it is important to understand that the decline in turnout occurred *despite* increasing education levels and not because of them. Professors Paul R. Abramson, John H. Aldrich, and David W. Rohde estimate that turnout would have declined even more, about 15 percent, had education levels not increased.[21]

What are the reasons for the decline? The "baby boomers" born in the mid-1940s and the 1950s entered the electorate in the mid-1960s and 1970s. They enlarged the pool of eligible voters but reduced the proportion of those who vote because, as previously noted, young people tend to vote with less regularity than their elders. (See Table 3–2.) They are more mobile; they have fewer economic interests and looser political ties to the community in which they live and vote; and they have not developed the habit of voting or, in some cases, even of identifying with a political party.

Similarly, advances in medicine have prolonged life and increased the number of senior citizens, particularly those over seventy-five. They, too, tend to vote less regularly, primarily for reasons of health. In short, the "youthing" and aging of the electorate contributed to lower voter turnout, but other factors, such as the weakening of partisan attitudes, contributed as well.

For the last three decades, the strength of partisan loyalties has declined, and the proportion of the electorate identifying themselves as independent has grown. Since party allegiances are a motivation for voting, a weakening of partisan attitudes could be expected to decrease turnout. And it has. Moreover, parties have become less important influences on the campaign and provide less sturdy linkage to voters.

As the parties have become more personalized and factionalized and as campaigns become more candidate centered, the election becomes more confusing to voters. It is harder to discern whose election is in their own interests. The difficulty of making this calculation has contributed to nonvoting among those with less education, who tend to have less information and less highly developed analytical skills.

People have also become more disillusioned about the political system and, correspondingly, less confident that their vote matters, or that they can change the way government works or public officials behave. This lower sense of efficacy has also depressed the vote. Abramson and colleagues argue that the decline in turnout from 1960 to 1988 can be attributed primarily to the combined effects of weaker partisan affiliation and feelings of less political effectiveness.[22]

A class bias also exists in voting that is related to negative feelings people have about their own ability to influence events and the trust they place in political leaders. The decline in turnout has been greatest among those in the lowest socioeconomic groups, thereby enlarging the participation gap between the haves and have nots.[23] This has resulted in an electorate that is less representative of the population as a whole, an electorate that is better educated and has higher incomes than the general public. To the extent that government responds to the electorate rather than to the general population, its policies take on a "have" coloration.

This class bias in voting produces a tragic irony in American politics. Those who are most disadvantaged, who have the least education, and who need to change conditions the most actually participate the least. Those who are the most advantaged, who benefit from existing conditions and presumably from public policy as it stands, vote most often. These trends in voting behavior work to reflect, even to perpetuate, the status quo.

Generational and racial divisions accentuate the problem. Younger people and racial minorities are disproportionately found in the lower socioeconomic strata. According to census data, there is an 8 to 10 percent difference in turnout between white and African Americans. In the last two presidential elections, moreover, the rate of turnout among whites increased more rapidly than among African Americans.[24]

What caused the overall increase in turnout in 1992? The recession, which may have energized some of those adversely affected by it; Perot's candidacy, which appealed to independents who are less likely to vote;

and new media formats, which reached and informed new voters, may have contributed to the increase. Whether the increase is permanent should become clearer after the 1996 election.

Turnout and Partisanship

Turnout has partisan implications as well. Since the Democratic party draws more of its electoral support from those in the lower socioeconomic groups, those with less formal education, and those with fewer professional opportunities, the lower turnout tends to hurt them more than the Republicans. In 1992, however, it did not. The increase in turnout was greater among Democrats than Republicans, thereby eliminating the partisan advantage the Republicans usually have from turning out a larger proportion of their partisans to vote. In the 1994 mid-term elections, however, the Republicans gained back their advantage.

Republicans have also benefited from greater financial resources, which have enabled them to mount more effective campaigns to identify and register new voters. They have tended to employ an individualized targeting approach to get out their vote, whereas the Democrats have had to adopt a more generalized strategy that directs mass appeals to key Democratic areas.

Despite the demographic differences between voters and nonvoters, some evidence suggests that results of elections, of at least the last two presidential elections, would not have been any different if more people had voted. Nonvoters surveyed after the 1988 and 1992 elections indicated that they preferred Bush to Dukakis and Clinton to Bush and Perot by approximately the same percentage as the national averages in these elections. One reason that nonvoters follow the dominant mood of the electorate is that they tend to be influenced by shorter-term factors that affect the outcome of the election, perhaps even more so than voters whose partisan allegiances can more easily resist these short-term forces. To understand the impact of partisanship on turnout we now turn to the partisan basis of politics.

THE PARTISAN BASIS OF POLITICS

Why do people vote as they do? Considerable research has been conducted to answer this question. Initially, much of it was done under the direction of the Center for Political Studies at the University of Michigan. Beginning in 1952, the center began conducting nation-wide surveys during presidential elections.[25] The object of these national election studies has been to identify the major influences on voting behavior. A random sample of the electorate is interviewed before and after the election. Respondents are asked a series of questions designed to reveal their attitudes toward the parties, candidates, and issues. On the basis of the answers to these questions, researchers have amassed a wealth of data to explain the voting behavior of the U.S. electorate.

A Model of the U.S. Voter

One of the earliest and most influential theories of voting behavior was presented in a book entitled *The American Voter* (1960). The model on which the theory is based assumes that individuals are influenced by their partisan attitudes and social relationships in addition to the political environment in which the election occurs. In fact, these attitudes and those relationships condition the impact of that environment on individual voting behavior.

According to the theory, people develop attitudes early in life, largely as a consequence of interacting with their families, particularly their parents. These attitudes, in turn, tend to be reinforced by neighborhood, school, and religious associations. The reasons they tend to be reinforced lie in the psychological and social patterns of behavior. Psychologically, it is more pleasing to have beliefs and attitudes supported than challenged. Socially, it is more comfortable to associate with "nice," like-minded people—those with similar cultural, educational, and religious experiences—than with others. This desire to increase one's "comfort level" in social relationships explains why the environment for most people tends to be supportive much of the time.[26]

Attitudes mature and harden over the years. The older people become, the less amenable they are to change. They are more set in their ways. Consequently, their behavior is more predictable. Political attitudes are no exception to this general pattern of attitude formation and maintenance. They, too, are developed early in life, are reinforced by association, grow in intensity, and become more predictable with time.

Of all the factors that contribute to the development of a political attitude, an identification with a political party is one of the most important. It affects how people see the campaign and how they vote. Party identification operates as a conceptual mechanism, a lens through which the campaign is evaluated. It provides cues for interpreting the issues, for judging the candidates, and for deciding whether and how to vote. The stronger these attitudes, the more compelling the cues; conversely, the weaker the attitudes, the less likely they will affect perceptions during the campaign and influence voting on election day.[27]

When identification with party is weak or nonexistent, other factors, such as the personalities of the candidates and their issue positions, are correspondingly more important. In contrast to party identification, which is a long-term stabilizing factor but one that can be changed over time, candidate and issue orientations are short term, more variable, often shifting from election to election. Of the two, the image of the candidate has been viewed as more significant most of the time.

Candidate images turn on performance and policy dimensions. People tend to form general impressions about candidates on the basis of what they know about the candidates' personal experience, their leadership capabilities, and their character. For an incumbent seeking reelection, accomplishments in office provide much of the criteria for an evaluation—how well the president has done. Other characteristics, such as trustworthiness, integrity, and candor, are also important. For the challenger, it is the potential for office as demonstrated by experience, knowledge, confidence, and assertiveness, plus a host of personal qualities that help determine qualifications for a leadership position such as president.[28]

Candidates' stands on the issues, however, seem less critical to the proponents of this voting behavior model than do their partisanship and performance in office. The principal explanation for downgrading the importance of issues has been the low level of information and awareness that much of the electorate possesses. To be important, issues must be salient. They must attract attention; they must hit home. Without personal impact, they are unlikely to be primary motivating factors in voting. To the extent that issue positions are not known or distinguishable between the principal candidates, their respective images become a stronger influence on the vote.

Ironically, that portion of the electorate that can be more easily persuaded—weak partisans and independents—tends to have the least information.[29] Conversely, the most committed tend to be the most informed. They use their information to support their partisanship.

The relationship between degree of partisanship and amount of information has significant implications for a democratic society. The traditional view of a democracy holds that information and awareness are necessary to make an intelligent judgment on election day. The finding, however, that those who have the most information are also the most committed, and that those who lack this commitment also lack the incentive to get more information, has upset some of the assumptions about the motivation for acquiring information and using it to vote intelligently.

A Refined Theory of Voting

The model of voting behavior first presented in 1960 has engendered considerable controversy. Critics have charged that the theory presumes that most of the electorate is uninformed and vote habitually rather than rationally. One well-known political scientist, the late V. O. Key, even wrote a book dedicated to "the perverse and unorthodox argument . . . that voters are not fools."[30] Key studied the behavior of three groups of voters between 1936 and 1960: switchers, stand-patters, and new voters. He found those who switched their votes to be interested in and influenced by their own evaluation of policy, personality, and performance. In this sense, Key believed that they exercised an intelligent judgment when voting.

Key's conclusion that most voters were not automatons and that most of their voting decisions were not solely or even primarily the product of their psychological dispositions and social pressures is accepted today by most students of electoral behavior. Even though voters may have limited information, they use it to arrive at political judgments. They reason, taking into account their present situation, their beliefs about government, and their assessments of how the country is doing under its current leadership and will do in the future. In the words of political scientist, Samuel Popkin:

> They consider not only economic issues but family, residential, and consumer issues as well. They think not only of their immediate needs, but also of their needs for insurance against future problems; not only about private good but also about collective goods.[31]

How do they do this? What criteria do they use in making judgments?

Morris Fiorina in his provocative study, *Retrospective Voting in American National Elections* (1981) tries to answer these questions. Utilizing a rational choice model adopted from economics, Fiorina argued that voting decisions are calculations people make on the basis of their accumulated political experience. They make these calculations by assessing the past performance of the parties and their elected officials in light of the promises they made and political events that have occurred. Fiorina calls this a *retrospective evaluation.*[32]

Retrospective evaluations are not only important for influencing voting in a given election; they are also important for shaping partisan attitudes, which Fiorina defines as "a running tally of retrospective evaluations of party promises and performance."[33] In other words, the running tally is a summary judgment of how well the parties and their leaders have done and are doing.

As a political attitude, partisanship is fairly stable. It can change but usually does not do so quickly. The discussion that follows examines the principal changes in partisan attitudes that have taken place over the last three decades and their impact on voting behavior.

Partisan Voting Patterns

The initial model of voter behavior was based on research conducted in the 1950s. Since that time, the U.S. electorate has experienced a divisive, unsuccessful war in Southeast Asia, a cohesive, successful one in the Persian Gulf, a major scandal (Watergate) that led to the resignation of a president, other smaller scandals involving public officials, large-scale social movements for equal rights and opportunities involving racial minorities and women, and periods of economic recession, inflation, and prosperity. Naturally, these events and the reaction of public officials to them have had an impact on the partisan attitudes of the electorate.

Three major trends stand out. First, there has been a reduction in the number of people who identify with a party and, conversely, an increase in the number of self-proclaimed independents. Second, there has been a decline in the strength of partisan identities. Third, there has been a shift in partisan loyalties, with the Democratic party losing adherents and the Republican party gaining them. Each of these changes has important long- and short-term implications for electoral politics.

Table 3–3 lists the percentage of party identifiers and independents. As the table indicates, during the forty-year period, 1952 to 1992, there has been a 13-percent decline in people who identify with a political party and a 16-percent increase in the number of self-proclaimed independents. Most of the shift occurred after 1964. The table also suggests that the decline was principally in the strong partisan category through the 1970s.

Although partisanship has weakened, with some strong partisans becoming weaker partisans, and weak partisans considering themselves independent, how independently voters behave on election day is another matter. Truly independent voting has increased far less rapidly than has independent identification by the electorate. In other words, a sizable portion claim that they are independent but continue to vote for candidates of the same party. They appear in Table 3–3 as independent but leaning in a partisan direction.[34]

The decline in partisanship and the growth of independents have produced a more volatile and manipulable electorate. With weaker partisan allegiances and more independent identifiers, the campaign, the candidates, and the issues seemingly have become more important influences on the vote.

Partisan Deviations

There has been a dramatic rise in split-ticket voting. According to Arthur H. Miller and Martin P. Wattenberg, about three times as many people divide their vote today as did in the 1950s.[35] The defections come primarily from weak partisans. Figure 3–1 presents the rates of defection among party identifiers from 1952 to 1992.

Defections from partisan voting patterns have tended to help the Republicans more than the Democrats. Without votes from Democratic defectors, the GOP could not have won seven presidential elections since 1952. Much of the help, however, has been short term. Although the Republicans have won all but two elections at the presidential level since 1968, they still do not command the loyalty of a plurality of the electorate. In 1992, defections among Republicans were actually higher than among Democrats.

TABLE 3-3

Party Identification, 1952–1994* (in percentages)†

Party Identification	1952	1956	1960	1964	1968	1972	1976	1980	1984	1988	1992	1994
DEMOCRAT
Strong	22	21	20	27	20	15	15	18	17	18	17	14
Weak	25	23	25	25	25	26	25	23	20	18	18	22
INDEPENDENT†
Leaning Democrat	10	6	6	9	10	11	12	11	11	12	14	12
Nonpartisan	6	9	10	8	11	13	15	13	11	11	12	13
Leaning Republican	7	8	7	6	9	11	10	10	12	13	13	10
REPUBLICAN
Strong	14	14	14	14	15	13	14	14	15	14	15	18
Weak	13	15	16	11	10	10	9	9	12	14	11	11
APOLITICALS
"Don't know"	4	4	3	1	1	1	1	2	2	2	—	—

* The survey question was, "Generally speaking, do you usually think of yourself as a Republican, a Democrat, an Independent, or what?" If Republican or Democrat, "Would you call yourself a strong (R) (D) or a not very strong (R) (D)?" If Independent, "Do you think of yourself as closer to the Republican or Democratic party?"

† Percentages may not equal 100 due to rounding.

‡ The people who fall into this category are those who declare themselves to be independent, but in follow-up questions indicate that they may lean in a partisan direction.

Source: National Election Studies, Inter-University Consortium for Political and Social Research, Center for Political Studies, University of Michigan, 1952–1992; General Social Surveys, National Opinion Research Center.

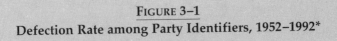

FIGURE 3–1
Defection Rate among Party Identifiers, 1952–1992*

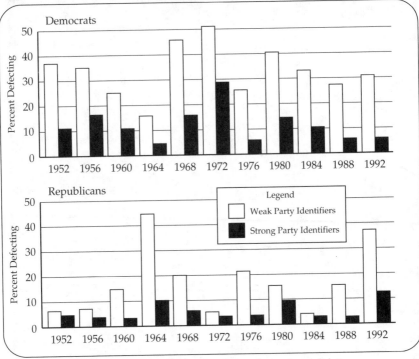

*Includes partisans who voted for Perot or the other major party candidate.

Source: National Election Studies, Inter-University Consortium for Political and Social Research, Center for Political Studies, University of Michigan.

The gap between self-identified Republicans and Democrats has narrowed, however. In 1952, the Democrats enjoyed a 20-percent advantage in party identification. Twenty years later that advantage had declined to 18 percent. The 1980s witnessed an even greater reduction in the partisan differential. By 1992, the Democratic lead in party identifiers was only 9 percent and 10 percent when partisan leaners are considered. (See Table 3–3.) When turnout is also taken into account, the Democratic lead among likely voters is a little less.

Partisan ties have also become weaker than they were thirty or even twenty years ago. The weakening of partisan loyalties, in turn, has produced more candidate-oriented voting and, to a lesser extent, more issue-oriented voting, especially at the presidential level. Why have these trends developed?

The reaction to Vietnam and Watergate and to the credibility gaps and political abuses of the so-called imperial presidents generated feelings of mistrust and hostility that were directed at politicians and their parties. Those who became eligible to vote, particularly during the 1970s during this period were less willing to identify with a political party. The unhappiness with parties has continued.[36] Moreover, the salience of social and cultural issues rendered the traditional partisan alliances, which had been built on an economic base, much less relevant.

A second reason for the drop in partisan identification has been the lowering of the voting age to eighteen. Over the last thirty years, the percentage of the electorate twenty-four years of age and under has nearly doubled. Since party identification tends to develop and harden over time, the youthing of the electorate has contributed to the decline in partisanship and growth of independents. This trend may change as the electorate gets older.

A third factor has to do with contemporary modes of campaigning and the declining role of the party in that capacity. In the past, the political party came between the voter and the candidate. Political parties provided the organization, planned the campaign, and made the partisan appeal. In doing so, they trumpeted their own cause. Today, much of the information comes directly from the candidate's organization via television. The party no longer mediates as it did in the pretelevision age.

Nonetheless, it is premature to write an obituary for partisanship and its impact on the electorate. The proportion of the population that continues to identify with a party remains significant and that identification either directly or indirectly influences their voting behavior.[37] In 1988, the relationship between partisanship and presidential voting was stronger than in any of the previous six presidential elections.[38] This relationship was weaker in 1992 because of the presence of a strong independent candidate and high levels of dissatisfaction with the nominees of both major parties.

Partisanship is no longer as good a predictor of the vote as it was in the past. It is not as strong an influence on how people evaluate the candidates or the issues and ultimately, on how they vote. Partisan ties have weakened, but they have not been eliminated, nor have they been replaced. The impact that the weakening of these ties has on the parties' electoral coalitions is discussed in the next section.

THE SOCIAL BASIS OF POLITICS

The New Deal Realignment

Political coalitions form during periods of partisan realignment. The last time such a classic realignment occurred was in the 1930s. Largely as a consequence of the Great Depression, the Democrats emerged as the dominant party.[39] Their coalition, held together by a common economic concern that the government play a more active role in dealing with the nation's economic problems, supported Franklin Roosevelt's New Deal program. Those who saw government involvement as a threat to the free enterprise system opposed much of Roosevelt's domestic legislation. They remained Republican in attitude and voting behavior.

The Democrats became the majority party during this period by expanding their coalition. Since the Civil War, the Democrats had enjoyed southern support. White Protestants living in rural areas dominated the southern electorate; African Americans were largely excluded from it. Only in the election of 1928, when Al Smith, the Catholic governor of New York, ran as the Democratic candidate, was there a sizable southern popular and electoral vote for a Republican candidate at the presidential level. Being a Catholic and an opponent of prohibition made Smith unacceptable to many white Protestant fundamentalists who lived in the South.

As a group, Catholics also voted Democratic before the 1930s. Living primarily in the urban centers of the North, they became increasingly important to the Democrats as their numbers grew in the population. Poor economic and social conditions, combined with the immigrant status of many Catholics, made them dependent on big-city bosses, who were able to deliver a sizable Democratic vote. In 1928, for the first time, a majority of the cities in the country voted Democratic. Catholic support for Smith and the Democratic party figured prominently in this vote.

The harsh economic realities of the Great Depression enabled Roosevelt to expand Democratic support in urban areas still further, especially to those in the lower socioeconomic strata. Outside the South, Roosevelt's political coalition was differentiated along class lines. It attracted people with less education and income and those with lower-status jobs. Organized labor, in particular, threw its support to Roosevelt. Union members became a core group in the Democratic coalition.

In addition to establishing a broad-based, blue-collar, working-class coalition, Roosevelt also lured specific racial and ethnic groups, such as African Americans and Jewish Americans, from their Republican affiliation. African Americans, who lived outside of the South, voted Democratic primarily for economic reasons, and Jewish Americans supported Roosevelt's liberal domestic programs and his anti-Nazi foreign policy. Neither of these groups provided the Democratic party of the 1930s with a large number of votes, but their loyalty to it and long-term impact on it have been considerable.

In contrast, during the same period the Republican party shrank. Not only were Republicans unable to attract new groups to their coalition, but they were unable to prevent the defection of some supporters whose economic situation affected their partisan loyalties and influenced their vote. Although the Republicans did retain the backing of a majority of business and professional people, they lost the support of much of the white

Protestant working class. Republican strength remained concentrated in the Northeast, particularly in the rural areas.

Evolving Political Coalitions

The coalition that formed during the New Deal held together, for the most part, until the 1960s. During this period, African Americans and Jewish Americans increased their identification with and support of the Democratic party and its candidates. Catholics tended to remain Democratic, although they fluctuated more in their voting behavior at the presidential level. Nonsouthern white Protestants continued to support the Republicans.

Some changes did take place, however, mainly along socioeconomic lines. Domestic prosperity contributed to the growth of a larger middle class. Had such a class identified with the Republicans for economic reasons, the Democratic majority would have been threatened. This identification did not occur, however. Those who gained in economic and social status did not, as a general rule, discard their partisan loyalties. The Democrats were able to hold on to the allegiance of a majority of this group and improve their position with the professional and managerial classes, which had grown substantially during this period. The Republicans continued to maintain their advantage with those in the upper socioeconomic strata. The economic improvement in the country had the effect of muting the class distinctions that were evident during the 1930s and 1940s.[40]

Partisan attitudes, however, were shifting in the South. White southerners, particularly those who first voted after 1940, began to desert their party at the presidential level, largely over civil rights issues. In 1948, Harry Truman won 52 percent of the southern vote, compared with Roosevelt's 69 percent four years earlier. Although Adlai Stevenson and John Kennedy carried the South by reduced margins, the southern white Protestant vote for president went Republican for the first time in 1960.

Major shifts in the national electorate began to be evident in the mid-1960s and have continued into the 1990s. (See Table 3–4.) The continued defection of southern white Protestants to Republican candidates, not only at the presidential level but at the other levels as well, has been the most significant and enduring of these changes.

Since 1952, the decline in the partisan loyalty of southern whites has been substantial. In that year 85 percent of them identified with the Democratic party; by 1992 that proportion had shrunk to less than forty percent with the ratio of Democrats to Republicans in the South declining from approximately 6 to 1 to less than 2 to 1.[41] Moreover, in the 1994 mid-term elections, Republican congressional candidates won a majority of the southern vote, the first time that has happened since Reconstruction.[42]

TABLE 3-4

Vote by Groups in Presidential Elections, 1952–1992 (in percentages)

	1952		1956		1960		1964		1968			1972	
	Adlai Stevenson	Dwight Eisenhower	Adlai Stevenson	Dwight Eisenhower	John Kennedy	Richard Nixon	Lyndon Johnson	Barry Goldwater	Hubert Humphrey	Richard Nixon	George Wallace	George McGovern	Richard Nixon
National total, by sex	44.6%	55.4%	42.2%	57.8%	50.1%	49.9%	61.3%	38.7%	43.0%	43.4%	13.6%	38%	62%
Male	47	53	45	55	52	48	60	40	41	43	16	37	63
Female	42	58	39	61	49	51	62	38	45	43	12	38	62
Race													
White	43	57	41	59	49	51	59	41	38	47	15	32	68
Nonwhite	79	21	61	39	68	32	94	6	85	12	3	87	13
Education													
College	34	66	31	69	39	61	52	48	37	54	9	37	63
High School	45	55	42	58	52	48	62	38	42	43	15	34	66
Grade School	52	48	50	50	55	45	66	34	52	33	15	49	51
Occupation													
Professional and business	36	64	32	68	42	58	54	46	34	56	10	31	69
White collar	40	60	37	63	48	52	57	43	41	47	12	36	64
Manual	55	45	50	50	60	40	71	29	50	35	15	43	57
Age (years):													
Under 30	51	49	43	57	54	46	64	36	47	38	15	48	52
30–49	47	53	45	55	54	46	63	37	44	41	15	33	67
50 & older	39	61	39	61	46	54	59	41	41	47	12	36	64
Religion													
Protestant	37	63	37	63	38	62	55	45	35	49	16	30	70
Catholic	56	44	51	49	78	22	76	24	59	33	8	48	52
Politics													
Republican	8	92	4	96	5	95	20	80	9	86	5	5	95
Democrat	77	23	85	15	84	16	87	13	74	12	14	67	33
Independent	35	65	30	70	43	57	56	44	31	44	25	31	69
Region													
East	45	55	40	60	53	47	68	32	50	43	7	42	58
Midwest	42	58	41	59	48	52	61	39	44	47	9	40	60
South	51	49	49	51	51	49	52	48	31	36	33	29	71
West	42	58	43	57	49	51	60	40	44	49	7	41	59
Members of labor union families	61	39	57	43	65	35	73	27	56	29	15	46	54

TABLE 3–4 (continued)

	1976			1980			1984		1988		1992[†]			
	Jimmy Carter	Gerald Ford	Eugene McCarthy	Jimmy Carter	Ronald Reagan	John Anderson	Walter Mondale	Ronald Reagan	Michael Dukakis	George Bush	Bill Clinton	George Bush	Ross Perot	Other/ Undecided
National total, by sex	50%	48%	1%	41%	51%	7%	41%	59%	46%	54%	44%	37%	14%	5%
Male	53	45	1	38	53	7	36	64	44	56	39	36	19	5
Female	48	51	*	44	49	6	45	55	48	52	48	36	10	6
Race														
White	46	52	1	36	56	7	34	66	41	59	40	40	15	5
Nonwhite	85	15	*	86	10	2	87	13	82	18	76	12	4	8
Education														
College	42	55	2	35	53	10	39	61	42	58	43	39	14	4
High School	54	46	*	43	51	5	43	57	46	54	45	37	12	6
Grade School	58	41	1	54	42	3	51	49	55	45	43	35	15	7
Occupation														
Professional and business	42	56	1	33	55	10	34	66	—	—	—	—	—	—
White collar	50	48	2	40	51	9	47	53	—	—	—	—	—	—
Manual	58	41	1	48	46	5	46	54	—	—	—	—	—	—
Age (years):														
Under 30	53	45	1	47	41	11	40	60	37	63	38	44	14	4
30–49	48	49	2	38	52	8	40	60	45	55	43	35	17	5
50 & older	52	48	*	41	54	4	41	59	49	51	46	37	11	6
Religion														
Protestant	46	53	*	39	54	6	39	61	42	58	—	—	—	—
Catholic	57	42	1	46	47	6	39	61	51	49	—	—	—	—
Politics														
Republican	9	91	*	8	86	5	4	96	7	93	7	77	13	3
Democrat	82	18	*	69	26	4	79	21	85	15	82	8	7	3
Independent	38	57	4	29	55	14	33	67	43	57	38	28	23	11
Region														
East	51	47	1	43	47	9	46	54	51	49	47	33	15	5
Midwest	48	50	1	41	51	7	42	58	47	53	45	35	13	7
South	54	45	*	44	52	3	37	63	40	60	40	42	13	5
West	46	51	1	35	54	9	40	60	46	54	43	36	15	6
Members of labor union families	63	36	1	50	43	5	52	48	63	37	—	—	—	—

* Less than 1 percent.

[†] Final three-way presidential poll (conducted November 1–2, 1992).

In 1992, the categories were college grads, college inc., and no college.

Source: Gallup Opinion Index, November 1992, p. 9. Reprinted with permission.

Despite Republican gains in the South, it is still not as solidly Republican today as it was Democratic from 1876 through 1944. According to political scientists Earl and Merle Black, Franklin Delano Roosevelt averaged 78 percent of the southern vote during his four presidential elections compared with 57 percent for Republican presidential candidates from 1972 to 1988.[43]

In 1988 and 1992, southern whites were less apt to vote for the Democratic presidential candidate than were whites in any other region of the country. Arkansas Democrat, Bill Clinton, received only 30 percent of the southern, white vote compared with 53 percent for George Bush and 17 percent for Ross Perot. Had it not been for the growth of the African American electorate in the South and its overwhelming support for Democratic candidates, the defection of the southern states from the Democratic camp would have been even more dramatic. In 1992, African Americans constituted 14 percent of southern voters.[44]

Another potentially important shift has been occurring among new voters, particularly younger ones. During the 1980s, a plurality of this group turned to the Republican party after being more Democratic than their elders since the 1950s. In 1984, those between the ages of eighteen and twenty-nine supported Ronald Reagan in his reelection bid just as strongly as did those over thirty. (See Table 3–4.) Their support of George Bush in 1988 was even greater. In 1992, however, the vote of younger Americans more closely reflected national voting trends, halting, at least temporarily, the tendency of this youngest age cohort to vote more for the Republicans than the Democrats.[45]

While Democrats have lost the allegiance of southern whites at the presidential level and have lost support from southern voters generally, they also saw electoral support dwindle from several of their key coalitional groups. Organized labor is a good example. In six of the eight presidential elections between 1952 and 1976, this group favored the Democratic candidate by an average of nearly 30 percentage points. Since 1984, the results have been closer although the Democrats still enjoy an advantage. Not only have the Democrats suffered from decreasing labor support, but as a group organized labor has declined as a proportion of the total population. Members of union households made up 25 percent of the electorate in 1952; today they constitute only 15 percent.

Catholic allegiance to the Democratic party has also weakened. The Democratic vote of this group has declined from its high of 78 percent in 1960 to a low of 39 percent in 1984. Dukakis and Clinton recovered some of these losses in 1988 and 1992. Nonetheless, the bad news for the Democrats is that the proportion of Catholics identifying with the Republican party has increased in the past decade, particularly among the young. Only the constant loyalty of older Catholics, particularly those over 65, has enabled the Democrats to maintain their advantage among this group.[46]

Jewish voters have evidenced a much smaller decline in their Democratic partisan sympathies and voting behavior. Approximately two-thirds of this group identify with the Democratic party, and three-fourths have voted for its presidential candidates since 1928. Between 1928 and 1988, the average Jewish vote for president has been 75 percent Democratic.[47] The only election since World War II in which a majority of Jews did not vote Democratic occurred in 1980 when 47 percent cast ballots for President Carter. Independent candidate John Anderson was a principal beneficiary of this defection, winning 14 percent of the Jewish vote. As a group, Jewish Americans returned to their traditional voting patterns after that election with approximately two-thirds supporting the Democratic presidential candidates in 1984 and 1988 and around 80 percent in 1992.

The Democratic electoral coalition has also retained and even increased the support of other key groups, notably African Americans and Hispanics. In recent decades, African Americans have become even more loyal to the Democratic party than they were in the past. Few Republican identifiers are left among African American voters in contrast to the late 1950s when almost 25 percent of this group considered themselves Republican. Today, more than 75 percent of African Americans consider themselves Democrats and less than 10 percent Republicans.[48]

In presidential elections since 1964, between 85 and 90 percent of the African American vote has gone to the Democratic presidential candidate. Moreover, turnout has also improved, exceeding the national average in 1984 and 1988 but not in 1992[49] (See Table 3–2). In 1984, one out of every four Mondale voters was African American; in 1992, one out of six Clinton voters was.

Hispanic voters have also become an important component of the Democrats' electoral coalition. With the exception of Cuban Americans concentrated in south Florida, a majority of Hispanic voters identify with the Democratic party and two-thirds of them tend to vote for its candidates on a regular basis.[50]

Since 1980, there have been discernible differences in the partisan identities and electoral voting patterns of men and women. This differential has produced what some have referred to as a "gender gap," with women more likely to identify and vote Democratic and men more likely to prefer the Republican party and its candidates. The gap has been in the range of 4 to 8 percent. It is larger among whites than nonwhites, larger among those in the higher socioeconomic brackets than in the lower groups, and larger among those with more formal education than less.[51] It is also greater between those who are unmarried than those who are married.

In the light of these shifts, how can the Democratic party's electoral coalition be described today? The Democrats have become a diverse party in which ethnic and racial minorities constitute core constituencies.

Democrats still receive overwhelming support from those with the lowest incomes and those who live in the cities. However, the relatively small size of the latter two groups compared with the population as a whole and their lower turnout make them less important components of the total electorate than they were in the past. On the other hand, other traditional Democratic-oriented groups, such as organized labor and Catholics, have weakened in their backing of Democratic candidates. Southern whites have exited in the largest proportions. Additionally, young voters in the 1980s have not identified with the Democratic party nor voted for its candidates in anywhere near the proportions that they did a decade or two ago.

Although the Democratic New Deal coalition has eroded, the groups within that coalition, with the exception of southern whites, have not become Republican. They have simply provided less support for the Democrats. Although the Republican party has gained adherents, it has not done so by virtue of a major exodus of groups from one party to the other.

As a party, the Republicans have become more white, more middle class, and more suburban. They have gained support in the South and Southwest, the so-called Sunbelt. Additionally, they have gained adherents from white evangelical groups which had supported the Democratic party and voted for its candidates through 1976. By the end of the 1980s a plurality of this group thought of themselves as Republican, with 80 percent voting for George Bush in 1988 and 63 percent in 1992. White evangelicals now constitute a core bloc within the Republican party's electoral coalition perhaps as important to the GOP as African Americans are to the Democrats.[52]

The shift of white evangelical Protestants who constitute approximately one-fourth of the population to the Republican party has offset some of the reduction in Republican support from mainline Protestants. The presidential votes of members of this group declined in 1992 as did their identification with the Republican party. In general regular church goers within both evangelical and mainline Protestant groups are more Republican in their party identification and voting behavior than those who do not attend regularly. Nonchurch goers, those who think of themselves as secular and rarely attend religious services, have become the least Republican of all.[53]

The contemporary Republican party thus consists of racial and religious majorities, those in the higher socioeconomic brackets, and those in the professional and managerial positions.

What conclusions can we draw about the social basis of politics today? It is clear that the old party coalitions have evolved and, in the Democrats' case, severely weakened. Although class, religion, and geography are still related to party identification and voting behavior, they are not as strongly related as they had been. Today, voters seem to be less influenced by group cues. They exercise a more independent judgment on election day, a judgment that is likely to be influenced by factors that condition the environment in which the election occurs and by the campaign itself. These changes explain why the Republicans' chances have improved although they have not become a majority of the electorate.

A New Partisan Majority?

Are Republican gains evidence of a new realignment of voters? Will the GOP soon emerge as the partisan majority? The answer is still unclear, but two basic trends stand out: one relates to the contemporary dealignment of the partisan attitudes of the electorate over time; the other pertains to the narrowing of the gap that had developed between Democratic and Republican identifiers.

Dealignment. Dealignment is a weakening in the attachment people feel toward political parties. It has produced more split-ticket voting, which has helped Republican presidential candidates more than their Democratic counterparts. It has also led more people to think of themselves as independents. The Republicans have usually been the beneficiaries of the independent vote as well although not in 1992.

Dealignment, in short, has enabled the Republicans to win an electoral majority in five of the last seven presidential elections. It also enabled independent candidate Ross Perot to receive 20 percent of the vote in 1992. It has reduced but not eliminated the Democrats' partisan advantage.

Realignment. There is some evidence that a gradual partisan realignment may also be occurring. It may, however, be less meaningful than the one that took place in the 1930s. With the exception of white southerners who have switched their partisan allegiances from Democrat to Republican, this realignment has not involved wholesale shifts from one electoral coalition to another in the rest of the country.[54] Nor has it involved overwhelming proportions of new voters who ally themselves with one party. Rather it consists of a gradual hemorrhaging of Democratic support.[55] If these trends persist, they may eventually result in the emergence of a new Republican majority, but they have not done so already.

A partisan realignment that occurs during an era of weaker partisan attachments for adherents to both parties may not have the same effect as one that occurred during a period in which partisan loyalties were stronger and more predictive of the vote. If people have generally less confidence in parties and weaker partisan allegiances, then their affiliation is not likely to matter as much. In the words of Martin Wattenberg, a keen student of partisan attitudes and behavior, "such a realignment is hollow when the two parties involved continue to have a weak image in the public mind and an uncertain role in the future of American government."[56]

SUMMARY

The electorate is not neutral. People do not come to campaigns with completely open minds. Rather, their preexisting attitudes and accumulated experiences color their perceptions and affect their judgment, much as stimuli from the campaign affect those attitudes and experiences.

Of the political beliefs people possess, partisanship has the strongest impact on voting. It provides a perspective for evaluating the campaign and for deciding whether and how to vote. It is also a motive for being informed, for being concerned, and for turning out to vote.

Between 1960 and 1988, there was a decline in the proportion of the population that voted. This decline can be partially attributed to the weakening of party ties, to the increasing proportion of younger voters, and to the cynicism and apathy of the electorate, a cynicism and apathy that has been particularly evident among those in the lower socioeconomic groups and those with the least formal education. The economic recession, the Perot candidacy, and the new media contributed to a reversal of this trend in 1992.

Partisan attitudes have also eroded since the 1960s. The percentage of people identifying with a party has declined. One consequence has been the increasing importance of short-term factors on voting. A second has been more split-ticket ballots. The weakening of partisan ties has produced a vote that either party can win. It has produced a presidential vote that has less carryover to congressional and state elections. And it has produced an electorate that is more volatile. These shifts have tended to help the Republicans more than the Democrats.

Group ties to the parties have also loosened. Their coalitions have shifted. The Democratic party, which became dominant during the New Deal period, has lost the support of a majority of southern whites in presidential elections and has suffered defections from other groups. That some of these groups have also declined as a proportion of the population or have lower than average turnout has further aggravated the Democrats' problem. Racial minorities, such as African Americans and Hispanics, have, however, retained their loyalty to the Democrats as have Jewish Americans. Women have become more supportive of Democratic candidates and men more supportive of Republicans.

Naturally, the Republicans have benefited from the fraying of the Democrats' electoral coalition. Looser partisan ties have given them greater electoral opportunities, and they have been successful in taking advantage of them.

The Republicans have gained in the South, benefited from the increased social and economic conservatism of a growing middle and upper-middle class, and made strides among younger voters. They have won five of the last seven presidential elections but have not thus far been able to expand their electoral coalition into a partisan majority.

These changes within the political environment have important implications for presidential politics. The weakening of partisan attitudes and the splintering of the New Deal coalitions augur a new era in electoral politics. It is clear that a dealignment has occurred. It is not clear whether a permanent realignment is taking place or, if it is, how important that realignment will be to the future of American politics. Partisan attitudes seem to be less compelling influences on voting behavior than they were in the past.

NOTES

1. An estimated 58.5 percent of the voting-age population *who were citizens* actually voted. Paul R. Abramson, John H. Aldrich, and David W. Rohde, *Change and Continuity in the 1992 Elections* (Washington, D.C.: Congressional Quarterly, 1994), p. 104.
2. Turnout percentages for the states were estimated by the Committee for the Study of the American Electorate, 421 New Jersey Ave., SE, Washington, D.C., 20003.
3. Abramson, et al., *Change and Continuity in the 1992 Elections*, p. 110.
4. Ronald P. Formisane, "Deferential-Participant Politics: The Early Republic's Political Culture, 1789," *American Political Science Review* 68 (June 1974): 473–487.
5. Walter Dean Burnham, "The Turnout Problem," in *Elections American Style*, ed. A. James Reichley (Washington, D.C.: Brookings Institution, 1987), pp. 112–116.
6. Although some states initially permitted all landowners to vote, including women, by 1807 every one of them limited voting to men. Michael X. Delli Carpini and Ester R. Fuchs, "The Year of the Woman: Candidates, Voters, and the 1992 Election," *Political Science Quarterly*, 108 (Spring 1993): 30.
7. Ibid.
8. Earl Black and Merle Black, *The Vital South: How Presidents Are Elected* (Cambridge, Mass.: Harvard University Press, 1992), p. 217.
9. The territory of Wyoming was the first to grant women the vote in 1867.
10. In the case of *Smith* v. *Allwright* (321 U.S. 649,1944), the Supreme Court declared the white primary unconstitutional. In its opinion the Court rejected the argument that parties were private associations and thus could restrict participation in their selection processes.
11. In 1992, women were about 2.1 percent more likely to vote than men. Abramson, et al., *Change and Continuity in the 1992 Elections*, p. 102.
12. Ruy A. Teixeira, *The Disappearing American Voter* (Washington D.C.: Brookings Institution, 1992), p. 8.
13. David P. Glass, Peverill Squire, and Raymond E. Wolfinger, "Voter Turnout: An International Comparison," *Public Opinion* 5 (December/January 1984): 49–55.
14. The period during which people can register, the places they have to go to do so, even the dates and hours when registration is permitted vary from state to state.
15. Teixeira, *The Disappearing American Voter*, pp. 106–147. Raymond E. Wolfinger and Steven J. Rosenstone, *Who Votes?* (New Haven, Conn.: Yale University Press, 1980), p. 73.
16. Approximately half the states had motor-voter laws of their own prior to the enactment of federal legislation.

17. Angus Campbell, Philip E. Converse, Warren E. Miller, and Donald E. Stokes, *The American Voter* (New York: John Wiley, 1960), p. 102.

18. Wolfinger and Rosenstone, *Who Votes?*, pp. 13–26.

19. Ibid., pp. 18–20, 35–36.

20. Teixeira describes "social connectedness" as the "interpersonal, community, and general social ties [that] provide a substantial proportion of an individual's motivation to vote." *The Disappearing American Voter*. (p. 36). He adds that demographic characteristics that usually reflect connectedness are marital status, church attendance, and age. Ibid., p. 37.

    See also Abramson, et al., *Change and Continuity in the 1992 Elections*, p. 115.

21. Ibid.

22. Ibid., p. 118.

23. Turnout for those with incomes under $10,000 was 37.6 percent in 1992; for those with incomes over $50,000 it was 81.8 percent. Ibid.

24. Ibid., p. 106.

25. Actually, a small interview-reinterview survey was conducted in 1948, but the results were never published. In contrast to the emphasis on political attitudes of the large-scale interview projects in the 1950s, the project in 1948 had a sociological orientation.

26. Campbell, et al., *The American Voter*, pp. 146–152.

27. Ibid., pp. 133–136. Party identification is determined by the following question: "Generally speaking, do you usually think of yourself as a Republican, Democrat, an Independent, or what?" To discern the strength of the identification, a second question is asked: "(if Republican or Democrat), Would you call yourself a strong (R) (D) or a not very strong (R) (D)? (If Independent), Do you think of yourself as closer to the Republican or Democratic party?"

    In examining the concept of party identification, Michigan analysts have stressed two dimensions: direction and strength. Others, however, have criticized the Michigan model for overemphasizing party and underemphasizing other factors, such as social class, political ideology, and issue positions. For a thoughtful critique, see Jerrold G. Rusk, "The Michigan Election Studies: A Critical Evaluation," (Paper presented at the annual meeting of the American Political Science Association, New York, September 3–6, 1981).

28. For a more extensive discussion of desirable presidential images, see Chapter 6 of this book and Benjamin I. Page, *Choices and Echoes in Presidential Elections* (Chicago: University of Chicago Press, 1978), pp. 232–265.

29. Campbell, et al., *The American Voter*, pp. 143 and 547. Independents who lean in a partisan direction tend to be better informed than those who do not. These independent leaners have many of the characteristics of party identifiers including loyalty to the party's candidates. They do not, however, identify themselves as Republicans or Democrats.

30. V. O. Key, Jr., *The Responsible Electorate* (Cambridge, Mass.: Harvard University Press, 1966), p. 7.

31. Samuel L. Popkin, *The Reasoning Voter* (Chicago: University of Chicago Press, 1991), p. 43.

32. Morris P. Fiorina, *Retrospective Voting in American National Elections* (New Haven: Conn.: Yale University Press, 1981), pp. 65–83.

33. Ibid., p. 84.

34. For an analysis of independents and their voting patterns, see Bruce E. Keith, et al., *The Myth of the Independent Voter* (Berkeley, Calif.: University of California Press, 1992).

35. Arthur H. Miller and Martin P. Wattenberg, "Policy and Performance Voting in the 1980 Election," (Paper presented at the annual meeting of the American Political Science Association, New York, September 3–6, 1981).

36. A CBS News/*New York Times* poll fielded nine days before the 1994 midterm election found 57 percent of those surveyed felt the country needed a new political party. See *New York Times,* November 3, 1994, p. 8A. A poll conducted for the *Times Mirror Center for the People and the Press* during the period April 6–9, 1995 found similar results.: "News Release," *Times Mirror Center for the People and the Press,* p. 66.

37.Warren E. Miller, "Party Identification, Realignment, and Party Voting: Back to the Basics," *American Political Science Review* 85 (June 1991): 559.

38. Abramson, et al., *Change and Continuity in the 1988 Elections* (Washington, D.C.: Congressional Quarterly, 1990) p. 212.

39. This description of the New Deal realignment is based primarily on the discussion in Everett Carll Ladd, Jr. with Charles D. Hadley, *Transformations of the American Party System* (New York: W. W. Norton, 1975), pp. 31–87.

40. Ibid., pp. 93–104.

41. Black and Black, *The Vital South,* p. 27.

42. Thomas B. Edsall, "Huge Gains in South Fueled GOP Vote in '94," *Washington Post,* June 27, 1995, p. A8.

43. Ibid.

44. Ibid., *The Vital South,* p. 217.

45.There is a discrepancy between the final Gallup Poll and election day exit polls. The latter show a larger youth vote for Clinton. see Table 8–2 on p. 270.

46. Everett Carll Ladd, "The 1992 Vote for President Clinton: Another Brittle Mandate?" *Political Science Quarterly,* 108 (Spring 1993): 5.

47. Lee Sigelman, "Jews and the 1988 Election: More of the Same?" in *The Bible and the Ballot Box,* eds. James L. Guth and John C. Green (Boulder, Colo.: Westview Press, 1991), p. 190. Neal Riemer, "Jewish Voters and Presidential Elections: The Record, the Reasons, the Future," (Paper presented at the annual meeting of the American Political Science Association, Washington, D.C., September 1–4, 1993), pp. 1–3.

48. Ladd, "The 1992 Vote for Clinton." p. 4.

49. Political scientist, Katherine Tate, suggests that support for Jesse Jackson in 1984 and opposition to Ronald Reagan that same year inflated the vote of this group. The absence of these two polarizing figures in 1988, brought turnout back to its more normal levels.
    For a discussion of turnout among African Americans in 1984 and 1988 see Katherine Tate, "Black Political Participation in the 1984 and 1988 Presidential Elections." *American Political Science Review,* 85 (December 1991): 1159–1176.

50. Ladd, "The 1992 Vote for President Clinton." p. 4.

51. Abramson, et al., *Change and Continuity in the 1988 Elections,* pp. 123–126.

52. The conservative policy orientation of this group has also colored the Republicans' position on some important and divisive social issues. For an excellent discussion of the religious right and its impact on the 1992 election see Lyman A. Kellstedt, John C. Green, James L. Guth, and Corwin E. Smidt, "Religious Voting Blocs in the 1992 Election: The Year of the Evangelical?" (Paper presented at the annual meeting of the American Political Science Association, Washington, D.C., September 1–4, 1993).

53. Ibid., pp. 7, 8, 11, 18, and 21.

54. Miller, "Party Identification." p. 562.

55. Changes in partisan identification are evident between elections. They may result from short-term factors such as an economic recession or longer-term trends that affect particular groups of voters. For a discussion of the causes of shifts in partisanship see Herbert Weisberg with David C. Kimball, "The 1992 Presidential Election: Party Identification and Beyond," (Paper presented at the annual meeting of the American Political Science Association, Washington, D.C., September 1–4, 1993), p. 2.
56. Martin P. Wattenberg, *The Decline of American Political Parties, 1952–1988* (Cambridge, Mass.: Harvard University Press, 1990).

SELECTED READINGS

Black, Earl, and Merle Black. *The Vital South: How Presidents Are Elected.* Cambridge, Mass.: Harvard University Press, 1992.

Burnham, Walter D. "The Turnout Problem," in A. James Reichley (ed.), *Elections American Style.* Washington, D.C.: Brookings Institution, 1987. pp. 97–133.

Campbell, Angus, Philip E. Converse, Warren E. Miller, and Donald E. Stokes. *The American Voter.* New York: John Wiley, 1960.

Carmines, Edward G., and James A. Stimson. *Issue Evolution: Race and the Transformation of American Politics.* Princeton, N.J.: Princeton University Press, 1989.

Clubb, Jerome M., William H. Flanigan, and Nancy H. Zingale. *Partisan Realignment: Voters, Parties, and Government in American History.* Boulder, Colo.: Westview Press, 1990.

Fiorina, Morris, P. *Retrospective Voting in American National Elections.* New Haven, Conn.: Yale University Press, 1981.

Keith, Bruce, David B. Magleby, Candice Nelson, and Elizabeth Orr. *The Myth of the Independent Voter.* Berkeley, Calif.: University of California Press, 1992.

Ladd, Everett Carll, "The 1992 Vote for President Clinton: Another Brittle Mandate?" *Political Science Quarterly,* 108 (Spring 1993): 1–28.

Ladd, Everett Carll, Jr., with Charles D. Hadley. *Transformations of the American Party System.* New York: W. W. Norton, 1978.

Leege, David, and Lyman A. Kellstedt. *Rediscovering the Religious Factor in American Politics.* New York: M. E. Sharpe, 1993.

Miller, Warren E. "Party Identification, Realignment, and Party Voting: Back to the Basics," *American Political Science Review,* 85 (June 1991): 557–570.

Nie, Norman H., Sidney Verba, and John R. Petrocik. *The Changing American Voter.* Cambridge, Mass.: Harvard University Press, 1976.

Niemi, Richard G., and Herbert F. Weisberg. *Controversies in Voting Behavior.* 3rd ed. Washington, D.C.: Congressional Quarterly, 1993.

Piven, Frances Fox, and Richard A. Cloward. *Why Americans Don't Vote.* New York: Pantheon, 1988.

Popkin, Samuel L. *The Reasoning Voter: Communication and Persuasion in Presidential Campaigns.* Chicago: University of Chicago Press, 1991.

Tate, Katherine. "Black Political Participation in the 1984 and 1988 Presidential Elections," *American Political Science Review,* 85 (December 1991): 1159–1176.

Teixeira, Ruy A. *The Disappearing American Voter.* Washington, D.C.: Brookings Institution, 1992.

Wattenberg, Martin P. *The Decline of American Political Parties: 1952–1988.* Cambridge, Mass.: Harvard University Press, 1990.

Wolfinger, Raymond E., and Steven J. Rosenstone. *Who Votes?* New Haven, Conn.: Yale University Press, 1980.

PART II

The Nomination

Chapter 4

Delegate Selection

INTRODUCTION

Presidential nominees are selected by the delegates to their party's national convention. The way those delegates are chosen, however, influences the choice of nominees. It also affects the influence of the state and its party leadership.

Procedures for delegate selection are determined by state law. Today, these procedures also have to conform to the general guidelines and rules established by the national party. Prior to the 1970s, they did not. Under the old system, statutes passed by the state legislature reflected the needs and desires of the political leaders who controlled the state. Naturally, these laws were designed to buttress that leadership and extend its clout.

Primary elections in which the party's rank and file chose the delegates were discouraged, co-opted, or even circumvented. Favorite son candidates, tapped by the leadership, prevented meaningful contests in many states. Although primaries were held, many of them were advisory; the actual selection of the delegates was left to caucuses, conventions, or committees, which were more easily controlled by party officials. There were also impediments to potential delegates' getting on the ballot: high fees, lengthy petitions, and early filing dates. Winner-take-all provisions gave a great advantage to the organization candidate, as did rules requiring delegates to vote as a unit.

Popular participation in the selection of convention delegates is a relatively recent phenomenon in the history of national nominating conventions. It was the Democrats who took the lead in encouraging their partisans to become involved in the nomination process by adopting a series of reforms that affected the period during which delegates could be selected, the procedures for choosing them, and ultimately their behavior at the convention. Although these Democratic party rules limited the states' discretion, they did not result in uniform primaries and caucuses. Considerable variation still exists in how delegates are chosen, how the vote is apportioned, and who participates in the selection.

This chapter explores these rules and their consequences for the nomination process. It is organized into four sections. The first details the changes in party rules. The second considers the legal challenges to these rules and the Supreme Court's decisions on these challenges. The third section examines the impact of the rules changes on the party and the electorate, and the fourth discusses how they have affected the candidates and their campaign strategies.

REFORMING THE NOMINATION PROCESS

Historically, states set their own rules for nominating candidates with relatively little guidance from the national party. Some rules discouraged popular participation; others encouraged it but made no effort to translate public opinion of the candidates into delegate support for them. In very few states was the delegation as a whole representative, demographically or ideologically, of the party's electorate within that state.

Democratic party reforms have attempted to change this situation. The party had two primary objectives in altering its rules to promote more internal democracy. Democrats wanted to encourage greater rank-and-file participation and to select delegates who were more representative of the party's supporters. The problem has been how to achieve these goals and still win elections.

The Democratic party has gone through two stages in reforming its delegate selection procedures. During the first, 1968–1980, it adopted a highly structured set of national rules aimed at achieving its two principal aims: greater participation and more equitable representation. It imposed these rules on the states. Since that time the party has modified these rules to improve the chances of its nominees in the general election. Unlike the Democrats, the Republican party has not mandated national rules on its state parties. Republican state parties, however, have been affected by Democratic reforms, particularly in states whose legislatures were controlled by the Democrats.

Democratic Rules, 1968–1980

The catalyst for the rules changes was the tumultuous Democratic convention of 1968, a convention in which Senator Hubert Humphrey won the nomination without actively campaigning in the party's primaries. Yet the primaries of that year were very important. They had become the vehicle by which Democrats could protest the Johnson administration's conduct of the war in Vietnam.

Senator Eugene McCarthy, the first of the antiwar candidates, had challenged Lyndon Johnson in the New Hampshire primary. To the surprise of many political observers, McCarthy received 42.4 percent of the vote, almost as much as the president, who got 49.5 percent. Four days after McCarthy's unexpectedly strong showing, Senator Robert Kennedy, brother of the late president and political rival of Johnson, declared his candidacy for the nation's highest office. With protests against the war mounting and divisions within the Democratic party intensifying, Johnson bowed out, declaring that he did not want the country's involvement in Southeast Asia to become a partisan political issue.

Johnson's withdrawal cleared the way for Hubert Humphrey, the vice-president, to run. Humphrey, however, waited almost a month to announce his intentions. His late entrance into the Democratic nomination process intentionally precluded a primary effort since filing deadlines had expired in most of the states. Like Johnson, Humphrey did not want to become the focal point of antiwar protests. Nor did he have the grass roots organization to match McCarthy's and Kennedy's. What he did have was the support of many Democratic leaders, including the president.

The last big-state primary in 1968 was California's. In it, Kennedy scored a significant victory, but during the celebration that followed, he was assassinated. His death left McCarthy as the principal antiwar candidate, but he was far short of a convention majority. Despite the last-minute entrance of Senator George McGovern, who hoped to rally Kennedy delegates to his candidacy, Humphrey won the nomination easily. To make matters worse for those who opposed Humphrey and the administration's war efforts, an amendment to the party platform calling for an unconditional end to the bombing of North Vietnam was defeated. McCarthy and Kennedy delegates felt victimized by the process and the result. They were angry. They demanded reform and eventually got it. A divided convention approved the establishment of a party committee to reexamine the rules for delegate selection with the goals of providing greater participation by the rank and file and more equitable representation.

Compounding the divisions within the convention were demonstrations outside of it. Thousands of youthful protestors, calling for an end to the war, congregated in the streets of Chicago. The police, under orders from Mayor Richard Daley to maintain order, used strong-arm tactics to disperse the crowds. Clashes between police and protesters followed. Television news crews filmed these confrontations, and the networks showed them during their convention coverage. The spectacle of police beating demonstrators further inflamed emotions and led to calls for reform, not only from those who attended the convention but from those who watched it on television.

After the election, a commission, chaired initially by Senator George McGovern, was appointed to study procedures for electing and seating convention delegates and to propose ways of improving them. The commission recommended that delegate selection be a *fair reflection* of Democratic sentiment within the state and implicitly, less closely tied to the wishes of state party leaders. Rules to make it easier for individuals to run as delegates, to limit the size of the districts from which they could be chosen, and to require that the number of delegates elected be proportional to the popular vote that they or the candidates to whom they were pledged received, were approved by the party. A requirement that delegates be chosen no earlier than the calendar year of the election was also approved.

Additionally, Democrats tried to prevent independents and, especially, partisans of other parties, from participating in the selection of Democratic delegates. The difficulty, however, was to determine who was a Democrat, since some states did not require or even permit registration by party. When implementing this rule, the party adopted a very liberal interpretation of Democratic affiliation. People identifying themselves as Democrats at the time of voting, or those requesting Democratic ballots, were viewed as Democrats. This process of identification effectively permitted *crossover* voting, allowing Republicans or independents to cross over and vote in the Democratic primary. The only primaries that the Democratic rules effectively prohibited were *open primaries*, those in which voters are given the ballots of both major parties, discard one, and vote the other.

In addition to translating public preferences into delegate selection, another major objective of the reforms was to equalize representation on the delegations themselves. Three groups in particular—African Americans, women, and youth—had protested their underrepresentation on party councils and at the conventions. Their representatives and others who were sympathetic to their plight pressed hard for more power and better representation for women and minorities. The reform commission reacted to these protests by proposing a rule requiring that all states represent these particular groups in reasonable relationship to their presence in the state population. Failure to do so was viewed as prima facie evidence of discrimination. In point of fact, the party had established quotas.

Considerable opposition developed to the application of this rule during the 1972 nomination process, and it was subsequently modified to require that states implement affirmative action plans for those groups that had been subject to past discrimination.[1] The party went one step further with respect to women. Beginning with its 1980 nominating convention, it required that each state delegation be equally divided between the sexes.

Still another goal of the reforms, to involve more Democrats in the selection process, was achieved not only by the fair reflection rule but by making primaries the preferred method of delegate selection. To avoid a challenge to the composition of their delegation, states switched to primaries in which delegates were elected directly by the people.[2]

Caucuses in which party regulars selected the delegates were still permitted, but they, too, were redesigned to encourage greater rank-and-file participation. (See Box 4–1, "The Iowa Caucus: How It Works.") No

---

BOX 4–1

The Iowa Caucus:
How It Works

DATE	**STAGES**
February	1. Caucuses are held in 2,166 precincts to choose more than 1,500 delegates to 99 county conventions.
March	2. Conventions are held in counties to choose 3,000 delegates to the six congressional district conventions.
May	3. Conventions are held in congressional districts to elect district-level delegates to national party conventions. The same delegates also attend the state convention.
June	4. State conventions elect at-large delegates to national party convention. Democrats also select their state party and elected official delegates.

PROCEDURES FOR THE FIRST-ROUND PRECINCT CAUCUSES

Democrats: Only registered Democrats who live in the precinct and can vote may participate. Attendees are asked to join preference groups for candidates. A group must consist of at least 15 percent of those present to be viable. Nonviable groups are dissolved, and those who were members of them may join other viable groups. Much lobbying occurs at this stage of the meeting. Delegates are allocated to candidates strictly on the basis of the group's proportion to the caucus as a whole.

Republicans: Attendees cast a presidential preference vote by secret ballot. Delegates to the county convention are then selected by whatever method the caucus chooses, either by direct election (winner take all) or proportionally on the basis of the straw vote.

longer could a state party leader cast a large number of proxies for the delegates of his or her choice. Caucuses had to be publicly announced with adequate time given for campaigning. Moreover, they had to be conducted in stages, and three-fourths of the delegates had to be chosen in districts no larger than those for members of Congress.

Other consequences, not nearly so beneficial to the goal of increased participation, were a lengthening of the process, escalating its costs, fatiguing its candidates, boring the public, and dividing the party. Since the contests at the beginning of the quest for the nomination received the most attention from the news media, candidates, and public alike, states began moving their primaries forward, "front-loading" the schedule and forcing candidates to start their campaigns in the year prior to the election, another trend that has continued.

Primaries and caucuses affected the type of delegate selected as well. They made it more difficult for elected officials and party leaders automatically to attend the nominating conventions. To participate, they too had to run as delegates. This, in turn, forced them to endorse a candidate or run as an unpledged delegate. Some chose not to do so, and others supported unsuccessful candidates. As a consequence the number of party leaders who attended the national nominating convention following the adoption of the rules changes declined substantially. The absence of these leaders generated and extended cleavages between the nominees and their electoral coalitions and the party's organization and its leadership.

These cleavages created serious problems, adversely affecting the chances of its nominees' in the general election, and if successful, in governing the country. During the presidential campaign, the divisiveness impaired a unified organizational effort, tarnished the images of party candidates, and increased defections from straight partisan voting. After the election, it made agenda and coalition building more difficult.

In short, the early party reforms produced unintended consequences. These consequences—the proliferation of primaries, the lengthening of the process, the divisiveness within the party, the poor representation of elected leaders, and, most importantly, the failure to win elections and govern successfully—prompted the Democrats to reexamine and modify their rules for delegate selection beginning in the 1980s.

Democratic Rules, 1981–Present

After each presidential election, party commissions, composed of a cross section of party officials, interest group representatives, and supporters of leading candidates for the nomination, have met and proposed a series of rules for the next party nomination. Each commission has tinkered with the rules.

The rule changes that have been made fall into three categories: those that affect the time frame and procedures of the selection process, those that affect the representation of public officials and party leaders, and those that govern the behavior of delegates at the convention itself.

The objective of the original reforms, to encourage participation by rank-and-file party supporters and to reflect their sentiment in the allocation of delegates, was impeded by three problems:

1. The states that held their primaries and caucuses early seemed to exercise disproportionate influence. This situation created an incentive for other states to front-load the process, for candidates to expend most of their resources at the beginning of the campaign or as soon as they got them, and for participants to turn out more regularly in March than in May.

2. A relatively small percentage of the vote in a state, known as a *threshold,* was needed for candidates to win delegates. This small percentage encouraged multiple candidacies, factionalizing the party and providing incentive for those without national experience, reputation, and even party ties, to run. By obtaining the votes of as little as 15 percent of those who participated in a primary or caucus, relatively unknown candidates could win delegates, gain recognition, and use this recognition to build a constituency and become a national figure.

3. The application of the proportional voting rule in some instances did not fairly reflect the popular vote. Moreover, even in instances in which it did reflect the popular vote, it produced unintended and undesirable consequences for the national party, for its state affiliates, and for the candidates seeking the nomination. For the national party, proportional voting extended the nomination process, disadvantaging it and its nominees in the general election. For the state parties, proportional voting diffused power and reduced the collective influence of party officials. For the candidates, proportional voting sometimes discouraged them from investing resources in districts that were highly competitive and from which they could gain only minimal advantage and encouraged them to concentrate on less competitive districts in which they enjoyed the most support. This concentration of resources adversely affected turnout and representation.

To modify the first of these problems, the party has tried to impose a "window" during which primaries and caucuses could be held. Initially the official period extended from the second Tuesday in March to the second Tuesday in June. Beginning in 1992, it was moved one week earlier to the first Tuesday in March, but continued until the second Tuesday in June.

What to do with those states, such as Iowa and New Hampshire, whose laws require that they choose their delegates before others, has been a perennial issue. Believing that it could not conduct its own selection process in these states, the national party decided that the best it could do was establish the window and grant these states an exception but require them to hold their contests closer to the designated period than in the past. Under current party rules Iowa is permitted to schedule its contest no earlier than 15 days before the window opens, whereas New Hampshire's primary cannot occur more than one week before and Maine's first-tier caucuses no earlier than two days prior to the official beginning of the nomination period.[3]

Front-loading still remains a problem, however, more so now than ever. In 1992, twenty-four states held Democratic primaries or the first round of their caucus selection process and fifteen states held Republican primaries or caucuses by the second Tuesday of March, known as Super Tuesday. Approximately one-third of all the Democratic delegates in 1992 and almost 37 percent of all the Republican delegates came from those states that held their contests at the very beginning of the nomination process.

There is even greater front-loading in 1996. To get into the action and have an impact on the selection of the nominees, many states have moved their primaries forward to the month of March. These include California, New York, Illinois, Ohio, and Michigan. As a consequence, approximately two-thirds of the convention delegates will be selected within a 44 day period beginning mid-February and continuing through March 26, 1996. (See Appendix D, Tentative Primary and Caucus Dates.)

Another change has been the modifications to the so-called fair reflection rule. One modification affected the minimum percentage of the vote necessary to be eligible for delegates; the other pertained to the methods by which the primary vote is converted into delegates. Both have been controversial.

In 1984, the Democrats raised the minimum vote needed to obtain delegates to 20 percent in caucuses and up to 25 percent in primaries. This change was designed to advance nationally known candidates such as Walter Mondale and reduce the factionalizing effect that a large number of people contesting for the nomination can have on the party. Democrats hoped the change would enable the eventual winner, preferably someone of national prominence, to emerge earlier and be better positioned to challenge the Republicans in the general election.

Naturally, these changes disadvantaged those who were not as well known. They also hurt minority candidates such as Jesse Jackson. With his supporters concentrated in districts with large minority populations and urban areas, Jackson was unable to reach the minimum percentage needed to win delegates in many predominantly white districts. Although he received 19 percent of the vote in the 1984 primaries, he obtained only 10 percent of the delegates selected in them. Owing to pressure from Jackson and others, the Democrats lowered the threshold in 1988 to 15 percent in primaries and caucuses and have kept it there since then.

Jackson was also victimized by another rule governing the delegate selection process—the formulas states were permitted to use when converting the popular vote into delegate support. Instead of adhering strictly to a straight proportional vote, the Democrats had permitted states some flexibility in applying that rule. This flexibility advantaged front-runners such as Walter Mondale and Michael Dukakis. In 1984, Mondale won 40 percent of the popular vote but 53 percent of the delegates who were directly elected; in 1988, Dukakis received 49 percent of the popular vote but 62 percent of the delegates who were directly elected. Jackson, was the principal casualty. Following the 1988 election the Democrats prohibited flexibility in applying the proportional voting rule. Today candidates receive delegates in Democratic primaries solely on the basis of the proportion of the vote they receive.

Another reform of the 1980s has been the addition of party leader and elected official delegates (PLEOs), known as *superdelegates.* Unhappy with the decreasing number of its party leaders and elected officials who attended the convention as delegates in the 1970s, the party wished to ensure that its leadership participated in conventions that selected its nominees. The absence of this leadership, particularly national elected officials, was thought to have contributed to the lack of support that the nominees received during the campaign and after the election. Jimmy Carter's difficulties in dealing with Congress were cited as evidence of the need for closer cooperation between party leaders and their presidential standard-bearer.

To facilitate closer ties, the Democrats established a new category of *add-on* delegates to be composed of PLEOs. One group of these add-on delegates, chosen from designated party leaders (including all members of its national committee) and from those who held high elected positions in government (including all Democratic governors and members of Congress plus a number of other national, state, and local officials), were to be unpledged. It was thought that this group of distinguished Democrats might be in a position to hold the balance of power if the convention were divided. Additionally, the party also provided for the selection of pledged add-on delegates equal to 15 percent of the state's base delegation. (See Table 4–1.)

Although these superdelegates have not been in a position to broker a divided convention, they have had an impact on the delegate selection process, an impact that reinforces the front-runner's advantage.[4] Naturally this advantage has incurred criticism from non-front-runners who desire the selection process to be open and not dominated by national legislators and party officials. A proposal by Jesse Jackson to decrease the number of PLEOs by eliminating the automatic inclusion of members of the party's national committee, however, was rejected by the Democratic National Committee in 1990. Approximately 18 percent of the delegate votes in 1996 will be cast by superdelegates.

Finally, the Democrats have reversed a rule adopted in 1980 that delegates who are publicly committed must vote for the candidate to whom

TABLE 4–1

Delegate Selection Rules for 1996

	Democrats	Republicans
Rank-and-file participation	Open to all voters who wish to participate as Democrats.	No national rule.*
Apportionment of delegates within states	75 percent of base delegation elected at congressional district level or lower; 25 percent elected at-large on proportional basis.	No national rule; may be chosen at large.
Party leaders and elected officials delegates	Current members and former chairs of the national committee, all Democratic members of Congress, former House Speakers and Senate leaders, current and past presidents and vice-presidents, all Democratic governors.	None.
Composition of delegations	Equal gender division; No discrimination; affirmative action plan required with goals and time tables for specified groups (African Americans, Native Americans, and Asian/Pacific Americans).	No gender rule but each state is asked to try to achieve equal gender representation. "Positive action" to achieve broadest possible participation required.
Time frame	First Tuesday in March to second Tuesday in June. Exceptions: Iowa, New Hampshire, and Maine.	No national rule.
Allocation of delegates	By proportional vote. Only in primaries or caucuses.	May be selected in primaries, caucuses, or by state committee on basis of proportional vote or by direct election within congressional districts or on an at-large basis.
Threshold	15 percent.	No national rule.
Delegate voting	May vote their conscience.	No national rule.
Enforcement	Automatic reduction in state delegation size for violation of time frames, allocation, or threshold rules.	Each state party to enforce its own rules, although certain types of disputes may be appealed to the national party.

* Republican national rules prescribe that selection procedures be in accordance with the laws of the state.

they are pledged. Democratic delegates today can vote their consciences, although their initial selection as pledged delegates must still have the approval of the candidate to whom they are committed. It is unlikely under the circumstances that many delegates will change their minds at the convention, unless their candidate encourages them to do so.

Republican Rules

The Republicans have not changed their rules after each recent national convention as the Democrats have. Nor can they do so. It is the Republican convention itself that approves the rules for choosing delegates for the next Republican convention. Under normal circumstances, these rules cannot be altered by the Republican National Committee or by special commissions the party creates.

Republicans, however, have been affected by the Democratic rules changes. Since state legislatures enact laws governing party nominations, and since the Democrats have controlled many of these legislatures in the 1970s and 1980s, they literally forced some of their reforms on the Republicans. Moreover, the Republicans have also made changes of their own. A committee of delegates and organizations, appointed in 1969, recommended that delegate selection procedures encourage greater participation in states that used conventions to pick their delegates; that more information about these procedures be promulgated to the party's electorate; and that voting by proxy be prohibited. These recommendations, adopted by the 1972 Republican convention, remain in effect today.

Unlike the Democrats, the Republicans have not chosen to mandate national guidelines for their state parties. Although they do not have a window period during which all primaries and caucuses must be held, their nominations process is still heavily front-loaded.

Whereas the Democrats prescribe a minimum threshold to receive delegate support, the Republicans do not. Their threshold varies from state to state. Whereas the Democrats impose proportional voting, the Republicans do not. They permit winner-take-all voting within districts or within the state. Such a voting system greatly advantages front-runners. In the last closely contested Republican nomination in 1988, George Bush won 59 percent of the popular vote in states holding some type of winner-take-all voting on Super Tuesday but won 97 percent of the delegates, giving him an almost insurmountable lead over his principal opponent that year, Robert Dole.

Finally the Republicans do not have special categories of delegates for party leaders and elected officials, although their state and national leaders have traditionally attended Republican conventions in greater proportion than their Democratic counterparts. (See Table 4–6.) Nor do the Republicans require that 50 percent of each state delegation be women. Since the 1980s the proportion of women at Republican conventions has ranged from a low of 29 percent to a high of 44. In 1992, 43 percent of the delegates were women.

A summary of delegate selection rules for the 1996 nomination appears in Table 4–1.

THE LEGALITY OF PARTY RULES

As previously mentioned, party reforms, to be effective, must be enacted into law. Most states have complied with the new rules. A few have not, sometimes resulting in confrontation between these states and the national party. When New Hampshire and Iowa refused to move the dates of their respective primary and caucuses into the Democrats' window period in 1984, the national party backed down. But previously, when Illinois chose its 1972 delegates in a manner that conflicted with new Democratic rules, the party sought to impose its rules on the state.

In addition to the political controversy that was engendered, the conflict between the Democratic National Committee and Illinois also presented an important legal question: which body—the national party or state—was the higher authority? In its landmark decision, *Cousins* v. *Wigoda* (419 U.S. 477, 1975), the Supreme Court sided with the national party. The Court stated that political parties were private organizations with rights of association protected by the Constitution. Moreover, choosing presidential candidates was a national experience that states could not abridge unless there were compelling constitutional reasons to do so. Although states could establish their own primary laws, the party could determine the criteria for representation at its national convention.

But another issue, crossover voting in open primaries, prompted still another court test between the rights of parties to prescribe rules for delegate selection and the rights of states to establish their own election law. Democratic rules prohibit open primaries. Four states had conducted this type of election in 1976. Three voluntarily changed their law for 1980. The fourth, Wisconsin, did not. It permitted voters, who participated in the primary, to request the ballot of either party. The national party's Compliance Review Commission ordered the state party to design an alternative process. It refused. The case went to court.

Citing the precedent of *Cousins* v. *Wigoda,* the Supreme Court held in the case of *Democratic Party of the U.S.* v. *Wisconsin ex. rel. La Follette* (450 U.S. 107, 1981) that a state had no right to interfere with the party's delegate selection process unless it demonstrated a compelling reason to do so. It ruled that Wisconsin had not demonstrated such a reason; hence, the Democratic party could refuse to seat delegates who were selected in a manner that violated its rules.[5]

Although these Court decisions have given the political parties the legal authority to design and enforce their own rules, the practicality of doing so is another question. Other than going to court if a state refuses to change its election law, a party, particularly a national party, has only two viable options: require the state party to conduct its own delegate selection process in conformity to national rules and penalize it if it does not do so, or grant the state party an exemption so that it can abide by the law of the state. In 1984, the Wisconsin Democratic party was forced by the national Democratic party to adopt a caucus mode of selection since the Republican-controlled legislature refused to change the state's open primary system. Turnout declined in the Wisconsin caucus. Subsequently, the Democrats have given Wisconsin and Montana, the only other state with a tradition of open primaries, exemptions to the closed primary rule. Other states are still precluded from switching to an open primary.

Despite the intraparty agitation over open primaries and others in which partisans are permitted to cross over and vote for candidates of the other party, there is evidence to suggest that this fear may be overblown. One study of 16 primaries on Super Tuesday in 1988 found little evidence of this phenomenon occurring.[6]

The party rule that seems to have had more of an impact on the nomination process, particularly on how the candidates allocate their resources, is the apportionment of delegates among the states.[7] Here the Republicans have had more controversy than the Democrats. The formula Republicans use to determine the size of each state delegation consists of three criteria: statehood (six delegates), House districts (three per district), and support for Republican candidates elected within the previous four years (one for a Republican governor, one for each Republican senator, one if the Republicans won at least half of the congressional districts in one of the last two congressional elections, and a bonus of four and one-half delegates plus 60 percent of the electoral vote if the state voted for the Republican presidential candidate in the last election).

This apportionment formula effectively discriminates against the larger states in two ways. First, it awards many of the bonus delegates to a state without regard to its size. Thus, the voting strength of the larger states is proportionally reduced by the bonuses while that of the smaller states is increased. Second, since the larger states are more competitive, they are less likely to be awarded bonus delegates on a recurring basis. Particularly hard hit are states in the Northeast and Midwest, such as New York and Pennsylvania, and smaller states, such as Massachusetts and Minnesota. California will also be hurt in 1996 since it voted Democratic in the 1992 presidential election.

The Ripon Society, a moderate Republican organization, has twice challenged the constitutionality of this apportionment rule, but it has not been successful.[8]

The Democratic apportionment formula has also been subject to some controversy. Under the plan used since 1968 and modified in 1976, the Democrats have allotted 50 percent of each state delegation on the basis of the state's electoral vote and 50 percent on the basis of its average Democratic vote in the last three presidential elections. The rule for apportionment was challenged in 1971 on the grounds that it did not conform to the "one person, one vote" principle, but the Court of Appeals asserted that it

TABLE 4–2

Delegate Apportionment, 1992 and 1996

State	Democrats†		Republicans*	
	1992	*1996*	*1992*	*1996*
Alabama	62	66	38	39
Alaska	18	19	19	19
Arizona	47	52	37	39
Arkansas	43	48	27	20
California	382	423	201	163
Colorado	54	58	37	27
Connecticut	61	65	35	27
Delaware	19	21	19	12
District of Columbia	29	38	14	14
Florida	160	177	97	98
Georgia	88	92	52	42
Hawaii	26	30	14	14
Idaho	24	24	22	23
Illinois	183	194	85	69
Indiana	86	89	51	52
Iowa	57	56	23	25
Kansas	42	41	30	31
Kentucky*	62	61	35	26
Louisiana*	69	76	38	27
Maine	30	32	22	15
Maryland	80	85	42	32
Massachusetts	107	114	38	37
Michigan	148	158	72	57
Minnesota	87	92	32	33
Mississippi*	45	49	34	32
Missouri	86	93	47	35
Montana	22	25	20	14
Nebraska	31	33	24	24
Nevada	23	27	21	14

* May be increased by 1 if a Republican governor is elected in 1995.

† Includes Democratic National Committee, Democratic members of Congress, governors, and other distinguished party leaders.

did not violate the equal protection clause of the Fourteenth Amendment. The Democratic formula results in even larger conventions than the Republican. Table 4–2 lists the apportionment of Republican and Democratic convention delegates for 1992 and 1996.

TABLE 4–2 *(continued)*
Delegate Apportionment, 1992 and 1996

State	Democrats[†]		Republicans*	
	1992	1996	1992	1996
New Hampshire	24	26	23	16
New Jersey	117.	120	60	48
New Mexico	33	34	25	18
New York	268	288	100	102
North Carolina	93	98	57	58
North Dakota	20	22	17	18
Ohio	167	171	83	67
Oklahoma	52	53	34	38
Oregon	53	56	23	23
Pennsylvania	188	195	91	73
Rhode Island	28	31	15	16
South Carolina	50	52	36	37
South Dakota	20	23	19	18
Tennessee	77	83	45	37
Texas	214	231	121	123
Utah	28	30	27	28
Vermont	19	22	19	12
Virginia	92	96	55	53
Washington	80	91	35	36
West Virginia	38	42	18	18
Wisconsin	91	93	35	36
Wyoming	19	19	20	20
American Samoa	5	6	4	4
Democrats abroad	10	9	—	—
Guam	5	6	4	4
Puerto Rico	57	58	14	14
Virgin Islands	5	4	4	4
Unassigned superdelegates[†]	262	777	—	—
Totals	4,286	4,298	2,210	1,981

THE IMPACT OF THE RULES CHANGES

The new rules adopted by the parties have produced some of their desired effects. They have opened up the nomination process by allowing more people to participate. They have increased minority representation at the conventions. But they have also decreased the influence of state and national party leaders over the selection of delegates, ultimately weakened the power of party leaders in the presidential electoral process, and have produced divisions within the party itself.

Turnout

One objective of the reforms was to involve more of the party's rank and file in the delegate selection process. This goal has been achieved. Turnout has increased. In 1968, before the reforms, only 12 million people participated in primaries, approximately 11 percent of the voting-age population (VAP). In 1972, the first nomination contest after changes were made, that number rose to 22 million. It has climbed steadily since then, declining only in 1984, when Ronald Reagan ran unopposed for the Republican nomination. In 1988 it peaked. With two contested nominations, turnout increased to almost 37 million, approximately 21 percent of the voting-age population. In 1992, approximately 20 million people voted in the Democratic primaries and 13 million in the Republican primaries.

Although more people have participated in their party's nomination, the level of participation has not been uniform. It has been greater in primaries than caucuses, greater in states that hold their contests early than those that hold them later in the process, and greater in states in which there is more competition than in those in which there is less. For both parties in 1992 as well as in 1988, New Hampshire turnout exceeded the national average. It attracted 167,819 Democrats and 174,165 Republicans in 1992.[9]

There have been variations in levels of participation among groups within the electorate as well. The better-educated, higher-income, older members of the society vote more often than do those who lack these characteristics. In general, the lower the turnout, the greater the demographic differences between voters and nonvoters. Although this pattern of participation has persisted in recent elections, the success of the Jackson campaigns in 1984 and 1988 in attracting minority voters and, to a much lesser extent, the campaign of Pat Robertson in appealing to white, evangelical Protestants, especially Pentecostals and Charismatics, have muted in those elections some of the differences that had existed between primary voters and their party's electorate.

There have also been claims that primary voters tend to be more ideologically extreme in their political beliefs than the average party voter, with Democrats being more liberal and Republicans more conservative than their party as a whole. Strong empirical evidence has not been found to support this contention although studies have shown southern Democrats who participate in their party's primary tend to be more moderate than the southern electorate as a whole.[10] In general for most of the country, primary voters do not appear to be more ideologically extreme than people who voted in the general election.[11] (See Table 4–3 for a profile of the Democratic party's primary electorate in 1992.)

Representation

A principal goal of the reforms was to make the national nominating convention more representative of those who identified with the party. Before 1972, the delegates were predominantly white, male, and well educated. Mostly professionals whose income and social status placed them considerably above the national mean, they were expected to pay their own way to the convention. Large financial contributors, as well as elected officeholders and party officials, were frequently in attendance.

In 1972, the demographic profile of convention delegates began to change. The proportion of women rose substantially. Youth and minority participation, especially in Democratic conventions, also increased. Since 1976, when the Democrats changed from a quota system to an affirmative action commitment, the representation of minorities has remained fairly constant. The percentage of women has increased, largely as a consequence of the Democratic rule that half the delegates be women. But attendance by those under age thirty, who have been removed from the specified minorities list, has declined. (See Table 4–4.)

Despite the changes in composition, the income and educational levels of the delegates have remained well above the national average. In 1992, 68 percent of the Democratic delegates and 75 percent of the Republican delegates had family incomes over $50,000 compared with 22 percent for the population as a whole.[12] Similarly, most of the delegates had much more formal education than did their party's rank and file. Thirty-three percent of the Republicans and 44 percent of the Democrats had completed college and had some postgraduate work compared with only 6 percent of the entire population.[13] Clearly the 1992 convention delegates enjoyed a much higher standard of living and much greater educational opportunities than did most Americans.

It is more difficult to determine the extent to which ideological and issue perceptions of recent delegates differed from those of their predecessors and from the electorate as a whole. In general, convention delegates tend to be more conscious of issues than their party's rank and file, with Republican delegates being more conservative than Republicans as a whole, and Democratic delegates more liberal than Democrats are generally.

TABLE 4–3

The Democratic Primary Electorate, 1992

Percentage of Total Vote		Voted for		
		Clinton	*Brown*	*Tsongas*
100	Total, 29 states	50%	21%	20%
	Gender			
47	Men	50	22	20
53	Women	51	20	21
	Race			
80	Whites	47	23	25
14	Blacks	70	15	8
4	Hispanics	51	30	15
	Age			
12	18–29 years	47	24	19
33	30–44 years	45	26	22
25	45–59 years	51	19	20
30	60 and older	59	15	18
	Religious affiliation			
50	Protestant	55	14	21
30	Catholic	44	24	24
6	Jewish	45	15	33
	Education			
8	Without a high school diploma	67	14	10
27	High school graduate	61	17	15
27	Some college	48	23	18
20	College graduate	42	24	26
18	Some postgraduate education	38	23	28
	Family income			
15	Less than $15,000	62	17	13
25	$15,000–29,999	55	19	18
30	$30,000–49,999	48	23	21
18	$50,000–74,999	45	23	25
11	$75,000 and over	38	23	29
	Those who identify themselves as . . .			
67	Democrats	57	19	17
29	Independents	36	25	27
4	Republicans	34	18	32
35	Liberals	47	26	20
45	Moderates	54	18	19
20	Conservatives	48	17	23
	Those who say their family's financial situation is . . .			
14	Better today than four years ago	44	24	22
39	Same today as four years ago	50	20	20
45	Worse today than four years ago	53	20	18

Source: This table constructs a Democratic primary electorate for the nation from exit polls conducted in twenty-nine Democratic primary states from February to June by Voter Research and Surveys. *New York Times* (July 12, 1992), p. 18.

TABLE 4-4
The Demography of National Convention Delegates, 1968–1992

	1968 Dem.	1968 Rep.	1972 Dem.	1972 Rep.	1976 Dem.	1976 Rep.	1980 Dem.	1980 Rep.	1984 Dem.	1984 Rep.	1988 Dem.	1988 Rep.	1992 Dem.	1992 Rep.
Women	13%	16%	40%	29%	33%	31%	49%	29%	50%	44%	48%	33%	48%	43%
Blacks	5	2	15	4	11	—	15	3	18	4	23	4	16	4
Under thirty	3	4	22	8	15	7	11	5	8	4	4	3	—	3
Median age (years)	(49)	(49)	(42)	—	(43)	(48)	(44)	(49)	(43)	(51)	(46)	(51)	—	—
Lawyers	28	22	12	—	16	15	13	15	17	14	16	17	—	6
Teachers	8	2	11	—	—	4	15	4	16	6	14	5	—	4
Union members	—	—	16	—	21	3	27	4	25	4	25	3	—	—
Attended first convention	67	66	83	78	80	78	87	84	74	61	65	68	45	—
College graduate	19	—	21	—	21	27	20	26	20	28	21	32	20	35
Postgraduate*	44	34	36	—	43	38	45	39	51	35	52	34	52	33
Protestant	—	—	42	—	47	73	47	72	49	71	50	69	47	71
Catholic	—	—	26	—	34	18	37	22	29	22	30	22	30	27
Jewish	—	—	9	—	9	3	8	3	8	2	7	2	10	2

* Includes those in the category of college graduates.

Source: CBS News Delegate Surveys, 1968 through 1980. Characteristics of the public are average values from seven CBS News/*New York Times* polls, 1980. Warren J. Mitofsky and Martin Plissner, "The Making of the Delegates, 1968–1980," *Public Opinion* (December–January 1980): 43. Reprinted with the permission of American Enterprise Institute. 1984 and 1988 data for delegates and public opinion supplied by CBS News from its delegate surveys and reprinted with permission of CBS News. 1992 data published in the *New York Times* (July 13, 1992), p. B 6 and the *Washington Post* (August 16, 1992), p. A 19. This table also appears in Stephen J. Wayne, G. Calvin Mackenzie, David M. O'Brien, and Richard L. Cole, *The Politics of American Government* (New York: St. Martin's Press, 1995, p. 337).

Surveys of the ideological perspectives of convention delegates at recent conventions support these generalizations. They reveal clear distinctions between the delegates of the major parties. (See Table 4–5.) Moreover, the issue stands of the delegates tend to confirm their ideological cleavage. Republican and Democratic delegates consistently take more conservative and liberal positions, respectively, on a range of policy matters. If these positions were plotted on an ideological continuum, they would appear to be more consistent (or ideologically pure) than the partisan electorate they represented and much more consistent (or pure) than the general public.

The delegate selection process seems to have contributed to the purity of these perspectives by encouraging activists, who have less of a tie to the party and more of a tie to a candidate and that candidate's ideological and issue positions, to get involved and run for delegate. To the extent that this trend has resulted in the election of more issue purists and fewer partisan pragmatists, compromise has become more difficult and party unity more elusive. One object of the creation of superdelegates by the Democrats was to reverse this trend.

In summary, despite the reforms, there continue to be differences between the ideological and demographic characteristics of convention delegates and those of their parties and of the electorate as a whole. Convention delegates reflect some demographic characteristics of their party's rank and file more accurately than in the past, but they are not necessarily more ideologically representative. In fact, delegates have tended to exaggerate the differences between the beliefs and attitudes of Republicans and Democrats. Whether this trend makes contemporary conventions more or less representative is difficult to say. One thing is clear: it is difficult to achieve representation, reward activism, maintain an open process, unite the party, and win elections, all at the same time.

TABLE 4–5

The Ideology of National Convention Delegates, 1976–1992

Ideology	1976		1980		1984	
	Dem.	Rep.	Dem.	Rep.	Dem.	Rep.
Liberal	40%	3%	46%	2%	48%	1%
Moderate	47	45	42	36	42	35
Conservative	8	48	6	58	4	60

Source: CBS News Delegate Surveys, 1976 through 1980. Characteristics of the public are average values from seven CBS News/*New York Times* polls, 1980. Warren J. Mitofsky and Martin Plissner, "The Making of the Delegates, 1968–1980," *Public Opinion* (December–January 1980): 43. Reprinted with the permission of American Enterprise Institute. 1984 and 1988 data for delegates and public opinion supplied by CBS News from its delegate

Party Organization and Leadership

Although increasing turnout and improving representation have been two desired effects of the reforms, weakening the state party structures and their leadership have not. Yet these two developments seem to have been an initial consequence of the increasing number of primaries. By promoting internal democracy, the primaries helped devitalize party organizations already weakened by new modes of campaigning and party leadership already weakened by the loss of patronage opportunities and the growth of social services by state and local governments.[14] Although the growth of caucuses has enhanced participation in the general election by enlarging the pool of people who are more likely to stay involved and vote, it has also contributed to struggles for control of the party organization and ultimately produced more divisions within it.[15] Moreover, the rules changes have encouraged the proliferation of candidates, which in turn has led to the creation of separate electoral organizations that can rival the regular party organization.

The power of elected party leaders has also been weakened. No longer able to control their state's delegation, party officials now have to compete with the supporters of the successful candidate for influence over the campaign. And prior to the creation of delegate slots for party leaders and elected officials, they had to run in the primaries and caucuses and win to ensure their attendance at the national conventions. Table 4–6 indicates the decreasing proportion of these VIPs who became delegates from 1968 through 1976, particularly at Democratic conventions.

State party organizations and state party leaders seem to be making a comeback, although most have not attained the preeminent position they enjoyed prior to the rules changes. Their control over the expenditure of

TABLE 4–5 *(continued)*
The Ideology of National Convention Delegates, 1976–1992

Ideology	1988		1992		1992 General Population
	Dem.	*Rep.*	*Dem.*	*Rep.*	
Liberal	43%	0%	47%	1%	27%
Moderate	43	35	44	28	38
Conservative	5	58	5	70	32

surveys and reprinted with permission of CBS News. 1992 data published in the *New York Times* (July 13, 1992), p. B 6, and the *Washington Post* (August 16, 1992), p. A 19. This table also appears in Stephen J. Wayne, G. Calvin Mackenzie, David M. O'Brien, and Richard L. Cole, *The Politics of American Government* (New York: St. Martin's Press, 1995), p. 338.

TABLE 4–6

Representation of Major Elected Officials at National Conventions, 1968–1992* (in percentages)

	1968	1972	1976	1980	1984	1988	1992
Democrats							
Governors	96%	57%	44%	74%	91%	100%	96%†
U.S. Senators	61	28	18	14	56	85	81†
U.S. Representatives	32	12	14	14	62	87	88†
Republicans							
Governors	92	80	69	68	93	82	81
U.S. Senators	58	50	59	63	56	62	42
U.S. Representatives	31	19	36	40	53	55	30

* Figures represent the percentages of Democratic or Republican officeholders from each group who served as delegates.

† Unpledged delegates (i.e., "superdelegates") only, not including those officeholders who went to the Democratic convention by other means.

Source: Figures provided by the Democratic and Republican National Committees.

soft money has provided them some of the leverage that they had lost in the 1970s. The increasing importance of state and local committees in providing funds and organizational support for the general election has also benefited these state party officials.

Winners and Losers

Rules changes are never neutral. They usually benefit one group at the expense of another. Similarly, they tend to help certain candidates and hurt others. That is why candidates have tried to influence the rules and why the rules themselves have been changed so frequently. Candidate organizations and interest groups have put continuous pressure on the Democratic party to amend the rules to increase their own clout in the selection process.

Clearly, the prohibition of discrimination, the requirement for affirmative action, and the rule requiring an equal number of men and women in state delegations have improved representation for women and minorities. These changes also have reduced the proportion of white males. For candidates seeking their party's nomination, this change has necessitated that slates of delegates supporting a candidate be demographically balanced to ensure that a multitude of groups are included.

The openness of the process and the greater participation by the party's rank and file have encouraged those who have not been party regulars to become involved. These changes forced aspirants for the nomination to depend more on the organizing capacities of their own campaign supporters and less on the energies, endorsements, and organizations of state party leaders. The continuing front-loading of the process, however, may actually be reversing this trend by increasing the dependence on the organizational support of "friendly" state party leaders for candidates who cannot create grass roots organizations in all of the states holding early contests.

Finally, the requirement for allocating delegates in proportion to the popular vote has also had profound effects on the Democrats. It has fragmented the party and lengthened the nomination process. The longer, more open nomination process may in turn have encouraged candidates to make more promises to more groups.

All of this has affected the candidates' quest for the nomination and their ability to govern. It has made campaigning more arduous and governing more difficult. Take Bill Clinton, for example. To win he had to make many promises such as lowering taxes for the middle class, ending discrimination against homosexuals in the military, and admitting Haitian refugees into the United States. Once in office, he soon found that he could not redeem these promises and had to delay, modify, or abandon them. Moreover, he had to endure character accusations that continued to plague him as president. Although all of Clinton's problems cannot be attributed to the nomination process, some of them can be. The point is that the quest for the nomination and what it takes to win may ultimately weaken a president by hyping performance expectations and then generating discontent when these expectations cannot be realized.

CAMPAIGNING FOR DELEGATES

The rules changes, finance laws, and television coverage have affected the strategies and tactics of the candidates. Prior to the 1960s, entering primaries was optional for leading candidates and necessary only for those who did not enjoy party support or national recognition. Today, entering primaries is essential for everyone, even an incumbent. No longer can a front-runner safely sit on the sidelines and wait for the call. The winds of a draft may be hard to resist, but, more often than not, it is the candidate who is manning the bellows.

In the past, candidates carefully chose the primaries they entered and concentrated their efforts where they thought they would run best. Today, they have much less discretion. By allocating delegates on the basis of a proportional vote, the nomination process now provides incentives for campaigning in as many states as possible for as long as possible.

Strategy and tactics have naturally evolved. There are now new answers to the old questions: when to declare, where to run, how to organize, what to claim, and how to win. Before 1972, it was considered wise to wait for an opportune moment in the spring of the presidential election year before announcing one's candidacy. Adlai Stevenson did not announce his intentions until the Democratic convention. John F. Kennedy made his announcement two months before the New Hampshire primary. It was also considered wise to restrict primary efforts, obtain the backing of the state party leaders, and work through their organizations. The successful candidates were those who could unify the party. They took few chances. The object of their campaign was to maintain a winning image.

Basic Strategic Guidelines

Plan far ahead. Much of the old conventional wisdom is no longer valid. Today it is necessary for all candidates to plan their campaigns early. Creating an organization, devising a strategy, and raising the amount of money necessary to conduct a national campaign all take time. These needs prompted George McGovern to announce his candidacy for the 1972 presidential nomination in January 1971, almost a year and a half before the Democratic convention, and Jimmy Carter to begin his quest in 1974, two years before the 1976 Democratic convention. Republican candidates for 1996 announced in the winter and spring of 1995.

Regardless of the date the official announcement is made, it is now common practice to start campaigning several years before the nomination. Republicans Robert Dole and Phil Gramm established exploratory committees and leadership PACs in 1994, two years before the 1996 Republican convention. Each of the candidates for the party's 1996 nomination made numerous trips to Iowa and New Hampshire before their caucuses and primary.

The quest for the 1992 presidential nomination, however, was an exception to the "early declare, early campaign" rule. The war in the Persian Gulf muted partisan politics for the latter half of 1990 and the first half of 1991 and resulted in approval ratings of nearly 90 percent for the incumbent. Bush's popularity discouraged prominent Democrats from seeking their party's nomination and Republicans from challenging the president. It was not until April 30, 1991, that the first candidate for the Democratic nomination, former Senator Paul E. Tsongas (Massachusetts), announced his candidacy. The president waited until December 1991 before declaring he was a candidate for reelection. Had conservative columnist, Pat Buchanan, not run against him, it is likely Bush would have waited even longer. (See Box 4–2, "Bush's Letter to Republican Party Chairman Richard Bond.")

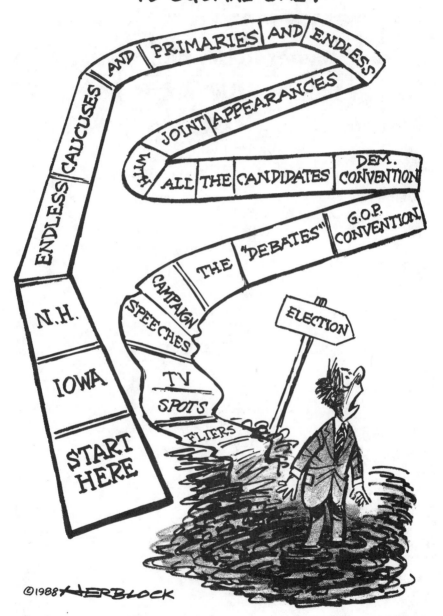

Unfortunately for the president, his delay in beginning the reelection campaign proved costly. Slow to develop a programmatic response to the recession, Bush found himself in the midst of a challenge that impeded his

---

BOX 4–2

Bush's Letter to Republican Party
Chairman Richard Bond

                                             EYES ONLY

                        GEORGE BUSH
                      October 31, 1991

    Dear Rich,

    I have asked son George to very quietly make
    some soundings for me on 1992. I'd appreciate
    it if you'd visit with him on your innermost
    thoughts about how to best structure the cam-
    paign organization. I have asked him not to
    share any information gleaned from anyone with
    any person other than me, and I'm asking him
    to talk to about eight to ten trusted political
    confidants.

    My plan is still to wait--defer final campaign
    structuring decisions until after the first of
    the year at least; but there seems to be a fair
    amount of churning around out there, and I need
    the unvarnished, frank views of my most trusted
    political confidants. If you prefer not to
    discuss this with him, I will understand. I
    have concluded he is the best one to help me
    gather this information together. I don't know
    when George will call, but he will.

    Off to Houston . . .

                              Sincerely,

                                 GB

    Mr. Richard Bond
    Box 577
    37B Westmoreland Drive
    Shelter Island, New York   11965

ability to communicate that program effectively to the American people. In the words of Charles Black, a senior adviser to the Bush campaign:

> What we needed to do in that first quarter, in order to win the general election, was to re-establish his [Bush's] credibility on the economy, show that he understood the problem, that he had some connection with people's problems, and that he had a plan. We couldn't do it. We presented the plan but it was obscured by the primary coverage and by the horse-race coverage, and by Pat [Buchanan] very effectively and articulately pointing out that the President wasn't on top of the economy.[16]

Concentrate efforts in the early contests. Doing well in the initial caucuses and primaries and qualifying for matching funds are the principal aims of most candidates today. The early contests are particularly important for lesser-known aspirants, less for the number of delegates they can win than for the amount of publicity they can generate and the public recognition they can gain as a consequence.[17]

By tradition the first official selection of delegates occurs in Iowa. Jimmy Carter in 1976, George Bush in 1980, and Gary Hart in 1984 got great boosts from their unexpectedly good showings in this state. Conversely, Ronald Reagan in 1980, John Glenn in 1984, and George Bush in 1988 were hurt by their disappointing performances.

Doing well in Iowa can enhance the fortunes of a lesser-known candidate. A good example was Gary Hart's performance in 1984. He received only 16.5 percent of the Democratic vote, compared with front-runner Walter Mondale's 48.9 percent, former nominee George McGovern's 10.3 percent, and Senator John Glenn's 3.5 percent. But Mondale's victory was expected; Hart's second-place finish was not. As a consequence, Hart shared the media spotlight with Mondale but profited from more laudatory coverage. Similarly, Pat Robertson's surprising second-place finish ahead of Vice-President George Bush in 1988 in Iowa generated favorable media coverage for Robertson. His gain was Bush's loss. It also reduced the attention given to Robert Dole's victory in that state. Robertson received more television coverage than Dole following the Iowa caucus.[18]

The Carter, Bush (1980), and Hart victories have inflated the importance of Iowa for non-front-running candidates of both parties. That importance may be short-lived, however. Changes in the scheduling of primaries since 1984 have shortened the period during which those who do well in Iowa can parlay their success into raising more money, building larger organizations, and generating more volunteers and endorsements. With New Hampshire eight days later and an increasing number of primaries occurring in early or mid-March, there is simply not enough time to gain a lot from a strong showing in Iowa. Moreover, the "winners" face another problem. Expectations of their future performance increase and media coverage tends to become more negative. In the words of Craig Allen Smith, the Iowa caucuses:

> have been a Venus fly-trap for presidential candidates. Dramatic logic lures them to the sticky leaves of the precinct caucuses where, prodded by journalists and Iowans, they pour more and more of their time, money, people, and strategic options into the gaping mouth of the plant until, at the very moment of victory, it snaps shut on their ability to win subsequent contests. Iowa provides no significant delegates, its New Hampshire momentum is soon reversed, its Super Tuesday momentum is transient, and the resources it devours are rarely recovered.[19]

The Iowa caucus was neither significant nor newsworthy in 1992. George Bush was not challenged, and Democrats conceded the election to home-state senator, Tom Harkin.[20] Because it was expected, Harkin's victory received little media coverage outside the state. Had he lost, it would have been news. With Robert Dole well known and the favorite to win in Iowa in 1996, the news focus is also likely to be the unexpected if it occurs—a Dole defeat or narrow victory—or the order in which the rest of the candidates finish.

When Iowa is not a factor as in 1992 and perhaps 1996, attention turns to New Hampshire. New Hampshire is traditionally important because it is the first state to hold a primary in which the entire electorate participates. It is thus the first popular test of a candidate's electability.

Candidates who do surprisingly well in this primary have benefited enormously. Eugene McCarthy in 1968, George McGovern in 1972, Jimmy Carter in 1976, Gary Hart in 1984, and Bill Clinton in 1992 all gained visibility and credibility from their New Hampshire performances, although none had a majority of the vote and only Carter had a plurality. Bill Clinton actually came in second with 25 percent of the vote, 8 percent less than former Massachusetts senator, Paul Tsongas. Clinton's relatively strong showing, however, in the light of allegations of marital infidelity and draft dodging made his performance more impressive in the eyes of the news media than Tsongas' expected win.

Republican Pat Buchanan also played the expectations game in New Hampshire to his advantage. Bay Buchanan, the candidate's sister and campaign manager, articulated her brother's New Hampshire strategy this way:

> Winning New Hampshire was never in the cards, but New Hampshire would give us momentum maybe to carry it through Georgia and then possibly an outside chance, in our wildest dreams, to make it through Super Tuesday. Winning New Hampshire for us was just doing well. It was doing better than it was perceived we would do. . . .

What we needed to do was make certain that those expectations were kept as low as possible. So we were up there saying, geez, you know, we're at nine. We hope to get to the teens. One of the Bush people made the mistake of saying "They won't break 30."[21]

Buchanan actually received 34 percent of the vote. A glitch in the early exit polls announced by the media on the night of the election, however, reported that his vote percentage would be even higher, thereby embarrassing the president before a large viewing audience and enhancing Buchanan's own credibility in the process.

Like Iowa, New Hampshire also receives extensive media attention. Together with Iowa, it accounted for approximately one-third of all the prenomination television coverage on the national news in 1988. With the Iowa caucus essentially uncontested in 1992, there was less coverage, but there were still 190 campaign stories on the evening news of the three major networks from January through the New Hampshire primary in 1992.[22] (See Figure 4–1.) Is it any wonder that candidates spend so much time, money, and effort in these early states?

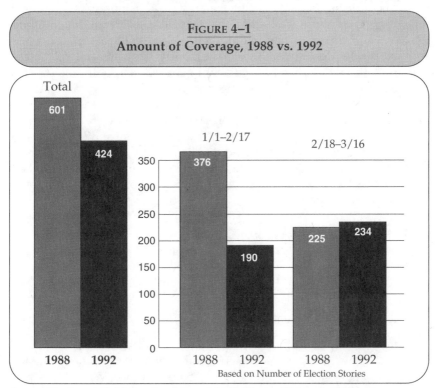

FIGURE 4–1
Amount of Coverage, 1988 vs. 1992

Based on Number of Election Stories

Source: "The Parties Pick Their Candidates," *Media Monitor* VI (March 1992), p. 2.

For non-front-runners there are few options to contesting these initial contests. The stakes are high, but the odds are not good. The failure to stand out may force them to drop out. On the other hand, winning is no guarantee of future success; it is simply an opportunity to continue.

For front-runners, the needs and opportunities are different. The early caucuses and primaries present a situation in which their superior resources can be used to eliminate or preclude competition, demonstrate electability, perhaps even invulnerability, and build a delegate lead. Winning confirms the front-runner's status; losing jeopardizes it, but recovery is possible, as Ronald Reagan demonstrated in 1980, Walter Mondale in 1984, and George Bush in 1988. An early loss, however, can raise questions about a front-runner's viability, as it did for Bush in 1988.

Raise and spend big bucks early. Having a solid financial base at the outset of the nomination process provides a significant strategic advantage. It allows a presidential campaign to plan ahead, to decide where to establish its field organizations, how much media advertising to buy, where to focus it and on which groups. It is no coincidence that those candidates who raise and spend the most money tend to do best.

The impact of early money is particularly significant for candidates who do not begin the quest for their party's nomination with a national reputation, candidates such as Michael Dukakis in 1988, Bill Clinton in 1992, and all the Republican candidates in 1996 with the exception of senate majority leader, Robert Dole. The ability to raise relatively large amounts of money early, particularly in comparison with one's rivals gives a candidate an edge in gaining recognition and organizational support.

Michael Dukakis and Bill Clinton used their superior fund raising to build and staff large organizations in New Hampshire and key southern states, develop and target their media to key groups, and focus their personal efforts on campaigning, whereas their principal opponents lacked the resources to do so competitively. In the words of Tsongas' campaign manager, Dennis Kanin:

> In 1991 we raised about $19,000 a week, which is a pitiful amount. . . .
> It was not for lack of trying, but people made the rational choice not
> to throw their money away on a candidate who could not win. So by
> the end of 1991, after ten months in the race, we had raised a million
> dollars. After three months in the race, Clinton had raised about $3
> million.[23]

Similarly, Republican contenders for their party's 1996 presidential nomination have engaged in a furious competition to raise money in 1995. Their campaign goals range from $10 to 25 million each. When combined with the federal matching grants they expect to receive at the beginning of

1996 and additional fundraising they will have to do during the period of primaries and caucuses, some might have a war chest in excess of $40 million dollars to mount their nomination campaign. After just the first four months of 1995, well before the first official contest, Gramm had raised $13 million, Dole $4.4 million, Alexander $5.2 million, Specter $1.2 million, and Buchanan almost $1 million. They had also spent large amounts with Gramm's expenses totalling $4.7 million and Dole's $1.9 million.

Another advantage of having money up front is that the news media interpret it as a sign of strength. The campaign's organization and financial resources are seen as indicators of its electoral potential. Well-financed candidates receive more news media coverage and can purchase more time for their speeches and advertisements. As a consequence, they can become better known more quickly. In 1988, Pat Robertson's organizational and financial strength made him a viable candidate despite his status as a political novice and his narrow political base within the Republican party.[24]

Two principal consequences follow from the need for early money: the financial campaign in the years before the nomination has assumed greater importance than in the past, and non-front-runners are disadvantaged even more than they were previously. The odds against a little-known outsider using Iowa and New Hampshire as a stepping stone to the nomination have increased in recent years.

Develop a deep and wide organization. The concentration of primaries and caucuses requires that candidates create a deep and wide organization, one that can attend to the multiple facets of the campaign and do so in many states simultaneously. But doing so has become increasingly difficult with the front-loading of the primaries, even for well-financed candidates. That is why attempts are made to supplement organizations with those of state party leaders whose endorsements have been obtained.

George Bush benefited enormously from the backing and organizational support of state parties in New Hampshire, South Carolina, and Illinois in 1988.[25] Similarly, Bill Clinton owed his first primary victory in Georgia in 1992 to the active campaign of Governor Zell Miller and his party organization. In general, Clinton exploited his position as head of the Democratic Leadership Conference to gain a strong base for his candidacy, particularly in the South. In Texas, for example, he had the backing of many of Texas' elected Democratic leaders and had a substantial field organization compared with Paul Tsongas' single volunteer coordinator prior to the New Hampshire primary.[26] In the quest for the 1996 Republican nomination, Robert Dole has had the most success in gaining endorsements from state and national party leaders. In Ohio, New York, and South Carolina he has received broad support from top state officials and intends to rely on their political networks in his campaign in those states' primaries.

The major task of any organization is to mobilize voters. This is especially important in caucuses in which candidate organizations are necessary to get supporters and sympathizers to the precinct meetings. In both caucuses and primaries, telephone banks must be established, door-to-door canvassing undertaken, and appropriate material mailed or hand delivered. It is also necessary to create the impression of broad public support and generate excitement. These activities involve a large volunteer effort. A major assumption of the Robertson campaign in 1988 was that the 3 million people who signed petitions urging him to run for president would be a continuing source for voluntary campaign activities and for fund raising.

There are many other examples. Eugene McCarthy and George McGovern recruited thousands of college students to help in 1968 and 1972. Jimmy Carter had his "Peanut Brigade," a group of Georgians who followed him from state to state; in 1976. Mondale benefited from the support of organized labor in 1984. Jesse Jackson effectively used African-American churches to recruit volunteers and raise money for his presidential campaigns in 1984 and 1988.

Monitor public opinion. With intentions clear, money in hand, and an organization in place, it is necessary to ascertain public sentiment, appeal to it, and try to manipulate it. To achieve the first goal, polling is essential.

The use of polls by candidates is a midtwentieth century phenomenon. Republican Thomas E. Dewey was the first to have private polling data available to him when he tried unsuccessfully to obtain the Republican nomination in 1940. John F. Kennedy was the first candidate to engage a pollster in his quest for the nomination. Preconvention surveys conducted by Louis Harris in 1960 indicated that Hubert Humphrey, Kennedy's principal rival, was potentially vulnerable in West Virginia and Wisconsin. On the basis of this information, the Kennedy campaign decided to concentrate time, effort, and money in these predominantly Protestant states. Victories in both helped demonstrate Kennedy's broad appeal, thereby improving his chances for the nomination.

Today, all major presidential candidates commission their own polls. These private surveys are important for several reasons. They provide information about the beliefs and attitudes of voters, their perceptions of the candidates, and the kinds of appeals that are apt to be most effective, and which ones seem to be working. Bill Clinton used polls to great advantage in 1992 to develop and target an economic appeal and to respond to allegations about his personal character. They were especially important early, according to his pollster, Stan Greenberg:

> In September we did some initial research in New Hampshire. Interpretations of the results of that research led us into this race. We concluded that the normal assumption that the New Hampshire primary

electorate is liberal and that a moderate candidate would not face good prospects was wrong-headed. But, more importantly, voters didn't care about ideology; they did not respond to anything we tested about "a new kind of Democrat"; . . . The bread and butter issues were all New Hampshire voters wanted to hear about.[27]

Poll results are also used to build momentum, increase morale, and affect media coverage. The amount of coverage is important because the more coverage candidates have, particularly during the early months, the more volunteers they can attract and the more money they can raise. The benefits of appearing to be popular and electable suggest why candidates have also used their private polls for promotional purposes. A good example is Nelson Rockefeller, who in 1968, tied his quest for the Republican nomination to poll data. Since he did not enter the primaries, Rockefeller's aim was to convince Republican delegates that he, not Richard Nixon, would be the strongest candidate. Private surveys, conducted for Rockefeller in nine large states, five important congressional districts, and the nation as a whole one month before the Republican convention, indicated that he would do better against potential Democratic candidates than Richard Nixon. Unfortunately for Rockefeller, the final Gallup preconvention poll, fielded two days after former President Dwight Eisenhower endorsed Nixon, did not support these findings. The Gallup results undercut the credibility of Rockefeller's polls as well as of another national poll that had Rockefeller in the lead and thus effectively ended his chances for the nomination.

Another use of private polls is to raise money. Contributors are more motivated to give to candidates who stand a reasonable chance of winning. Thus, the release of poll data to potential donors and even to the news media is often designed to demonstrate a candidate's electability.

Although polls directly affect a candidate's strategy, tactics, and fund raising, their impact on the general public is less direct. Despite the fear of many politicians, there are few empirical data to suggest that polls generate a "bandwagon effect," a momentum for a candidate that causes people to jump on board. There is, however, some evidence of a relationship between a candidate's standing in the polls, success in the primaries, and winning the nomination. What is unclear is whether the public opinion leaders win because they are more popular or whether they are more popular initially because they are better known and ultimately because they look like winners.

Design and target a distinctive appeal. The information obtained from polls is used to create and shape leadership images and to target these images to sympathetic voters. In designing an appeal, candidates must first establish their credentials, then articulate a general approach, and finally discuss specific policy problems and solutions. For lesser-known candidates the initial emphasis must be on themselves and their relevant experience.

Paul Tsongas, Bob Kerrey, Tom Harkin, and Douglas Wilder were hardly household names for most Americans in 1992. To be viable, each of these Democratic candidates had to gain national recognition and enlarge his political constituency by making a distinctive appeal. Jerry Brown and Bill Clinton were a little better known at the beginning of the Democratic nomination process, although they had or developed another problem— unfavorable images that they had to overcome.

Once the foundation had been laid, the Democratic candidates tried to make appeals that distinguished themselves from their opponents. Both Tsongas and Clinton emphasized their economic programs, articulating positions they had previously described in their respective books: *A Call to Economic Arms* and *A Plan for America's Future.* Kerrey spoke about the need for health reform, Brown government reform, and Harkin a return to old Democratic values and interests.

In articulating their messages, each candidate targeted a specific group of potential supporters. Tsongas appealed to the business community and to higher-income, better-educated Democrats who were concerned about their party's progovernment, antibusiness, policies. Clinton directed his remarks to the middle class and to racial minorities. Stan Greenberg, the candidate's pollster and strategist described it as a "bottom-up" strategy:

> We knew we were running bottom-up, that we were going to win with a black-white bottom-up coalition. We couldn't do it in New Hampshire, which has a very highly educated electorate. But as a strategy overall for the South and as a strategy for the industrial Midwest, we knew we were building bottom-up.[28]

Harkin targeted liberals, particularly organized labor, in his short-lived campaign, whereas Brown appealed to disaffected Democrats who had difficulty relating to their party and its current leadership.

On the Republican side in 1988 Buchanan directed his message to conservatives, unhappy with Bush's economic and social policies. As the incumbent, Bush made a national appeal. Initially he pointed to his foreign policy successes but as the recession deepened, he was forced to discuss his economic plans for the future.

The 1996 Republican candidates also sought to mount a distinctive appeal within the range of their party's political beliefs. Phil Gramm trumpeted his conservative economic positions, presenting himself as the heir to Reaganism. Robert Dole, viewed as a moderate senator, also stressed his conservative credentials, pledging not to raise taxes and to reduce the role of the national government. A much publicized speech by Dole criticized the entertainment media for its emphasis on violence and its debasing of community and family values. Lamar Alexander, running as a Washington outsider, reiterated the Republican anti-national-government theme, promising to return power to the people and their elected state officials. Richard Lugar stressed his foreign policy competence but also advanced the idea of a flat tax with few exemptions when he announced his candidacy in mid-April 1995, two days after federal income taxes were due. Pat Buchanan, Robert Dornan, and Alan Keyes tried to gain attention by using strident ideological rhetoric that emphasized their social conservatism and neo-isolationist nationalism. Arlen Specter, painted himself as the only true moderate, railing against the policy positions and political ascendancy of the Christian right in the Republican party. Pete Wilson emphasized his economic and social conservatism—balance the budget, cut welfare, restrict immigration, and eliminate affirmative action—, but he supported a pro-choice position on abortion.

In conveying these messages and appeals, candidates utilize news media. Most who can afford radio and local television advertising use it to reach the largest possible audience. The Democratic ads during the early part of the 1992 nomination process were designed primarily to gain name recognition and to associate the candidates with their principal themes and issues. (See Box 4–3, "Pre-New Hampshire Television Advertising.")

As the campaign progresses and public recognition grows, negative or oppositional advertising begins to appear with greater frequency. The Clinton-Brown contest in New York saw a barrage of attack advertising in which each candidate criticized his opponent's credibility and record and defended his own, often in the same ad. (See Box 4–4, "Negative Democratic Advertising.")

The media campaign for the Republicans in 1992 was both harsher and shorter. Running against an incumbent president, Buchanan immediately established himself as a protest candidate, providing reasons for voting against President Bush. In one ad, he accused the president of " . . . investing tax dollars in pornographic and blasphemous art" as pictures of gay men in suggestive positions, wearing leather-clad garb, flashed on the screen. Another Buchanan commercial, aired before the Michigan primary, accused Bush's top political aides of having worked as lobbyists for foreign interests. The implication was clear; they were selling America out. Bush responded in kind. One of his ads alluded to Buchanan's criticism of U. S. involvement in the Persian Gulf; another to his criticism of American automobiles and to the fact that he drove a Mercedes Benz. (See Box 4–5, "Negative Republican Advertising.")

In addition to the advertising, a staple of contemporary presidential campaigns, other methods are also used to reach voters. In 1992, these included video news releases produced by the candidates, satellite interviews with local news media, and telephone, specifically the use of the 800 number to raise money and gain volunteers.

Box 4–3

Pre-New Hampshire Television Advertising

KERREY: PROMOTING VISION AND COURAGE

Script: Narrator: "He came to the Senate to fight for health care for all Americans. Now his Health U.S.A. bill is the best hope for national health insurance. Bob Kerrey: He'll never run from a fight. He volunteered for Vietnam, was a Navy Seal, and leading a commando raid, an enemy grenade cost him his leg. His bravery that night won him the Medal of Honor, the highest award for valor. In the hospital he learned to walk again. Home in Nebraska, he ran a marathon, and starting with nothing, built a business that employs 900 people.

"For him, politics is a cause, not a career. An outsider who defeated an incumbent governor, he wiped out a deficit, helped his state through a farm depression, then despite record popularity, refused to run for a second term.

"Now, in a time of crisis, his cause is fundamental change. National health insurance. Get tough with Japan on trade. A tax cut for the middle class. A national industrial policy to fight for American jobs. Fight back, America."

On the screen: Picture of the Senator talking to voters, as a Navy Seal receiving the Medal of Honor, running and taking the oath as Governor. The commercial ends with the Senator speaking with New Hampshire residents as statements of his goals flash on the screen. (60-second commercial.)

Scorecard: The ad seeks to convey that Mr. Kerrey has a vision for the country and the courage to carry it out, trying to capitalize on voter distaste for conventional politicians. It is tough not to be impressed by Mr Kerrey's résumé. Several close-up shots seem intended to emphasize Mr. Kerrey's all-American good looks.

Accuracy: People who followed Mr. Kerrey's 1988 Senate race in Nebraska say that health care did not, in fact, figure heavily in the campaign. Details of his personal history are not the object of debate. It is true that he gave up the Governor's office when, by all accounts, he could have been re-elected easily.

Source: Elizabeth Kolbert, "The Ad Campaign," *New York Times* (February 11, 1992), p. A 22.

BROWN: CAPITALIZING ON "OUTSIDER" ROLE

Script: Interviews with people, identified at the end of the half-hour "infomercial" as Brown campaign workers, who denounce Washington and politicians with remarks like these:
"They don't give a hoot about us, except to get us to vote for them."
"I think they're all the same, Republicans and Democrats. They're in it for themselves."
"The process is pretty corrupt."
Narrator (Sally Kellerman):
"Finally somebody not beholden to partisan politics who knows the system from the ground up and wants to change it."
Edmund G. Brown Jr.: "Our democracy has been the object of a hostile takeover engineered by a confederacy of corruption, careerism and campaign consultants. And money has been the lubricant greasing the deal."
Mr. Brown narrates a program-within-a-program on the Revolutionary War, urging voters to be "winter patriots," and pitches his toll-free number for donation.

On the screen: Declaration of Independence with "We the People" prominent, and the faces of citizens—black, white, brown, Asian, male, female, elderly and young—superimposed. Various views of Mr. Brown speaking and being interviewed. Newspaper headlines citing his policies when he was Governor of California. The Revolutionary War through paintings. (30-minute commercial.)

Accuracy: Most of Mr. Brown's claims are at least in part accurate. He promoted women and members of minorities in record numbers and his concerns about the environment are now widely held.

Scorecard: The documentary-style commercial portrays Mr. Brown as an outsider who has always bucked insiders to benefit ordinary people. It suggests that policies for which he was once criticized, or even ridiculed, turned out to be sound. The program-length commercial is written in segments so viewers tuning in midway will get the message. It is a cost-saving device since the rates for such "infomercials" are " less than for standard advertising.

Source: Karen De Witt, "The Ad Campaign," *New York Times* (February 12, 1992), p. A 20.

BOX 4–3 *(continued)*
Pre-New Hampshire
Television Advertising

TSONGAS: DISDAIN FOR RIVALS' PLANS

Script: Narrator: "Some candidates want to give you a tax cut of 97 cents a day. But will that create jobs? One candidate knows it's gimmicks and bigger deficits that got us into this mess. Paul Tsongas offers straight answers. He'll declare an economic emergency immediately to get America moving: Get business to invest in new jobs and plants. Rebuild industry. And make our workers the most skilled and productive in the world.

"Paul Tsongas won't short-change our future. He'll LEAD America back."

On the screen: Slow motion of coins representing the 97 cents that Mr. Tsongas estimates the various tax-cut plans of his rivals would save the average family. Stills of an "out-of-business" sign, workers standing in unemployment lines. Video of a Tsongas speech. A final shot of coins with Mr. Tsongas's book *A Call to Economic Arms* landing on top. (30-second commercial.)

Accuracy: The message is essentially consistent with his performance in the Senate, when Mr. Tsongas was one of 11 Senators who voted against the 1981 Reagan plan to cut taxes. Just before he left the Senate in 1984, he sponsored an amendment to freeze government spending.

Scorecard: The ad extends the Tsongas campaign strategy of dismissing rival economic proposals including President Bush's tax-cut plans, as "gimmicks" that will only worsen the economic slump. It emphasizes Mr. Tsongas's disdain for certain tax cuts and deficit spending, which he blames for the current economic malaise. Mr. Tsongas presents himself as strong enough to push through plans that, even though unpopular, would energize the economy.

Source: Karen De Witt, "The Ad Campaign," *New York Times* (February 12, 1992), p. A 21.

CLINTON: THE PERSONAL APPROACH

Script: Narrator: "This is the story of a young man. Born in a small town called Hope. Hope, Arkansas. The son of a widow who taught him that anything was possible with hard work, faith and determination. This is the real story of Bill Clinton.

"He worked his way through Georgetown and Yale Law School, became a Rhodes Scholar, and then set out to make a difference for others in one of the poorest states in our country. And against all odds, made progress.

"First, he tackled the schools, standards, accountability, smaller class sizes, and now the highest graduation rate in the region.

"Build the economy, one of the highest growth rates in new jobs of any state in the nation. Manufacturing jobs created at 10 times the national rate. It isn't a miracle. It's just progress. And, a bit of hope."

Bill Clinton: "That's what this election's about and it's about your future. I want you to send a message to this country about what kind of country we're going to have, about what kind of future you want, about what kind of leadership you believe in and about how we can win again."

Narrator: "This is the time. New Hampshire is the place. This is our country. Let's take it back."

On the screen: Black and white photographs of Bill Clinton growing up, in classrooms, talking with construction workers, wading through a crowd. His words are from a recent New Hampshire speech. Bill and Hillary Clinton are shown hugging and waving with crowd in the background (60-second commercial.)

Accuracy: In 1989, Arkansas stopped computing high school graduation rates because they did not reflect migration patterns. The Southern Regional Educational Board, representing 16 Southeastern states, rated Arkansas first in the region in 1987 and second in 1988. Arkansas was rated 17th in the nation in 1988 by the Department of Education.

From 1985 to 1989, Arkansas rated 22d nationally in total employment growth, the U.S. Department of Labor said. It ranked 10th in new manufacturing jobs. The national growth rate in such jobs was 0.9 percent; in Arkansas it was 10.2 percent, the Department said.

Scorecard: Given the past few weeks of discussion about Mr. Clinton's character, his strategists have decided to present a fuller biographical picture. Voters who were initially impressed had little to fall back on when personal questions arose.

Source: Gwen Ifill, "The Ad Campaign," *New York Times* (February 11, 1992), p. A 22.

Box 4–4

Negative Democratic
Advertising

BROWN: COUNTERING THE IMAGE OF "FLAKINESS"

Script: "As Governor of California, Jerry Brown refused to take a pay raise, cut taxes for working people, created over two million new jobs, and appointed unprecedented numbers of women and minorities.

"Governor Clinton's Arkansas? A right-to-work state, ranks dead last in worker safety, its wages among the lowest in the country. And while Bill Clinton plays golf at a restricted all-white club, Arkansas remains one of only two states with no civil rights act."

"Now that's slick, but we want real change."

On the screen: Film and still images of Governor Brown change to a still shot of Governor Clinton in a golf cart. The image of Mr. Clinton is gradually reduced to the size of a golf ball, which then appears to be knocked off the screen, as though struck by a golf club.

Accuracy: Governor Brown did oppose a proposed $11,000 increase in his salary, which was $49,000, for the 1975–76 budget year. Much of California's tax decrease in his terms [are] the result of Proposition 13, the voter initiative enacted in 1978, which Governor Brown opposed until it was passed at the polls. By 1982, when Mr. Brown left office, the lost revenue, plus a national recession, had created a $1 billion state budget shortage.

In Governor Brown's second term, jobs in the state increased about an average of 1 percent a year, but the work force increased about twice as fast.

The claim about "unprecedented" minority appointees is impossible to verify, since such statistics were not kept before Governor Brown. By mid-1982, he had appointed 1,707 women, compared with 510 in Gov. Ronald Reagan's eight years and 309 in Mr. Brown's father's eight years before that.

Scorecard: The ad attempts to counter charges of "flakiness" by portraying Mr. Brown as both a man of the people and an effective Governor. It paints Governor Clinton as an enemy of unions, a charge that while not necessarily fair, could be effective in a highly unionized state like New York. It takes advantage of what Governor Clinton himself has called a mistake, his golf playing at an all-white country club.

Source: Bruce Weber, "The Ad Campaign," *New York Times* (March 29, 1992), p. A 15.

CLINTON: TAKING AIM AT BROWN

Script: "Jerry Brown says he wants to change. But *Newsday* says his tax changes would, quote, 'Stick it to the very people he claims to help.'

"Our Senator Moynihan calls Brown's plan 'unconscionable' because it would destroy the Social Security Trust Fund.

"Citizens for Tax Justice says that Brown would triple taxes on the poor, raise taxes on the middle class and add a new 13-cent sales tax. In the *Daily News,* Brown's plan is called the greatest single rip-off of working people in history.

"Only Bill Clinton is fighting for a better deal for all of us. He'll put people first."

On the screen: Pictures of newspaper clippings in black and white. Color film of Mr. Clinton, workers and families.

Accuracy: The quotations in the commercial are accurate. Mr. Brown, however, disputes the analysis of his plan by groups like Citizens for Tax Justice.

Scorecard: Public opinion research shows that voters react negatively to the details of Mr. Brown's tax proposal, so the Clinton campaign, trying to head off a large protest vote for Mr. Brown, is attacking him where he is most vulnerable.

Source: Elizabeth Kolbert, "The Ad Campaign," *New York Times* (March 29, 1992), p. A 16.

One of the distinctive aspects of the 1992 nomination campaign was the propensity of candidates, particularly the Democrats, to circumvent the national media whenever possible. They did so in a variety of ways. The Clinton campaign, for example distributed between 25,000 and 30,000 video tapes about the candidate to New Hampshire Democrats.[29] Video news releases were also given to local media by several of the candidate organizations. And about 10 percent of the local stations used them on their news shows, in some cases without even revealing the source.[30]

Box 4–5

Negative Republican

Advertising

"MICHIGAN HAS TOO MUCH AT STAKE TO TRUST PAT BUCHANAN"

Candidate: President Bush

Contest: Michigan Primary

Producer: Mike Murphy, Don Sipple, and Alex Castellanos

Time: 30 seconds

Audio: The issue: Michigan jobs. Pat Buchanan tells us, America first. But while our auto industry suffers, Pat Buchanan chose to buy a foreign car. A Mercedes-Benz. Pat Buchanan called his American cars, quote, "lemons." Pat Buchanan. It's "America first" in his political speeches, but a foreign-made car in his driveway. Michigan has too much at stake to trust Pat Buchanan.

Background: This is a classic protectionist appeal based on a symbol—Buchanan's German car—that is likely to be offensive to auto workers and other union members in Michigan. It taps into the growing "buy-America" movement and uses the conservative commentator's own words to paint him as a hypocrite. The ad also echoes the theme of an earlier Bush spot that Buchanan's protectionist policies would hurt American jobs. While the Mercedes has nothing to do with how Buchanan would perform as president, the ad reminds viewers that this street-fighting candidate is also a well-heeled Washington pundit.

Satellite technology has also been used extensively in the last two nomination processes. In 1992, nearly half of the local news media conducted interviews with the candidates for their party's nomination compared with only 20 percent four years earlier.[31] Of the Democrats Jerry Brown gave the most interviews followed by Bill Clinton.[32] Even George Bush engaged in this form of campaigning despite his ability to make news as president and his campaign's ability to buy air time.

The candidates also took advantage of free television on national talk-

"REGISTERED AGENT: CHARLES R. BLACK— BUSH STRATEGIST"

Candidate: Patrick Buchanan

Contest: Michigan Primary

Producer: Ian and Betsy Weinschel

Time: 30 seconds

Audio: Many of George Bush's top political advisors show up in Justice Department files as foreign agents. Bush strategist Charles R. Black: registered agent. Firm represented Japanese official. Communications director James H. Lake: registered agent. Japan auto parts. Republican chairman Richard N. Bond: registered agent. Government of Panama. No wonder Michigan has lost 73,000 jobs. Put Americans first!

Background: Buchanan cleverly uses the foreign lobbying issue to cast unpatriotic aspersions on the President's team. Bond is not even part of the campaign, and he represented Panamanians opposed to former dictator Manuel Antonio Noriega. But the notion of presidential strategists being paid by Japanese interests is sure to strike a chord in a state with a battered auto industry. There is, of course, no demonstrable link between the advisers' lobbying work and Michigan's job loss, but it fits neatly into the politics of resentment.

Source: "30-Second Politics," *Washington Post* (March 14, 1992), p. A 12.

entertainment shows. Clinton appeared on twenty-one of these shows from January to July, and Perot, once he got into the race, was on four.[33] Jerry Brown made the most extensive use of radio talk shows. In doing so, he always repeated his 800 telephone number to raise money and solicit volunteers, a device Ross Perot used as well when he launched his presidential campaign. Brown raised approximately $5 million from 250,000 people primarily through this device; Perot received more than 2 million calls during the first phase of his campaign.[34]

The candidates were back on the airwaves for the 1996 nomination and election but even earlier in the process. Lamar Alexander bought $300,000 of air time in Iowa and New Hampshire to run two 60 second biographical commercials, beginning in June 1995, in order to introduce himself to the voters of those states. President Clinton's reelection committee spent $2.6 million to create and broadcast three 30 second ads in key states also in the summer of 1995. The ads, with commentaries by police officers, present the president's ban against assault weapons.

All of these factors—timing, finance, organization, and communications—affect the quest for delegates. They help shape the candidates' strategies and tactics for the nomination. Generally speaking, there have been two successful contemporary prototypical strategies, one for lesser-known aspirants, the other for front-runners. Jimmy Carter used the first of these strategies successfully in his initial quest for the nomination in 1976. In his run four years later, Carter adopted the second. Since that time, most of the principal contenders have employed one of these strategies or a variation of them in their attempts to win their party's nomination.

The Non-Front-Runner Strategy: Stepping Stones to Prominence

Non-front-runners lack the resources for victory: money, media, and organization. Their objective must be to obtain them and to do so as quickly as possible. The only way to do this is to run hard and fast at the outset, entering the first contests, doing well, gaining media attention, demonstrating electability, generating momentum, and eventually building a delegate base.

This was Jimmy Carter's strategy in 1976, and it has become the non-front-runner model since then. Hamilton Jordan, Carter's campaign manager, designed the basic game plan two years before the election. He described the early preconvention strategy as follows:

> The prospect of a crowded field coupled with the new proportional representation rule does not permit much flexibility in the early primaries. No serious candidate will have the luxury of picking or choosing among the early primaries. To pursue such a strategy would

cost that candidate delegate votes and increase the possibility of being lost in the crowd. I think that we have to assume that everybody will be running in the first five or six primaries.

A crowded field enhances the possibility of several inconclusive primaries with four or five candidates separated by only a few percentage points. Such a muddled picture will not continue for long as the press will begin to make "winners" of some and "losers" of others. The intense press coverage which naturally focuses on the early primaries plus the decent time intervals which separate the March and mid-April primaries dictate a serious effort in all of the first five primaries. Our "public" strategy would probably be that Florida was the first and real test of the Carter campaign and that New Hampshire would just be a warm-up. In fact, a strong, surprise showing in New Hampshire should be our goal which would have tremendous impact on successive primaries.[35]

The goal was achieved. Dubbed the person to beat after his victories in the Iowa caucuses and New Hampshire primary, Carter, with his defeat of George Wallace in Florida, overcame a disappointing fourth place in Massachusetts a week earlier and became the acknowledged front-runner.

The efficiency of the Carter organization, the effectiveness of his personal style of campaigning, and the lack of strong opposition helped him to win eight of the next nine primaries. These victories gave him approximately 35 percent of the delegates selected by early May, more than double that of his nearest competitor. Although Carter lost ten out of the last seventeen primaries, he was able to continue to build a delegate lead over the field. By the end of the primaries, his nomination had become a foregone conclusion.

The Carter effort in 1976 became the strategic plan for George Bush in 1980 and Gary Hart in 1984 and for most of the Democratic contenders in 1988 and 1992. Concentrating their efforts in Iowa and New Hampshire and other early contests, candidates campaigned vigorously in these states and used the media, particularly local media, to increase their name recognition. They visited the states frequently and tried to build deep organizations.

Whereas Iowa paid off for Carter, the front-loading of the selection process, particularly the holding of a southern regional primary on the second Tuesday of March, has reduced the "bump" that Iowa can give to a victorious non-front-runner. New Hampshire, however, has remained important. It is still considered essential to non-front-runners because it is the first popular election in the nomination cycle. There has been only one person elected president who has not won the New Hampshire primary—Bill Clinton. His second place finish, however, was described by his handlers and interpreted by the news media as a moral victory. (See Box 4–7, "The Clinton 1992 Nomination Strategy.")

To summarize, the task for lesser-known aspirants is to increase their public recognition and, at the same time, to demonstrate their effectiveness as candidates. A win in the early caucuses and primaries, no matter how slight, confounds the odds, surprises the news media, embarrasses the front-runner, and energizes the non-front-runner's candidacy. Media coverage expands; fund raising is made easier; volunteers join the organization; endorsements become more likely; and momentum can be generated, at least in the short run.[36]

On the other hand, early losses for non-front-runners doom their candidacy, forcing them to withdraw, usually on the pretext of having insufficient funds to continue. There is no prize for coming in second except perhaps a prime-time convention speech. News media often speculate that candidates who demonstrate some popular appeal would make good vice-presidential candidates, but the fact of the matter is that successful nominees rarely choose their opponents to run with them. The only recent exception to this rule was Reagan's selection of Bush—not his first choice—in 1980.

Another Non-Front-Runner Approach: Using the Campaign Pulpit

Jesse Jackson was not a typical non-front-runner in 1984 and 1988, and, to some extent, neither were Pat Robertson in 1988 and Jerry Brown and Pat Buchanan in 1992 and again in 1996. Jackson and Brown did not employ the prototypical challenger strategy although Robertson and Buchanan did. Neither Jackson nor Brown had large paid organizations nor could afford extensive paid media. Robertson and Buchanan relied more heavily on advertisements and in Robertson's case, a paid field organization. What all these candidates had in common, however, was a large cadre of grass roots supporters but little realistic chance of winning their party's nomination. Why then did they campaign for it?

They each had several overlapping objectives: to use the campaign as a pulpit for presenting their ideas and as a vehicle for mobilizing their constituencies to promote the interests of those who were not well represented in the party and its hierarchy, to be considered as members of that hierarchy with considerable political power, and to influence the party and its platform. In the words of Bay Buchanan:

> There were a number of reasons why we were going to run, the least of which is that we wanted to win. . . . First, we felt very strongly that the President was the heir to the Reagan legacy, that he had taken the country in a certain direction, and it was assumed it was the direction the conservatives would have taken. Pat thought that we needed a spokesperson to represent conservatives, to say this *isn't* the direction we think is in the best interest of conservatives. . . . Second was

eminent domain. David Duke, who had been made a national figure, was speaking about some of those issues that we thought were ours legitimately. He was being made the ultimate spokesperson for conservatives, a development which was going to do incredible damage to the conservative movement. . . . The third was to actually move the President, force him to keep to the issues that we felt were right and proper for the Reagan legacy.[37]

To achieve their objectives, each of these candidates needed above all else to campaign. They also needed to demonstrate their political strength by winning elections if they were to remain active candidates. Jackson and Brown continued to the convention even though Dukakis and Clinton had each built up huge delegate leads. Robertson and Buchanan dropped out after Bush effectively wrapped up the nomination. They lacked the money to continue, but they had made their points. All four candidates reiterated and defended their campaign positions in addresses at their respective party conventions.

Others have also used the campaign to focus attention on themselves and their ideas. Ellen McCormick ran as an antiabortion candidate for the Democratic nomination in 1976. Lyndon LaRouche has used the Democratic primaries in 1980 and 1984 as a pretext for expounding his philosophy and increasing his supporters. George McGovern entered the 1984 nomination sweepstakes and Gary Hart reentered in 1988 in large part to participate in the public forum generated by the campaign and to try to resuscitate their damaged political images and reputations.

Republicans Bucahnan, Dornan, and Keyes fall into the pulpit candidacy category in 1996. Each wishes to use the nomination campaign as a platform for his issue agenda and ideological perspective as well as a vehicle for extending his name recognition and political influence.

With television being the primary vehicle for conducting a large-scale nomination campaign, and with candidates having distinctive perspectives and appeals attracting public attention, it is likely that the preconvention process will continue to be used for purposes other than solely winning the nomination.

The Front-Runner Strategy: Amassing Delegates

For front-runners the task is different. They do not need to gain recognition or establish their credentials. They do need to maintain their credibility and electability and extend their constituencies. What they need most is delegates. Thus, the strategy is simple and straightforward—acquire as many delegates as quickly as possible and build an insurmountable lead.

The principal advantages front-runners have occur at the beginning of the process. A key element of their strategy must be to maximize these advantages. They need to make use of the benefits of a superior

Box 4–6

The Bush 1992
Nomination Strategy

The Bush strategy was designed in August 1991 even before the president had indicated his intention to seek renomination and almost four months before the Buchanan challenge. It was a straightforward, front-runner strategy in which the superior financial, organizational, and political resources available to an incumbent president seeking reelection would be used to set the foundation on which the president would campaign against his Democratic challenger.

The plan was to articulate a national agenda, first by noting the president's foreign policy successes and then turning to his economic and domestic programs for the next four years. As Mary Matalin, Bush's political director, put it,

> We knew that this election was going to be on the economy and domestic affairs, but we thought it was quite legitimate to launch from our foreign policy achievements. We wanted to make the connection that the leadership required for foreign policy achievements is transferable to domestic problems, and make the case that foreign policy successes abroad meant economic prosperity at home.[38]

Unfortunately, Bush was not able to make that case. The media focused on his challenge from the right not his plans for the future. The

organization, financial base, media coverage, political endorsements, and volunteer efforts to overwhelm their opposition. The front-loading of the primaries provides added impetus to striking a knockout blow in the early rounds, when the lesser-known opponents are least able to compete with them.

Walter Mondale pursued this strategy in 1984, George Bush did so in 1988 and again in 1992, and Robert Dole in 1996. Michael Dukakis and Bill Clinton used variations of this approach. They all spent heavily up front, had large paid staffs, and sought (and received) political endorsements. These resources produced early payoffs—delegate leads that encouraged most of their opponents to drop out and gave them as front-runners a hedge against any future losses against the candidates who remained. (See Box 4–6, "The Bush 1992 Nomination Strategy," and Box 4–7, "The Clinton 1992 Nomination Strategy.")

deepening recession and the president's slowness in responding to it made him an easy target for the Democrats running for their party's nomination. And to make matters worse, after Bush had defeated Buchanan, Ross Perot got into the race as an independent candidate, lashing out at the president. All of this put Bush on the defensive. He was unable to convince voters that the future would be any different than the past.

The emergence of a strong Perot candidacy in the spring of 1992 placed the Bush campaign in a strategic dilemma. Should the president and his aides attack Clinton on vulnerable character issues, turn to his record as Arkansas governor, and criticize his policy positions or go after Perot? The decision was to focus on Perot, who in early June led both major party candidates in public opinion polls. Opposition research collected by the Republican party, much of it leaked to the media, was used to discredit Perot's personal character, outsider image, and leadership capabilities. The anti-Perot campaign was successful; Perot's popular support declined, and he withdrew from the race in mid-July. But the Republican attack against Perot also gave Clinton a vital respite, which he used to great advantage. By the end of the preconvention period, Clinton was back on his feet, Bush had still not articulated an economic program to the satisfaction of most Americans, and the incumbent president continued to encounter dissatisfaction within his own party.

SUMMARY

The delegate selection process has changed dramatically since 1968. Originally dominated by state party leaders, it has become more open to the party's rank and file as a consequence of the reforms initiated by the Democratic party. These reforms, designed to broaden the base of public participation and increase the representation of the party's electorate at its nominating convention, have affected the Republicans as well, even though the GOP has not chosen to mandate national guidelines for its state parties, as the Democrats have. Supreme Court decisions that give the national parties the authority to dictate rules, new state laws that conform to these rules, and public pressure to reflect popular sentiment and improve representation have led to a greater number of primaries and more delegates selected in them for both parties.

Box 4–7

The Clinton 1992
Nomination Strategy

Although Bill Clinton did not begin as a front-runner, he emerged as one before the New Hampshire primary. Once New York governor, Mario Cuomo, decided not to be a candidate in December 1991, the news media dubbed Clinton the person to beat, noting the relative strength of his organization and financial position compared with those of the other declared candidates. They also saw his centrist policy as advantageous.

Initial preparation for the Clinton campaign began in the fall of 1991. A major debate within the campaign organization was whether to cast Clinton as a regional candidate, a moderate who would build on his southern base, or as a national leader who would emphasize middle-class values and interests. The consensus decision was to run a national campaign and demonstrate broad appeal for the centrist positions Clinton espoused. Three major speeches on economic, domestic, and foreign policy given at Georgetown University in Washington D.C., Clinton's alma mater, set the thematic structure of the campaign.

The first primary, New Hampshire, posed a difficult challenge for the candidate. Even before the character issues dominated headlines and put Clinton on the defensive, he faced the problem of competing against a regional New England candidate, Paul Tsongas, and a Vietnam hero, Senator Bob Kerrey. Clinton's advisers assumed he would be in third place for most of the New Hampshire campaign, hoped that he would pick up strength toward the end by stressing economic issues, but were ready to move quickly to other primaries regardless of the result.[39]

Allegations of marital infidelity and draft dodging, which surfaced in the month prior to the New Hampshire vote, forced Clinton to defend himself. It was decided to tackle the infidelity issue immediately with the candidate and his wife appearing on the popular CBS television-magazine program, "60 Minutes." In his brief appearance, which was seen by millions because the program followed the Superbowl, Clinton admitted that he and his wife had marital difficulties, but stated that these difficulties were a thing of the past. The campaign's quick televised response to the accusations limited their political fall-out and elevated Clinton's stature. He then returned to substantive policy issues, delivering a major economic address following the taped "60 Minutes" interview.

The draft-dodging issue was not handled nearly as well nor did the campaign react to it as quickly or as directly. "We made some big mistakes there," stated campaign strategist, James Carville. "The biggest mistake, I think was that I just didn't insist, let's get a suite at the Ritz-Carlton in Boston and just stay in the news mix in New Hampshire. . . . There was just a lot of resistance to the idea. He and Hillary really wanted to go home. He hadn't seen [his daughter] Chelsea."[40]

The genius of the Clinton campaign was that it was able to neutralize at least one character issue that had forced Gary Hart to end his candidacy four years earlier. In fact, on the night of the New Hampshire primary, campaign spokespersons actually turned the character issues to Clinton's advantage. Appearing before the press, the candidate's advisers referred to him as the "Comeback Kid" in New Hampshire; his second-place finish was described as a victory in the light of the problems he faced.

Having successfully survived New Hampshire, the next objective of the campaign was to blunt any momentum that Paul Tsongas may have generated by coming in first in that state. The strategy was to beat Tsongas in the Georgia primary, which had been moved forward a week at the request of the Clinton campaign, and to defeat him in Colorado. Both objectives were achieved. With the help of Georgia governor, Zell Miller, and his political organization, Clinton easily won that state. Tsongas came in a distant second. By focusing on the issue of nuclear energy, of concern to Colorado Democrats, Clinton provided an opportunity for Californian Jerry Brown to defeat Tsongas. Only in Maryland did Tsongas win. The split verdict broke Tsongas' momentum and positioned Clinton perfectly for Super Tuesday.

Clinton crushed his opponents in the southern regional primaries and built a large delegate lead. His victory was made even more impressive by Tsongas' decision to challenge Clinton in Florida and several other southern states in order to demonstrate his own national appeal and not concede so many delegates to Clinton.[41]

Fresh from his victory on Super Tuesday, the Clinton campaign moved to the Midwest, to Illinois and Michigan. His superior organization and financial position made him the favorite in both states. Tsongas' last hurrah came in Illinois. Clinton was leading, but according to Tsongas' campaign manager, Dennis Kanin, the former Massachusetts senator was gaining in the polls. Here's how Kanin described what happened:

> We just started to get the feeling that this thing was turning around. I don't know if it's true or not, but that's certainly what our polling showed. Then came the debate on Sunday night, which I think was critical. The final turning point was when Brown attacked Hillary Clinton at the end of the debate, and Clinton effectively stood up for Hillary. More important it dominated the last several minutes of the debate. Paul was kind of off there somewhere and not part of the battle.

(continued)

Box 4–7 *(continued)*

The Clinton 1992
Nomination Strategy

I know that those of us who were in the room thought, these guys look like they're going at each other, and [Tsongas] is the only one that you know, looks responsible and presidential.

My wife had a different reaction. She said, "I'm sick about it." I asked why. She said, "People like a guy who stands up for his wife. "And all day on Monday, all the news programs and CNN had this every 15 minutes, Clinton standing up for Hillary. We were gone.[42]

With his wins in Illinois and Michigan, Clinton became the prohibitive favorite, but it did not end the campaign. Brown's refusal to bow out did not threaten Clinton's nomination, but his criticism affected Clinton's stature in the eyes of the voters. Although he won the New York primary, Clinton's image was severely damaged by Brown's attacks. Polls indicated that 60 percent of those surveyed believed that Clinton did not possess the honesty and integrity to be president.[43] To counter this perception, the Clinton campaign reintroduced their candidate to the electorate in a series of biographical ads that presented the hardships and struggles that this poor boy from Arkansas encountered growing up and ultimately surmounted in his rise to political prominence. These commercials, combined with talk show appearances in which Clinton reminisced about his upbringing, gradually muted his negative image.[44]

The development of the Perot campaign and the decision by the Republicans to attack Perot in June and July enabled Clinton to get back on his feet before the Democratic Convention. As pollster/strategist Stan Greenberg put it:

We came out of the primaries in very difficult shape . . . our negatives were very high. I think the principal advantage that we gained from Perot was his being on the scene in June and our having the space to use that period to rebuild our candidacy. Without Perot, we assumed that, as you had with Dukakis, . . . [the Republicans] would have been on attack in June and it would have been hard for us to rebuild in that period.[45]

An important component of Clinton's strategy during this period was to ignore Perot in the hopes that he would self-destruct or that the Republicans would destroy him. Again, that part of the strategy proved correct. Clinton's popularity was building as he approached the Democratic convention.

Public participation has increased although turnout levels have varied with the date of the contest, the level of intraparty competition, the amount of money spent, and other candidate-related factors. The delegates have been demographically more representative than those of the prereform era. Larger percentages of women and minorities have been chosen. The delegates seem to be more ideologically conscious, consistent, and extreme in their views, however, than do rank-and-file partisans.

There have been other effects, most of them not beneficial to the parties. Candidacies have proliferated. The parties, particularly the Democrats, have become more factionalized at the national level. These unintended consequences have generated still other reforms, such as the imposition of a window period and the creation of superdelegates, designed to produce more cohesiveness within the party without at the same time abolishing the original goals of reform. They have also been designed to strengthen the influence of party leaders and elected officials.

The strategy for seeking delegates has also been affected by the rules changes. The basic tenets of this strategy include

1. Plan far ahead.
2. Concentrate efforts in the early contests.
3. Raise and spend big bucks early.
4. Create a deep and wide organization.
5. Monitor public opinion.
6. Design and target a distinctive appeal.

Tactical decisions on how to mobilize and allocate sufficient resources to build and maintain delegate support depend on the particular circumstances of individual candidates.

In general, there have been two successful prototypes to winning the nomination: the come-from-nowhere approach of the non-front-runner, and the heavy and continuous pounding strategy of the leading candidates. Non-front-runners need stepping stones to the nomination. Their initial goal must be to establish themselves as viable candidates. At the outset, the key is recognition. Over the long haul, it is momentum. Recognition is bestowed by the news media on those who do well in the early caucuses and primaries; momentum is achieved through a series of prenomination victories that demonstrate electability. Together, recognition and momentum compensate for what the non-front-runners lack in reputation and popular appeal. That is why non-front-runners must concentrate their time, efforts, and resources in the first few contests. They have no choice. Winning will provide them with opportunities; losing will confirm their secondary status.

For the front-runners, the task is different and easier. They have to maintain their position as likely nominees, not establish it. This purpose provides them with a little more flexibility at the outset, but it also requires a broad-based campaign with major resources raised and spent early. Front-runners must take advantage of their organizational and financial base to build a quick and insurmountable lead. For them the name of the game is delegates, delegates, and more delegates.

In the end, it is the ability to generate a popular appeal among the party's electorate that is likely to be decisive. Only one person in each party can amass a majority of the delegates, and that is the individual who can build a broad-based coalition. Although specific groups may be targeted, if the overall constituency is too narrow, the nomination cannot be won. That is why most candidates tend to broaden and moderate their appeal over the course of the prenomination process even before they begin the general election campaign.

NOTES

1. The groups that were initially singled out were Native Americans, African Americans, and youth. Subsequently, the list of affected groups has been altered by the addition of Hispanics, Asian/Pacific Americans, and women, and by the deletion of youth. In 1992, the party also added those with physical handicaps to the groups protected against discrimination.
2. Some states still hold a presidential preference vote with a separate election of delegates by a convention. Others connect the presidential vote and delegate selection on an at-large or district basis. By voting for a particular candidate or delegates pledged to that candidate (or both), voters may register their presidential choice and delegate selection at the same time and by the same vote. The number of these primaries has increased as a consequence of the rules changes. A third alternative is to cast separate votes for president and for convention delegates.
3. Iowa and New Hampshire both have state laws that *require* their contests to be the first caucus and primary, respectively. Democratic party rules take these laws into consideration by the exceptions granted to these two states. The perennial problem for the Democrats, however, has been that other states, such as South Dakota, Wyoming, and Delaware have also enacted legislation that schedules their nomination contests before the official period begins, thereby forcing Iowa and New Hampshire to move their selection date even further ahead—all in violation of party rules.
4. The front-runner advantage was particularly evident in 1984 when the rule specified that 80 percent of the Democratic members of Congress were to be chosen as PLEOs. Their selection before the caucuses and primaries had occurred prompted complaints that the popular vote had been preempted and that nonestablishment candidates were disadvantaged. The party has subsequently revised its rules to include all Democratic members of Congress.
5. A more recent decision by the Supreme Court, also involving open primaries, has further enhanced the power of parties, in this case state parties, to establish rules for nominating candidates. In December 1986 the Supreme Court, in the case of *Tashjian* v. *Republican Party of Connecticut* (107 S. Ct. 544, 1986), voided a Connecticut law that prohibited open primaries. Republicans, who were in the minority in Connecticut, had favored such a primary as a means of attracting independent voters. Unable to get the Democratic-controlled

legislature to change the law, the state Republican party went to court, arguing that the statute violated First Amendment rights of freedom of association. In a 5-to-4 ruling, the Supreme Court agreed, and struck down the legislation.

6. Priscilla L. Southwell, "Open versus Closed Primaries: The Effect on Strategic Voting and Candidate Fortunes (Super Tuesday 1988)," *Social Science Quarterly,* 72 (December 1991): 795.

7. Paul-Henri Gurian, "The Influence of Nomination Rules on the Financial Allocations of Presidential Candidates," *The Western Political Quarterly,* 43 (September 1990): 684.

8. The first of these challenges, initiated in the form of a lawsuit, was declared moot when a decision was delayed until after the 1972 Republican convention. A second case, begun in 1975, challenged the formula on the grounds that it violated the Supreme Court's "one person, one vote" rule. This argument was rejected by the U.S. Court of Appeals for the District of Columbia, and the Supreme Court refused to intervene. The Ripon Society has continued to contest the rules within the party, but to no avail.

9. *Congressional Quarterly,* "Guide to the 1992 Democratic National Convention," (July 4, 1992): 70–71; *Congressional Quarterly,* "Guide to the 1992 Republican National Convention," (August 8, 1992): 63.

10. Earl Black and Merle Black, *The Vital South: How Presidents Are Elected* (Cambridge, Mass.: Harvard University Press, 1992), p. 268.

11. Barbara Norrander, "Ideological Representativeness of Presidential Primary Voters," *American Journal of Political Science* 33 (August 1989): 570–587.

12. "Who Are the Delegates?" *Washington Post* (July 12, 1992), p. A 13; "Delegates: Who They Are?," *Washington Post* (August 16, 1992), p. A 13.

13. Ibid.

14. Howard L. Reiter maintains that the reforms routinized and legitimized long-term changes that were occurring to the party system. Of these changes he mentions "the advent of electronic media, civil service reforms which undercut the patronage system, the rise of the educated middle class and assimilation of immigrants, government social welfare programs, new campaign techniques, and the nationalization of politics." Howard L. Reiter, "The Limitation of Reform: Changes in the Nominating Process," *British Journal of Political Science* 15 (1985): 399–417.

15. Walter Stone Jr., Lonna Rae Atkeson, and Ronald B. Rapoport, "Turning On or Turning Off? Mobilization Efforts of Participating in Presidential Nominations,"*American Journal of Political Science* 36 (August 1992): 688.

16. Quoted in Charles T. Royer (ed.). *Campaign for President: The Managers Look at '92* (Hollis, N.H.: Hollis Publishing Co., 1994), p. 108.

17. The news media give disproportionate coverage to these early contests. In 1988, with both parties having contest nominations, there were a total of 601 campaign stories on the three major networks' evening news shows between January 1 and the middle of March; in 1992, there were 424. In comparison there were a total of 1,559 evening news stories on the entire nomination process from January 1, 1992 through the Republican convention on August 21. "Battle of the Sound Bites: TV News Coverage of the 1992 Presidential Election Campaign," *Media Monitor* (March 1992), p. 2.

18. S. Robert Lichter, Daniel Amundson, and Richard E. Noyes, *The Video Campaign: Network Coverage of the 1988 Primaries,* (Washington, D.C.: American Enterprise Institute, 1988), pp. 95–96.

19. Craig Allen Smith, "The Iowa Caucuses and Super Tuesday Primaries Reconsidered: How Untenable Hypotheses Enhance the Campaign Melodrama," *Presidential Studies Quarterly* 22 (Summer 1992): 524.
20. Running in one's home state or home region is usually a great advantage. In a study of presidential nominations from 1976 to 1988, Professor Barbara Norrander found that home-state and regional pride inflated the vote of two-thirds of the candidates who sought their party's nomination, with Democrats benefiting more than Republicans. Barbara Norrander, "Nomination Choices: Caucus and Primary Outcomes, 1976–1988," *American Journal of Political Science* 37 (May 1993): 347.
21. Quoted in Royer, *Campaign for President*, p. 117.
22. "Amount of Coverage: 1988 vs. 1992," *Media Monitor* (March 1992): 2.
23. Quoted in Royer, *Campaign for President*, pp. 38–39.
24. Professor Barbara Norrander notes that in nomination contests between 1976 and 1988 some of the biggest spenders on the Republican side have also been the biggest losers. Pat Robertson and Robert Dole in 1988 are two examples. Norrander found that the Republicans who did win within this period did so regardless of how much money they spent. In short, it appears that the prospective losers tried to compensate for their secondary status by spending more, and it did not work. Norrander, "Nomination Choices," p. 361.
25. New Hampshire was the comeback state for Bush after his Iowa defeat; South Carolina, occurring three days before Super Tuesday, was the candidate's springboard into the South; and midwestern Illinois was the final victory that sealed Dole's fate and ensured Bush's nomination.
26. David Broder, "Tsongas Forced to Play Organizational Catch-Up," *Washington Post* (March 8, 1992), p. A 19.
27. Quoted in Royer, *Campaign for President*, p. 14.
28. Ibid., p. 90.
29. David Wilhelm as quoted in Royer, *Campaign for President*, p. 77.
30. John Pavlik and Mark Thalhimer, "From Wausau to Wichita: Covering the Campaign via Satellite," in Martha FitzSimon (ed.). *Covering the Presidential Primaries*, (New York: The Freedom Forum Media Studies Center, 1992) p. 41.
31. Ibid., pp. 36–37.
32. Ibid., p. 39.
33. Dirk Smillie, "Rating an Uncertain Season," in FitzSimon (ed.). *Covering the Presidential Primaries*, p. 20.
34. Mark A. Thalhimer, "An Uncertain Season," in FitzSimon (ed.). *Covering the Presidential Primaries*, p. 28.
35. Hamilton Jordan, "Memorandum to Jimmy Carter, August 4, 1974," in *Running for President 1976*, Martin Schram (New York: Stein & Day, 1977), pp. 379–380.
36. According to Larry M. Bartels, momentum is a product of personal preferences that are projected onto expectations. Bartels argues that momentum can best be achieved by a little-known candidate who scores unexpected successes in situations where there is no clear front-runner. What happens is that people who have little substantive information about this candidate project their own desires for an ideal candidate onto this new winner. This result increases expectations and contributes to momentum. "Expectations and Preferences in Presidential Nominating Campaigns," *American Political Science Review* 79 (1985): 804–815.
37. Quoted in Royer, *Campaign for President*, p. 24.
38. Ibid., p. 18.
39. Stan Greenberg, p. 34.

40. Ibid., p. 71.
41. Dennis Kanin, p. 87.
42. Ibid., p. 95.
43. Frank Greer, p. 100.
44. Betsy Wright, a senior campaign aide who had previously served as chief of staff for Clinton when he was governor of Arkansas, described one incident in the difficult process of getting the candidate back in touch with the painful experiences of his younger years:

    I gave him this one letter saying, "This is not going to be easy, but you have to read this letter." It was from a classmate of his in Hot Springs High School who was in Vietnam in the Marine Corps, telling him, don't come here, and if you come here don't come in the Marines. It contained pages of description about the emotional feeling of what it's like to kill your first person and to watch your buddies getting killed. . . . In the envelope with the letter was the guy's obituary—he was killed in action. The letter to Bill was the last letter he ever wrote. Bill looked at me, "don't make me do this," tears in his eyes too, "don't make me do this." Quoted in Royer, *Campaign for President*, p. 188.
45. Greenberg quoted in Royer, *Campaign for President*, pp. 184–185.

SELECTED READINGS

Bartels, Larry M. *Presidential Primaries and the Dynamics of Public Choice.* Princeton, N. J.: Princeton University Press, 1988.

Buell, Emmett H., Jr., and Lee Sigelman (eds.). *Nominating the President.* Knoxville, Tenn.: University of Tennessee Press, 1991.

Greer, John G. *Nominating Presidents: An Evaluation of Voters and Primaries.* New York: Greenwood, 1989.

Gurian, Paul-Henri, and Audrey A. Haynes, "Campaign Strategy in Presidential Primaries, 1976–1988," *American Journal of Political Science,* 37 (February 1993): 335–341.

Mayer, William G. (ed.) *In Pursuit of the White House: How We Choose Our Presidential Nominees.* Chatham, N.J.: Chatham House, 1995.

Norrander, Barbara. "Ideological Representativeness of Presidential Primary Voters." *American Journal of Political Science* 33 (August 1989): 570–587.

Plissner, Martin, and Warren J. Mitofsky. "The Making of the Delegates, 1968–1988." *Public Opinion* 3 (September/October 1988): 45–47.

Polsby, Nelson W. *The Consequences of Party Reform.* New York: Oxford University Press, 1983.

Royer, Charles T. (ed.). *Campaign for President: The Managers Look at '92.* Hollis, N.H.: Hollis Publishing Company, 1994.

Shafer, Byron E. *Quiet Revolution: The Struggle for the Democratic Party and the Shaping of Post-Reform Politics.* New York: Russell Sage Foundation, 1983.

Left: *A symbol of Theodore Roosevelt's Bull Moose Party, which was formed in 1912 after the Republican National Committee joined conservative Republicans in supporting William Howard Taft for reelection.* **Right:** *A Republican campaign emblem for Dwight Eisenhower.*

Chapter 5

The Convention

INTRODUCTION

Political conventions are almost as old as political parties. (See Chapter 1 for a history of presidential nominations.) They have symbolic as well as practical importance for the parties and for the country. They are ritual—part of the American political tradition. They are a show piece for the party leaders and elected officials. They are a mechanism by which nominees are formally chosen, platforms drafted, and presidential campaigns launched.

Although conventions are important to parties, they have become less significant as newsworthy events. The reason for this has as much to do with the media's perception of what is newsworthy as it does with changes in the nomination process itself, changes which have reduced the convention's decision-making capabilities and increased its decision-ratifying role. Today, national nominating conventions are mostly theater, pure and simple.

Prior to 1956, they were decision-making bodies. Majorities were constructed within them to make the critical decisions. Party leaders, who exercised considerable control over the selection of their state delegations, debated among themselves. Once they agreed on the candidates, they cast the votes of their delegates in favor of their particular choice.

The last brokered conventions occurred in 1952.[1] In that year Democratic and Republican leaders wheeled and dealed in "smoke-filled rooms" to select Governor Adlai Stevenson of Illinois and General Dwight

Eisenhower as their respective nominees. Since those conventions, the delegate selection process has dictated the nominees.

Another indication of the decline of the brokered convention has been first-ballot phenomena that have characterized all recent conventions. In fact, since 1924, when the Democrats took 103 ballots to nominate John W. Davis, there have been only four conventions (two Democratic and two Republican) in which more than one ballot has been needed. In 1932, the Democrats held four roll calls before they agreed on Franklin Roosevelt, and three in 1952 to nominate Adlai Stevenson. In 1940, Republican Wendell Willkie was selected on the eighth ballot, breaking a deadlock among Thomas Dewey, Arthur Vandenberg, and himself. Eight years later, Dewey was nominated on the third ballot.

A variety of factors have reduced the convention's decision-making capabilities. State party leaders no longer control the composition or behavior of their delegations. The involvement of the party's rank and file in the selection process enhances the prospects that the delegates will be publicly committed to a candidate and that their votes for the nominee will be known long before they are cast in the convention. In fact, the major television networks, newsmagazines, and newspapers regularly conduct delegate counts during the preconvention stage of the nomination process and forecast the likely winners.

The broadcasting of conventions by radio and later, television has also detracted from the delegates' ability to bargain with one another effectively. It is difficult to compromise before a television camera, especially during prime time. Public exposure has forced negotiations off the convention floor and even out of "leaky" committee rooms.

Size is another factor that has affected the proceedings. Conventions used to be relatively small. In 1860, 303 delegates nominated Democrat Stephen Douglas, and 466 chose Republican Abraham Lincoln. Today, the participants run into the thousands. Table 5–1 lists the number of delegate votes at Democratic and Republican conventions since 1940. When alternates and delegates who possess fractional votes are included, the numbers grow even more. In 1996, the Republicans will have around 2,000 delegates, and the Democrats, augmented by the add-on delegates of party leaders and elected officials, will have around 4,900 delegates.[2]

Because of the large number of delegates, divisions within the parties have been magnified. These divisions, in turn, have produced the need for more efficient organizations, both within the groups desiring recognition and by party officials and candidate representatives seeking to maintain order and to create the image of a unified party. For the party leaders and the prospective nominee, the task has become one of orchestration; their goal is to conduct a huge pep rally replete with ritual, pomp, and entertainment—a made-for-TV production. From the perspective of the party and its nominees, the convention now serves primarily as a launching pad for the general election.

TABLE 5–1

Delegate Votes at Nominating Conventions, 1940–1996*

Year	Republicans	Democrats
1940	1,000	1,100
1944	1,059	1,176
1948	1,094	1,234
1952	1,206	1,230
1956	1,323	1,372
1960	1,331	1,521
1964	1,308	2,316
1968	1,333	2,622
1972	1,348	3,016
1976	2,259	3,008
1980	1,994	3,331
1984	2,234	3,933
1988	2,277	4,160
1992	2,210	4,286
1996[†]	1,981	4,298

* The magic number, the number of votes needed for nomination, equals one more than half.

[†] Tentative numbers—the final number of votes will be determined by each party after the 1995 elections.

Source: Richard C. Bain and Judith H. Parris, *Convention Decisions and Voting Records,* 2nd ed. (Washington, DC: Brookings Institution, 1973), Appendix C. Updated by author.

This chapter explores that pep rally goal and the tension it has created—tension between the party and its nominees on one hand and media representatives, activist delegates, and defeated candidates on the other. The first part of the chapter describes the official convention, the one in which the delegates participate. Here the organization and themes of the meeting are discussed. The second section examines the issues that most frequently divide the convention—credentials, rules, and platforms. The third part of the chapter details the selection of the nominees: the strategy and the tactics of the candidates and the characteristics of the successful nominees. Throughout these three sections, procedural, substantive, and personnel issues are presented as barometers of party cohesiveness and as indicators of the support the nominees can expect to receive from their own party in the general election.

The mediated convention, the one the people of the United States see on television, serves as the prime focus of the fourth part of the chapter. The principal questions examined in this section include: How do the parties script and stage their show? and How does the media react to that orchestration? The impact the convention has on the electorate and ultimately on the government is the subject of the final section.

THE OFFICIAL CONVENTION

Preliminary decisions on the convention are made by the party's national committee, usually on the recommendation of its chair and appropriate convention committees. An incumbent president normally exercises considerable influence over many of these decisions: the choice of a convention city, the selection of temporary and permanent convention officials, and the designation of the principal speakers. Both the Democrats and the Republicans have traditionally turned to national party leaders, primarily members of Congress, to fill many of the positions. The technicalities of scripting and staging the event are left to professionals.[3]

In choosing a site, many factors must be considered: the size, configuration, and condition of the convention hall, transportation to and from it, financial inducements, the political climate, and the cultural ambiance of the city itself. These factors weighed heavily in the Democrats' choice of Chicago for its 1996 convention and the Republicans' choice of San Diego. Both cities are located in states and regions critical to electoral success.

Chicago, a Democratic bastion, has been host to 24 major party conventions since 1860.[4] The one potential drawback to Chicago is the memory of its last political convention in 1968 with civil disturbances on the streets and raucous political divisions among the delegates on the floor of the convention. In choosing Chicago, the Democrats hope to make a not-so-subtle comparison between the state of the party and the country in 1968 and 1996.

San Diego also offers Republicans many of the amenities of a large metropolitan area; a hospitable political environment, including a Republican state governor and city mayor; and much local publicity in the state that has the most electoral votes and one that the Republican lost in 1992.

Organizing the Meeting

Over the years, a standard agenda has been followed by both parties. The first day is devoted to greetings by national party officials, elected officials from the city and state in which the convention occurs, and speeches by other party leaders. The keynote address is also usually given during prime viewing hours on the opening night.

The basic purpose of the keynote is to unify the delegates, smoothing over the divisions that may have emerged during the preconvention campaign, and to rouse them and the public for the coming election. The address ritually trumpets the achievements of the party, eulogizing its heroes and criticizing the opposition for its ill-conceived programs, inept leadership, and general inability to cope with the nation's problems. The keynoter for the party that does not control the White House sounds a litany of past failures and suggests that the country needs new leadership. Naturally, the keynoter for the party in office reverses the blame and praise. Noting the accomplishments of the administration and its unfinished business, the speaker urges a continuation of the party's effective leadership.[5]

The tone of the speech, however, can vary considerably. In 1984 Governor Mario Cuomo of New York, the Democratic keynoter, sounded a sober theme. Describing the United States as a tale of two cities, he chided the Reagan administration for pursuing policies that benefited the rich at the expense of the poor. In contrast, Ann Richards, then treasurer of Texas, who gave the 1988 keynote address, was more folksy, upbeat, and humorous. Criticizing George Bush for being aloof, insensitive, and uncaring, she concluded sarcastically, "he can't help it. He was born with a silver foot in his mouth."[6] In 1992, the Democrats had three first-night keynoters: Senator Bill Bradley (New Jersey), Governor Zell Miller (Georgia), and former Representative Barbara Jordan (Texas); the Republicans had one: Senator Phil Gramm (Texas). Although none of their addresses was particularly notable, all articulated the themes the party wished to emphasize in its forthcoming campaign. (See Box 5–1, "Excerpts from the 1992 Keynotes and Other Major Speeches.")

The more newsworthy and memorable speeches in 1992 were given by others. Pat Buchanan gave one of his rousing campaign speeches on opening night of the Republican convention. Endorsing the president for reelection, Bush's former challenger unleashed a scathing attack on the Democrats and Bill Clinton. The delegates loved the speech, but the news media saw it as harsh and mean-spirited conservative rhetoric.[7] In contrast, former President Reagan's speech, which followed Buchanan's, was lauded for its eloquence and optimism.

Reagan's speech continued the recent practice of allowing party leaders, including ex-presidents, to address the convention. With the convention's promotional activities for the party and its nominees eclipsing its decision-making functions, prime-time exposure has become one of its most treasured prizes. In recent conventions the Democrats have even traded this exposure to unsuccessful candidates in exchange for their public commitment to support the ticket in the election. That was the deal given Edward Kennedy in 1980, Jesse Jackson and Gary Hart in 1984, and Jackson again in 1988 and 1992 as well as Paul Tsongas. Jerry Brown, however, who refused to endorse the 1992 Democratic ticket, could only talk under party rules that permitted candidates with delegate support to address the convention for no more than 20 minutes. Moreover, Brown's remarks were scheduled before prime-time coverage by the major networks began.

Reports from the major committees (credentials, rules, and platform) are usually on the agenda on the second day of the convention although the Republicans approved their platform on the opening day in 1992. Often the product of lengthy negotiations, these reports to the convention represent the majority's voice on the committees. For a minority to pre-

---

Box 5–1

Excerpts from the 1992 Keynotes and Other Major Speeches

DEMOCRATS

Zell Miller
Americans cannot walk our streets in safety, because our "tough-on-crime" President has waged a phony war on drugs, posing for pictures while cutting police, prosecutors and prisons.

And George Bush doesn't get it?

Four years ago, Mr. Bush told us he was a quiet man, who hears the voices of quiet people.

Today, we know the truth: George Bush is a timid man who hears only the voices of caution and the status quo.

Jesse Jackson
All of us are not born giants with silver spoons in our mouths and gold slippers on our feet. Some of us are born short—short of hope, short of opportunity, abandoned, neglected, homeless, motherless, teeth crooked, eyes tangled, dreams busted, hurt. But somebody has to measure their giantness, not by leaping up but by reaching back and reaching out and loving and caring and sharing.

Democrats, if we pursue that ethic, that love ethic, that care ethic, we will win.

And deserve to win.

Stand tall. Never surrender. Keep hope alive. Keep hope alive.

---

sent its views, 25 percent of the committee in question must concur in the minority report. Membership on the committees tends to reflect support for the candidates in the convention as a whole. Thus, when the majority that backs the perspective nominee is unified and effectively coordinated, there is little the minority can do, as was the case in both parties in 1992.

The third day is devoted to the presidential nomination and balloting. In an evenly divided convention, this period is clearly the most exciting. Much ritual has surrounded the nomination itself. In early conventions, it was customary for delegates simply to rise and place the name of a candidate in nomination without a formal speech. Gradually, the practice of nominating became more elaborate. Speeches were lengthened. Ritual required that the virtues of the candidate first be extolled before the candidate's identity was revealed. Today, with public speculation beginning

REPUBLICANS

Phil Gramm

Ronald Reagan sighted the Kremlin in the cross hairs, but it was George Bush who pulled the trigger. . . .

Leadership is the difference. It has changed the world and it has brought us more than peace; George Bush's leadership has brought us victory.

Pat Buchanan

George Bush is a defender of right to life and a champion of the Judeo-Christian values and beliefs upon which this America was founded. Mr. Clinton, however, has a different agenda.

At its top is unrestricted, unrestricted abortion on demand. . . a militant leader of the homosexual rights movement could rise at that convention and say: "Bill Clinton and Al Gore represent the most pro-lesbian and pro-gay ticket in history." And so they do. . .

Elect me, and you get two for the price of one, Mr. Clinton says of his lawyer-spouse.

And what does Hillary believe? Well, Hillary believes that 12-year-olds should have the right to sue their parents.

And Hillary has compared marriage and the family as institutions to slavery and life on an Indian reservation.

Well, speak for yourself, Hillary.

months before and the selection of the nominee a foregone conclusion, the practice of withholding the name has been abandoned.

Demonstrations normally follow the nomination. The advent of television, however, has changed the character of these demonstrations. No longer spontaneous, they are now carefully staged and timed to indicate enthusiasm for the nominee but also to keep convention events moving during the prime-time viewing hours.

Once all nominations have been made, the balloting begins. The secretary of the convention calls the roll of states in alphabetical order, with the chair of each delegation announcing the vote. A poll of the delegation may be requested by any member of that delegation. In 1988, the Democrats installed an electronic system to ensure a fast and accurate count. After the delegation is polled, the chair records the vote of the state on a terminal connected to the podium.

Vice-presidential selection, followed by the nominees' acceptance speeches, are the final order of business. They occur on the last day of the convention. In their early years, nominating conventions evidenced some difficulty in getting candidates to accept the vice-presidential nomination. Because of the low esteem in which the office was held, a number of prominent individuals, including Henry Clay and Daniel Webster, actually refused it. In Webster's words, "I do not propose to be buried until I am really dead and in my coffin."[8]

Today, the vice-presidency is coveted, especially as a stepping stone to the presidency. In the twentieth century six vice-presidents have become president through succession (either death or resignation); two, Richard Nixon and George Bush, have been elected to the presidency (although Nixon was not elected directly from the vice-presidency); and two others, Hubert Humphrey and Walter Mondale, have been presidential candidates.

Despite the appeal of the vice-presidency, it is almost impossible to run for it directly. There are no vice-presidential primaries and no government matching funds for vice-presidential candidates. Only one "vote" really counts—the presidential nominee's. Since the prospective nominee normally has sufficient delegates to control the convention, the presidential standard-bearer can and does dictate the selection. Although most delegates accept the recommendation, there have been a sprinkling of protest votes over the years by delegates who do not like the person selected or who use the vice-presidential nomination to signify opposition to a policy position or perspective that the presidential nominee has adopted.

Only once in recent history, however, has the convention had to make more than a proforma decision on the vice-presidential nomination. In 1956, Democrat Adlai Stevenson professed to have no personal preference. He allowed the convention to choose between Estes Kefauver and John Kennedy. The convention chose Kefauver, the most popular Democrat in the public opinion polls at the time of his nomination.

Since the choice of a vice-presidential nominee is usually not difficult or particularly controversial, a great deal of time is not set aside for it. Moreover, the convention vote on the nomination is frequently made on the afternoon of the last day, to leave the prime viewing hours for the acceptance speeches of the vice-presidential and presidential nominees. These speeches are intended to be the crowning event of the convention. They are the time for displays of enthusiasm and unity. They mark the beginning of the party's presidential campaign.

Articulating the Themes

The custom of giving acceptance speeches was begun in 1932 by Franklin Roosevelt. Before that time, conventions designated committees to inform the presidential and vice-presidential nominees of their decisions. Journeying to the candidate's home, the committees would announce the selection in a public ceremony. The nominee, in turn, would accept in a speech stating his positions on the major issues of the day. The last major party candidate to be told of the nomination in this fashion was Republican Wendell Willkie in 1940.

Today, acceptance speeches can be occasions for great oratory: they are both a call to the faithful and an address to the country. They articulate the principal themes for the general election.

Harry Truman's speech to the Democratic convention in 1948 is frequently cited as one that helped to fire up the party. Truman chided the Republicans for obstructing and ultimately rejecting many of his legislative proposals and then adopting a party platform that called for some of the same social and economic goals. He electrified the Democratic convention by challenging the Republicans to live up to their convention promises and pass legislation to achieve these goals in a special session of Congress that he announced he was calling. When the Republican-controlled Congress failed to enact that legislation, Truman was able to pin a "do-nothing" label on it and make that label the basic theme of his successful presidential campaign.

In 1984, Democratic candidate Walter Mondale made a mammoth political blunder in his acceptance speech. Warning the delegates about the United States budget deficit that had increased dramatically during Reagan's first term, Mondale said that he would do something about it if he were elected president: "Let's tell the truth. Mr. Reagan will raise taxes, and so will I. He won't tell you. I just did."[9] Democratic delegates cheered his candor, directness, and boldness; the public did not. He and his party were saddled with the tax issue throughout the *entire* campaign.

The 1992, acceptance addresses continued the practice of reiterating and articulating campaign themes. Clinton, who had spent much of the previous months trying to reshape his personal image, began his speech by talking about his upbringing and personal struggles.[10] In addition to providing a personal dimension, Clinton sought to achieve two other objectives in his speech: to lay out his goals and articulate the programs that accompanied them and to blunt expected Republican criticism of him, his experience as Arkansas governor, and his proposals for public policy. Saying that he wished to conclude a "New Covenant" with the American people, Clinton promised "a new choice" based on old values."[11]

In accepting renomination by the Republicans, Bush touted his foreign policy achievements, chided the congressional Democrats for obstructing his domestic program, and raised the issues of trust and experience with respect to his Democratic challenger. He implored his audience: "I ask not just for your support for my agenda but for your commitment to renew and rebuild our nation."[12]

Both speeches were intended to launch the candidates in their respective campaigns. Clinton, taking advantage of the momentum generated by the Democratic convention, immediately took his campaign on the road. With vice-presidential nominee, Al Gore, and their wives, a Democratic bus caravan visited small towns in the Midwest, reenforcing Clinton's moderate agenda aimed at middle-class voters and maintaining the media's focus on him and his campaign. In contrast, Bush did not follow up his acceptance speech with a campaign that reemphasized its principal message, thereby allowing that message to dissipate in the period that followed the Republican convention.

CREDENTIALS, RULES, AND PLATFORMS

There have been frequent challenges at national party conventions. In one way or another they involve the leadership and the successful nominees and concern the delegates pledged to these nominees, the rules that got them there and will enable them to control the proceedings, and the policies they have advocated and are likely to pursue. Those who initiate the challenges are the unsuccessful candidates and their supporters. Desiring to exercise influence in a convention in which they are in the minority, they use these challenges as a means of forcing the leadership and the nominees to acknowledge their claims and to give them something in exchange for their support in the forthcoming election. These challenging delegates, who are likely to be activists and who represent others with similar views and desires, do not want to leave the convention empty-handed, even though they have lost the nomination.

Challenging Credentials

All delegates must present proper credentials to participate at national nominating conventions. Disputes over credentials have occurred from time to time. Twice in the twentieth century, Republican conventions have witnessed major credential changes that ultimately determined their nominee. William Howard Taft's victory over Theodore Roosevelt in 1912 and Dwight Eisenhower's over Robert Taft in 1952 followed from convention decisions to seat certain delegates and reject others. In both cases, grass roots challenges to old-line party leaders generated competing delegate claims. The convention in 1912 rejected these challenges and seated the regular party delegates, producing a walkout by Roosevelt's supporters and giving the nomination to Taft. Forty years later the delegates denied the nomination to Taft's son by recognizing the credentials of delegates pledged to Eisenhower and rejecting those supporting Senator Taft.

Democratic conventions have also witnessed credentials fights. In 1968 and again in 1972, these challenges were based on allegations that certain party members had been excluded from caucuses and conventions, that certain state delegations did not possess sufficient minority representation, and that some of those delegations were chosen in a manner that did not conform to party rules.

The California challenge at the 1972 Democratic convention illustrates the last of these complaints. George McGovern had won the primary and, according to California law at the time, was entitled to all the delegates. The credentials committee, however, decided that the state's delegates should be divided in proportion to the popular vote because the commission that had revised the Democratic rules for 1972, a commission McGovern initially headed, had affirmed the principle of proportional voting although it did not require states to change their law to conform to this principle until 1976. McGovern challenged the ruling and won on the convention floor, thereby making his nomination all but certain. There have been no serious delegate challenges at either convention since 1972 largely because of the reforms that have established clear procedures for delegate selection and eliminated the discretion state party leaders had exercised in choosing them.

Adopting the Rules

Rules govern the manner in which the convention is conducted; they also can affect the next delegate selection process four years down the road. Convention rules are interpreted by the chair of the convention, with the convention itself having final authority. The Rules Committee can propose changes in these internal procedures, but these changes must be approved by the delegates.

In formulating the rules, there is often tension between the desire of the minority to be heard and the interest of the majority, especially the leadership, to run an efficient convention. A humorous incident at the 1956 Republican convention illustrates this tension. In the nomination for vice-president, Richard Nixon was expected to be the unanimous choice. A movement to dump him from the ticket, led by perennial candidate Harold Stassen, had failed. When the roll of states was called for nominations, a delegate from Nebraska grabbed the microphone and said he had a nomination to make. "Who?" said a surprised Joseph Martin, chair of the convention. "Joe Smith," the delegate replied. Martin did not permit the name of Joe Smith to be placed in nomination, although the Democrats were later to contend that any Joe Smith would have been better than Nixon.

For the most part, convention rules have not caused much wrangling. Those that have generated the most controversy have concerned voting for the party's nominees. Until 1936, the Democrats operated under a rule that required a two-thirds vote for winning the nomination. James K. Polk's selection in 1844 was a consequence of Martin Van Buren's failure to obtain the support of two-thirds of the convention, although Van Buren had a majority. The two-thirds rule in effect permitted a minority of the delegates to veto a person they opposed.

The Democratic party also permitted the unit rule, a requirement that some states adopted to maximize their voting strength. The rule obligated all members of a delegation to vote for the majority's candidate or position on a pending issue regardless of their own views. Beginning in 1968, the Democratic convention refused to enforce unit voting any longer. The elimination of this majority-take-all principle obviously reduced the probability that state delegations would vote as units and, ultimately, weakened the power of the state party leaders. The Republicans never sanctioned nor prohibited unit voting. When the Mississippi delegation decided to vote as a unit at the 1976 convention to enhance its influence and perhaps tip the balance to President Ford, there was little that challenger Ronald Reagan could do or party officials would do.

Among the recent rules controversies that have divided Republican conventions, two stand out. In 1952, when Eisenhower supporters challenged the credentials of a sizable number of Taft delegates from southern states, the convention adopted a "fair play" rule that prohibited contested delegates from voting on any question, including their own credentials. This rule, which effectively prevented many Taft delegates from voting, swung the challenges and eventually the nomination to Eisenhower.

The other recent dispute that became a precursor of the presidential vote occurred during the 1976 Republican convention, when the Reagan organization proposed a rules change that would have required Gerald Ford to indicate his choice for vice-president before the vote for president, as his opponent, Ronald Reagan had done. Ford's supporters strongly opposed and subsequently beat this amendment. As a consequence, there was no way for Reagan to shake the remaining delegates loose from Ford's coalition. Ford won the presidential vote 1,187 to 1,070—a margin almost identical to that of his rules victory.

An even more acrimonious division over party rules occurred in 1980 at the Democratic convention. At issue was a proposed requirement that delegates vote for the candidate to whom they were publicly pledged at the time they were chosen to attend the convention. Trailing Jimmy Carter by about six hundred delegates, Ted Kennedy, who had previously supported the requirement, urged an open convention in which delegates could vote their consciences rather than merely exercise their commitments. This change in the rules would have required rejection of the pledged delegate rule. Naturally, the Carter organization favored the rule and lobbied strenuously and successfully for it. By a 600-vote margin the convention accepted the binding rule, thereby ensuring President Carter's renomination. The Democrats have subsequently repealed this rule, requiring instead that delegates reflect in good conscience the sentiments of those who elected them.[13]

Drafting the Platform

Traditionally, the platform has been the object of most of the challenges and controversies. The ideological orientation of activist delegates and the pragmatic political needs of the leadership and the party's nominees make controversy almost inevitable. Two often conflicting aims lie at the heart of the platform-drafting process. One has to do with winning the election, and the other with pleasing the party's core constituency. The goal of accommodating as many people as possible has been accomplished by moderating the language and, occasionally, by increasing the level of ambiguity on the most controversial and emotionally charged issues. When appealing to the party's dominant coalition, on the other hand, traditional images have been presented and certain economic and social positions stressed.

The tension resulting from these conflicting goals has caused real problems for platform drafters. The resulting documents contain high-sounding rhetoric, self-praise, and unrealistic goals that open them to criticism that they are substantially meaningless and politically unimportant, that they bind and guide no one. There may be some truth to these criticisms, but they also overstate the case.

Promises and performance. Contrary to popular belief, platforms are important. They are the party's principal attempt to define itself; to state what it stands for and why its candidates should be elected. Although platforms contain rhetoric and self-praise, they also articulate goals and policy positions that differentiate one party from the other. In an examination of the Democratic and Republican platforms between 1944 and 1976, Gerald Pomper found that most of the differences were evident in the planks incorporated by one party but not by the other.[14] Over these years the Republicans, who were in the minority, emphasized national security and general governmental matters, whereas the Democrats, the majority party during this period, stressed economic issues, particularly those that pertained to labor and social welfare.

Party platforms are directed to broad constituencies. The Republican party has traditionally tried to expand its electoral base by appealing to independents and Democrats on the basis of national issues, ideological concerns, and social (family) values, whereas the Democrats have usually designed their platforms to appeal to many of the specific groups that comprise their electoral coalition by emphasizing domestic economic matters.

Beginning in 1988, the Democrats toned down their liberal rhetoric in an attempt to make their platforms more appealing to middle-class voters disaffected by the party's social and economic policies in the 1970s and 1980s. In contrast, the Republicans have moved to the right, becoming more conservative, more ideological, and more exclusive.

Contrasts in the 1992 Party Platforms

DEMOCRATS	REPUBLICANS
Abortion	
Democrats stand behind the right of every woman to choose, consistent with *Roe* v. *Wade*, regardless of ability to pay, and support a national law to protect that right.	We believe the unborn child has a fundamental individual right to life which cannot be infringed.
Health Care	
All Americans should have universal access to quality, affordable health care—not as a privilege but as a right.	Republicans believe government control of health care is irresponsible and ineffective. We believe that health care choices should remain in the hands of the people, not government bureaucrats.
Homosexual Rights	
We will . . . provide civil rights protection for gay men and lesbians and an end to Defense Department discrimination.	We oppose any legislation or law which legally recognizes same-sex marriages and allows such couples to adopt children or provide foster care. . . .
Energy and the Environment	
We reject the Republican myth that energy efficiency and environmental protection are enemies of economic growth.	We believe that recreation, forestry, ranching, mining, oil and gas exploration, and production on our public lands can be conducted in a way compatible with their conservation.

There have also been substantial differences in content between the party's platforms. (See Box 5–2, "Contrasts in the 1992 Party Platforms.") These differences in turn have produced different public policies because elected officials of both parties have a relatively good record of meeting their pledges.

DEMOCRATS	REPUBLICANS
Immigration	
Democrats support immigration policies that promote fairness, nondiscrimination and family reunification and that reflect our constitutional freedoms of speech, association and travel.	Our Nation of immigrants continues to welcome those seeking a better life. . . . Illegal immigration . . . undermines the integrity of border communities and already crowded urban neighborhoods.
Taxes	
We will relieve the tax burden on middle-class Americans by forcing the rich to pay their fair share. We will provide long-overdue tax relief to families with children.	We will cut the capital gains tax rate to 15 percent—zero in enterprise zones—and index it so government cannot profit from inflation by taxing phantom capital gains, . . .
Welfare	
Welfare should be a second chance, not a way of life. We want to break the cycle of welfare by adhering to two simple principles: No one who is able to work can stay on welfare forever, and no one who works should live in poverty.	Today's welfare system is anti-work and anti-marriage. . . . It cannot be merely tinkered with by Congress; It must be re-created by states and localities.

Source: Democratic Party Platform as appears in *Congressional Quarterly* (July 4, 1992): 59–67; Republican Party Platform as appears in the *New York Times* (August 18, 1992), p. A 10.

Although approximately three-quarters of party platforms are high-sounding rhetoric, about one-fourth contains fairly specific promises. Of these, Pomper found that almost 75 percent have been kept.[15] To illustrate. *The Washington Times*, a persistent critic of the Clinton presidency found that the administration had redeemed 47 percent of the campaign and platform promises that the Democrats had made in its first 10 months in office.[16] Another more sophisticated analysis of party platforms and federal expenditures between 1948 and 1985 found federal spending priorities to be closely linked to the emphases laid down within party platforms.[17]

A principal reason that so many of the convention promises have been acted on is that elected officials participate in the drafting of platforms; in fact, they hold many of the key committee positions. For the party in power, the incumbent president seeking reelection, usually takes the lead, exercising the most influence over the composition of the platform committee and the product it produces. For the party out of power, the chair of the national committee usually selects the leadership of the platform committee, and the successful nominee controls a majority of the delegates.[18]

Accommodations and disagreements. The platform-drafting process has traditionally been designed to accommodate outside groups and partisan interests in such a way as to maximize the leadership's control over the final document. In the first stage, public hearings are held. These hearings provide an opportunity for group representatives to be heard, to present their positions, and to make their claims. The Democrats held only one such public hearing in 1992, whereas the Republicans held four.

After the hearings have been concluded, staff chosen by the committee chair in consultation with the chair of the national committee, draft a working paper that is presented to one or several drafting subcommittees, which review and finalize the draft for the full committee's consideration. The platform committees of both parties meet the week before their respective conventions to debate the draft and to agree on a platform to be presented to the entire convention. Within the platform committee and on the floor of the convention, amendments can be offered. Convention rules make it difficult for a small minority to be successful, however.[19] Here as elsewhere, the drafting process is controlled by the prospective nominees through their designated representative.

The Republican platform-drafting process was more open and participatory than the Democrats in 1992. Members of the Republican platform committee were given more latitude in speaking their minds and framing the platform than were their Democratic counterparts. Unfortunately for the Republicans, the news media interpreted this openness as a sign that Bush was weak, could not control the committee, and was forced to accept a more conservative platform than he would have preferred. This evaluation fueled the dominant storyline of a conservative takeover of the Republican convention.[20]

In general the more open the platform-drafting process, the more divisive it appears to be. Prior to 1988, the Republicans, the more homogeneous of the two parties, suffered less than the Democrats from this divisiveness. In 1992, they suffered more.

PRESIDENTIAL AND VICE-PRESIDENTIAL SELECTION

Strategies and Tactics

There are a number of prizes at nominating conventions. The platform contains some of them. The rules can also be important, but the big prize is the presidential nomination itself. When that is in doubt, all the efforts of the leading contenders must be directed at obtaining the required number of votes to be nominated. When it is not in doubt, the leading contenders can concentrate on uniting the party, articulating their themes, and converting the convention into a huge campaign rally for themselves. In 1976, the Reagan organization focused its attention on winning the nomination; in 1980 it sought to present a united front; in 1984 it orchestrated a coronation ceremony that was repeated by George Bush in 1988 but with less success in 1992.

In recent Democratic conventions the front-runners have tried to heal the wounds of the nomination contest by appealing to disaffected delegates to join them and the party for the fall campaign. This is precisely what Michael Dukakis did in 1988. Making peace with his principal opponent, Jesse Jackson, Dukakis conceded the rules changes and some of the platform proposals Jackson wanted in exchange for Jackson's public support of the Democratic ticket at the convention and during the campaign. In 1992, the Clinton campaign appealed to Tsongas delegates and to Perot supporters when the latter first dropped out of the presidential race on the day Clinton accepted the Democratic nomination. Brown's desire to bring his campaign to the convention even though he had no chance of getting the nomination and his refusal to endorse the Democratic ticket, created the opposite effect—a refusal by Clinton delegates to consider any of his proposals for reform and to deny him a prime-time opportunity to address the convention.

A key to success, regardless of the objective, is organization. Recent conventions have seen the operation of highly structured and efficient candidate organizations. Designed to maximize the flow of information, regulate floor activity, and anticipate and control roll call votes, these organizations usually have elaborate communications systems linking floor supporters to a command center outside the convention hall. Key staff members at the command center monitor reports, articulate positions, and make strategic decisions.

In addition to having an effective organization, candidates need goals and a strategy for achieving them. (See Box 5–3, "1992 Convention: Goals and Strategies.") Both are ultimately shaped by the party's and candidate's status at the time of the convention. The objective for leading candidates is to maintain the momentum, win on the first ballot, and prepare for the general election with minimum dissent and diversions. For those

---

Box 5–3

1992 Convention:

Goals and Strategies

DEMOCRATS

Each of the prospective nominees had their basic goals and strategies for their nominating convention. For Clinton, it was to continue the process of reintroducing himself and his candidacy. Describing himself as a "New Democrat" with new policy based on old values, Clinton reiterated his principal goals and programs. A second objective was to redefine his party, discarding its liberal label, particularly in the economic arena, in favor of a more moderate, mainstream, middle-class approach. Finally, he desired to convince voters that the Democrats could govern effectively given the experience of the previous Democratic administration, Jimmy Carter's. Having an orderly and unified convention was important toward achieving this latter objective.

In pursuing its agenda, the Clinton organization exercised tight control over convention proceedings, including the platform debate and the speeches. Only those who endorsed the ticket were given prime-time speaking opportunities. The speeches themselves were synchronized by the Clinton speech-writing team under the direction of Paul Begala to ensure that they articulated the themes of the forthcoming campaign.

The Democratic effort succeeded in part because the media chose to interpret the proceedings in the context of past conventions. The news was that the 1992 Democratic convention was less acrimonious and more unified than previous ones. This news was also part of the message the Democrats wished to convey to the viewing audience.

---

who are behind, the goal is to challenge the certainty of the initial balloting, despite public predictions to the contrary, and to demonstrate the ability to win the nomination and the election. Thus, although Gary Hart trailed Walter Mondale by hundreds of delegates going into the 1984 convention, he continued to maintain the possibility of his receiving the Democratic nomination until the actual balloting put Walter Mondale over the top.

For non-front-runners still seeking the nomination, there are two immediate needs: to indicate the vulnerability of the front-runner, and to emphasize their own capacity to win. Two tactics have been employed by challengers to accomplish these ends. One is to release polls, such as Rockefeller did in 1968, showing the strength of the non-front-runner and the weakness of the convention leader in the general election. The objective here is to play on the delegates' desire to nominate a winner.

REPUBLICANS

The Republicans had a different set of goals. The first was to restore their partisan base by appealing to conservatives to come home. Polls indicated that approximately one-third of Republican voters, mostly conservatives, were disaffected with President Bush. A second objective was to set the thematic context for the campaign, and in so doing, present the president in a positive light to the American voters. The plan here was to structure the convention's thematic content from the broad to the specific, ending with the spotlight on George Bush. Thus, the theme of the first day was the world and the success of U.S. policy over the last 12 years. For the second day the focus was on the nation. Traditional values and community and family issues were the topic for the third night, and on the fourth the focus was on the nominees, Bush and Quayle, and their acceptance speeches.

Whereas the Democrats gained from comparison to their previous conventions, the Republicans suffered. The news media evaluated the Republican convention as a conservative *coup d'etat* with Bush as its principal captive. The media's message was that Republican policy as articulated at the convention was not mainstream as party leaders claimed but was extremist, uncompromising conservatism. It was that message, not the one advanced by George Bush in his acceptance speech, that echoed in the minds of much of the electorate as the general election campaign began.

A second tactic is to create an issue before the presidential balloting and win on it. If the issue affects the rules that affect the vote, so much the better. Reagan in 1976 and Kennedy in 1980 tried this ploy but without success. Their defeats on key votes confirmed their status as also-rans and forced them to focus on the platform to influence the party and its nominee, to save face, and to position themselves for the next battle in four years.

Front-runners, on the other hand, must avoid taking unnecessary risks. Ford followed this strategy in 1976, as Carter did in 1980, Mondale in 1984, and Dukakis in 1988. They compromised where possible on policy and other issues but maintained their positions on those challenges that could have jeopardized their nomination or injured their presidential campaign. Clinton and Bush both gave ground on the platform, but otherwise were able to exercise sway over the delegates at their respective conventions.

Although it may be necessary for front-runners to show their strength, they must be careful not to flaunt it and accentuate divisions created by the nomination process. Once the nomination is ensured, the object of front-runners is to unify the faithful and present a united front for the general election. Achieving unity requires the victorious candidate to reach out to disaffected members of the party.

Characteristics of the Nominees

The nominations of relatively obscure governors by the Democrats in 1976, 1988, and 1992 and a former movie actor and California governor by the Republicans in 1980 indicate that changes in the preconvention process have affected the kind of people chosen by their parties. In theory, many are qualified. The Constitution prescribes only three formal criteria for the presidency: a minimum age of thirty-five, a fourteen-year residence in the United States, and native-born status. Naturalized citizens are not eligible for the office.

In practice, a number of informal qualifications have limited the pool of potential nominees. Successful candidates have usually been well known and active in politics, and have held high government positions. Of all the positions from which to seek the presidential nomination, the presidency is clearly the best. Only five incumbent presidents (three of whom were vice-presidents who had succeeded to the office) have failed in their quest for the nomination. It should be noted, however, that several others were persuaded to retire rather than face tough challenges.

Over the years, there has been a variety of paths to the White House. When the congressional caucus system was in operation, the position of secretary of state within the administration was regarded as a stepping stone to the nomination if the incumbent chose not to seek another term. When national conventions replaced the congressional caucus, the Senate became the incubator for most successful presidential candidates. After the Civil War, governors emerged as the most likely contenders, particularly for the party that did not control the White House. Governors of large states in particular possessed a political base, a prestigious executive position, and leverage by virtue of their control over their delegations.

The position of governors as potential candidates weakened with the development of national television networks in the 1950s. With most statehouses outside of major population centers, governors did not get as much exposure as Washington-based officials. Lacking national media coverage in an age of television and national political experience at the time the role of government in Washington was expanding, most governors also did not possess the staffing resources that the White House and Senate provided. It is no wonder that between 1960 and 1972 all party nominees came from the upper legislative chamber or the White House.[21]

The nominations of Carter, Reagan, Dukakis, and Clinton have broken this trend. New party rules, finance legislation, and strong anti-Washington sentiment have once again increased the opportunities for governors although they have not eliminated the advantage a national reputation can provide for those seeking their party's presidential nomination.

There are other informal criteria, although they have less to do with qualifications for office than with public prejudices. Only white males have ever been nominated by either of the major parties although African Americans have sought the Democratic nomination. Until 1960, no Catholic had been elected, although Governor Alfred E. Smith of New York was chosen by the Democrats in 1928. Michael Dukakis was the first candidate whose ancestry could not be traced to northern Europe, a surprising commentary on a country that has prided itself on being a melting pot.

Personal matters, such as health and family life, can also be factors. After Alabama governor, George Wallace, was crippled by a would-be assassin's bullet, even his own supporters began to question his ability to withstand the rigors of the office. Senator Thomas Eagleton was forced to withdraw as the Democratic vice-presidential nominee in 1972 when his past psychological illness became public. Today, presidential and vice-presidential candidates are expected to release detailed medical reports on themselves.

Family ties have also affected nominations and elections. There have been only two bachelors elected president, James Buchanan and Grover Cleveland.[22] During the 1884 campaign, Cleveland was accused of fathering an illegitimate child and was taunted by his opponents with "Ma, Ma, Where's my Pa? Gone to the White House, Ha! Ha! Ha!" Cleveland admitted responsibility for the child, even though he was not certain he was the father.

Until 1980, no person who was divorced had ever been elected. Andrew Jackson, however, married a divorced woman, or at least a woman he thought was divorced. As it turned out, she had not been granted the final court papers legally dissolving her previous marriage. When this information was became public during the 1828 campaign, Jackson's opponents asked rhetorically, "Do we want a whore in the White House?"[23] Jackson and Cleveland both won.

In more recent times, candidates have been hurt by marital problems, allegations of sexual misconduct, or other personal frailties. The dissolution of Nelson Rockefeller's marriage and his subsequent remarriage seriously damaged his presidential aspirations in 1964. That Adlai Stevenson was divorced also did not improve his chances, particularly after his former wife spoke out against him. Senator Edward Kennedy's marital problems and his driving accident on Chappaquiddick Island, off the coast of Massachusetts, in which a young woman riding with the senator was drowned, were serious impediments to his presidential candidacy in

1980. Similarly, Gary Hart's alleged "womanizing" forced his withdrawal in 1988, whereas the length of the period between Pat Robertson's marriage and the birth of his first son raised some eyebrows and was a topic of conversation and concern among some of his religious followers. Bill Clinton's election despite the allegations of marital infidelity, marijuana smoking, and draft dodging suggest that the electorate is more concerned about contemporary conditions and behavior than they are with relationships and behavior that have occurred in previous years, especially in the distant past.

The informal qualifications of the presidential nominee have in general been matched by those of the vice-presidential candidate as well. The nomination of a woman, Geraldine Ferraro, by the Democrats in 1984 and the continued speculation of former General Colin Powell as a possible presidential or vice-presidential candidate, however, have made gender and race seem less of a barrier today than they were in the past.

The vice-presidential search has traditionally been affected by the perceived need for geographic and ideological balance. Presidential aspirants have tended to choose vice-presidential candidates primarily as running mates and only secondarily as governing mates. Despite statements to the contrary, most attention is given to how the prospective nominee would help the ticket.

The choice of Dan Quayle in 1988 is a good example. Needing to bolster his standing among conservative Republicans and to appeal to younger voters, Vice-President Bush, who was then sixty-four years old, had been born and raised in Connecticut, had moved to Texas, and still vacationed at his home in Maine, chose a forty-one-year-old senator from the Midwest (Indiana) on the advice of his media and polling consultants.[24]

In contrast, Bill Clinton chose Al Gore in 1992 not so much to balance the ticket as to emphasize his centrist policy positions, southern roots, and generational appeal to the baby boomers. Gore did provide some policy balance in the environmental and national security areas where Clinton was perceived by some as weak. (For lists of Democratic and Republican party conventions and nominees, see Tables 5–2 and 5–3.)

THE MEDIATED CONVENTION

Radio began covering national conventions in 1924. Television broadcasting commenced in 1956. Because conventions in the 1950s were interesting and unpredictable events in which important political decisions were made, they attracted a large audience, one that increased rapidly as the number of households having television sets expanded. During the 1950s and 1960s, about 25 percent of the potential viewers watched the conventions, with the numbers swelling to 50 percent during the most significant part of the meetings. The sizable audience made conventions important

Table 5-2
Republican Party Conventions and Nominees, 1900–1996

Year	City	Dates	Presidential Nominee	Vice-Presidential Nominee	Number of Presidential Ballots
1900	Philadelphia	June 19–21	William McKinley	Theodore Roosevelt	1
1904	Chicago	June 21–23	Theodore Roosevelt	Charles Fairbanks	1
1908	Chicago	June 16–19	William Taft	James Sherman	1
1912	Chicago	June 18–22	William Taft	James Sherman, Nicholas Butler*	1
1916	Chicago	June 7–10	Charles Evans Hughes	Charles Fairbanks	3
1920	Chicago	June 8–12	Warren Harding	Calvin Coolidge	10
1924	Cleveland	June 10–12	Calvin Coolidge	Charles Dawes	1
1928	Kansas City	June 12–15	Herbert Hoover	Charles Curtis	1
1932	Chicago	June 14–16	Herbert Hoover	Charles Curtis	1
1936	Cleveland	June 9–12	Alfred Landon	Frank Knox	1
1940	Philadelphia	June 24–28	Wendell Willkie	Charles McNary	6
1944	Chicago	June 26–28	Thomas Dewey	John Bricker	1
1948	Philadelphia	June 21–25	Thomas Dewey	Earl Warren	3
1952	Chicago	July 7–11	Dwight Eisenhower	Richard Nixon	1
1956	San Francisco	August 20–23	Dwight Eisenhower	Richard Nixon	1
1960	Chicago	July 25–28	Richard Nixon	Henry Cabot Lodge, Jr.	1
1964	San Francisco	July 13–16	Barry Goldwater	William Miller	1
1968	Miami Beach	August 5–8	Richard Nixon	Spiro Agnew	1
1972	Miami Beach	August 21–23	Richard Nixon	Spiro Agnew	1
1976	Kansas City	August 16–19	Gerald Ford	Robert Dole	1
1980	Detroit	July 14–18	Ronald Reagan	George Bush	1
1984	Dallas	August 20–23	Ronald Reagan	George Bush	1
1988	New Orleans	August 15–18	George Bush	Dan Quayle	1
1992	Houston	August 17–21	George Bush	Dan Quayle	1
1996	San Diego	August 10–16			1

* The 1912 Republican convention nominated James Sherman, who died on October 30. The Republican National Committee subsequently selected Nicholas Butler to receive the Republican electoral votes for vice-president.

Source: Updated from *National Party Conventions, 1831–72* (Washington, D. C.: *Congressional Quarterly*, 1976), pp. 8–9. Copyrighted materials reprinted with permission of Congressional Quarterly, Inc.

TABLE 5–3
Democratic Party Conventions and Nominees, 1900–1996

Year	City	Dates	Presidential Nominee	Vice-Presidential Nominee	Number of Presidential Ballots
1900	Kansas City	July 4–6	William Jennings Bryan	Adlai Stevenson	1
1904	St. Louis	July 6–9	Alton Parker	Henry Davis	1
1908	Denver	July 7–10	William Jennings Bryan	John Kern	46
1912	Baltimore	June 25–July 2	Woodrow Wilson	Thomas Marshall	1
1916	St. Louis	June 14–16	Woodrow Wilson	Thomas Marshall	43
1920	San Francisco	June 28–July 6	James Cox	Franklin Roosevelt	103
1924	New York	June 24–July 9	John Davis	Charles Bryan	1
1928	Houston	June 26–29	Alfred Smith	Joseph T. Robinson	4
1932	Chicago	June 27–July 2	Franklin Roosevelt	John Garner	Acclamation
1936	Philadelphia	June 23–27	Franklin Roosevelt	John Garner	1
1940	Chicago	July 15–18	Franklin Roosevelt	Henry Wallace	1
1944	Chicago	July 19–21	Franklin Roosevelt	Harry Truman	1
1948	Philadelphia	July 12–14	Harry Truman	Alben Barkley	1
1952	Chicago	July 21–26	Adlai Stevenson, Jr.	John Sparkman	3
1956	Chicago	August 13–17	Adlai Stevenson, Jr.	Estes Kefauver	1
1960	Los Angeles	July 11–15	John Kennedy	Lyndon Johnson	1
1964	Atlantic City	August 24–27	Lyndon Johnson	Hubert Humphrey	Acclamation
1968	Chicago	August 26–29	Hubert Humphrey	Edmund Muskie	1
1972	Miami Beach	July 10–13	George McGovern	Thomas Eagleton, Sargent Shriver*	1
1976	New York	July 12–15	Jimmy Carter	Walter Mondale	1
1980	New York	August 11–14	Jimmy Carter	Walter Mondale	1
1984	San Francisco	July 16–19	Walter Mondale	Geraldine Ferrarro	1
1988	Atlanta	July 18–21	Michael Dukakis	Lloyd Bentsen	1
1992	New York	July 13–16	Bill Clinton	Al Gore	1
1996	Chicago	August 26–29			1

* The 1972 Democratic convention nominated Thomas Eagleton, who withdrew from the ticket on July 31. On August 8 the the Democratic National Committee selected Sargent Shriver as the party's candidate for vice-president.

Source: Updated from *National Party Conventions, 1831–72* (Washington, D. C.: *Congressional Quarterly,* 1976), pp. 8–9. Copyrighted materials reprinted with permission of Congressional Quarterly.

for fledgling television news organizations, which were beginning to rival newspapers for news coverage during this period.

Initially, the three major networks provided almost gavel-to-gavel coverage. They focused on the official events, that is, what went on at the podium. Commentary was kept to a minimum.

The changes in the delegate selection process that occurred in the 1970s and 1980s had a major impact on the amount and type of television coverage as well as the size of the viewing audience. As the decision-making capabilities of conventions declined, their newsworthiness decreased, as did the proportion of households that tuned in.[25]

The major networks subsequently reduced their coverage. In 1992 they limited prime-time viewing to one or two hours. Only CNN, PBS, and C-Span provided more extensive viewing.[26]

Not only has the coverage decreased, but it has also become more inventive. Correspondents hunt for news and engage in endless analysis. Thus, the convention seen by most viewers is often quite different from the one experienced by the delegates.

The network's orientation, which highlights the more dramatic and entertaining aspects of the convention rather than broadcasting its official, predictable, and often boring proceedings, has interfered with the party's desire to present a united front and to use the convention to launch its presidential campaign. The clash between these two conflicting goals has resulted in a classic struggle for control between the news media and the politicians. The more convention managers are successful in orchestrating their meeting and presenting a unified front and favorable images for their party and its nominees, the less newsworthy the news media find the convention. The more the news media can report on drama, conflict, and human interest, the less the convention meets the party's political objectives.

The network analysis of the 1992 Republican convention is a case in point. The delegates responded enthusiastically to the speeches of most of their leaders, including those of Pat Buchanan, Marilyn Quayle, and Phil Gramm, but the networks described these very same speeches as old-style, conservative rhetoric, preaching to the faithful. Moreover, the pictures they showed confirmed the story they told of fanatical right-wing delegates mesmerized by highly charged conservative oratory. During Pat Buchanan's speech, for example, a speech which CBS commentator, Dan Rather, referred to as "raw meat," the camera showed Rev. Jerry Falwell, Phyllis Schlafly, and others in rapt and approving attention; it then cut away to show young Republicans "pumping their fists into the air in a militaristic show of support."[27]

Scripting the Convention as Theater

Assuming that the more unified the convention, the greater its impact on the electorate, party leaders take television coverage into account when planning, staging, and scheduling national nominating conventions. The choice of a convention site, the selection of speakers, and the instructions to the delegates are all made with television in mind. Conventions are now highly scripted and staged by armies of professionals from the decorations of the hall, to the entertainment package, to the speeches of the candidates and the order in which they are presented.

Movie stars regularly make appearances. Films about the party and its recent presidents are shown. Entertaining while they inform, these films provide an additional benefit for the party; they require a darkened hall, which makes it more difficult for the networks to interview unhappy delegates. The newspeople are forced to carry the movie on their networks, substitute their own clippings and reports, or to retreat to the quiet of anchor booths to evaluate events. Either way, what is being broadcast minimizes the divisiveness that a variety of opinions often suggests and the turmoil that thousands of people milling about on the convention floor can convey.

The films themselves have exacerbated the tension between party officials and the network news producers who view such visual presentations as propaganda, not news. In 1984, a film designed to introduce President Reagan by citing the accomplishments of his administration was not carried by two of the three major networks on precisely these grounds. Similarly, in 1992, CBS and NBC substituted their own films on Clinton for the one prepared by his backers and shown to the convention.

Conventions have also become faster-paced than in the past, primarily because the three major commercial networks have reduced the amount of coverage they provide. Major addresses are scheduled during the time when the largest audience is likely to be tuned in. A delay can result not only in a smaller television audience, but in no coverage if the networks choose to revert to their late-evening programming. A 10:30 PM (eastern daylight saving time) acceptance speech is considered ideal and is now standard fare. In 1972, however, a debate over party rules and the nomination of several candidates for the Democratic vice-presidential nomination delayed McGovern's speech until 2:48 A.M., prime time only in Hawaii and Guam!

Whereas major unifying events are timed to increase the number of viewers, potentially disruptive and discordant situations are scheduled to minimize them. Raucous debates, likely to convey the image of a divided party, are delayed, if possible, until after the evening viewing hours. In the 1964 Republican convention, for example, when Goldwater partisans got wind of a series of minority platform amendments favored by Nelson Rockefeller and George Romney, they arranged to have the majority report read in its entirety to postpone the amendments until early morning in the East, when most potential supporters of the minority position would not be watching. In the 1964 Democratic convention, President Johnson rescheduled a movie paying tribute to President John Kennedy

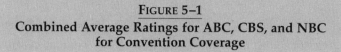

FIGURE 5–1

Combined Average Ratings for ABC, CBS, and NBC for Convention Coverage

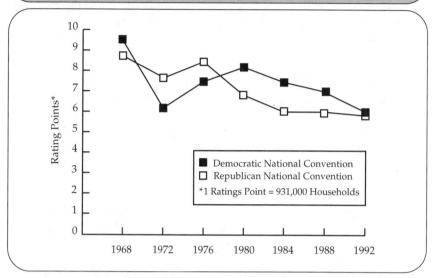

Source: Nielsen Media Research as appears in Wendy Zeligson Adler, "The Conventions on Prime Time," in *The Homestretch: New Politics. New Media. New Voters?* eds. Martha FitzSimon and Edward C. Pease (New York: Freedom Forum Media Studies Center, 1992), p. 56.

until after the vice-presidential nomination had been concluded, to preclude any bandwagon effect for Robert Kennedy for that position. In 1984 and again in 1988, the Democrats scheduled debate on minority platform planks introduced by Jesse Jackson for the afternoon before the major networks were to begin their coverage. In 1992, however, they scheduled a less-divisive platform debate for an evening session in the hopes of enlivening the show and thereby keeping the viewing audience from switching to the major-league baseball All-Star game, which was being shown on one of the networks.

Covering the Convention as News

Initially, when conventions were considered newsworthy events, the proportion of the audience that tuned in was extensive.[28] (See Figure 5–1). That proportion has substantially declined. In 1992, more people watched an entertainment show on Fox and the All-Star game on CBS than the Democratic convention on the other major networks; similarly, more watched a rerun of "Roseanne" on the second night of the Republican convention than watched the convention on the three major networks combined![29]

The reason for the decline in the viewing audience is fairly obvious. For many people, even those interested in politics, conventions are boring to watch; the prospective nominees are known; the speeches, and even the platform, contain few surprises. Lack of viewer appeal is the reason that the networks have reduced their coverage. In 1988, the three major networks provided about sixty hours of evening coverage; in 1992 they provided only about half that amount.[30]

Moreover, only about half of the coverage that is provided is devoted to the official convention—the speeches, films, reports, and votes. The remainder focuses on the delegates, the party, the unsuccessful and successful nominees, and the general election. Only those who subscribe to cable, can see the entire convention proceedings.[31]

As an action medium, television constantly scans the floor for dramatic events and human interest stories. Delegates are pictured talking, eating, sleeping, parading, even watching the convention on television. Interviews with prominent individuals, rank-and-file delegates, and family and friends of the prospective nominee are conducted. To provide a balanced presentation, supporters and opponents are frequently juxtaposed. To maintain the audience's attention, the interviews are kept short, usually focusing on reactions to actual or potential political problems.

Take the 1992 Democratic convention, for example. A relatively harmonious affair, the media focused on what little discord it could find. Here is how Howard Kurtz, *Washington Post* media analyst, described coverage of those events:

> Faced with the most carefully orchestrated Democratic convention in modern history, television tonight settled for whatever scraps of conflict it could find.
>
> CNN carried repeated updates on a demand by some supporters of Edmund G. "Jerry" Brown, Jr. that he be allowed to address the convention. Reporter Gene Randall stationed himself amid placard-waving delegates from California, a small group that loomed larger when it filled the television screen.
>
> When CNN landed a live interview with Bill Clinton, anchor Bernard Shaw's first question was, "What about Jerry Brown? Are you going to let him speak?" Shaw even asked Clinton about a minor seating dispute in the Virginia delegation.[32]

Where there is little discord, the media and even the convention organizers and its presidential nominee try to create tension as a device to hold the audience's attention. The most frequent unresolved question is, who will be the party's vice-presidential nominee? Unless an incumbent president and vice-president are seeking renomination, the vice-presidential recommendation of the presidential nominee has often not been revealed until the morning of the final day. To heighten the drama in 1964 Lyndon Johnson invited the two most likely candidates to join him in Washington for the helicopter trip to the convention in Atlantic City, New Jersey.

The vice-presidential charade reached new heights in 1980. Throughout the first three days of the Republican convention, network correspondents speculated on who Ronald Reagan's running mate would be. On the second day of the convention, unbeknownst to the public, officials of the Reagan organization approached former President Gerald Ford, who had expressed interest in the vice-presidential nomination. As private talks were being conducted, Ford indicated his willingness to consider the vice-presidency during a television interview. This interview immediately fueled public speculation and turned the news media focus from the convention proceedings on the platform to the Reagan/Ford negotiations. To follow these negotiations the delegates had to watch television from the convention floor. So great were the expectations for this so-called dream ticket that when it failed to materialize, Reagan had to come to the convention himself to whip up support for his second choice, George Bush.

For a variety of reasons, including the desire for suspense, presidential candidates did not until recently make in-depth inquiries about their running mates. Their failure to do so has had serious repercussions. In 1972, Thomas Eagleton, the Democratic vice-presidential nominee, was forced to leave the ticket after his history of mental depression became known. George McGovern had not been aware of Eagleton's past illness when he picked him. The Democrats were also hurt in 1984 when allegations of campaign irregularities and incomplete financial disclosures by Geraldine Ferraro in her congressional campaigns and allegedly improper real estate transactions by her husband were made at the start of the general election campaign. Similarly in 1988, the critical scrutiny that Republican vice-presidential nominee, Dan Quayle, received diverted attention from the convention and raised questions about Bush's judgment. After the firestorm subsided, however, Bush's choice of Quayle resulted in only minor damage to the ticket. The choice of Al Gore by the Democrats in 1992 produced the opposite effect: a media glow that worked to the Democrats' advantage.

The news media tend to inflate the coverage of the vice-presidential nomination in the absence of other news. This was particularly evident in 1988, when vice-presidential designee Dan Quayle received more coverage during the Republican convention than did presidential nominee Bush and twice as much as President Reagan.[33]

Even more controversial than television coverage *in* conventions was the networks' coverage *outside* of them, particularly television's reporting of the 1968 Chicago demonstrations. Not only were the networks charged with overemphasizing the disruptions to the detriment of their convention coverage; they were seen as helping to incite the demonstrators by the mere presence of their live cameras in the streets. Claiming that the events were newsworthy and certainly not of their own creation, the networks responded by denying that they gave disproportionate coverage to them. CBS News reported that it had devoted only thirty-two minutes to these events out of more than thirty-eight hours of total convention coverage.[34]

ASSESSING THE CONVENTION'S IMPACT

Does coverage such as the kind the Democrats received in 1968 or the Republicans received in 1992 have a negative impact? Was that coverage partially responsible for each party's defeat in those elections? Do conventions affect voting behavior? Do they influence the electorate's perception of the candidates and their evaluations of their messages?

The answer to these questions is a qualified yes. There seems to be a relationship between convention unity and electoral success. Since 1968 the party that appears to have had the most harmonious convention has emerged victorious.[35] It is difficult, however, to say how much or even whether the unity contributed to the result or simply reflected the partisan environment that fostered the particular outcome.

In the short run, conventions almost always boost the popularity of their nominees and decrease that of their opponents. Only George McGovern in 1972 did not gain as a consequence of the Democratic convention coverage. The boost, however, may be short-lived as it was for George Bush in 1992. His small rise in the polls had all but dissipated in the week that followed. Table 5–4 indicates the levels of support for the nominees before and after the 1992 Democratic and Republican nominating conventions.

TABLE 5–4
Impact of Conventions on Candidate Popularity, 1992

	Before Both Conventions*	After Democratic Convention	After Republican Convention
1992			
Democrat (Bill Clinton)	40%	56%	52%
Republican (George Bush)	48	34	42
Other/Undecided	12	10	6

* This poll (before both conventions) was conducted on July 6–8, before Ross Perot withdrew from the campaign. Here Perot voters have been assigned to the candidate named as their second choice.

Source: The Gallup Poll Monthly (August 1992), p. 25.

Political scientists have suggested three major effects of conventions on voters: (1) they heighten interest, thereby increasing turnout; (2) they arouse latent feelings, thereby raising partisan awareness; (3) they color perceptions, thereby affecting personal judgments of the candidates and their issue stands.[36] The perceptions that Clinton was a new, moderate-type Democrat who led a unified party but that Bush had been captured by the conservatives within his own party contributed to the electorate's judgment about each of them.

Conventions can have a powerful psychological impact on their viewers, making them more inclined to follow the campaign and vote for a party's candidates. They can energize participants. They can also have an organizational effect, fostering cooperation among the different and frequently competing groups within the party, encouraging them to submerge their differences and work toward a common goal.

Studies have also shown that convention watchers tend to make their voting decisions earlier in the campaign.[37] Whether they make those decisions because they watch the convention or whether they watch the convention because they are more partisan and politically aware is unclear, however. Nonetheless, about one-fifth of the electorate claim that they decide for whom they will vote at the time of the convention.

For all these reasons convention planners take no chances. They try to produce an upbeat, harmonious, enthusiastic convention in order to improve the political environment for the party's nominees in the fall.

SUMMARY

Presidential nominating conventions have existed since the 1830s. Picking the party's nominees, determining its platform, and unifying the party remain the principal tasks. There have been changes, however. Caused primarily by the reforms in the delegate selection process and, secondarily, by news media coverage of the conventions, these changes have resulted in greater emphasis placed on the public aspects of conventions and less on internal party matters.

That national nominating conventions continue to be marred by some controversy is not surprising considering that they are composed of delegates chosen in a divisive selection process to represent different preferences and perspectives within the party. Although the big prize, the presidential nomination, is usually preordained by the results of the primaries and caucuses, the other prizes, the party's rules and its policy positions, are not. Disputes over the credentials of the delegates, the rules of selection, or procedures of the convention are usually fought among candidate organizations and affect the presidential vote, if not at the current meeting, then during the delegate selection process four years hence. Platform issues, on the other hand, tend to reflect infighting within the party's electoral coalition. These policy-oriented controversies tend to be generated by organized interests within the parties and the desire of these interests to obtain recognition and their policy goals.

In addition to the tension between the needs of these groups and the goals of the party, tension has also been created between the news media and party leaders. To attract and maintain their viewing audience, the media need a newsworthy convention. They find it in the drama and conflict they emphasize. To launch its general election campaign, the party needs an interesting, convincing, and unified convention. Its organizers attempt to achieve these objectives by orchestrating the meeting, emphasizing their campaign themes, giving podium opportunities to their candidates, and using various theatrical devices such as made-for-convention movies.

The results of the party's efforts can be measured in the short run by the boost their nominees receive in public approval following the conventions. But many things can happen between the convention and election day that can mute or reinforce the themes and images presented in and projected by the convention. As the first major event of a presidential campaign, conventions affect the start of the race; they can heighten interest, color perceptions, and reinforce attitudes.

Finally, the changes in the delegate selection process have enlarged the selection zone for potential nominees. It is unlikely that a Democratic convention before 1972 would have chosen a McGovern, Carter, Dukakis, or Clinton or that a Reagan would have come as close as he did to defeating an incumbent president in 1976. Moreover, the selection of a woman by the Democrats in 1984 indicates that gender may no longer be as important a consideration—at least for second place on the ticket. Other barriers, such as race and religion, are probably less important as well.

To party professionals especially, the best evidence of future success is past success. Factors that might detract from such success, whether political, ideological, or personal, lessen the odds of getting the nomination. As a result, many presidential nominees possess similar social and political attributes. In politics, the norm is frequently considered the ideal. Deviations from that norm can be dangerous and must be adequately explained.

NOTES

1. Byron E. Shafer, *Bifurcated Politics: Evolution and Reform in the National Party Convention* (Cambridge, Mass.: Harvard University Press, 1988), pp. 17–18.
2. The Democratic figure includes more than 4,300 delegates plus another 605 alternates who will excerise between them around 4,300 votes. The final figure is subject to change as a consequence of the 1995 elections in some states and special elections, resignations, and deaths.
3. These include ". . . managers, entertainment directors, communication liaisons, publicity personnel, satellite network producers, even specialists in seat arrangements, balloon drops, demonstration choreographers, and 'hand-

painted sign' artists." Larry David Smith and Dan Nimmo, *Orchestrating National Party Conventions in the Telepolitical Age* (New York: Praeger, 1991), p. 226.

4. Chicago has a new convention center, a large number of first-class hotels and restaurants, and excellent transportation to and within the city. To attract the thousands of Democrats, media correspondents, and other interested parties who are expected to spend millions of dollars in their four-day meeting, Chicago offered the Democrats $32 million in services and facilities, more than any other of the competing cities. Richard L. Berke, "Democrats Pick Chicago for Convention," *New York Times* (July 20, 1994), p. A 8.

5. Perhaps the most famous of all keynote addresses was William Jennings Bryan's. A relatively unknown political figure, Bryan at the age of thirty-six electrified the Democratic convention of 1896 with his famous "Cross of Gold" speech. His remarks generated so much enthusiasm that the delegates turned to him to lead them as standard-bearer. He did, and lost.

6. Ann Richards, Address to the Democratic convention, Atlanta, Georgia, July 18, 1988, *Congressional Quarterly*, 46 (July 23, 1988): 2024.

7. Buchanan had agreed to submit a copy of his speech to Bush's managers 24 hours in advance of delivery to ensure that it was consistent with the campaign's themes and did not preempt former President Ronald Reagan who was to follow Buchanan. Fearful that the campaign organization would leak the speech, however, Buchanan decided to give another address, one which was only shown to convention coordinator, Craig Fuller and faxed to Bob Teeter, Bush's pollster and strategist. Bay Buchanan quoted in Charles T. Royer, ed. *Campaign for President: The Managers Look at '92* (Hollis, N.H.: Hollis Publishing Company, 1994) p. 208.

8. Quoted in Malcom Moos and Stephen Hess, *Hats in the Ring* (New York: Random House, 1960), pp. 157–158.

9. Walter Mondale, Address to the Democratic convention, San Francisco, California, July 19, 1984 as reprinted in the *New York Times*, July 20, 1984, p. A 12.

10. A short video biography of the candidate was shown to the delegates prior to Clinton's address.

11. Bill Clinton, Address to the Democratic convention, New York, New York, July 16, 1992, reported in *Congressional Quarterly*, 50 (July 18, 1992): 2129.

12. George Bush, Address to the Republican convention, Houston, Texas, August 20, 1992 reported in *Congressional Quarterly* (August 22, 1992): 2559.

13. This requirement means in essence that the convention does not force pledged delegates to exercise their pledges; however, presidential aspirants still have the right to approve delegates identified with their candidacies. Once the delegates have been approved, however, they cannot be removed if they threaten to vote against the candidate to whom they were committed.

14. Gerald M. Pomper, "Control and Influence in American Politics," *American Behavioral Scientist* 13 (November/December 1969): 223–228; Gerald M. Pomper with Susan S. Lederman, *Elections in America* (New York: Longman, 1980), p. 161.

15. Naturally, the party controlling the White House has an advantage in accomplishing its goals. According to Pomper, between 1944 and 1968 the party in office achieved about four-fifths of its program, but even the losers gained some of their objectives. During the Nixon administration, the Democrats actually fulfilled more of their pledges than did the Republicans. Pomper with Lederman, *Elections in America*, p. 161.

16. J. Jennings Moss, "Promises, promises: A Clinton report card at the 1-year mark," *The Washington Times*, January 20, 1994, p. A 9.

17. Ian Budge and Richard I. Hofferbert, "Mandates and Policy Outputs: U.S. Party Platforms and Federal Expenditures," *American Political Science Review*, 84 (March 1990): 129.

18. The actual makeup of the committee is determined by party rules and is designed to reflect the demographic and geographic characteristics of the party. In 1992, the Democratic platform committee consisted of 161 delegates plus two cochairs; the Republican resolutions committee, the committee that drafts its platform, had 107 members who were convention delegates plus 7 officials. A majority of the delegates on both committees supported their respective presidential nominees, Bill Clinton and George Bush.

19. Democratic rules specify that a minimum of 20 percent of the members of its standing committees are needed to propose a minority report. The Republican rules are even more restrictive. Offering a minority plank on the floor of the Republican convention requires the sponsorship of 27 resolution committee members or a majority of six state delegations.

20. For an excellent description of the platform-drafting process for both parties in 1992 see L. Sandy Maisel, "The Platform-Writing Process," *Political Science Quarterly*, 108 (Winter 1993–1994): 671–698.

21. The House of Representatives has not been a primary source of nominees. Only one sitting member of the House, James A. Garfield, has ever been elected president, and he was chosen on the thirty-fifth ballot. In recent nomination contests, however, a number of representatives have sought their party's nomination. Representative Morris Udall finished second to Jimmy Carter in 1976; Representative John Anderson competed for the Republican nomination in 1980 before running as an independent candidate in the general election. In 1988, Representatives Jack Kemp and Richard Gephardt were candidates for their party's nomination. There were no serious House candidates for either party in 1992. In 1996 Representative Robert Dornan sought the Republican nomination while Speaker Newt Gingrich did not close the door on a potential draft movement for his nomination.

22. Historian Thomas A. Bailey reports that in his quest for the presidency, Buchanan was greeted by a banner carried by a group of women that read, "Opposition to Old Bachelors." *Presidential Greatness* (New York: Appleton-Century Crofts, 1966), p. 74.

23. Ibid.

24. George Bush chose Dan Quayle for another reason. In the words of his son, George Bush, Jr., "Dad felt comfortable with him." The implication here is that he didn't feel as comfortable with other Republicans, such as senate leader Robert Dole; his wife, Elizabeth Dole, who was a cabinet secretary during the Reagan administration; Jack Kemp, member of the House of Representatives and popular among conservatives; or some of the big-state Republican governors who were mentioned as possible vice-presidential nominees. After standing in Reagan's shadow for eight years, Bush wanted a vice-president who would do the same for him. He did not want a prominent Republican with his or her own political base drawing attention or decreasing support from his leadership in his administration. Quayle fit the bill.

25. Approximately 34 million people saw Clinton's and Bush's acceptance speeches in 1992, 27.3 million on the major networks and 7 million on CNN

and PBS. "34 Million View Final Session," *New York Times* (August 22, 1992), p. 6.

26. NBC News did combine with the public broadcasting system for PBS coverage from 8 to 10 P.M. but then split off to provide its own hour of prime-time coverage after that. The arrangement, however, enabled PBS to provide more in-depth reporting and analysis with the addition of NBC correspondents. NBC, in turn, could record events as they occurred for later broadcasting.

27. Elizabeth Kolbert, "Networks Focus on Convention's Move to the Right," *New York Times*, (August 19, 1992), p. A 14.

    Another example of this conflict between the news media and party leaders occurred on the opening night of the Republican convention. The Republican script called for an early Monday evening appearance by President Bush in the convention city of Houston, his first public event of the week. The timing of what proved to be a rousing Bush speech, evoking the memories of Harry Truman's come-from-behind presidential victory in 1948, was set to coincide with the airing of the evening news. Unfortunately for Bush, none of the networks broke away from their regular newscasts to carry the speech live; instead they showed only brief clips of it. Thus as Bush's speech was reaching its dramatic climax, NBC's Tom Brokaw was telling his audience about Woody Allen's affair with Mia Farrow's adopted daughter, not about George Bush's political comeback. Howard Kurtz, "TV Coverage Ignores GOP Script," *Washington Post* (August 18, 1992), p. A 15.

28. The first television coverage of a national convention occurred in 1940 when NBC broadcast the Republican convention to viewers within a 50-mile radius of its transmitter atop the Empire State Building in New York City. Wendy Zeligson Adler, "The Conventions on Prime Time," in *The Homestretch: New Politics. New Media. New Voters?* eds. Martha FitzSimon and Edward C. Pease (New York: The Freedom Forum Media Studies Center, 1992), p. 55.

29. Ibid.

30. Ibid.

31. The Cable News Network (CNN) provided gavel-to-gavel coverage, as did C-Span, the public service channel, which broadcast the official proceedings with no commentary. In 1992, a number of other cable alternatives also targeted the convention to their specific audiences: Black Entertainment Television, Comedy Central, MTV, and Nostalgia Television.

32. Howard Kurtz, "Brush Fires in the Forest of Newsmakers," *Washington Post* (July 14, 1992), p. A 18.

33. S. Robert Lichter and Linda S. Lichter, "Covering the Convention Coverage," *Public Opinion* 11 (September/October 1988): 41.

34. "Republicans Orchestrate a Three-Night TV Special," *Broadcasting* (August 28, 1972), p. 12.

35. Shafer, *Bifurcated Politics*, p. 161.

36. Thomas E. Patterson, *The Mass Media Election* (New York: Praeger Publishers, 1980), pp. 72–74.

37. Ibid., p. 103.

SELECTED READINGS

Adler, Wendy Zeligson. "The Conventions on Prime Time,"in Martha FitzSimon and Edward C. Pease (eds.) *The Homestretch: New Politics. New Media. New Voters?* New York: The Freedom Forum Media Studies Center, 1992, pp. 55–57.

Cammarano, Joseph and Jim Josefson, "Putting it in Writing: An Examination of Presidential Candidate Platforms in the 1992 Election," *Southeastern Political Review*, 23 (June 1995): 187–204.

Davis, James W. *National Conventions in an Age of Party Reform.* Westport, Conn.: Greenwood Press, 1983.

Maisel, L. Sandy. "The Platform-Writing Process," *Political Science Quarterly,* 108 (Winter 1993–1994): 671–698.

Pavlik, John V. "Insider's Guide to Coverage of the Conventions and the Fall Campaign," in FitzSimon and Pease, *The Homestretch,* pp. 40–54.

Shafer, Byron E. *Bifurcated Politics: Evolution and Reform in the National Party Convention.* Cambridge, Mass.: Harvard University Press, 1988.

Smith, Larry David and Dan Nimmo. *Cordial Concurrence: Orchestrating National Party Conventions in the Telepolitical Age.* New York: Praeger, 1991.

Sullivan, Denis, Jeffrey Pressman, and F. Christopher Arterton. *Exploration in Convention Decision Making.* San Francisco: Freeman, 1976.

PART III

The Campaign

Left, the symbol of the American Party—The Know Nothings—in the 1856 presidential elections. When asked about their motives or the platform of their organization, party members would respond, "I know nothing." Their candidate, former President Millard Fillmore, placed third behind James Buchanan (Dem.) and John Fremont (Rep.).

Chapter 6

Organization, Strategy, and Tactics

INTRODUCTION

Elections have been held in the United States since 1789; campaigning by parties for their nominees began soon thereafter. It was not until the end of the nineteenth century, however, that presidential candidates actively participated in the campaigns. Personal solicitation was viewed as demeaning and unbecoming of the dignity and status of the presidency.

Election paraphernalia, distributed by the parties, first appeared in the 1820s; by 1828 there was extensive public debate about the candidates. Andrew Jackson, and to a lesser extent, John Quincy Adams, generated considerable commentary and controversy. Jackson's supporters lauded him as a hero, a man of the people, "a new or second Washington"; his critics referred to him as "King Andrew the first," alleging that he was immoral, tyrannical, and brutal.1 Adams was also subjected to personal attack. Much of this heated rhetoric appeared in the highly partisan press of the times.

The use of the campaign to reach, entertain, inform, and mobilize the general electorate began on a large scale in 1840. Festivals, parades, slogans, jingles, and testimonials were employed to energize voters. The campaign of 1840 is best remembered for the slogan, "Tippecanoe and Tyler too," promoting Whig candidates General William Henry Harrison, hero of the battle of Tippecanoe in the War of 1812, and John Tyler, and for its great jingles:

187

What Has Caused This Great Commotion?
(Sung to the tune of "Little Pig's Tail")

What has caused this great commotion, motion, motion,
Our country through?
It is the ball a rolling on, on.

Chorus
For Tippecanoe and Tyler too- Tippecanoe and Tyler too,
And with them we'll beat little Van, Van, Van, [Martin Van Buren]
Van is a used up man,
And with them we'll beat little Van.[2]

The successful Whig campaign made it a prototype for subsequent presidential contests.

The election of 1840 was also the first in which a party nominee actually campaigned for himself. General William Henry Harrison made 23 speeches in his home state of Ohio.[3] He did not set a precedent that was quickly followed, however. It was 20 years before another presidential candidate took to the stump and then under the extraordinary conditions of the onset of the Civil War and the breakup of the Democratic party.

Senator Stephen A. Douglas, Democratic candidate for president, spoke out on the slavery issue to try to heal the split that it had engendered within his party. When doing so, however, he denied his own personal ambitions. "I did not come here to solicit your votes," he told a Raleigh, North Carolina, audience. "I have nothing to say for myself or my claims personally. I am one of those who think it would not be a favor to me to be made President at this time."[4]

Abraham Lincoln, Douglas's Republican opponent, refused to reply, even though he had debated Douglas two years earlier in their contest for the Senate seat from Illinois, a contest Douglas won. Lincoln, who almost dropped out of public view when the campaign was underway, felt that it was not even proper for him to vote for himself.[5] He cut his own name from the Republican ballot before he cast it for others in the election.[6]

For their part, the Republicans mounted a massive campaign on Lincoln's behalf. They held what were called "Wide Awake" celebrations in which large numbers of people were mobilized. An account of one of these celebrations reported that

the Wide-Awake torch-light procession is undoubtedly the largest and most imposing thing of the kind ever witnessed in Chicago. Unprejudiced spectators estimate the number at 10,000. Throughout the whole length of the procession were scattered portraits of Abraham Lincoln. Banners and transparencies bearing Republican mottoes, and pictures of rail splitters, were also plentifully distributed. Forty-three bands of music were also in the procession.[7]

Presidential candidates remained on the sidelines until the 1880s. Republican James Garfield broke the tradition by receiving visitors at his Ohio home. Four years later in 1884, Republican James Blaine made hundreds of campaign speeches in an unsuccessful effort to offset public accusations that he profited from a fraudulent railroad deal. Benjamin Harrison, Republican candidate in 1888, resumed the practice of seeing people at his home, a practice that has been referred to as front-porch campaigning. Historian Keith Melder writes that Harrison met with 110 delegations consisting of almost 200,000 people in the course of the campaign.[8] William McKinley saw even more visitors over the course of his front-porch campaign in 1896. He spoke to approximately 750,000 people who were recruited and in some cases transported to his Canton, Ohio home by the Republican party.[9]

McKinley's opponent, William Jennings Bryan, actually traveled around the country making speeches. By his own account, he traveled more than eighteen thousand miles and made more than six hundred speeches, and, according to press estimates, he spoke to almost 5 million people.[10] He nearly collapsed from exhaustion at the end of the campaign.

In 1900, Republican vice-presidential candidate, Theodore Roosevelt took on Bryan, "making 673 speeches, visiting 567 towns in 24 states, and traveling 21,209 miles."[11] Twelve years later, ex-president Theodore Roosevelt, once again took to the hustings, only this time he was trying to defeat a fellow Republican president, William Howard Taft, for his party's nomination. Roosevelt won nine primaries, including one in Ohio, Taft's home state, but was denied the nomination by party leaders. He then launched an independent candidacy in the general election, campaigning on the Progressive, or "Bull Moose," ticket. His Democratic opponent, Woodrow Wilson, was also an active campaigner. The Roosevelt and Wilson efforts augured the end of passive presidential campaigning. The last front-porch campaign was waged by Warren G. Harding in 1920.

Harding's campaign was distinguished in another way; he was the first to use radio to speak directly to voters. This new electronic medium and television, which followed it, radically changed presidential campaigns.

Initially, candidates were slow to adjust their campaign style to the new techniques necessitated by radio. In one famous incident in 1928, the Democratic candidate, Al Smith, gave a speech in Oklahoma City on the subject of religion. Smith, the first Roman Catholic to receive his party's nomination for president, tried to defuse the religious issue by addressing it in this speech. His heavy New York accent and rasping voice were faithfully captured on the airwaves, to his detriment; the thunderous applause he received sounded like a disturbance. Listeners could not tell whether Smith was being cheered or jeered.[12]

Franklin Roosevelt was a master of radio, and he employed it skill-fully in all his presidential quests. He also utilized the "whistle-stop" campaign train, which stopped at railroad stations along the route to allow the candidate to address the crowds that came to see and hear him. In 1932, Roosevelt, who personally took a train to Chicago to accept his nomination, visited thirty-six states, traveling some thirteen thousand miles in his presidential campaign. His extensive travels, undertaken in part to dispel a whispering campaign about his health—he had polio as a young man, which left him unable to walk or even stand up unaided—forced President Herbert Hoover onto the campaign trail.[13]

Instead of giving the small number of speeches he had originally planned, Hoover logged more than ten thousand miles, traveling across much of the country. He was the first incumbent president to campaign actively for reelection. Thereafter, with the exception of Franklin Roosevelt during World War II, personal campaigning became standard for incumbents and nonincumbents alike.

Harry Truman took incumbent campaigning a step further. Perceived as the underdog in the 1948 election, Truman whistle-stopped the length and breadth of the United States, traveling thirty-two thousand miles and averaging ten speeches a day. In eight weeks, he spoke to an estimated 6 million people.[14] While Truman was rousing the faithful by his down-home comments and hard-hitting criticisms of the Republican-controlled Congress, his opponent, Thomas Dewey, was promising new leadership but providing few particulars. His sonorous speeches contrasted sharply and unfavorably with Truman's straightforward attacks.

The end of an era in presidential campaigning occurred in 1948. Within the next four years television came into its own as a communica-tions medium. The number of television viewers grew from less than half a million in 1948 to approximately 19 million in 1952, a figure that was deemed sufficient in the minds of campaign planners to launch a major television effort. The Eisenhower presidential organization budgeted almost $2 million for television, and the Democrats promised to use both radio and television "in an exciting, dramatic way."[15]

The potential of television was evident at the outset. Republican vice-presidential candidate, Richard Nixon, took to the airwaves to reply to accusations that he had appropriated campaign funds for his personal use and had received money and other gifts from wealthy supporters, includ-ing a black-and-white cocker spaniel by the name of Checkers. Nixon denied the charges but said that under no circumstances would he and his family give up the dog, which his children dearly loved. A huge outpour-ing of public sympathy for Nixon followed, effectively ending the issue, keeping him on the ticket, and demonstrating the impact television could have on a political career and a presidential campaign.

Television made a mass appeal easier, but it also created new obstacles for the nominees. Physical appearance became more important. Styles of oratory changed. Instead of just rousing a crowd, presidential aspirants had to convey a personal message to television viewers. Attention began to focus more on the images candidates projected, both of themselves and of their opponents, and less on the positions they presented.

Television had other effects as well. It eventually replaced the party as the principal link between the nominees and the voters. It decreased the incentive for holding so many election events—rallies, parades, speeches—since many more people could be reached through this mass medium. Finally, it required that campaign activities and events be carefully orchestrated and scripted, keeping in mind how they would appear on the screen and what images they would convey to voters.

The people who organized and ran campaigns were also affected. Public relations experts were called on to apply mass marketing techniques. Pollsters and media consultants supplemented and to some extent replaced savvy politicians in designing and executing strategies. Even the candidates seemed a little different. With the possible exception of Lyndon Johnson and Gerald Ford, both of whom succeeded to the presidency through the death or resignation of their predecessors, incumbents and challengers alike reflected the grooming and schooling of the age of mass communications. And where they did not, as in the cases of Walter Mondale and Michael Dukakis, they fared poorly.

This chapter and the one that follows discuss these aspects of modern presidential campaigns. Organization, strategy, and tactics serve as the principal focal points of this chapter, whereas image projection, election news coverage, and the impact of the media on campaigns are addressed in the next one.

The next section of this chapter describes the structures of modern presidential campaigns and the functions they perform. It examines attempts to create hierarchical campaign organizations but also notes the decentralizing pressures. The tensions between candidate organizations and the regular party structure are discussed as well.

The basic objectives that every strategy must address are explored in the section that follows. These include designing a basic appeal, creating a leadership image, sometimes coping with the incumbency factor, and building a winning geographic coalition. The last section of the chapter deals with tactics. It begins by describing the techniques for communicating the message, orchestrating the campaign, targeting and timing appeals, and finally, turning out the voters on election day.

ORGANIZATION

Running a campaign is a complex, time-consuming, nerve-racking venture. It involves coordinating a variety of functions and activities, including advance work, scheduling, press arrangements, issue research, speech writing, polling, media advertising, finances, and party and interest group activities. To accomplish these varied tasks, a large, specialized campaign organization is necessary.

All recent presidential campaigns have had such organizations. The organizations have similar features. There is a chairperson who presides over the organization and acts as a liaison among the candidate, the party, and the campaign; a manager who orchestrates the operation; a political director and several deputies charged with supervising day-to-day activities; usually an administrative head of the national headquarters; division chiefs for special operations; and a geographic hierarchy that reaches to the state and local levels. Every campaign also has a pollster, media consultants, strategists, grass roots organizers, plus an array of technical experts.

Within this basic structure, organizations have varied in style and operation. Some have been very centralized, with a few individuals making most of the major strategic and tactical decisions; others have been more decentralized. Some have worked through or in conjunction with national and state party organizations; others have disregarded these groups and created their own field organizations. Some have operated from a comprehensive game plan; others have adopted a more incremental, reactive approach. In some, the nominee has assumed an active decision-making role; in others, the candidate defers to the principal campaign advisers who collectively make major strategic and tactical decisions.

The Goldwater organization in 1964, the Nixon operation in 1972, the Reagan effort of 1984, the Bush campaign of 1988, and the Clinton campaign of 1992 exemplify the tight, hierarchical structure in which a few individuals control decision making and access to the candidate. In Goldwater's case, his chief advisers were suspicious of top party regulars, most of whom did not support the senator's candidacy. They opted for an organization of believers, one that would operate in an efficient military fashion.[16] This structure and the people chosen to run it produced tension between the regular Republican organization and the citizen groups that had helped Goldwater win the nomination.

Tensions arise in every campaign between the candidate's and the party's organizations, between the national headquarters and the field staff, and between the research and operational units. Some of these tensions are the inevitable consequence of ambitious people operating under severe time constraints and pressures. Some are the result of the need to coordinate a large, decentralized party system for a national campaign. Some result from limited resources and the struggle over who gets how much. In Goldwater's case, however, the tensions were aggravated by his circumvention of party regulars, by his concentration of decision making in the hands of a few, and by his attempt to operate with two separate campaign organizations in many states.

The same desire for control and for circumventing the party was evident in Richard Nixon's reelection campaign in 1972. Completely separated from the national party, even in title, the Committee to Reelect the President (known as CREEP) raised its own money, conducted its own public relations (including polling and campaign advertising), scheduled its own events, and even had its own security division. It was this division, which operated separately from the Republican party, that harassed the Democratic campaign of George McGovern by heckling his speeches, spreading dishonest rumors, and perpetrating other illegal acts, including the attempted wiretapping of the Democratic National Committee headquarters at the Watergate Office Building. The excesses perpetuated by individuals in the Nixon campaign illustrate both the difficulty of overseeing all the aspects of a large presidential campaign organization and the risk of placing nonprofessionals in key positions of responsibility. Had the more experienced Republican National Committee exercised more of an influence over the presidential campaign, there might have been less deviation from accepted standards of behavior.

The Reagan and Bush efforts in 1980, 1984, and 1988 operated more closely with state Republican party organizations than had either Goldwater's or Nixon's. Both were directed by separate campaign organizations, but each was linked to the party at both the national and the state levels. Fund-raising efforts and grass roots activities were primarily party affairs, whereas the presidential campaign organization exercised most of the control over the basic strategy, thematic content of the campaign, relations with the media, resource allocation, and the scheduling and appearances of the presidential and vice-presidential candidates.

Bush's organization in 1988 has received considerable praise for its tight-knit structure and efficient operating style. A small circle of advisers, each with designated areas of responsibility, ran the campaign and interacted with the nominee. By contrast, his 1992 organization was disjointed, uncoordinated, and internally competitive. Three separate groups, the White House, the reelection committee, and the campaign's media operation vied for power. James Baker, Bush's secretary of state who took over as White House chief of staff in August 1992, controlled presidential activities but was unable to provide a coherent policy focus for the campaign. The reelection committee developed themes and campaign activities but was unable to synchronize them with the White House. The media group, composed of Madison Avenue advertising executives, designed still other campaign appeals in their commercials, many of which were rejected by the other groups. It was not until the final weeks of the campaign that these three units seemed to mesh together in a concerted effort.

The principals on Bush's campaign staff included Robert Teeter, a Republican pollster who served as chairman, Frederick Malek, a businessman and former aide to President Nixon, who had the title campaign manager, Mary Matalin, political director, Charles Black, a Republican consultant who served as the primary strategist, David Carney, the head of field operations, and Fred Steeper, the campaign's pollster.

Democratic campaign organizations have tended to be looser in structure and more decentralized in operation than have the Republicans'. For many years the Democrats had stronger state parties and a weaker national base. As a consequence, their presidential candidates tended to rely more heavily on state party organizations. This is less true today.

In recent years Democratic candidates, like their Republican counterparts, have established separate organizations to run their presidential campaigns. They have used their regional and state coordinators to oversee activities, creating some tension with party regulars in the process. Moreover, there has been little coordination with the national committee or with congressional campaign committees. Major decisions have been made by presidential candidates and their inner circle of advisers.

In 1984 and 1988, the organizations of Walter Mondale and Michael Dukakis had difficulty carrying out coordinated campaign efforts. Their problems were partially structural. Mondale, who knew many party and elected officials, consulted with a wide range of policy experts and campaign supporters, often changing directions and reversing previous decisions in midstream. Michael Dukakis had the opposite problem. His campaign organization was too insular for too long. Democrats, who had worked in other presidential campaigns, were not quickly recruited and integrated into the Dukakis organization.

The Clinton organization of 1992 did not suffer from these problems. It was a tightly run operation, ostensibly headed by lawyer Mickey Kantor who had the title of campaign chairman. Day-to-day operations, however, were handled by James Carville who ran the infamous "war room," the focal point of the campaign's activities. It was in the war room that plans for strategy were developed and responses to Republican attacks initiated. David Wilhelm, campaign manager, coordinated state operations; George Stephanopoulous, communications director, designed and directed media strategy; Stan Greenberg, provided and interpreted polling data and was a major strategist; Betsey Wright, deputy campaign chair, anticipated and handled the "character" issues; Susan Thomases was the principal scheduler; Paul Begala was head speech writer; and Mandy Greenwald was the principal media consultant.

The relationship between the candidate's organization and the party's organization is important not only for winning the election but for governing. Candidates who circumvent their party and its elected officials in the planning and conduct of their presidential campaigns, as Richard Nixon did in 1972 and Jimmy Carter in 1976, find it more difficult to mobilize the partisan support needed to bridge the separation of powers and govern effectively. They have less inclination to build a strong national organization and more incentive to convert it into a personal following, responsive to their needs, particularly reelection. Frequently in these circumstances key party leaders are replaced by loyal supporters of the successful nominee. These supporters also staff key White House positions including the political office. When the president leaves office, however, these supporters lose their patron and ultimately their position although they may reappear in other campaigns or other administrations. When the party loses a presidential campaign, the candidate's organization disintegrates, and the party, blamed in part for the defeat, must try to rebuild itself. Not only does this situation contribute to frequent turnover among national party leaders, but it weakens the party.

STRATEGIC OBJECTIVES

Strategies are game plans, blueprints, calculated efforts to convince the electorate to vote for a particular candidate. They include a basic appeal as well as a plan for implementing it.

Certain decisions cannot be avoided when developing an electoral strategy. These decisions stem from the rules of the system, the costs of the campaign, the character of the electorate, and the environment in which the election occurs. Each of them involves identifying objectives, allocating resources, and monitoring and adjusting that allocation over the course of the campaign. That is what a strategy is all about: it is a plan for developing, targeting, and tracking campaign resources.

Most strategies are articulated before the race begins; others are forged during the election itself. In 1984, Reagan strategists designed an elaborate plan well before the Republican convention. The Bush plan in 1988 and the Clinton plan in 1992 were also designed before their respective conventions met to nominate them. In the words of James Carville, principal Clinton strategist in 1992:

> By the time the convention had come, we had spent a lot of time, a lot of money, a lot of research on determining what it was that we wanted to do. By mid-June, . . . we had a pretty good idea of the things that we needed to accomplish, of the nature and depth of our problems and how we wanted to solve them and accomplish our objectives.
>
> Strategically, we knew 85 percent of what we wanted to do by late June.[17]

In contrast, Humphrey's 1968 strategy, Dukakis's in 1988, and Bush's in 1992 emerged after their nominations and in the midst of their presidential campaigns.

Designing a Basic Appeal

The first step in constructing a campaign strategy is designing a basic appeal. This appeal has two principal components: one consists of the emphasis placed on party images and the other on key policy issues. The objective is to frame the electoral choice in as advantageous a manner as possible to the candidate and party.

Partisan images. All things being equal, the candidates of the dominant party have an advantage which they try to maximize by emphasizing their partisan affiliation, lauding their partisan heroes, and making a blatant partisan appeal. Democratic candidates have traditionally clothed themselves in the garb of their party since the realignment of the 1930s. Republican candidates, initially, did not. Eisenhower, Nixon, and Ford downplayed partisan references, pointing instead to their personal qualifications and positions on certain types of issues. As the gap between the two parties narrowed, however, Republican candidates have been more willing to label themselves as partisans.

Identifying with the party is only one way in which the partisan orientations of the electorate are activated and enforced. Recalling the popular images of the party is another. For the Democrats, common economic interests are still the most compelling link that unites their electoral coalition. Perceived as the party of the average person, the party that got the country out of the Great Depression, the party of labor and minority groups, Democrats have tended to do better when economic issues are salient as they were in 1992.

Democratic candidates emphasize "bread-and-butter" issues, such as jobs, wages, and benefits for the working and middle class. They contrast their orientation for the plight of the average American with Republican ties to the rich and especially to big business. The Democrat's sympathy for the less fortunate, however, has been a mixed blessing in recent years. Beginning in the 1970s and continuing into the 1990s, this sympathy has been perceived by much of the electorate as antithetical to the interests of the middle class. Exploiting this perception, Republicans have repeatedly criticized their "tax-and-spend" opponents.

Bill Clinton sought to reassert his party's middle-class appeal in his 1992 campaign. Calling himself a "New Democrat," Clinton took pains to distinguish his own moderate policy orientation from the more liberal views of his Democratic predecessors. He projected himself as a change-oriented candidate, but one who would accomplish that change in a manner that was consistent with the desires and interests of most Americans, including those who had defected from the Democratic party to vote for Reagan and Bush. His appeal was successful in the sense that he avoided the tax-and-spend label that had stuck to and stymied Democrat candidates in the 1980s and again in the 1994 midterm election.

Whereas economic issues have tended to unite the Democrats, social issues have not. Since the 1970s, Republican presidential candidates have successfully exploited social divisions within the Democratic party to their political advantage by focusing on such high-intensity issues as crime, welfare, busing, racial quotas, and other government-imposed solutions to social problems. In doing so, they have not only appealed to the fears and frustrations of moderate and conservative Democrats but have reaffirmed their own support for the traditional American values of individual initiative, family responsibility, and local autonomy.

In 1992, the Clinton campaign effectively countered this Republican imagery by taking policy positions that promoted family and community values, personal safety, and a less intrusive role for government. Occupying the middle ground, the Democrats successfully denied the Republicans *their* social issues. Only in the area of abortion and school prayer did the major party candidates and their parties offer clear-cut alternatives within the social realm to the voters.

When foreign and national security issues have been salient, Republican candidates have traditionally done better. This is why they tend to stress these issues in their campaigns. Not only does the more favorable perception Republicans have enjoyed in this area help their candidates, it also reduces the impact of partisanship on voting since international concerns have usually not engendered the same degree of partisanship that domestic issues have.

In 1952, Eisenhower campaigned on the theme "Communism, Corruption, and Korea," projecting himself as the candidate most qualified to end the war. Nixon took a similar tact in 1968, linking Humphrey to the Johnson administration and the war in Vietnam. Four years later, Nixon varied his message, painting George McGovern as the "peace at any price" candidate and himself as the experienced leader who could achieve peace with honor. Gerald Ford, though, was not nearly as successful in conveying his abilities in foreign affairs, in part because he was overshadowed by the expertise and statesmanship of his secretary of state and national security adviser, Henry Kissinger. In 1980, Reagan pointed to the Soviet invasion of Afghanistan and to the Iranian hostage situation to criticize the foreign policy of the Carter administration and to urge greater expenditures for defense; in 1984, he pointed to the increased defense capacity of the United States and to its success in containing the expansion of communism. Similarly, George Bush cited his experience in foreign affairs and his personal acquaintance with many world leaders in 1988. He was unable to "sell" his foreign policy prowess four year later, however. With the Cold War over, the Persian Gulf War concluded, and the public preoccupied with domestic issues, Bush's emphasis on his foreign policy presidency became a liability not an asset.

The general perception that the Democrats are weaker in foreign and military affairs has prompted some of their recent standard-bearers to talk even tougher than their opponents. In his 1976 campaign, Carter vowed that an Arab oil embargo would be seen by his administration as an economic declaration of war. In 1984, Walter Mondale supported the buildup of U.S. defenses, including Reagan's strategic defense initiative.

In 1988, Dukakis spoke about the need for the United States to be more competitive within the international economic arena as did Clinton in 1992.

Salient issue positions. The electoral environment affects the priorities and substance of a candidate's policy appeal. In 1992, the electorate was concerned mostly about the economy, particularly jobs and the federal budget deficit.[18] Here's how Fred Steeper, Bush's pollster, described the public mood in a memo to campaign chair Robert Teeter midway through the general election campaign:

> People's perceptions of the economy are mirroring the weakness measured in economic performance. The number of people who believe that the economy is "getting better" dropped from 28% in late May to just 10% in September. By more than three-to-one, those who believe the economy is getting worse now outnumber those who believe things are getting better (10% better, 33% worse).
>
> In addition, more people now believe that Democrats would do a better job than Republicans at keeping the country prosperous (33% Republican, 45% Democrat). This is the first time since the depths of the 1982 recession that the Democrats have had an advantage on this issue.[19]

Steeper's memo was intended to get the campaign to take these factors into consideration when tailoring the president's message in the final weeks of the campaign.

Economic issues are the most recurrent national issues. They "hit home" in a way that social and national security issues may not. A poor economy helps the party that is out of power and hurts an incumbent running for reelection. Ronald Reagan drove the economic problem home in 1980 with the question he posed at the end of his debate with President Jimmy Carter, a question directed at the American people: "Are you better off now than you were four years ago?" Similarly, James Carville, chief strategist of the 1992 Clinton campaign, kept a sign over his desk, "It's the economy, stupid." He did not want anyone in the Clinton organization to forget the primary issue.

Having a weak economy was a particularly severe problem for President George Bush in 1992 because he faced not one but two challengers who echoed the same theme—economic conditions were poor and the Bush administration was to blame for them. The emphasis on the economy placed Bush in a dilemma: either downplay the problem, which he had done in 1991 and open himself to the charge, "he just doesn't get it," or talk about it and propose a credible solution to the problem, thereby keeping the campaign focused on the economy. Bush did neither.

Although he did articulate a new economic program, he chose not to stress it, preferring instead to divert public attention to the character issues of his opponents. In the end the electorate did not judge these issues nearly as relevant as those that affected them in their everyday life.

Creating a Leadership Image

Regardless of the partisan imagery and thematic emphases, candidates for the presidency must stress their own qualifications for the job and cast doubt on their opponents'. They must appear presidential, demonstrating those personal characteristics and leadership qualities the voters consider essential for the position.[20]

In the past, projecting a presidential image was more difficult and important for the Republicans, given the partisan disadvantage they had within the electorate. Today, it is probably equally if not more important for the Democrats, given their heterogeneous composition, perceptions of their lack of competence and resolve in foreign affairs, and criticism of the leadership abilities of recent Democratic presidents, particularly Carter and Clinton.

Accentuating the positive. A favorable image, of course, cannot be taken for granted. It has to be created, or at least polished. Contemporary presidents are expected to be strong, assertive, and dominant. During times of crisis or periods of social anxiety, these leadership characteristics are considered absolutely essential. The strength that Franklin Roosevelt was able to convey by virtue of his successful bout with polio; Dwight Eisenhower by his military command in World War II; and Ronald Reagan by his tough talk, clear-cut solutions, and consistent policy goals contrasted sharply with the perceptions of Adlai Stevenson in 1956, George McGovern in 1972, Jimmy Carter in 1980, and Walter Mondale in 1984 as weak, indecisive, and vacillating.

When Gerald Ford and Jimmy Carter were criticized for their failure to provide strong leadership, their campaign organizations countered by focusing on their actions as president, emphasizing those situations in which they were in charge—giving orders, making decisions, announcing policies. George Bush tried to use the same strategy to overcome the perception that he equivocated on the issue of raising taxes and failed to design a program to deal with the economic recession. Bill Clinton's reelection campaign is also presenting him in similarly assertive, official capacity as president.

For challengers, the task of seeming to be powerful, confident, and independent (one's own person) can best be imparted by a no-nonsense approach, a show of optimism, and a conviction that success is attainable. John Kennedy's rhetorical emphasis on activity in 1960 and Richard Nixon's tough talk in 1968 about the turmoil and divisiveness of the late

1960s helped to generate the impression of a take-charge personality. Kennedy and Nixon were seen as leaders who knew what had to be done and would do it.

In addition to seeming tough enough to be president, it is also important to exhibit sufficient knowledge and skills for the job. In the public's mind, personal experience testifies to the ability to perform. In 1992, Bush contrasted his governing experience with that of his opponents; Perot emphasized his can-do qualities as a successful businessman; and Clinton pointed to his rise from a humble origin, his experience as governor, and his new ideas to demonstrate his sensitivity and capacity for the office.

Empathy is also an important attribute for presidential candidates. People want a president who can respond to their emotional needs, one who understands what and how they feel. As the government has become larger, more powerful, and more distant, empathy has become more important. Roosevelt and Eisenhower radiated warmth. Carter and Clinton were both particularly effective in generating the impression that they cared, creating a contrast with the stereotypical image of their Republican opponents. By comparison, McGovern, Nixon, and Dukakis appeared cold, distant, and impersonal.

Candor, integrity, and trust emerge periodically as important attributes in presidential image building. Most of the time these traits are taken for granted. Occasionally, however, a crisis of confidence, such as Watergate, dictates that political skills be downplayed and these qualities stressed. Such crises preceded the elections of 1952 and 1976. Dwight Eisenhower, a war hero, and Jimmy Carter, who promised never to tell a lie, both benefited from the perception that they were honest, decent men. In contrast, Richard Nixon in 1972 and Bill Clinton in 1992 were plagued with credibility problems that reenforced their politician images.

Highlighting the negative. Naturally, candidates can be expected to raise questions about their opponents. These questions assume particular importance if the public's initial impression of the candidates is fuzzy, as it may be with outsiders who win their party's nomination. When Republican polls revealed Dukakis' imprecise image in 1988, senior Bush advisers devised a strategy to take advantage of this situation and define Dukakis in ways that would discredit him. The strategy was based on the premise that the higher the negative perceptions of a candidate, the less likely that candidate would be to win.[21] Lee Atwater, architect of this strategy, put it this way: "When I first got into politics, I just stumbled across the fact that candidates who went into an election with negatives higher than 30 or 40 points just inevitably lost."[22]

In 1992, Bush also challenged the qualifications of his opponents. With Clinton's moderate policy positions making it difficult for Bush to paint him as liberal as he had done to Dukakis, Bush chose to emphasize the character issues of trustworthiness and candor. But here his campaign ran into a problem, adverse public reactions to his negative Dukakis campaign and to the allegations about Ross Perot that were leaked to the media by supporters of Bush. Fearing that his first negative commercials would be greeted by a "there he goes again response" by the media, the Bush campaign delayed their airing and then introduced them with a touch of humor to soften their effect.[23] Still, voters were leery. A survey conducted by the Times Mirror Center for People and the Press in early October 1992 found that 50 percent of those who saw the Bush advertisements felt that they were not truthful compared with 35 percent for Clinton's.[24]

Unlike Dukakis, who chose initially not to dignify Bush's attacks by replying to them, Clinton helped defuse the attacks against him by reacting quickly and directly. Describing Clinton's rapid response team, F. Christopher Arterton said

> When journalists pressed for the campaign's reaction to charges leveled by the president in a speech or by his campaign staff in their daily "fax attack," the Clinton response team would sift through their computerized data banks to develop a rebuttal based on contrary information. Press releases designed to discredit a Bush campaign charge were assembled and faxed to journalists from campaign headquarters in an effort to arrest a detrimental story within one news cycle. That is, the Clinton response team endeavored to reach journalists with their side of the story before the daily deadlines passed. They hoped to either kill the story or at least to ensure that the news reports would contain both the charge and their rebuttal. [25]

This rapid reaction not only deflected criticism, but it enabled the Clinton campaign to keep the media focus on *their* issue—the economy, not Bush's.

In summary, candidates try to project images of themselves that are consistent with public expectations of the office and its occupant. Traits such as inner strength, decisiveness, competence, and experience are considered essential for the office, and others such as empathy, sincerity, credibility, and integrity are viewed as necessary for the individual. Which traits are considered most important varies to some extent with the assessment of the strengths and weaknesses of the incumbent. The negative attributes of a sitting president become the essential traits for the next one.

Dealing with Incumbency

Claiming an image of leadership requires a different script for an incumbent than for a challenger. Until the mid-1970s when the media became more critical of presidential performance, incumbents were thought to

Box 6–1

An Incumbency Balance Sheet

ADVANTAGES

Prior to the mid-1970s being president was thought to help an incumbent in the quest for reelection. The advantages stemmed from the visibility of the office, the esteem it engenders, and the influence it provides. Being president guarantees recognition. The president is almost always well known. A portion of the population may even have difficulty at the outset in identifying the challenger although the primaries have now contributed to the name recognition of all the candidates.

Moreover, incumbents are generally seen as experienced and knowledgeable, as leaders who have stood the tests *of* the office *in* the office. From the public's perspective, this quality creates a climate of expectations that works to the incumbent's benefit more often than not. Since security is one of the major psychological needs that the presidency serves, the certainty of four more years with a known quality is likely to be more appealing than the uncertainty of the next four years with an unknown one— *provided the performance in office is viewed as acceptable.*

Translated into strategic terms, the public's familiarity and comfort with incumbents permits them to highlight their opponent's lack of experience, and contrast it with their own and their record in office. Carter used a variation of this tactic in 1980. He emphasized the arduousness of the job in order to contrast his energy, knowledge, and intelligence with Reagan's. Bush too stressed his competence, experience, and trustworthiness in 1992.

The ability of presidents to make news, to affect events, and to dispense the "spoils" of government can also work to their advantage. Presidents are in the limelight and can maneuver to remain there. The media focus is always on them. All recent presidents who have campaigned for reelection have tried to utilize the symbolic and ceremonial presidency, signing legislation into law in the rose garden of the White House, meeting heads of state in Washington or their own capitals, making speeches and announcements, holding press conferences, honoring military and civilians—all behind the presidential seal.

Presidents have another trump card. Presumably, their actions can influence events. They try to gear economic recoveries to election years. They also use their discretionary authority to distribute the resources at their disposal, such as grants, contracts, appointments, and emergency aid. They must be careful, however, not to seem overtly partisan. Actions that appear to be solely or primarily for political purposes, such as Ford's pardon of Nixon in 1974 or Carter's and Bush's announcements of juicy federal government contracts can backfire.

The incumbency advantages extend to vice-presidents seeking their party's presidential nomination but not necessarily to their general election campaign. They cannot easily propound their leadership credentials from the vice-presidency, a position of followership. The number two person is not free to dissent from unpopular, unwise, or unsuccessful administration policies; nor can a vice-president take credit for popular, wise, and successful ones. Thus, a vice-president is in the worst of two worlds, unlikely to receive support from those who dislike the administration and unlikely to inherit automatically the votes of those who do. Vice-President George Bush dealt with this dilemma by binding himself to President Reagan. He refused to indicate positions he had taken or advice he had given to Reagan, thereby casting his fate with his popular predecessor and forcing the electorate to judge him in 1988 on the basis of the performance *of the administration* rather than his performance *within* it.

DISADVANTAGES

Today these incumbency advantages are often offset by equally strong disadvantages. They stem from the dilemmas of contemporary presidents, the persistent media criticism, and the anti-Washington, antipolitician mood of the contemporary electorate.

In their campaigns for office, presidential candidates hype themselves, make promises, and create great expectations. Once in office, however, they find those expectations difficult to meet. With the constitutional system dividing authority; the political system decentralizing power; and public opinion fluid, ambiguous, often inconsistent, and compartmentalized, it is difficult for presidents to build and maintain a governing consensus. Yet their leadership role demands that they do so—hence the gap between expectations and performance.

Persistent media criticism has contributed to the president's problems. With radio and television talk-show hosts railing against presidents, with television and newspaper investigative reporters heightening public awareness of policy problems and inadequate governmental responses to them, with network news coverage more critical of incumbents, particularly during presidential campaigns, it has become increasingly difficult for presidents to project an image of successful leadership.

This news mix in turn has fueled public distrust of government and the people who run it. With confidence waning in government, in parties, and in contemporary political leaders, Washington experience has become a liability and not the asset it once was. Thus, contemporary incumbents no longer enjoy the advantages their twentieth-century predecessors had in seeking reelection.

have an advantage. (See Box 6–1, "An Incumbency Balance Sheet.") Between 1900 and 1972, thirteen incumbents sought reelection and eleven won. And the two that lost, Taft in 1912 and Hoover in 1932, faced highly unusual circumstances. In Taft's case he was challenged by the independent candidacy of former Republican president, Theodore Roosevelt. Together, Taft and Roosevelt split the Republican vote, enabling Democrat Woodrow Wilson to win with only 42 percent of the total vote. Hoover ran during the Great Depression, for which he received much of the blame.

Following the 1972 election, however, incumbents have fared poorly. All have sought reelection, but only Reagan has won. Adverse political and economic factors help explain the more recent defeats. The worst political scandal in the nation's history and the worst economic recession in forty years hurt Ford's chances, as did his pardon of the person who had nominated him for the vice-presidency, Richard Nixon. In 1980 and 1992, a weak economy, a loss of confidence in the president's leadership abilities, and an anti-Washington mood among the electorate contributed to Carter's and Bush's losses.

Today incumbents are advantaged or disadvantaged based on their perceived performance in office. Having a good record contributes to a president's reelection potential just as a poor record detracts from it. Bad times almost always hurt an incumbent. Rightly or wrongly, the public places most responsibility for economic conditions, social relations, and foreign affairs on the president. That a president may actually exercise little control over some of these external factors seems less relevant to the electorate than do negative conditions, the desire that they be improved, and the expectation that *the president* do something about them.

Thus, incumbency can be a two-edged sword, strengthening or weakening a claim to leadership. During the campaign incumbents point to their accomplishments, noting the work that remains, and sounding a "stay-the-course" theme, whereas challengers argue that it is time for a change and that they can do better.

Building a Winning Geographic Coalition

In addition to designing a general appeal and addressing the leadership/incumbency issues, a winning geographic coalition must be assembled. Geography is critically important in this regard. Since the election is decided by the Electoral College, the primary objective must always be to win a majority of the college, not necessarily a majority of the popular vote.

Electoral College strategies almost always require candidates to concentrate their resources in the large states with the most electoral votes. Failure to win a majority of these states make it extremely difficult to put together a winning coalition. The basic strategic consideration is how many resources should be expended in these states. The answer usually is, a lot, probably even more than the proportional share of the vote these states have in the Electoral College.[26]

In building their electoral coalitions, candidates begin from positions of strength, move to states in which they have some support, and compete in most of the large states regardless of the odds. Since the loss of their southern base in the 1960s, the Democrats have had to focus on the northeastern and midwestern states. New York, Pennsylvania, Ohio, Michigan, and Illinois form the core of their present geographic coalition.

The shift in population to the southern and western states has hurt the Democrats. In 1952, 278 electoral votes of a total of 531 were in the Northeast and Midwest;[27] in 1972, there were 265 votes out of 538; in 1992, there were only 223 (also out of 538). Thus, the Democrats' base has shrunk while the Republicans' has expanded.

Table 6–1 shows each party's electoral base. Thirteen states, which currently have a total of 98 electoral votes, have voted for the Republican candidate in each of the last seven presidential elections, whereas eleven states with 140 electoral votes have voted Republican in six of the last seven elections. During the same period only the District of Columbia, with 3 votes, has voted Democratic in the last seven elections and only Minnesota with 10 electoral votes has voted Democratic in six of them. Thus, other things being equal, the Republicans begin the campaign with a considerably larger geographic core than do the Democrats.

The Republican base was not always so imposing. In 1964, Goldwater was ready to concede the East and concentrate his efforts on the rest of the country. His strategy was to go for the states Nixon had won in 1960 plus several others in the South and Midwest. As one of Goldwater's aides put it: "It was a regional strategy based on the notion that little campaigning would be needed to win votes in the South, no amount of campaigning could win electoral votes in New England and on the East Coast, but that votes could be won in the Midwest and on the West Coast. As the Senator said, 'Go hunting where the ducks are.'"[28]

In 1968, Nixon strategists set their sights on ten battleground states, including the big seven—California, Illinois, Michigan, New York, Ohio, Pennsylvania, and Texas—plus New Jersey, Wisconsin, and Missouri, where Humphrey provided the main opposition—and on five peripheral southern states, where George Wallace was the principal foe.[29] In 1976, however, Ford found himself in a situation that required a broad-based national effort because the Democrats had nominated a southerner. Carter's strategy in that election was to retain the traditional Democratic states and regain the South. He achieved his goal and put together a narrow Electoral College majority. By 1980, however, his electoral coalition had disintegrated and was not reconstructed by the Democrats until 1992.

Reagan's strategy in both 1980 and 1984 was to rely on Republican

TABLE 6-1
Voting Blocks in the Electoral College, 1968–1992

Number of Elections

States Voting Democratic since 1968

Four		Five		Six		Seven	
Georgia	(13)	Hawaii	(4)	Minnesota	(10)	District of Columbia	(3)
Maryland	(10)	Massachusetts	(12)				
New York	(33)	Rhode Island	(4)				
		West Virginia	(5)				

States Voting Republican since 1968

Seven		Six		Five		Four	
Alaska	(3)	California	(54)	Alabama	(9)	Louisiana	(9)
Arizona	(8)	Colorado	(8)	Arkansas	(6)	Pennsylvania	(23)
Florida	(25)	Illinois	(22)	Connecticut	(8)	Washington	(11)
Idaho	(4)	Montana	(3)	Delaware	(3)	Wisconsin	(11)
Indiana	(12)	Nevada	(4)	Iowa	(7)		
Kansas	(6)	New Hampshire	(4)	Kentucky	(8)		
Nebraska	(5)	New Jersey	(15)	Maine	(4)		
North Dakota	(3)	New Mexico	(5)	Michigan	(18)		
Oklahoma	(8)	North Carolina	(14)	Mississippi	(7)		
South Dakota	(3)	South Carolina	(8)	Missouri	(11)		
Utah	(5)	Vermont	(3)	Ohio	(21)		
Virginia	(13)			Oregon	(7)		
Wyoming	(3)			Tennessee	(11)		
				Texas	(32)		

The state's electoral votes appear in parentheses.

Note: A majority of the Electoral College, needed to elect a president, is 270 votes.

support in the South and West and concentrate his campaign on the industrial heartland, specifically Michigan, Illinois, and Ohio. By saturating several key midwestern states with money, media, and appearances by the candidates and well-known boosters, Reagan's campaign advisers hoped to make it impossible for the Democratic ticket to obtain a majority in the Electoral College. The Reagan strategies in 1980 and 1984 provided the operational model for Bush in 1988.

The Bush strategy in 1992 was more difficult. Writing off California and New York, trailing in all the battleground states of the Midwest, challenged in the South, his strategists had to identify those states that they were likely to win and then others in which they could conceivably catch up. Only sixteen states, including Texas, Florida, Indiana, and Virginia, were thought to be solidly in the Republican camp at the beginning of the campaign. When others likely to go Republican were added to the list, the total amounted to only 192 electoral votes. To make up the difference, the Republicans had to target all the midwestern states. They ended up winning only Indiana.

In contrast, Clinton had the luxury of leading in five of the seven largest states at the beginning of the campaign and was competitive in the other two, Texas and Florida. Prior to the Democratic convention his campaign targeted the five large states in which he was ahead plus 15 others. Together these states had a total of 370 electoral votes. Clinton's targeting effort proved extremely accurate. Only one targeted state, North Carolina, voted Republican in the election and only one nontargeted state, Nevada, voted Democratic.

Carter's and Clinton's successful geographic strategies in 1976 and 1992 seem to offer the Democrats their best hopes of winning an Electoral College majority in the future. Key to any Democratic success is narrowing the Republican's geographic base. By competing in the South and the West, the Democrats force the Republicans to devote resources to these areas, resources that they might otherwise concentrate in the key battleground states. Thus, a Democratic candidate with popularity in either the South, West, or both, would seem to have an advantage over one whose recognition and appeal was primarily in the Northeast.

TACTICAL CONSIDERATIONS

Whereas the basic objectives set the contours of the campaign strategy, tactical considerations influence day-to-day decisions and activities. Tactics are the specific ways by which strategic objectives are achieved. They involve techniques to communicate, target, and time the message so that it has maximum impact. Unlike strategy, which can be planned well in advance, tactics change with the environment and events. The circumstances, in short, dictate different tactical responses.

Communicating Techniques

There are a variety of ways to convey a political message, including door-to-door canvassing, direct mail, and mass media. At the local level especially, door-to-door campaigning may be a viable option.

Personal contact is generally considered to have a greater influence on voters than any other kind of campaign activity. It is most effective in stimulating voting. To a lesser extent, it may also influence the decision on how to vote. The problem with personal contact is that it is time-consuming, volunteer-intensive, and reaches a limited number of people. Once candidates get by the early, small-state caucuses and primaries, it may not be cost-effective.

The Kennedy organization in 1960 was one of the first to mount a campaign on the local level. Using the canvass as a device to identify supporters and solicit workers, Kennedy's aides built precinct organizations out of the newly recruited volunteers. The volunteers, in turn, distributed literature, turned out the voters, and monitored the polls on election day. They were instrumental in Kennedy's narrow victory in several states.

In making contacts, candidate organizations usually rely on telephone banks to identify likely supporters and get them out to vote on election day. Telephone techniques have also been used to solicit volunteers, coordinate grass roots campaigns, and target media messages. The Perot campaign was particularly successful in using the telephone, specifically its 800-number, to organize potential voters. Unable to turn to lists of registered voters or past supporters as the major parties could, Perot publicized his 800-number, and his organization recorded the telephone number of all callers, used their names and addresses to compile a geographic map of areas of potential strength, and then proceeded to direct advertising to these areas.[30]

Direct mail, a technique frequently used in fund raising, has also been employed to distribute information about the candidate and the party. Personalized letters can be targeted to groups and individuals and tailored to address specific issues. The Republicans effectively employed direct mail in 1988. The party's extensive files of registered voters identified potential Republican supporters. Aides canvassed these people by telephone to determine their candidate preferences as well as their issue concerns. Letters signed by George Bush addressing the issue with which they were most concerned were then sent to each of these potential Republican voters. Lacking the information base that the Republicans had, the Democrats were forced to conduct mass mailings directed toward those who lived in key swing precincts or those areas populated by an ethnic, racial, or occupational group that was likely to support its nominees.

For conveying a substantive message to a specific audience, direct mail can be extremely efficient, although its effectiveness varies with the level of education of the group. It tends to have greater impact on those who are less educated, particularly those who do not receive a lot of other mail.

Another option is the electronic media—radio and television. Although impersonal and more costly than telephone and regular mail, it has the advantage of reaching large numbers of people simultaneously. Less taxing on the candidate than extensive personal campaigning, it also facilitates some control over the political environment. Although messages cannot be tailored as precisely as they can in individualized letters, they can be designed to create and project favorable images and can be targeted regionally and, on non-English language cable stations, ethnically. (Media advertising is discussed in Chapter 7.)

The reach of radio and television, the size of their potential audiences, and their ability to direct messages to sympathetic listeners or viewers explain why an increasing proportion of expenditures by the campaigns of the presidential candidates are spent on the production and airing of this form of advertising. In 1976, total expenditures on all forms of media accounted for approximately half the campaign budget; by 1992 it was about two-thirds, with television advertising being the largest single expenditure. (See p. 242 for details on these expenditures.)

Developments in the communications media, specifically satellite technology, have also enabled candidates to design and project their messages to local audiences. They can remain in their studios and be interviewed by local anchors around the country. Electronic town meetings and press conferences have now become standard fare.

No matter how extensive a candidate's use of mass media may be—and Perot's was extensive—a certain amount of personal campaigning is still necessary. Appearances by presidential hopefuls create news, often becoming media events themselves. They make the candidates seem real to the voters and testify to the candidates' concern for the people they are addressing. The problem with personal appearances is that they are personally wearing for the candidate, may have limited impact, and are not completely controlled even though extensive preparation goes into them and many precautions are taken.

Orchestrating the Campaign

Whether appearing in person or on television, much advance work is necessary. Jerry Bruno, who "advanced" Democratic presidential campaigns in the 1960s, described his tasks as an advance man, tasks that have not changed all that much over the years:

> It's my job in a campaign to decide where a rally should be held, how a candidate can best use his time getting from an airport to that rally, who should sit next to him and chat with him quietly in his hotel

room before or after a political speech, and who should be kept as far away from him as possible.

> It's also my job to make sure that a public appearance goes well—a big crowd, an enthusiastic crowd, with bands and signs, a motorcade that is mobbed by enthusiastic supporters, a day in which a candidate sees and is seen by as many people as possible—and at the same time have it all properly recorded by the press and their cameras.[31]

Bruno's efforts are indicative of the great lengths to which modern campaigns go to prevent uncontrolled and unanticipated events from marring a presidential candidate's appearance. The Clinton campaign took this preparation to new heights in 1992. The campaign had its own television cameras record rallies and speeches and provide favorable footage to local news media.

Even with all the advance preparations, things can go wrong. If the crowds are thin, if the candidate is heckled, if a prominent public figure refuses to be on the platform with the candidate or a controversial one does appear, or if the candidate makes a verbal slip, then the event may do more harm than good. Mondale got off to an embarrassing start in 1984 when an early hour Labor Day parade in which he was to appear drew relatively few onlookers. The news was the absence of spectators. Television cameras pictured Mondale walking down nearly-empty streets in New York City. The message was clear—his candidacy sparked little enthusiasm.

The Clinton campaign used its own television crew to minimize such embarrassments. As F. Christopher Arterton writes,

> If the camera angle showed a sparse crowd, or if a garishly clad spectator distracted the viewer's eye, or if the signs down front blocked the candidate's tie, or if the opposition's signs began showing up in the background, a quick call from Little Rock to the cellular phone of the on-site advance staff could correct the offending blemish.[32]

The arduous and exhausting schedules of modern campaigns have contributed to displays of emotion by candidates that have embarrassed them and damaged their public image. One of the most highly publicized of these incidents occurred during the 1972 New Hampshire primary. Senator Edmund Muskie, the Democratic front-runner, seemed to break into tears when defending his wife from the attacks of William Loeb, publisher of the state's *Manchester Union Leader*. In the minds of some, the incident made Muskie look weak and not presidential.[33]

Candidates have also made off-color or inappropriate remarks that have caused controversy. When addressing a group of supporters following his 1984 campaign debate with Democrat, Geraldine Ferraro, Vice-President George Bush stated that he had intended "to kick ass" during the debate. The comment, designed to show a macho George Bush, was greeted with enthusiasm by his supporters but not by his opponents.[34] Eight years later, then President Bush, carried away by his own rhetoric, referred to Bill Clinton and Al Gore as "waffle man" and Ozone. A couple of days later he called them "bozos." Criticized for using such language, Bush suggested that he was only trying to be funny.[35]

Some one-liners have worked to the candidate's advantage, at least in the short run. When Republican vice-presidential nominee Dan Quayle compared his Senate experience with John F. Kennedy's in his debate with Lloyd Bentsen, the Democratic candidate shot back, "I served with Jack Kennedy; I knew Jack Kennedy; Jack Kennedy was a friend of mine. Senator, you are no Jack Kennedy."[36] Quayle, shaken by Bentsen's blunt reply, remained on the defensive for the remainder of the debate. Bush's "Read my lips" pledge not to raise taxes enhanced his popularity during the 1988 campaign but made it more difficult for him to find an acceptable solution to the problem of the budget deficit once in office and came back to haunt him during the 1992 campaign.

Targeting Messages

Candidates are normally very careful about their public utterances. Knowing that the press focuses on inconsistencies and highlights controversies, presidential candidates tend to stick to a prepared script that coordinates themes, positions, pictures, and words. Reagan did this successfully in 1984. His campaign introduced a new theme every ten days to two weeks and keyed the president's speeches to it. Situations that might have distracted public attention or confused it were carefully controlled.

Speeches are tailored for specific groups. In appealing to ethnic voters, Dukakis referred to his Greek heritage and to his parents' immigration to the United States. "If this son of immigrants can seek and win the presidency with your help," he told voters, "then your kids and your grandkids, the kids and grandkids of immigrants all over this country, from every community, can do the same."[37]

Key to a targeting effort is polling. Candidates must identify those appeals that are likely to be most effective with the specific groups to whom they are directed. Then they must monitor their messages to assess their impact, fine-tuning them when necessary.

Computer technology is also used. F. Christopher Arterton describes the sophisticated computer mapping operation that the Clinton organization used to coordinate its media campaign with its grass roots, get-out-the-vote activities:

It began by superimposing media markets on a map of the United States. Week by week, each media market was ranked in terms of the number of persuadable voters in the market weighted by the Electoral College votes and the perceived strategic importance of the states reached in that market. The resulting map, in which the media markets were arrayed on an eight-point, color-coded scale, quickly revealed where the campaign needed to place its emphasis in travel, field organization, and media buys.[38]

Timing Appeals

In addition to the problem of whom to appeal to, what to say, and how to say it, decisions about when to make the appeal are important. Candidates naturally desire to build momentum as their campaigns progress. This goal usually dictates a phased effort, especially for the underdog.

Goldwater's campaign of 1964 illustrates the plight of the challenger. Having won the Republican nomination after heated primary contests against Nelson Rockefeller, the senator initially had to reunite the party. The first month of his campaign was directed toward this end. Endorsements were obtained; the party was reorganized; traditional Republican positions were articulated. Phase two was designed to broaden Goldwater's electoral support. Appeals to conservative Democratic and independent voters were made on the basis of ideology. The third phase was the attack. Goldwater severely criticized President Johnson, his Great Society program, and his liberal Democratic policies. In phase four, the Republican candidate enunciated his own hopes, goals, and programs for America's future. Finally, at the end of the campaign, perceiving that he had lost, Goldwater adhered to his views and became increasingly uncompromising in presenting his conservative beliefs.

In 1988, George Bush's strategy was also phased. The first stage of his campaign during the Republican convention was to establish his own qualifications for the office as an experienced national leader and a loyal vice-president but also a person with his own ideas. Cutting Dukakis down to size was the focus of stage two. In the third part of his campaign, Bush sought to accentuate the positive. The theme of his ads, "peace and prosperity," was designed to generate and maintain a positive feeling in the last month of the campaign.

The staging of the Bush campaign was less distinct and less successful in 1992. Although his initial plan was to articulate an economic policy agenda following his renomination by the Republican convention and reiterate it throughout the campaign, Bush got diverted by the character issues and spent most of his time criticizing his opponents. It is difficult for an incumbent to win by conducting such a negative campaign.

Turning Out Voters

When all is said and done, it is the electorate that makes the final judgment. Who comes out to vote can be the critical factor in determining the winner in a close election. Although turnout is influenced by a number of variables, including the demographic characteristics and political attitudes of the population, registration laws and procedures, the kind of election and its competitiveness, and even the weather (see Chapter 3), it is also affected by the campaign itself.

On balance, lower turnout has hurt the Democrats more than the Republicans, because a larger proportion of Democratic party identifiers have been less likely to vote. Thus, a key element in the strategy of most Democratic candidates since Franklin Roosevelt has been to maximize the number of voters by organizing large registration and get-out-the-vote drives.

Traditionally, the party organizations at the state and local levels, not the candidate's central headquarters, mount the drive. A party divided at the time of its convention can seriously damage its chances in the general election. A case in point was the Humphrey campaign of 1968. Humphrey received the nomination of a party that took until late October to coalesce behind his candidacy, too late to register a large number of voters for the November election. Had it not been for organized labor's efforts in registering approximately 4.6 million voters, Humphrey probably would not have come as close as he did.

Whereas Humphrey's loss in 1968 can be attributed in part to a weak voter registration drive, Carter's victory in 1976 resulted from a successful one. The Democratic National Committee coordinated and financed the drive. With the support of organized labor, Democrats outregistered Republicans. Labor's efforts in Ohio and Texas contributed to Carter's narrow victory in both states. A successful program to attract African American voters also helped increase Carter's margin of victory.

One of the most sophisticated registration efforts by either party occurred in 1984. The Reagan/Bush organization used the prenomination period to identify potential unregistered supporters. Lists of people, grouped by precinct, were supplied to state and local Republican committees for the purposes of enlarging the potential Republican vote. In contrast, the Democrats lacked the organizational mechanism and financial support to match the Republican effort that election, falling far short in their effort to register new voters. They were more successful in 1992 when Democratic turnout increased more than did Republican turnout.

SUMMARY

Campaigning by presidential nominees is a relatively recent phenomenon. Throughout most of the nineteenth century, presidential campaigns were run by the parties on behalf of their nominees. The goal was to energize and educate the electorate with a series of public activities and events. Beginning in the 1880s, presidential candidates became increasingly involved in the campaign. By the 1920s they had become active participants, using radio and later television to reach as many voters as possible. To some extent, the electronic media has replaced the parties as the critical link between candidates and voters.

Advances in transportation and communications have made campaigning more complex, more expensive, and more sophisticated. These advances required considerable activity by the candidates and their staffs. Campaign strategy and tactics are now more closely geared to the technology of contemporary politics.

Campaign organizations have increased in size and expertise. Supplementing the traditional cadre of party professionals are the professionals of the new technology: pollsters, media consultants, direct mailers, lawyers, accountants, and a host of other specialists. Their inclusion in the candidate's organization has made the coordination of centralized decision making more difficult but more necessary. It has also produced at least two separate organizations, one very loosely coordinated by the party's national committee and the other more tightly controlled by the candidates and their campaign staffs.

The job of campaign organizations is to produce a unified and coordinated effort. Most presidential campaigns follow a general strategy based on the prevailing attitudes and perceptions of the electorate, the reputations and images of the nominees and their parties, and the geography of the Electoral College. The strategy includes designing a basic appeal, creating a leadership image, dealing with incumbency (if appropriate), and allocating campaign resources in the light of Electoral College politics.

In designing a basic appeal, Democratic candidates have emphasized their party label and those "bread-and-butter" issues that have held their coalition together since the 1930s. Republican candidates, on the other hand, did not emphasize partisanship until the 1980s. Instead, they stressed foreign policy and national security issues. They also used economic issues to their advantage by contrasting domestic conditions during the Carter and Reagan administrations. The recession of 1992 made this comparison difficult and muted foreign policy issues, thereby forcing the GOP to concentrate on character issues.

Part of the strategy of every presidential campaign is to project an image of leadership. Candidates do this by trumpeting their own strengths and exploiting their opponent's weaknesses. They try to project a litany of traits that the public desires in their president, traits which are emblematic of the office and resonate with the public mood of the election period.

An established record, particularly by presidents seeking reelection, shapes much of that leadership imagery. Depending on the times, that record may contribute to or detract from the candidates' reelection potential. Until recently, incumbents were thought to have an advantage. Being president—making critical decisions, exercising the powers of the office—was viewed as evidence of the leadership that presidential candidates have to demonstrate. Disappointment with contemporary presidents, however, reenforced by persistent media criticism, has helped level the playing field for challengers.

When allocating resources, the geography of the Electoral College must be considered. Each party begins with a base of safe states. Since 1968 that base has been larger for the Republicans than for the Democrats. Population movements to the South and the West have resulted in a regional advantage for the Republicans, one that allows them greater flexibility in designing their geographic strategy. The Democrats have been forced to concentrate their resources in the larger states. A southern or western candidate helps the Democrats combat the Republican's strategic geographic advantage.

The candidates' strategies influence the conduct of their campaigns, but their tactics tend to have greater and more direct effect on day-to-day events. Key tactical decisions include what techniques are to be used, when, and by whom. They also include what appeals are to be made, how, when, and to whom.

Other than the belief that flexibility and rapid responses are essential, it is difficult to generalize about tactics. Much depends on the basic strategic plan, the momentum of the campaign, external conditions, and the unfolding of events. In the end, the methods that mobilize the electorate by getting people excited about a candidate are likely to be of the greatest benefit in turning out and influencing the vote. Much of the campaign is filtered through the mass media. The next chapter explores this mediation and its impact on the election.

NOTES

1. Keith Melder, *Hail to the Candidate: Presidential Campaigns from Banners to Broadcasts* (Washington, D.C.: Smithsonian Institution Press, 1992), pp. 70–74.
2. Ibid., p. 87.
3. Ibid., p. 88.
4. Quoted in Marvin R. Weisbord, *Campaigning for President* (New York: Washington Square Press, 1966), p. 45.
5. Historian Gil Troy writes that Lincoln's avoidance of anything that smacked of political involvement was in fact a political tactic that he used throughout the campaign, emphasizing passivity and partisanship. Gill Troy, *See How They Ran: The Changing Role of the Presidential Candidate* (New York: Free Press, 1991), p. 66.
6. Weisbord, *Campaigning for President*, p. 5.
7. Quoted in Melder, *Hail to the Candidate*, p. 104.
8. Ibid., p. 125.
9. Keith Melder, "The Whistlestop: Origins of the Personal Campaign," *Campaigns and Elections* 7 (May/June 1986): 49.

10. William Jennings Bryan, *The First Battle* (1896; reprint, Port Washington, N.Y.: Kennikat Press, 1971), p. 618.
11. Melder, *Hail to the Candidate*, p. 129.
12. Weisbord, *Campaigning for President*, p. 116.
13. Franklin Roosevelt had been crippled by polio in 1921. He wore heavy leg braces and could stand only with difficulty. Nonetheless, he made a remarkable physical and political recovery. In his campaign, he went to great lengths to hide the fact that he could not walk and could barely stand. The press generally did not report on his disability. They refrained from photographing, filming, or describing him struggling to stand with braces.
14. Cabell Phillips, *The Truman Presidency* (New York: Macmillian, 1966), p. 237.
15. Stanley Kelley, *Professional Public Relations and Political Power* (Baltimore: Johns Hopkins Press, 1956), pp. 161–162.
16. Karl A. Lamb and Paul A. Smith, *Campaign Decision-Making: The Presidential Election of 1964* (Belmont, Calif.: Wadsworth, 1968), pp. 59–63.
17. Quoted in Charles T. Royer, ed. *Campaign for President: The Managers Look at '92* (Hollis, N.H.: Hollis Publishing Company, 1994), p.194.
18. According to the National Election Studies, 43 percent of the voters cited the economy and jobs as the principal issue, 21 percent mentioned the budget deficit, and 19 percent listed health care. Values and taxes were cited by 15 and 14 percent, respectively, foreign policy by only 8 percent.
19. Fred Steeper, "Memorandum" October 28, 1992. Made available to the author by the Republican National Committee.
20. An excellent examination of presidential traits appears in Benjamin I. Page, *Choices and Echoes in Presidential Elections* (Chicago, Ill.: University of Chicago Press, 1978), pp. 232–265. The discussion that follows in the text draws liberally from Professor Page's description and analysis.
21. Following the Republican convention in August, when the public was just beginning to compare the candidates and form their initial impression of the nominees, Bush unleashed his anti-Dukakis campaign, painting his opponent as a free-spending liberal, soft on crime, weak on defense, and short on experience—a Democrat in the tradition of such unsuccessful and discredited Democratic candidates as George McGovern, Jimmy Carter, and Walter Mondale.

    Dukakis chose initially not to reply to Bush's attacks. His failure to do so compounded his problem, allowing the Republicans to shape early public perceptions of the Democratic nominee. By the time Dukakis did respond, his negative image had been established in the minds of the voters. The Dukakis experience served as a lesson to the Clinton campaign.
22. Quoted in Thomas B. Edsall, "Why Bush Accentuates the Negative," *Washington Post*, October 2, 1988, p. C 4.
23. Fred Steeper, in Royer, ed. *Campaign for President*, p. 192.
24. Times Mirror Center for The People & The Press, "The People, The Press & Politics, Campaign '92: Air Wars," October 8, 1992, p. 2.
25. F. Christopher Arterton, "Campaign '92: Strategies and Tactics of the Candidates," in *The Election of 1992*, Gerald Pomper, F. Christopher Arterton, Ross Baker and Walter Dean Burnham, et al. (Chatham, N.J.: Chatham House Publishers, 1993), p. 85.
26. A political scientist, Steven J. Brams, and a mathematician, Morton D. Davis, devised a formula for the most rational way to allocate campaign resources. They calculated that resources should be spent in proportion to the "3/2's power" of the electoral votes of each state. To calculate the 3/2's power, take

the square root of the number of electoral votes and cube the result. They offer the following example: "If one state has 4 electoral votes and another state has 16 electoral votes, even though they differ in size only by a factor of four, the candidates should allocate eight times as much in resources to the larger state." In examining actual patterns of allocation between 1960 and 1972, Brams and Davis found that campaigns generally conformed to this rational allocation rule. "The 3/2's Rule in Presidential Campaigning," *American Political Science Review*, 68 (1974): 113.

27. Alaska, Hawaii, and the District of Columbia did not cast electoral votes in 1952.

28. Quoted in Lamb and Smith, *Campaign Decision-Making*, p. 95.

29. Together, these states had 298 electoral votes. Nixon needed to win at least 153 of them, which combined with his almost certain 117 electoral votes from other Republican-oriented states, would make the Electoral College majority of 270. He actually won 190 electoral votes from the states he targeted.

30. Tom Steinert-Threlkeld, "High-tech Tactics by Perot Could Reshape Politics, Experts Say," *Dallas Morning News* (May 3, 1992), pp. 1, 15.

31. Jerry Bruno and Jeff Greenfield, *The Advance Man* (New York: Morrow, 1971), p. 299.

32. Arterton, "Campaign '92," p. 92.

33. George McGovern, who benefited from the Muskie episode, expressed his own frustration toward the end of his presidential campaign. When passing a vociferous heckler at an airport reception, McGovern told his critic, "Kiss my ass!" The press dutifully reported the senator's comment.

34. Another well-reported incident, this one involving Vice-President Nelson Rockefeller, occurred in 1976. It too was precipitated by heckling. The Republican vice-presidential candidate of that year, Senator Robert Dole, accompanied by Rockefeller, was trying to address a rally in Binghamton, New York. Constantly interrupted by the hecklers, Dole and then Rockefeller tried to restore order by addressing their critics directly. When this approach failed, Rockefeller grinned and made an obscene gesture, extending the middle fingers of each of his hands to the group. The vice-president's response was captured in a picture that appeared in newspapers and magazines across the country, much to the embarrassment of the Republican ticket.

35. In recent campaigns each of the major party candidates have made questionable statements that were highlighted by the media. In the midst of the Democratic primaries in 1976, Carter stated that he saw nothing wrong with people trying to maintain the "ethnic purity" of their neighborhoods. After some interpreted his remarks as racist, Carter indicated that he had made an error in his choice of words, promptly retracted them, and apologized. During his second debate with Carter, President Ford asserted that the Soviet Union did not dominate Eastern Europe. His comment, picked up and repeated by the media, led critics to wonder whether he really understood the complexities of international politics, much less appreciated the threat and influence of the Soviet Union.

36. Quoted in "Transcript of the Vice Presidential Debate," *Washington Post* (October 6, 1988), p. A 30.

37. Quoted in Edward Walsh, "Dukakis Is Wearing Ethnicity on His Sleeve," *Washington Post* (May 22, 1988), p. A 7.

38. Arterton, "Campaign '92," p. 87.

SELECTED READINGS

Aldrich, John H. and Thomas Weko, "The Presidency and The Election Campaign: Framing the Choice in 1992," in Michael Nelson (ed.) *The Presidency and the Political System*, Washington, D.C.: Congressional Quarterly Press, 1995, pp. 251–270.

Archer, J. Clark, Fred M. Shelley, Peter J. Taylor, and Ellen R. White. "The Geography of U.S. Presidential Elections. *Scientific American* 259 (July 1988): 44–51.

Arterton, F. Christopher, "Campaign '92: Strategies and Tactics of the Candidates," in Gerald Pomper, F. Christopher Arterton, Ross Baker, Walter Dean

Burnham, et al., *The Election of 1992*. Chatham, N.J.: Chatham House Publishers, Inc., 1993, pp. 74–109.

Goldman, Peter, Thomas M. DeFrank, Mark Miller, Andrew Murr, and Tom Mathews. *Quest For the Presidency 1992*. College Station, TX: Texas A&M Press, 1994.

McCubbins, Mathew D. (ed.). *Under the Watchful Eye: Managing Presidential Campaigns in the Television Era*. Washington, D.C.: Congressional Quarterly Press, 1992.

Melder, Keith. *Hail to the Candidate: Presidential Campaigns from Banners to Broadcasts*. Washington, D.C.: Smithsonian Institution Press, 1992.

Royer, Charles T. (ed.). *Campaign for President: The Managers Look at '92*. Hollis, N.H.: Hollis Publishing Company, 1994.

Troy, Gil. *See How They Ran: The Changing Role of the Presidential Candidate*. New York: Free Press, 1991.

White, Theodore H. *The Making of the President: 1960*. New York: Atheneum, 1988.

——. *The Making of the President, 1964*. New York: Atheneum, 1965.

——. *The Making of the President, 1968*. New York: Atheneum, 1969.

——. *The Making of the President, 1972*. New York: Atheneum, 1973.

——. *America in Search of Itself: The Making of the President, 1956–1980*. New York: Harper and Row, 1982.

ILSON'S
ISDOM
INS
ITHOUT
AR

To appeal to a nation that hoped to sit out the hostilities in Europe, the Democrats tried to capitalize on the solid, scholarly demeanor of Woodrow Wilson.

Chapter 7

Media Politics

INTRODUCTION

Media and politics go hand-in-hand. The press has served as an outlet for divergent political views from the founding of the Republic. When political parties developed at the end of the eighteenth century, newspapers became a primary means for disseminating their policy positions and promoting their candidates.

This early press was contentious and highly adversarial, but it was not aimed at the masses. Written for the upper, educated class, newspapers contained essays, editorials, and letters that debated economic and political issues. It was not until the 1830s that the elitist orientation of the press began to change. Technological improvements, the growth in literacy, and the movement toward greater public involvement in the democratic process all contributed to the development of the so-called "penny press," newspapers that sold for a penny and were directed at the general public.

The penny press revolutionized American journalism. Newspapers began to rely on advertising rather than subscriptions as their primary source of income. To attract advertisers, they had to reach a large number of readers. To do so, newspapers had to alter what they reported and how they reported it.

Prior to the development of the penny press, news was rarely "new"; stories were often weeks old before they appeared and were often rewritten or reprinted from other sources. With more newspapers aimed at the general public, a higher premium was placed on gathering news quickly and reporting it in an exciting, easy-to-read manner.

The invention of the telegraph helped in this regard, making it possible for an emerging Washington press corps to communicate information to the entire country. What was considered news also changed. Events replaced ideas, and human interest stories supplemented the official proceedings of government.

Sensational news—stories of crime, sex, and violence—captured the headlines and sold papers, not essays and letters on public policy. Joseph Pulitzer's *New York World* and William Randolph Hearst's *New York Journal* set the standard for this era of highly competitive "yellow journalism."[1]

Not all newspapers featured sensational news. In 1841, Horace Greeley founded the *New York Tribune* and ten years later, Henry Raymond began the *New York Times*. Both appealed to a more-educated audience who were interested in the political issues of the day. After a change in ownership, the *New York Times* became a paper of record. Operating on the view that news is not entertainment but valuable public information, the *Times* adopted the motto, "All the news that's fit to print." It published entire texts of important speeches and documents and detailed national and foreign news.

Toward the middle of the nineteenth century, newspapers began to shed their advocacy role in favor of more neutral reporting. The growth of news wire services, such as the Associated Press and United Press, and of newspapers that were not tied to political parties contributed to these developments.

As candidates became more personally involved in the campaign, they too became the subject of press attention. By the beginning of the twentieth century, the focus had shifted to the nominees, so much so that at least one candidate, Alton Parker, Democratic presidential nominee for 1904, angrily criticized photographers for their unyielding efforts to take pictures of him while he was swimming in the nude in the Hudson River.[2] Despite the intrusion into their personal lives, candidates began taking advantage of the press' interest in them, using "photo opportunities" and news coverage to project their image and extend their partisan appeal.

With the advent of radio in the 1920s and television in the 1950s, news media coverage of campaigns changed once again. Radio supplemented the printed press. Although it did not provide regular news coverage, radio excelled at covering special events as they were happening. The 1924 presidential election was the first to be reported on radio; the conventions, major speeches, and election returns were broadcast live that year. During the 1928 election, both presidential candidates, Herbert Hoover and Alfred E. Smith, spent campaign funds on radio advertising.

Radio lost its national audience to television in the 1950s, but remained a favorite communications medium of candidates seeking to target their messages to specific groups in specific locations. The cheapest and most accessible electronic medium today, it is used extensively during the nomination phase of the electoral process.

President Coolidge Poses
with Native Americans

President Coolidge used "Photo ops" to attract attention in an otherwise dull campaign in 1924.

Photo source: AP/Wide World Photos.

The influence of television on presidential elections was first felt in 1952. The most important news event of that presidential campaign was a speech by General Dwight Eisenhower's running mate, Richard Nixon. Accused of obtaining secret campaign funds in exchange for political favors, Nixon defended himself in a television address. He denied accepting contributions for personal use, accused the Democratic administration of being soft on communism, criticized his campaign opponents, and vowed that he would never force his children to give up their dog, Checkers, who had been given to the Nixon family by political supporters. The emotion of the speech, and particularly the reference to Checkers, generated a favorable public reaction, ended discussion of the campaign funds, kept Nixon on the Republican ticket, and demonstrated the power of television for candidates in their campaigns.

Paid television advertising by the political parties also first appeared in the 1952 presidential campaign. The marketing of candidates like commercial products was to revolutionize the electoral process, particularly the strategy and tactics of the campaign. It enabled those seeking office to craft and project their image as well as attack their opponents' and to do so before a large viewing audience.

Campaigns have now become made-for-TV productions. Rallies and speeches are staged as media events, and on-air interviews are also standard fare. Political advertising, designed to reinforce positive and negative candidate and party images, regularly consume more than half of the candidates' campaign budgets.

Nor has broadcast television programming become the last word. Communication satellites, laser fiber optics, integrated circuits for high-speed-transmission of digital images and data have opened additional channels for communicating during campaigns, and candidates are now beginning to take advantage of them. In addition, they are experimenting with new radio and television formats, new interactive mechanisms to solicit opinions, gain support, and raise money, and new techniques to influence the coverage of their campaigns.

This chapter examines these developments and their impact on presidential electoral politics. The next section discusses traditional "hard" news coverage of campaigns. It examines how network news organizations interpret political events and how candidates react to that interpretation. The "soft" news/entertainment format is explored in the second section. Here the chapter describes the techniques that candidates used in 1992 to circumvent the national press corps. The third section turns to another news/entertainment feature—presidential debates. It describes their history, structure, staging, and impact on the public. Political advertising is the subject of the fourth section, in which we present some of the most successful advertisements that have been aired, examine the increasing emphasis on negativity, and evaluate the effect of advertising on the electorate's perceptions of the candidates. The final section assesses the media's cumulative impact on voting choice.

TRADITIONAL COVERAGE: HARD NEWS

The modus operandi of news reporting is to inform and interest the public. But it does so with its own professional orientation—one that affects what is covered and how it is covered. Political scientist Thomas E. Patterson argues that the dominant conceptual framework in which the election is reported is that of a game. The candidates are the players and their moves (words, activities, images) are seen as strategic and tactical devices to achieve their principal goal—to win. Even their policy positions are frequently evaluated within this game schema, described as calculated attempts to appeal to certain political constituencies. Although Patterson argues that the game schema is most pronounced at the beginning of the presidential selection process, he sees it as an organizing principle for the news media throughout that process.[3]

Why do media use the game, often referred to as the "horse race," as a primary focus? The answer is that they are in the entertainment business. Viewing elections as a game heightens viewers' interest. Heightened interest, in turn, increases the size of the audience and, of course, the profits, since advertising revenue is based on the estimated number of people watching, hearing, or reading a particular program or paper.

There is another reason. The game format lends an aura of objectivity to reporting. Rather than presenting subjective accounts of the candidates' positions and their consequences for the country, it encourages the news media to present quantitative data on the public's reaction to the campaign. Public opinion surveys, reported as news, are frequently the dominant story during the primaries and caucuses and share the spotlight with other campaign issues, such as the candidates' character, strategies, and tactics, during the general election.

Covering campaigns as if they were sporting events is not a new phenomenon. In 1976, Thomas Patterson found about 60 percent of television election coverage and 55 percent of newspaper coverage was devoted to the campaign as a contest.[4] Michael J. Robinson's and Margaret Sheehan's analysis of the "CBS Evening News" during the 1980 election revealed that five out of six stories emphasized the competition.[5]

What seems to be different today is the increasing emphasis placed on the campaign game and the decreasing attention given to policy debate. Robinson and Sheehan found that CBS News devoted an average of only ninety seconds per program to issues of policy, approximately 20 to 25 percent of the total election coverage.[6] In 1984, no policy question received the attention that Geraldine Ferraro's finances or Ronald Reagan's age did.[7] Although policy issues received more attention in 1988, coverage declined four years later, a surprising finding in the light of the economic recession and concern about budget deficits, business competitiveness, and health care in 1992.[8] It was Clinton's trip to Russia when he was a Rhodes scholar; Perot's allegation of dirty tricks, particularly his charge that Republicans had threatened to disrupt his daughter's wedding; and Bush's participation in Iran-Contra, an allegation that resurfaced during the final week of the campaign, that garnered the headlines and the public's attention.[9]

Dr. Robert Lichter and his associates did a content analysis of 730 election stories on the evening news from September 7 (Labor Day) to November 2 (Election Day) in 1992. The results of their analysis are presented in Table 7–1.

TABLE 7–1

1992 Election Topics on the News

Type of Story	Number
Horserace	258
Campaign strategy	239
Candidate controversies	234
Policy issues	233

Source: "Clinton's the One," *Media Monitor* (November 1992): 3.

The Bad News Syndrome

Once the campaign begins, the principal candidates get approximately the same amount of coverage.[10] Contrary to popular belief, incumbents seeking reelection do not dominate the news.[11] They do tend to receive more negative treatment, however. In 1980, Jimmy Carter was treated more harshly than Ronald Reagan, and in 1984, Reagan was treated more harshly than Walter Mondale. Vice-President George Bush running for president in 1988 fared poorly as well. His saving grace was that his Democratic opponent, Michael Dukakis, received equally unfavorable coverage, about two negative comments for every positive one.

Much the same pattern emerged in 1992. In their analysis of network evening news coverage in 1992, Lichter and his associates found that 69 percent of the evaluations of Bush—his campaign, his positions, his performance, his general desirability—were negative. Bad news, however, was not restricted to incumbents in 1992. There was plenty of it to go around in that election. Sixty-three percent of all the comments about Clinton were negative compared with 54 percent negative for Perot.[12]

The bad news extended to the major parties and to the government as well. During the general election, 83 percent of network news stories on the Democratic party were negative compared with 87 percent for the Republicans.

What is the reason for the bad press? Does it represent an ideological bias? Most academic experts believe that it does not, pointing out that conservatives are treated no better nor worse than liberals. There does, however, appear to be a journalistic bias or orientation that shapes election news coverage and may help explain this bad news syndrome.

The question is, what is news? A fresh face winning and an experienced candidate losing are news; an experienced one winning and a new one losing are not. Similarly, the first time a candidate states a position, it is news; the second time it is not. Since candidates cannot give new speeches every time they address a group, the news media that cover the candidate look for other things to report.

Verbal slips, inconsistent statements, and mistakes often become the focus of attention. Kiku Adatto found, "only once in 1968 did a network even take note of a minor incident unrelated to the content of the campaign."[13] In recent elections there is much more frequent reporting of trivial slips. Roger Ailes, Bush's 1988 media director, explained this phenomenon in the following manner:

> Let's face it, there are three things that the media are interested in: pictures, mistakes, and attacks. That's the one sure way of getting coverage. You try to avoid as many mistakes as you can. You try to give them as many pictures as you can. And if you need coverage, you attack, and you will get coverage.
>
> It's my orchestra pit theory of politics. If you have two guys on stage and one says, "I have a solution to the Middle East problem," and the other guy falls in the orchestra pit, who do you think is going to be on the evening news?[14]

The news media's penchant for reporting embarrassing misstatements encourages the candidates *not* to be spontaneous, *not* to be candid, *not* to make mistakes.

Even a candidate's failure to provide the news media with information or pictures can be a source of admonishment. Take the comment that ABC correspondent Sam Donaldson made to Michael Dukakis, who was playing a trumpet with a local marching band in the midst of his 1988 presidential campaign. Donaldson reported, "He played the trumpet with his back to the camera." As Dukakis played the Democratic victory tune, "Happy Days Are Here Again," Donaldson could be heard saying off-camera, "We're over here governor."[15]

National news media correspondents also grumbled about Ross Perot who made himself practically unavailable to them during the latter phase of his presidential campaign. Just about the only way they could cover him was to watch his television ads or talk show appearances or call his campaign organization office for press releases.

Television news has an additional bias. As an action-oriented, visual medium, its content must move quickly and be capable of being projected as an image on a screen. It emphasizes pictures and deemphasizes words; less attention is devoted to what candidates say and more to how people react to their words and images. That is why campaign speeches are laden with sound bites, such as "Where's the beef?," "It is morning in America," or "Read my lips—No new taxes."

From the candidates' perspective the bad news is magnified by the fact that they do not get the opportunity to tell their own story in their own words on the news that is broadcast by the major networks. The average length of a quotation from candidates on the evening news in 1968 was 42.3 seconds. In 1988, it was 9.8 seconds; in 1992, it was an unbelievable 8.4 seconds. In their analysis of the evening news, Lichter and his associates found that the candidates accounted for only twelve percent of the airtime in campaign stories, whereas reporters were heard for 71 percent, "nearly 16 hours of speaking time."[16] It is the networks' anchors and correspondents, not the candidates, who present the election news of the day.

The Story Line

In addition to the presumption about the nature of news and the format in which it is presented, there is also a framework into which that news is fitted. According to Professor Patterson, a dominant story line emerges and much of the campaign is explained in terms of it. In 1992, it was Pat Buchanan's surprising showing against Bush that was news, not Bush's easy wins against his Republican rival; it was the conservative-controlled Republican convention and platform that garnered the headlines, not the adulation that greeted Bush and his running mate, Dan Quayle: it was the president's inability to turn the election around, to "hit a home run" during his debates with Clinton and Perot that was news rather than his plans for the future or even the character issues he raised about his opponents. In Patterson's words:

> Bush's bad press was mainly a function of journalistic values. The news form itself affected both the content and the slant of most of his coverage. Bush's story was that of a re-election campaign in deep trouble—much like the story of a baseball team that was favored to win the pennant but stumbled early and never regained its stride.[17]

Patterson describes this story line as the *likely-loser* scenario.[18] He adds that there are three other principal campaign stories. At least one has a happy ending. It involves the *front-runner* who has a lead and maneuvers to keep it. The media attributes superior resources, often including the perquisites of the office, as reason why the front-runner stays on top. Ronald Reagan's 1984 campaign illustrates the front-runner script.[19]

The other two narratives are of a *bandwagon* in which candidates build a lead and those that have them *losing ground*. In the first scenario, an image of strong and decisive leadership generates support; in the second, the image of a weak and vacillating leadership contributes to the erosion. Jimmy Carter's primary spurt in 1976 provides an illustration of the bandwagon; his decline in the general election exemplifies the losing-ground story.[20]

Patterson's point is that the press fits the news of the campaign into the principal story rather than creates a new story from the changing events of the campaign. Naturally, the perceptions of the news media affect the electorate's understanding of what is happening.

Impact of the News Media

What impact does the style and substance of election news coverage have on the voters? Studies of campaigning in the 1940s indicated that the principal impact of the news media was to activate predispositions and reinforce attitudes rather than to convert voters. Newspapers and magazines provided information, but primarily to those who were most committed. The most committed, in turn, used the information to support their beliefs. Weeding out opposing views, they insulated themselves from unfavorable news and from opinions that conflicted with their own.[21]

With the bulk of campaign information coming from print press in the 1940s, voters, particularly partisan voters, tended to minimize cross pressures and to strengthen their own preexisting judgments. In contrast, the less committed also had less incentive to become informed. They maintained their ignorance by avoiding information about the campaign. The format of newspapers and magazines facilitated this kind of selective perception and retention.

Television might have been expected to change this because it exposed the less committed to more information and the more committed to other points of view. Avoidance became more difficult, although the use of remote control devices has rendered viewers less captive to the picture on a particular channel than they were when television first began to cover presidential campaigns.

Television news also compartmentalizes more than the print press. The evening news fits a large number of stories into a thirty-minute broadcast (which includes only twenty-three minutes of news). Of necessity, this time frame restricts the coverage that can be given to each item. Campaign stories average ninety seconds on the evening news, the equivalent of only a few paragraphs of a printed account. Their brevity helps explain why viewers do not retain much information from television coverage of them.

Nonetheless, television news coverage is still influential if only because more people follow presidential campaigns on television than through any other medium. It is the prime source of news for approximately two-thirds of the population.[22] Newspapers are a distant second, with only 20 percent of the population listing them as their principal source of news. Radio and magazines trail far behind. (See Table 7–2.)

Television news helps set the agenda for the campaign. Its emphasis or lack of emphasis on certain issues affects the content of the debate, the attention that the candidates must give to specific policy and character issues, and to some extent, the kinds of responses they have to provide. Media expert, Michael J. Robinson, believes that this agenda-shaping

TABLE 7-2

Public Use of Media to Follow Presidential Campaigns, 1952–1992 (percent)

Media	1952	1956	1960	1964	1968	1972	1976	1980	1984	1988	1992
READ NEWSPAPER ARTICLES ABOUT THE ELECTION											
Regularly			44	40	37	26	28	27	24	—	—
Often*	39	69	12	14	12	14	17	29	34	—	—
From time to time†	40		16	18	19	16	24	17	19	—	—
Once in a great while‡			7	6	7	4	10				
No	21	31	21	22	25	40	22	27	23	—	—
ATTENTION PAID TO NEWSPAPER ARTICLES ABOUT THE PRESIDENTIAL CAMPAIGN											
Great deal									8	6	9
Quite a bit									14	12	15
Some									28	22	20
Very little									20	9	6
None									31	52	50
LISTEN TO SPEECHES OR DISCUSSIONS ON RADIO											
Good many§	34	45	15	12	12	8	12	14	10	5	7
Several¶	35		17	23	16	21	20	22	20	10	11
One or two**			10	12	12	13	16	15	16	17	18
No	30	55	58	52	59	59	52	50	55	69	64
WATCHED PROGRAMS ABOUT THE CAMPAIGN ON TELEVISION											
Good many§	32	74	47	41	42	33	37	28	25	—	31
Several¶	19		29	34	34	41	38	37	37	—	39
One or two**			11	13	13	16	15	22	24	—	19
No	49	26	13	11	11	9	10	13	14	—	11

ATTENTION PAID TO TELEVISION NEWS ABOUT THE PRESIDENTIAL CAMPAIGN

Response			
Great deal	17	15	20
Quite a bit	24	26	29
Some	28	29	28
Very little	11	13	11
None	20	17	13

READ ABOUT THE CAMPAIGN IN MAGAZINES

Response										
Good many[§]	15	—	12	10	9	7	12	7	7	—	—
Several[¶]	—	31	15	16	12	15	24	19	16	—	—
One or two[**]	26	—	13	13	15	14	15	12	11	—	—
No	60	69	59	61	64	64	49	62	66	—	—

ATTENTION PAID TO MAGAZINE ARTICLES ABOUT THE PRESIDENTIAL CAMPAIGN

Response			
Great deal	3	3	4
Quite a bit	4	6	7
Some	7	11	10
Very little	2	3	3
None	84	76	77

Note: "—" indicates question not asked.

* "Quite a lot, pretty much" in 1952; "yes" in 1956; "good many" in 1980–1984.

† "Not very much" in 1952; "several" in 1980–1984.

‡ "One or two" in 1980–1984. "Quite a lot, pretty much" in 1952.

¶ "Yes" in 1956.

** "Not very much" in 1952.

Source: National Election Studies codebooks. Center for Political Studies. Institute for Social Research, University of Michigan, Ann Arbor, Mich. Reprinted from Harold W. Stanley and Richard G. Niemi, *Vital Statistics on American Politics* (Washington, D.C.: *Congressional Quarterly*, 1994), pp. 72–73. Reprinted by permission of Congressional Quarterly, Inc.

function directly affects the political elites. He argues that the press influences *how* political elites "relate" to the mass public and *how* those elites communicate political options.[23] In this way the news media affect the conduct of the campaign, which in turn influences the decisions of the electorate.

The news media may have a direct influence on voters as well. They color their perceptions of the candidates and parties, particularly the candidates' qualifications for leadership. That is why candidates do their utmost to shape the coverage they receive.

From the perspective of those running for office, the news coverage is harsh and the news media adversarial. The candidates' motives are questioned, their speeches are summarized into a very few points or sound bites, their misstatements are highlighted, their character frailties emphasized, and their policy positions criticzed. Is it any wonder that candidates also try to circumvent the national press corps to reach their audiences directly?

NONTRADITIONAL COVERAGE: SOFT NEWS

One of the major changes in media politics in the 1990s has been the use of a soft news format by the major party candidates. Pioneered by Ross Perot on television and Jerry Brown on radio, this new format provides a more candidate-friendly environment in which to engage the electorate. Appearances on the morning and evening television talk and entertainment shows (such as CBS' "This Morning," ABC's "Good Morning America," NBC's "Today," "Phil Donahue," "Larry King Live," the "Arsenio Hall Show" and MTV) have now become commonplace. In all, presidential candidates and their running mates were on thirty-nine separate talk/entertainment programs during the 1992 campaign. Even President Bush appeared in this format, despite his initial misgivings, although he did not appear at ease while doing so. According to one group of analysts, Bush, who had granted an interview to MTV's Tabitha Soren, . . . "looked about as comfortable as a father talking to his teenage daughter about safe sex."[24]

Clinton's appearance on the "Arsenio Hall Show" before the Democratic convention, wearing sun glasses and playing his saxophone, was another story. To many watching the show, he appeared to be a real kind of guy, someone with whom they could identify.

For Perot, talk show appearances constituted much of his "live" campaign, beginning with his original announcement that he might run for president on the "Larry King Live" show. In 1995, Republicans Richard Lugar and Pete Wilson followed Perot's example, also announcing their intention to seek their party's nomination on "Larry King Live."

The use of the talk/entertainment format has several advantages for candidates. They are treated better, more like celebrities than politicians.

Clinton on the "Arsenio Hall Show"

To reach larger, less politically involved audiences in 1992, presidential candidates appeared on entertainment shows. Here Bill Clinton plays his saxophone for Arsenio Hall. This appearance, like one on MTV, contrasted the younger, "swinging" Clinton with George Bush—a contrast that worked to Clinton's advantage.

Photo source: AP/Wide World Photos.

Their hosts tend to be more cordial and less adversarial than news commentators and reporters. Moreover, their audience is also different. Those who watch these shows tend to be less oriented toward politics, and particularly partisan politics, and thus may be more amenable to influence by the candidates who appear on these programs.

Variations of talk/entertainment format are town meetings and call-in programs in which candidates answer questions posed by average citizens. By interacting with ordinary people, presidential candidates can demonstrate their responsiveness, sincerity, and empathy with the problems people face. Bill Clinton was particularly effective in such a setting.

There are other benefits of the soft news format. For one thing, it distances candidates from the aggressive "got-ya" style of reporting in which national correspondents frequently engage. Instead of being asked very specific, often tricky, "hardball" questions, that focus on personality, image, and horserace issues, interviewers, audience, or call-in participants tend to ask "softer" questions that are more straightforward, issue-oriented, and easier to answer, questions which may even have been screened in advance by program producers. And the candidates can give longer answers that are broadcast in their entirety rather than in one or two sound bites. In fact, the programs themselves are often newsworthy, generating an even larger impact for the candidates when clips of their comments are rebroadcast or summarized on the news. Nor are the expenses associated with appearance on these shows comparable to the costs of staging a major media event.

The larger audience, the higher comfort level, and the greater ability of candidates to project their desired images and present seemingly spontaneous but often carefully crafted answers suggest that this soft news format will continue to be used by presidential campaigns to circumvent the national press corps and reach a portion of the general public directly.

PRESIDENTIAL DEBATES

Debates represent another "entertainment" component of presidential campaigns, one which candidates, particularly those who are behind, find useful. They see them as an opportunity to improve their own image and damage their opponent's. Unlike most of their campaign rhetoric—speeches, statements, and responses to questions—debates are live and unedited although the formats limit the time for the response. Nonetheless, they give candidates greater latitude to present their thoughts as they wish them presented. That is why they like them.

The news media also like the debate format because it generates interest and facilitates comparison among the candidates. It is a newsworthy event that fits within the game motif.

The first series of televised debates occurred in 1960. John Kennedy used them to counter the impression that he was too young and inexperienced. Richard Nixon, on the other hand, sought to maintain his stature as Dwight Eisenhower's knowledgeable and competent vice-president and the obvious person to succeed his "boss" in office.

In the three elections that followed, Lyndon Johnson and then Nixon, both ahead in the polls, saw no advantage in debating their opponents and refused to do so. Gerald Ford, however, trailing Jimmy Carter in preelection polls in autumn of 1976, saw debates as his best opportunity to win in November. The Carter camp, on the other hand, saw them as a means of crystallizing their support. In 1980, the rationale was similar. From Reagan's perspective, it was a way to reassure the electorate about himself and his qualifications for office. For Carter, it was another chance to emphasize the differences between himself and Reagan, between their parties, and between their issue and ideological positions.

By 1984, presidential debates had become so much a part of presidential campaigns that even incumbents could not avoid them without making their avoidance a major campaign issue. Thus, Ronald Reagan was forced by the pressures of public opinion to debate Walter Mondale, even though he stood to gain little and could have lost much from their face-to-face encounter. And in the 1992 election, George Bush's initial refusal to accept a plan for a series of campaign debates put forth by the Commission on Presidential Debates, a nonpartisan group that had organized the 1988 presidential and vice-presidential debates, hurt him politically. Bill Clinton chided the president for his refusal to debate him and did so at the site and time of their first proposed debate. Speaking beside an empty chair, intended to remind people of Bush's absence, he said: "If I had the worst record of any president in fifty years, I wouldn't want to defend that record either."[25] After Democratic partisans, dressed as chickens, appeared at Bush's rallies, the president gave in. "I am tired of looking like a wimp," he told his handlers.[26]

One reason that debates have become such an integral component of the presidential electoral process is that they regularly attract many viewers, more than any other single event of the entire campaign. By bringing the candidates together on the same stage at the same time, the debates become major campaign stories, routinely covered by the news media.[27]

It is estimated that more than half the adult population of the United States watched all the Kennedy/Nixon debates and that almost 90 percent saw one of them.[28] The first Carter/Ford debate in 1976 attracted an estimated 90 to 100 million viewers, and the Carter/Reagan debate and Mondale/Reagan debates had audiences of over 100 million. Audience estimates of the 1992 debates range around 90 million per presidential debate and a little lower for the vice-presidential debate.[29] These large audiences have been maintained despite the increasing availability of alternative programming at the time of the debate on local broadcasting stations, cable, and satellite channels.

Although presidential debates are here to stay, their number, scheduling, and format are still subject to negotiation between the principal contenders and their staffs. In these negotiations incumbents tend to have an advantage. President Carter refused to include independent John Anderson in the 1980 debate; in 1984, President Reagan set the parameters for the debates with Mondale as did Vice-President Bush for Dukakis in 1988. It was a different story, however, in 1992. With President Bush trailing in the polls, the campaign moving into the late-September–early-October period, and Clinton making an issue of Bush's refusal to

TABLE 7–3

Presidential Debates, 1960–1992

1960	**John Kennedy v. Richard Nixon**
September 26	Chicago, Ill.
October 7	Washington, D.C.
October 13	Split screen:
	Kennedy in New York, N.Y.
	Nixon in Hollywood, Calif.
October 21	New York City
1976	**Jimmy Carter v. Gerald Ford**
September 23	Philadelphia, Pa.
October 6	San Francisco, Calif.
October 15, vice-presidential candidates:	Houston, Tex.
Walter Mondale v. Robert Dole	
October 22	Williamsburg, Va.
1980	**Jimmy Carter v. Ronald Reagan**
October 18	Cleveland, Ohio
1984	**Walter Mondale v. Ronald Reagan**
October 7	Louisville, Ky.
October 11, vice-presidential candidates:	Philadelphia, Pa.
Geraldine Ferraro v. George Bush	
October 21	Kansas City, Mo.
1988	**Michael Dukakis v. George Bush**
September 25	Winston-Salem, N.C.
October 5, vice-presidential candidates:	Omaha, Nebr.
Lloyd Bensen v. Dan Quayle	
October 13	Los Angeles, Calif.
1992	**George Bush v. Bill Clinton v. Ross Perot**
October 11	St. Louis, Missouri
October 13, vice-presidential candidates:	Atlanta, Georgia
Dan Quayle v. Al Gore v. James Stockdale	
October 15	Richmond, Virginia
	(town meeting format)
October 19	East Lansing, Michigan

debate, the president could not dictate the terms and had to accept a compromise that included formats that he and advisers initially opposed.[30] (See Table 7–3.)

Preparation

Despite the appearance of spontaneity, debates are highly scripted, carefully orchestrated events. Representatives of the candidates study the locations, try to anticipate the questions, and prepare written answers for their candidates. Mock studios are built and the debate environment simulated. The opponent's speeches and interviews are carefully studied for content, style, and other nuances.[31] They are then used in dress rehearsals by stand-ins who imitate the opponents. Here's how *Newsweek* reporters described Clinton's preparation before his first debate in 1992:

> His first informal run-through, three days before the opening debate in Saint Louis, was a shambles. The winner, on most scorecards in the suite, was "Perot," as played by Congressman Mike Synar of Oklahoma; . . . The more discouraging outcome was that Clinton hadn't even managed to outpoint Robert Barnett, the Washington lawyer standing in for Bush. . . .

> His people checked a videotape of the proceedings, then sat down with Clinton around a big conference table the next morning. It was Friday. There were two days left, and their gladiator wasn't ready. Tom Donilon, who had been put in charge of the prep sessions, . . . [said to Clinton], "Ask yourself at the beginning of each question, can we achieve a strategic goal? You want to take control of the question, not be a *prisoner* of the question."

> "There are three points we want to concentrate on," Stan Greenberg said. "First, George Bush means continued economic decline. Second, Bill Clinton is for average people, versus George Bush for the few. Third, you want to draw the contrast between George Bush, who won't do anything, versus Bill Clinton, who will use government to help people. . . . "

> I'd distill it even harder," James Carville said. "Change versus more of the same, and Bill Clinton is a different kind of Democrat."[32]

In the first actual debate, Bill Clinton used the word "change" twelve times, four times in his opening statement.

Perot and Bush went through less elaborate preparations. Perot met with several of his advisers on the day before the debates to go over possible questions and examined his briefing books. He did not prepare his actual responses, however. On the day of the debate when the other candidates were closeted with their advisers, Perot went horseback riding with his grandchildren.

Bush consulted with his advisers and briefing books, went through a trial run the day before the first debate, and then studied his briefing book on the flight to St. Louis, the debate site.[33]

Box 7–1

Debate Questions and Answers:

Memorandum to Clinton, 1992

MEMORANDUM

TO: GOVERNOR CLINTON

FROM: PAUL BEGALA, MIKE DONILON

RE: TOUGH QUESTIONS, TOUGH ANSWERS

ETHICS/CHARACTER

Q: GOVERNOR, AS A PUBLIC OFFICIAL HAVE YOU EVER TOLD A LIE? UNDER WHAT CIRCUMSTANCES IS IT PROPER FOR AN ELECTED OFFICIAL TO WITHHOLD THE TRUTH FROM THE AMERICAN PEOPLE?

A: Every human being makes mistakes, but the last 25 years have seen an unprecedented breach of faith between the government and the people. From Vietnam to Watergate to Iran-Contra to the arming of Saddam Hussein, people are losing faith. Because of this loss of faith, I think the only time it is defensible for a President to withhold information from the American people is when our national security— American lives and American interests— are in immediate peril.

Q: WHAT MAKES YOU THINK YOU HAVE THE CHARACTER TO BE PRESIDENT?

A: I think character is developed and revealed by showing strength through adversity. In my years as an Attorney General and a Governor I've seen my share of tough times and had to make a lot of difficult decisions. The toughest test of character I've ever had to face came in the form of a phone call from the State Police to the Governor's Mansion late one night. It was my brother Roger. He was messed up in drugs. They wanted my authorization to arrest him in a sting. I approved it, and Roger went off to prison. At first he wouldn't speak to me. But now Roger's recovered. He's off drugs and out of prison and doing well with his career. And I couldn't be more proud of him.

Q: AS A YOUNG MAN, YOU TOOK EXTRAORDINARY STEPS TO AVOID GOING TO VIETNAM. AS AN ADULT POLITICIAN, YOU'VE TOLD SEVERAL DIFFERENT STORIES ABOUT THAT TIME IN YOUR LIFE. AS PRESIDENT, WHAT WILL YOU SAY TO YOUNG MEN WHO WON'T WANT TO GO WHEN *you* CALL THEM TO SERVE— AND WHAT DO YOU SAY NOW TO THE FAMILIES WHO LOST LOVED ONES IN A WAR YOU WOULDN'T SERVE IN?

A: I opposed the Vietnam War. I thought that war weakened and divided America then, and I think that now. I would say that to any family who lost a loved one: I mourn their loss and respect the service of everyone who went to Vietnam. But as President I will not commit America to any more Vietnams. I do not relish the prospect of sending men into battle. Nor do I shrink from it. But when I am President we will go into battle for clear and convincing reasons—with clear goals and objectives. We will send our troops in well-armed and well-trained and well-equipped. It's time we put the past behind us and focused on the future.

Q: GOVERNOR, YOU'VE HAD MANY SHIFTING STORIES ON YOUR ACTIONS TO AVOID MILITARY SERVICE IN VIETNAM. ONCE AND FOR ALL, WITH ALL AMERICA WATCHING: WHAT DID YOU DO DURING THE WAR?

A: I [arranged to enroll in] an ROTC unit, then thought better of it and submitted myself for the draft. I got a high lottery number and was never called. If some people want to vote against me for that, that's their right. But it won't make their lives one bit better the day after the election.

Q: YOU AND MRS. CLINTON WERE INVOLVED IN AN INVESTMENT WITH A MAN NAMED JAMES MCDOUGAL, WHO OWNED A SAVINGS-AND-LOAN. MRS. CLINTON REPRESENTED THE S&L BEFORE THE STATE BANKING COMMISSION. IS SUCH AN INVESTMENT PROPER? DOESN'T IT AT LEAST RAISE THE APPEARANCE OF IMPROPRIETY?

A: No. One of the things I am proudest of is that even after 12 years of Governor, even my opponents have to admit we've had a scandal-free Administration. I wish I could say the same about the last 12 years of Presidential Administrations. But about that investment: we lost money on the deal, so it wasn't smart from that standpoint. But you should understand that at the time we invested with Mr. McDougal he didn't own an S&L and I wasn't the Governor. By the time he did own an S&L and I was the Governor we were losing money hand over fist—and it would have been impossible to find a buyer for a failed real estate deal.

Source: Excerpted from "Memorandum to Governor Clinton," from Paul Begala and Mike Donilon as reprinted in Peter Goldman, Thomas M. DeFrank, Mark Miller, et al., *Quest for the Presidency: 1992*, (College Station, TX.: Texas A&M Press, 1994), pp. 723–725.

In general, all debate participants with the possible exception of Richard Nixon, in his first debate with Kennedy, and the memorable exception of Admiral James Stockdale in the 1992 vice-presidential debate, have been well prepared.[34] But not all have been feeling well. Nixon had bumped his knee on a car door going into the television studio for that first debate and was in considerable pain. Dukakis had a viral flu, with a fever of 101, and a sore throat during his second debate with Bush, Clinton was hoarse with a scratchy throat in the days preceding the first of the 1992 presidential debates.[35]

Strategy and Tactics

Much calculation goes into debate strategy and tactics. Candidates need to decide what issues to stress and how to stress them; how to catch their opponents off guard or goad them into an error; whether and how to respond to a personal attack and to criticism of their policy positions. (See Box 7–1, "Debate Questions and Answers: Memorandum to Clinton, 1992.")

Debate style can be particularly important. Kennedy and Carter talked faster than their opponents to create an action-oriented psychology in the minds of the viewers. Both tried to demonstrate their knowledge by citing many facts and statistics in their answers. Ford and Reagan spoke in more general terms, expressing particular concern about the size and structure of government. Reagan's wit and anecdotes in 1980, Bush's manner in 1988, and Perot's down-to-earth language and self-deprecating humor conveyed a human dimension with which viewers could identify in contrast to their opponents less "identifiable" responses. Dukakis was particularly hurt by his reply to the question, "if Kitty Dukakis were raped and murdered, would you favor an irrevocable death penalty for the killer?"[36] His matter of fact, rambling response sealed his technocratic, ice-man image.

In his debates with Bush, Clinton had three broad objectives: stay focused on the economy, respond to any personal attack, and ignore Perot. Since he was in the lead, Clinton wanted to avoid making a big mistake. He played it safe. To present a knowledgeable, presidential image, he cited statistics and specific policy proposals in his first debates although he became more general by the last one. In every debate, he swiftly responded to any personal attacks against him. In one particularly effective response to Bush's imputation about his patriotism for protesting against the Vietnam war as a Rhodes scholar at Oxford University in Great Britain, Clinton said:

> When [Sen.] Joe McCarthy went around this country attacking people's patriotism, he was wrong. . . . And a senator from Connecticut stood up to him named Prescott Bush. Your father was right to stand up to Joe McCarthy; you were wrong to attack my patriotism. I was opposed to the war, but I love my country.[37]

Bush looked away from his Democratic opponent and down at the podium as Clinton uttered these words about his father, indicating that Clinton's response hit home.

Clinton was extremely persuasive in the second town-meeting-style debate, empathizing with questioners and directing his responses to them. Bush, however, seemed ill at ease in this format. At one point near the end of the debate, television cameras caught him looking at his watch, thereby conveying the impression that he was uncomfortable and just wanted out.

Throughout the 1992 debates, the president was in the most difficult position of the three candidates. Trailing in the polls, he had to do well; "hit a home run" was the way the media put it by the third and final debate. Yet he faced not one but two critics who kept focusing on the problems that beset the country during his administration. As a consequence, Bush had to walk a tightrope, downplaying economic problems but at the same time proposing economic solutions to them. He emphasized his experience, but could not dwell on his foreign policy successes because domestic issues were much more salient.

Bush's problems were compounded by his style and rhetoric, particularly in the second debate in which members of the audience asked questions. Beginning his answers with such phrases as "I'm a little confused here, . . . I'm not sure that, . . . I'm not sure that I get it. Help me with the question and I will try to answer it," he seemed uncertain of himself and on the defensive. His hesitation, especially in response to a question on how the national debt affected him personally, reinforced the image that Democrats were trying to project that the president "just didn't get it." Only in the last debate did Bush seem animated, taking the offensive against Clinton.

Perot was in the best position of all during the debates. With high personal negatives and low ratings in the polls, he had little to lose and much to gain. Here's how George Stephanopoulos, director of communications for the Clinton campaign, saw it:

> We kind of knew, from our first practice session, that Perot had a very good chance of winning the first debate. The dynamics made him almost impossible to beat, because whenever we would get engaged in something with Bush, Perot had a choice. He could scold either one or both. He could pile on, or he could just pull out and do some kind of a one-liner, which he had always done, and make himself look apolitical or above politics, or outside of Washington.[38]

Portraying himself as a no-nonsense problem solver, Perot sought to distinguish his candidacy from that of his rivals by painting them as traditional politicians, part of the problem, people who lacked common-sense, private-sector solutions. Perot used business terminology to reinforce his credentials as a successful entrepreneur. He even used humor such as his comment, "I'm all ears," to show that he could laugh at himself. All of this seemed to work. Entering the debates with only 7 percent of the electorate saying that they would vote for him, he left them with 18 percent supporting his candidacy.

Evaluation and Impact

The news media have tended to assess debates in terms of winners and losers. Their evaluation help condition how the public judges the results since most people do not follow the content closely nor do they put much faith in their own evaluation.

In the past there seems to have been a two-stage debate reaction: the first, in the twenty-four hours following the debate and the second, a day or two later. In the first stage opinions were influenced primarily by partisan orientations and previously held views; in the second the news media and the public's reaction to the debates reinforced or altered the electorate's initial judgment. After that, the impact of the debate became more difficult to discern and faded into the general political setting of the campaign.

Ford's second debate with Carter is an excellent illustration of this two-stage effect. During that debate the president stated that the Soviet Union did not dominate the communist countries of Eastern Europe when in fact it did. News analysts made much of this faux pas, and Ford did not recant his comments for three days. In the interim his image, which had been initially enhanced by the second debate, was seriously damaged.[39] The debate reinforced the impression that he was not up to the job.

Today, instant polls and surveys of focus groups have shortened reactions to the debates and in the process reduced the ability of news media analysts and "spin doctors" to shape public opinion. In 1992, one network reported poll results of a preselected group of respondents 15 minutes after the debates were concluded. Table 7–4 indicates public opinion before and after the 1992 debates.

Even though Perot gained in public support, Clinton was able to use the debates to buttress his lead. As William Kristol, an adviser to Vice-President Quayle, put it:

> I think the debates made a huge difference. We were seven or eight points down after the Quayle/Gore debate and 14 down by Sunday after the Thursday night debate. Making up that deficit in three weeks was just too much. After he watched the performances on Thursday night, Dan Quayle believed the election was unwinnable.[40]

The Clinton experience testifies to the conventional wisdom that debates tend to solidify partisan support. Those who are more involved are more likely to watch the debates; those who are more knowledgeable

TABLE 7–4

Percentage of Public Support before, during and after the 1992 Debates*
(based on registered voters)

Dates	Bush	Clinton	Perot	Other/Undecided
September 28–30	35%	52%	7%	6%
October 4–6	35	47	10	8
October 8–10	33	51	10	6
(THE FIRST PRESIDENTIAL DEBATE: 10/11)				
October 13–15	34	47	13	6
(THE SECOND PRESIDENTIAL DEBATE: 10/15)				
(THE THIRD PRESIDENTIAL DEBATE 10/19)				
October 21–22	31	43	18	8
October 24–25	34	43	17	6
October 26–27	38	40	16	6
October 28–29	40	41	14	5
October 30–31	36	43	15	6
October 31–November 1	36	44	14	6

*The percentage of people answering the question: "If the Presidential election were being held today, would you vote for the Republican ticket of George Bush and Dan Quayle, for the Democratic ticket of Bill Clinton and Al Gore, or for the independent candidates, Ross Perot and James Stockdale?"

Source: Based on *The Gallop Poll Monthly,* (September and October, 1992).

are more likely to learn from them; those who are more partisan are more apt to be convinced by them. People root for their own candidates. The debate reconfirms their initial perceptions and predilections.

For weaker partisans and independents, the debates can increase interest and can clarify, color, or even change opinions about the candidates. Before debating, Kennedy was thought by many to be less knowledgeable and less experienced than Nixon; Carter was seen as an enigma, as fuzzier than Ford; Reagan was perceived to be more doctrinaire and less informed than his first Democratic opponent, President Carter. Perot was seen as self-serving, autocratic, and arrogant. The debates helped each of these candidates to overcome these negative perceptions.

The experiences of Kennedy in 1960, Carter in 1976, Reagan in 1980, and Clinton in 1992 suggest why debates tend to help challengers more than incumbents. Being less well known, challengers have more questions raised about them, their competence, and their capacity to be president. The debates provide them with an opportunity to satisfy some of these doubts in a believable setting and on a comparative basis. By appearing to be at least the equal of their incumbent opponents, the challenger's image as a potential president is enhanced. Also incumbents have to defend their record, whereas challengers can go on the offensive.

CAMPAIGN ADVERTISING

Candidates are marketed much like any other commercial product. Advertising is used to gain attention, make a pitch, and leave an impression. The end, of course, is to get the electorate to do something—vote for specific candidates on election day.

Media Consultants

Advertising professionals are hired to supplement regular campaign staff and to design, produce, and target the advertisements. In 1988, the Bush organization turned to Roger Ailes, an experienced political consultant, to oversee its media efforts. Ailes had been in charge of advertising for Richard Nixon's campaign of 1968. His ads that year helped resurrect the image of Nixon, who had been defeated for president in 1960 and for governor of California in 1962. Ailes was given a similar assignment in 1988— develop a positive presidential image for George Bush and a negative one for his opponent, Michael Dukakis, an assignment that he pursued aggressively and successfully.

Ailes was unavailable in 1992, so Bush turned to a team of Madison Avenue advertising executives, dubbed the November Company, to do his media. Headed by Martin Puris, the group did not have much experience in the political arena nor were they close to the president. When tensions and differences emerged between the advertising team and senior officials of the Bush reelection committee, the president was forced to replace his media director with a veteran of past Republican campaigns, Sig Rogich.

Clinton retained the Washington political consulting firm of Greer, Margolis, Mitchell, Greenwald, and Associates, which had designed, coordinated, and targeted his preconvention advertising. Perot employed executives from a local Dallas advertising firm to help develop, produce, and place his ads.

All three media groups were extremely busy. They spent over $100 million on advertising in 1992. According to Professor L. Patrick Devlin, Bush spent $38.5 million of his campaign funds, Clinton $35 million, and Perot, $40 million on television advertising. Additionally, Democratic and Republican party funds were expended on generic campaign advertising. [41]

Techniques and Timing

The advantage of paid advertising, particularly on television, is that candidates can say and do what they want. The problem, however, is to make the advertisement look real. Candidate-sponsored programs are not unbiased, and the public knows it. Generating interest and convincing viewers are more difficult for advertisers than newscasters.

Thus, for advertising to be effective, it must be presented in a believable way. Having a candidate interact with ordinary people is one way of achieving credibility. Not only must media presentations appear authentic; they must seem realistic. When candidates are placed in situations in which they do not fit, visual media can do more damage than good. Such was the case when Michael Dukakis's staff created a photo opportunity in which their candidate wore an army helmet and rode in a combat-ready tank.

The objective of the advertisement was to demonstrate Dukakis's support for the military and for a strong national defense policy. The situation, however, was so contrived and the candidate looked so silly that the Republicans countered with a commercial in which the Dukakis scene on tape was featured along with information about the Democratic candidate's opposition to a long list of military programs and weapons systems.

Political ads take many forms. Short spots are interspersed with other commercials in regular programming. Longer advertisements that preempt part of the standard fare and full-length productions, such as interviews, documentaries, and campaign rallies, have also been employed. The primary benefits of the short spots are that they make a point, are cheaper to produce and air, and are usually viewed by a larger audience. Longer programs, which may go into greater detail about the candidate's career, qualifications, and beliefs, are generally seen by fewer people although Ross Perot's novel media campaign in 1992 attracted and maintained a sizable audience even though most of his programs lasted 30 minutes or even longer.

In addition to length, timing is also a critical consideration of campaign advertisers. For the candidate who appears to be ahead, the advertising should be scheduled at a steady rate over the course of the campaign to maintain the lead. Nixon in 1968 and 1972, Carter in 1976, and Clinton in 1992 followed this practice. Reagan in 1984 and Bush in 1988 and 1992 did not. Both decided to hold much of their advertising for the final weeks. In Bush's case in 1992, it was too late. By the time of his final advertising spurt to the finish line, the debates had ended, public opinion had solidified, and Bush could not catch up.

Most campaign advertising must be sequenced as well. At the outset it is necessary to identify the candidate with information about his family, experience, and qualifications for the office. Once the personal dimension is established, the position of the candidate can be articulated in the second stage. In this argumentative phase the themes are presented and policy positions noted. In the third stage, the candidate frequently goes on the offensive by running a series of ads in which the reasons not to vote for the opponent are stressed. Candidates who are behind may frequently use their earlier stages to go negative as well. Most candidates like to end their campaign on a positive note. In the final phase, "feel good" commercials are shown. Replete with catchy and upbeat jingles, smiling faces, happy families, and much Americana, they strive to make voters feel good about supporting the candidate.[42]

Images and Messages

The name of the game is image making. With the emphasis on leadership, three dimensions of presidential qualities are usually stressed: one has to do with character and persona; another with issue positions and basic values; and a third with essential leadership skills—vision, charisma, decisiveness, and the capacity for getting things done.

Positivity. Positive campaign advertisements emphasize the strengths of a candidate. For presidents seeking reelection, or even vice-presidents running for the top office, one of those strengths is clearly experience in high office. Their advertising pictures them in a variety of presidential roles. One of Jimmy Carter's most effective 1980 commercials showed him in a whirl of presidential activities ending as darkness fell over the White House. A voice intoned, "The responsibility never ends. Even at the end of a long working day there is usually another cable addressed to the Chief of State from the other side of the world where the sun is shining and something is happening." As a light came on in the president's living quarters, the voice concluded, "And he's not finished yet."[43] Ronald Reagan in 1984 and George Bush in 1992 used a variation of the president-at-work ad.

Comparisons are also important. Although all candidates must demonstrate their presidential qualities, they also need to distinguish themselves from their opponents. In 1976, Carter emphasized his unusual leadership abilities. His slogan, "A leader, for a change," as well as his less formal appearance and even his decision to use green as the color of his literature in contrast to the traditional red, white, and blue, conveyed how different he was from old-style Washington politicians and the two Republican presidents who preceded him. In 1980, Reagan stressed the different kinds of solutions to the nation's old and persistent policy problems as did Perot in 1992. Perot's ads of that campaign were among the most distinctive ever used in a presidential campaign. Their amateurish quality was purposely designed to set them apart from the slick, smooth, professional commercials of his Republican and Democratic opponents. It was precisely this contrast that Perot wished to convey to the American people.

Negativity. Ads that exploit an opponent's weaknesses by focusing on character deficiencies, issue inconsistencies, or false leadership claims are

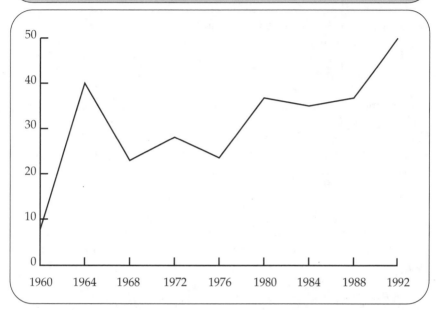

FIGURE 7–1
Percent of Negative Televised Presidential Advertisements,
1960–1992

Source: Lynda Lee Kaid and Anne Johnston, "Negative versus Positive Television Advertising in U.S. Presidential Campaigns, 1960–1988," *Journal of Communication* 41 (Summer
1991): 57; updated by the author from data provided in L. Patrick Devlin, "Contrasts in
Presidential Campaign Commercials of 1992," *American Behavioral Scientist*, 37 (November
1993): 288.

referred to as *confrontational, attack,* or *negative.* This type of advertising
has increased since the 1970s. (See Figure 7–1.)

Negative campaigning, of course, is nothing new. It is as old as presidential electoral politics. George Washington was called a philanderer
and a thief; Andrew Jackson was accused of marrying a prostitute; at the
outset of the Civil War, Abraham Lincoln was charged with being illegitimate and black; Theodore Roosevelt was said to be a drunkard, Herbert
Hoover a German sympathizer during World War I, and Franklin D. Roosevelt a lecher, lunatic, and a closet Jew whose real name was Rosenfeldt.

What seems to be different today is the increasing emphasis placed on
these negative ads by the candidates; the extent to which they seem
to have affected the tenor, agenda, and issues of the campaign; and the
widely held belief that they have had a major impact on the perceptions of
the electorate.

Instead of playing to a candidate's strengths, negative advertising
exploits the opposition's weaknesses, using ridicule and stereotyping to

drive the point home. As early as 1952 when political advertising first appeared on television, negative commercials were used to highlight potentially vulnerable positions and images of the opposition. One of the most famous (or infamous) of these early negative political spots was created by advertising executive Tony Schwartz in 1964 for use against Barry Goldwater. It was designed to reinforce the impression that Goldwater was a trigger-happy zealot who would not hesitate to unleash nuclear weapons against a communist foe. Pictured first was a little girl in a meadow plucking petals from a daisy. She counted to herself softly. When she reached nine, the picture froze on her face, her voice faded, and a stern-sounding male voice counted down from ten. When he got to zero there was an explosion, the little girl disappeared, and a mushroom-shaped cloud covered the screen. Lyndon Johnson's voice was heard: "These are the stakes—to make a world in which all of God's children can live, or go into the dark. We must either love each other, or we must die." The ad ended with an announcer saying, "Vote for President Johnson on November 3. The stakes are too high for you to stay home."

The commercial was run only once. Goldwater supporters were outraged and protested vigorously, but their protestations actually kept the issue alive. In fact, the ad itself became a news item, and parts of it were shown on television newscasts. The Democrats had made the point, and the news media helped reinforce it.

In the 1970s and 1980s, the Republican candidates also ran highly effective negative commercials.[44] One of the most successful of these commercials, "the people-in-the-street ad," features interviews with ordinary citizens who are asked about the candidates. The comments usually are edited to highlight a message. In Ford's 1976 ads, for example, most of people interviewed were from Carter's home state of Georgia. "He didn't do anything," stated one man from Atlanta. "I've tried, and all my friends have tried, to remember exactly what Carter did as governor, and nobody really knows." The commercial concluded with an attractive woman, also from Georgia, saying, in a thick southern accent, "It would be nice to have a President from Georgia—but not Carter." She smiled. The ad ended.[45]

Negative advertising has been used extensively in recent campaigns. In 1988, researchers estimated that anywhere from 40 to 60 percent of all the advertising broadcast was negative.[46] What distinguished the advertising in the 1988 campaign, however, was not its volume as much as the controversial nature of the ads themselves, which played on the fears and prejudices of the American people.

One ad in particular evoked a strong, emotional response. Directed against Michael Dukakis, it featured a mug shot of Willie Horton, an African American prisoner who had raped a white woman while on a weekend furlough from a Massachusetts jail. Aimed at those who were fearful of crime, of African Americans, and of liberals and their "do-good"

BOX 7–2

The Willie Horton Ad:
"Weekend Passes"

VIDEO	AUDIO
Side-by-side photographs	An announcer says, Bush and Dukakis on Crime,"
Photograph of Bush	"Bush supports the death penalty for first-degree murderers."
Photograph of Dukakis	"Dukakis not only opposes the death penalty, he allowed first degree murderers to have weekend passes from prison."
Mug shot of Willie Horton	"One was Willie Horton, who murdered a boy in a robbery, stabbing him nineteen times."

Photograph of convict being arrested.	"Despite a life sentence, Horton received ten weekend passes from prison. Horton fled, kidnapped a young couple, stabbing the man and repeatedly raping his girlfriend."
Photograph of Dukakis	"Weekend prison passes. Dukakis on crime."

Source: "A 30-Second Ad on Crime," *New York Times* (November 3, 1988) p. B 20.

social policies, the ad placed Dukakis squarely in the liberal, do-gooder camp. (See Box 7–2, "The Willie Horton Ad: 'Weekend Passes.'")

Sponsored by a political action committee supporting Bush, this commercial was supplemented by other PAC ads featuring relatives of the victims of Horton's crimes, including a man whose wife had been raped by Horton and a woman whose brother had been stabbed by him. More than $2 million was spent on speaking tours for these people who were personally touched by Horton's horrendous acts.[47] The Bush campaign also produced ads of its own to reinforce the crime issue.[48]

The cumulative impact of these crime ads was to leave the impression that Michael Dukakis released hardened criminals who then recommitted their heinous crimes on innocent victims. By the end of the campaign 25 percent of the electorate knew who Willie Horton was, what he did, and who furloughed him; 49 percent thought Dukakis was soft on crime.[49] The ads achieved their intended effect.

The amount of negative advertising increased in 1992. L. Patrick Devlin's analysis of candidate advertising in that election found that almost 70 percent of Clinton's ads were negative compared with 56 percent of Bush's. In all, Devlin reports that about half of the ads were negative.[50]

Voters, however, seemed more leery of the ads in 1992. Part of their skepticism stemmed from the legacy of 1988. Part of it also resulted from ad watching by major news organizations. Large newspapers, news services, and networks now regularly assign reporters to cover advertising and examine the accuracy of its claims. Political Scientist Darrell M. West reports a steady increase in this type of coverage.[51]

THE CUMULATIVE IMPACT OF MEDIA

The time, money, and energy spent on media by the candidates suggest that the mass media have a major impact on campaigns and elections. Why else would so many resources be devoted to them? Yet it is difficult to document their precise effect on voting behavior. That the public paid more attention to the 1992 campaign, knew more about the candidates in that election, and turned out in greater numbers than in previous years may be attributed in part to the use of the soft news format by the candidates, but there are undoubtedly other factors, such as the recession, the three candidates who were running, and their extensive campaign that contributed as well.

Much of the concern about the media focuses on news coverage. The negativism of the press, the tendency to highlight inconsistencies and misstatements, even the propensity to interpret rather than report events, has led many people, including candidates, to conclude that this coverage is biased, has adversely affected their campaigns, and unduly influences the results of the election. At some point during the 1992 presidential campaign each of the major candidates made such accusations.

Box 7–3
Advertising Strategies in 1992

The advertising strategies of the candidates differed significantly from one another in 1992. The distinctiveness of the Clinton effort was its timing and targeting. Aimed at local markets in key states, the Clinton ads first introduced the candidate in 60-second spots and then used 30-second commercials to address particular problems and the candidate's plans to deal with them.

In designing its ads, the Clinton media team made heavy use of focus groups to gage reaction to attacks on Clinton and his proposed responses to those attacks. The Clinton campaign was determined not to repeat the mistakes of the Dukakis campaign—allowing attacks to stand without an energetic and rapid reaction to them. So efficient was the Clinton team that they actually obtained some copies of Bush's ads or the scripts for those ads *before* they were actually broadcast. Howard Kurtz, media critic for the *Washington Post*, reported that one week before the election the Clinton campaign obtained the script for a Bush ad, designed and tested a response to it, and had it on the air within 24 hours of the Bush commercial![52]

Bush's media strategy was not nearly as well planned or executed as Clinton's. The initial goal of his media consultants was to present a series of testimonials about the president's accomplishments by leading personalities from the entertainment, business, and governmental communities. Internal staff disagreements about the testimonials, however, combined with the difficulty of obtaining permissions for them, impeded the effort and resulted in only a few of these ads being shown. As the convention neared, the focus changed from Bush's achievements to his conservative credentials. After the convention there was still another change of direction—this time to present the president's plan to end the recession, a plan he had articulated in a Detroit speech early in September. But instead of following this message with other ads reiterating an economic program, the media strategy shifted to attacks on Clinton's character and experience. In all, over 100 ads were produced for Bush, but many of them were never aired.

(continued)

Is the media, particularly the news media, really that powerful? Do they affect voter choice? The answer is probably yes although their impact may depend on the level of knowledge and strength of partisan attitudes of the electorate. For knowledgeable partisans, the primary media effect is to reinforce rather than challenge their inclinations to support their party's nominees. For those without strong partisan identities, and those who are marginally interested in the election, however, the media provide information; shape perceptions of the candidates, parties, and issues; and

Box 7–3 (*continued*)

Advertising Strategies in 1992

Attack and Response:
Bush and Clinton Ads in 1992

BUSH: TV SPOT HARSHLY DENOUNCES CLINTON'S RECORD

On the screen: Opens with gloomy black and white images of a rainy day, a deserted road, weeds rustling in the wind. Key phrases from the narration, and sources for the statistics, are superimposed over similarly depressing images. Closes with a tree and buzzard in the desert and these words, "America Can't Take That Risk."

Producer: The November Company.

Television script: Announcer: "In his 12 years as Governor, Bill Clinton has doubled his state's debt. Doubled government spending and signed the largest tax increase in his state's history. Yet his state remains the 45th worst in which to work. The 45th worst for children. It has the worst environmental policy.

"And the F.B.I. says Arkansas had America's biggest increase in rate of serious crime. And now Bill Clinton wants to do for America what he's done for Arkansas. America can't take that risk."

Accuracy: This ad is a case study in how accusations can be made and how facts can be used to bolster them or tear them down. The Bush campaign backs its accusations with statistics and cites its sources on screen. The Clinton campaign refutes every accusation with its own statistics.

For example, while it is true that Arkansas doubled government spending, most of that growth came from inflation. The Clinton campaign has also cited figures from the National Governors' Association showing that all but six states have doubled general spending since Mr. Clinton took office.

Scorecard: This ad takes facts out of context to paint Mr. Clinton as a governor who brought only misery to Arkansas. In reality, Mr. Clinton has been considered a better than average governor of a small, poor state. It tries to scare viewers into thinking that a Clinton administration would bring only gloom and doom to the whole country. In 30 seconds, the ad tries to hit Mr. Clinton on the hot-button issues of the environment, children, crime and taxes—all issues that Mr. Bush has been attacked on.

Source: Richard I. Berke, "Bush: TV Spot Harshly Denounces Clinton's Record," *New York Times* (October 30, 1992), p. A 19. Copyright ©1992 by The New York Times Company. Reprinted by permission.

CLINTON: ISSUING A QUICK RESPONSE

Less than a day after the Bush campaign began broadcasting its commercial attacking Arkansas, the Clinton campaign produced this 30-second response, for broadcast in select markets . . .

On the screen: Phrases appear that underscore the narration, like "Bush ads are misleading and wrong," and "Arkansas leads the nation in job growth." Beneath the words, in smaller type, appear sources for the phrases, like CBS, Bureau of Labor Statistics. Interspersed with the words are photographs of Gov. Bill Clinton at work in the Governor's office.

Producer: Clinton/Gore Creative Team.

Television script: Announcer: "CBS, CNN and newspapers across the country call George Bush's ads misleading and wrong. The fact is, under Bill Clinton's leadership Arkansas leads the nation in job growth, has the second-lowest tax burden and the lowest Government spending in the country.

"And he's balanced 12 budgets. They reduced infant mortality, and now have the highest graduation rate in the region. And in the past year, Arkansas's crime rate went down.

"No wonder *The Washington Post* says George Bush is lying about Bill Clinton's record, and why *The Oregonian* concluded, 'Frankly, we no longer trust George Bush.'"

Accuracy: While the Bush ad makers selectively used figures to attack Mr. Clinton's record, this ad selectively uses figures to build up his record and makes assertions out of context. The Clinton ad says Arkansas leads the nation in job growth, but the Bush campaign cites figures showing that has been true for only the last three months. While Mr. Clinton balanced 12 budgets, he was required to by state law.

The ad uses many citations to lend it credibility but sometimes goes overboard. It was not the institution of *The Washington Post* that said Mr. Bush was lying, but Judy Mann, a local columnist.

Scoreboard: This ad inundates viewers with documentation to try to lessen the impact of one of the Bush campaign's harshest attacks. The ad also tries to portray Mr. Clinton as a successful Governor and the President as a man who cannot be trusted.

Source: Richard L. Berke, "Clinton: Issuing a Quick Response," *New York Times* (October 30, 1992), p. A 19. Copyright 1992 by The New York Times Company. Reprinted by permission.

(continued)

Box 7–3 *(continued)*

Advertising Strategies in 1992

Perot's advertising was substantively different from both Bush's and Clinton's. His commercials were longer, less gimmicky, and shown in a more compressed time period, mostly in the last month of the campaign. Many of the ads featured Perot himself talking to the American people and illustrating his talk with computer-designed but simply staged graphics.

When Perot got back into the race and had high "negatives," his first group of ads, relatively short in length (60 seconds), emphasized the nation's economic problems. Most of them had a similar format, using a scroll technique in which the announcer assessed the issue and its consequences in words that also appeared on the screen. Although Perot did not appear in these, it was clear what the message was and who it was from.

Later in the campaign, Perot himself was featured. Long biographical ads, some lasting an hour, were produced to introduce the candidate to the voters. Designed to offset negative impressions about Perot when he dropped out of the race in July, these ads presented his human dimension and stressed his successful business career.

The third stage of Perot's advertising consisted of his so-called *infomercials*, half-hour media presentations on the economy, the deficit, trade imbalances, and America's declining competitiveness in world markets. Essentially unscripted, these ads were intended to demonstrate Perot's credibility and individuality. Large audiences tuned in despite the length of these programs and the absence of many pictures and action.[53]

may motivate people to vote. In general, the media are apt to be more influential during the preconvention period, when less is known about the candidates and when partisan affiliation is not a factor.

With the decline of strong partisanship in the electorate and the increase in the number of independents, the audience that may be affected during the general election has become larger and is potentially more malleable for a longer period. This is why candidates spend so much time, money, and effort to develop and execute media strategies from affecting the hard news coverage their receive, to utilizing soft news opportunities, to participating in campaign events such as debates, and to mounting effective advertising campaigns of their own. The mass media has become the primary conduit through which campaigns reach the voters and from which voters gain most of the information they need for making a judgment on election day.

SUMMARY

The mass media has a profound effect on presidential politics: on the organization, strategy, and tactics of the campaign; on the distribution of resources; and directly or indirectly on the electorate's voting decisions. That is why so much of presidential campaign is devoted to media-related activities.

First and foremost, candidates try to affect their news coverage. That coverage is not necessarily favorable. Candidates are often portrayed critically, their statements viewed with suspicion, and their strategies seen as manipulative.

The news media see and report the campaign as a game, fitting statements, events, and activities into various story lines. Their schema highlights drama and gives controversial statements and events the most attention but also downplays deep discussions of policy issues. They also play up personalities and give disproportionate attention to major blunders and conflicts.

Candidates naturally try to improve on this coverage. They orchestrate their campaigns for the news media. They choose their words carefully, minimize spontaneity, include sound bites into their speeches, create good visual images, and do all they can to prevent embarrassing situations from occurring. But even with all this preparation, the news of their campaign may not be sufficient, particularly in its initial phases, and from the candidates' perspective, it is never good enough.

For this reason candidates also try to circumvent the national news media to reach the voters directly. People like to be entertained, so candidates have resorted to various entertainment formats to convey a message, project an image, and energize their supporters. In the past, parades, rallies, and other campaign events were the principal vehicles by which these objectives were achieved. Today, radio and television talk/entertainment shows, town meetings, and presidential debates are the most frequently used devices to gain and maintain attention from a sizable segment of the population.

The soft news/entertainment programs have been particularly amenable to a conversational dialogue with the electorate, a dialogue that may itself become a news event. Within this less hostile format, candidates can be more expansive, seemingly more responsive, and better able to display positive attributes of themselves.

Town meetings are also useful in this respect. They have the additional advantage of allowing candidates to interact directly with the audience, to demonstrate their understanding of their problems and empathy for those who suffer from them, and to present their solutions on a level that the average person can understand and appreciate.

Debates constitute still another entertaining, educational opportunity, particularly for candidates who need to enhance their public recognition and personal images. Not only do debates permit candidates to present their positions on contemporary issues in their own words and often to a large audience, but they facilitate comparisons with their opponents. The news media play a role here as well, covering the debates and often participating in them, reporting the public's reaction as well as their own evaluation, and then integrating the debate into the ongoing campaign story.

Paid advertising is a fourth device, one which candidates have used extensively to sell themselves to the voters. The techniques that they employ, the strategy and tactics they use, even the people who develop and target the ads come from the advertising profession.

In recent presidential campaigns, at least fifty percent of a candidate's campaign budget is spent on media, primarily on the production, airing, and targeting of advertising. Although political commercials tap both positive and negative leadership dimensions, an increasing proportion of the ads have been negative. This negativity has produced some backlash within an electorate that has become increasingly leery about the claims of the ads and cynical about the merits of the candidates. News organizations have contributed to voters' skepticism by treating ads as campaign news and critically assessing their accuracy.

Most communications analysts believe that media campaigns have an impact. At the very least, they inform the electorate. They may energize supporters. They can affect perceptions of the candidates, parties, and issues, which in turn can influence vote choice. For strong partisans, the cumulative impact of the media is to reinforce predispositions and existing political attitudes; for weaker partisans and independents, however, the impact can also be to alter opinions although one election campaign does not usually change partisan attitudes on a permanent basis.

The proportion of the electorate that is actually influenced in their voting choice by hard and soft news coverage, presidential debates, and candidate advertising is difficult to assess with any certainty. But campaign managers take no chances. In a close election, influencing even a small number of voters can change the outcome. And from the candidates' and their managers' perspectives, that outcome is what the presidential election is all about.

NOTES

1. The term *yellow journalism* comes from the comic strip,"The Yellow Kid," which first appeared in Joseph Pulitzer's *New York World* in 1896. The kid, whose nightshirt was colored yellow in the paper, was an instantaneous hit and sparked a bidding war for the comic strip between Pulitzer and William Randolph Hearst. Although the strip's popularity lasted only a few years, the competition between these two media titans continued for decades.
2. David Stebenne, "Media Coverage of American Presidential Elections: A Historical Perspective," in *The Finish Line: Covering the Campaign's Final Days* ed.

Martha FitzSimon (New York: The Freedom Forum Media Studies Center, 1993), p. 83.

3. Thomas E. Patterson, *Out of Order* (New York: Alfred A. Knopf, 1993), pp. 53–133.
4. Thomas E. Patterson, "Television and Election Strategy," in *The Communications Revolution in Politics,* ed. Gerald Benjamin (New York: Academy of Political Science, 1982), p. 30.
5. Michael J. Robinson and Margaret A. Sheehan, *Over the Wire and on TV: CBS and UPI in Campaign '80* (New York: Russell Sage Foundation, 1983), p. 148.
6. Ibid., p. 146.
7. Thomas E. Patterson and Richard Davis, "The Media Campaign: Struggle for the Agenda," in *The Elections of 1984,* ed. Michael Nelson (Washington, D.C.: Congressional Quarterly, 1985), p. 119.
8. "Clinton's the One," *Media Monitor* (November 1992): 2.
9. Ibid.
10. Not only do the news media focus more on the candidates than their policies, but they focus primarily on the major party candidates. When running for their party's nomination, candidates receive coverage roughly in proportion to their popular standing, with the front-runners getting the most. After the conventions are over, it becomes primarily a two-person contest. Minor party and independent candidates tend to receive little, if any, attention, the exceptions being John Anderson in 1980 and Ross Perot in 1992.
11. James Glen Stovall, "Incumbency and News Coverage of the 1980 Presidential Campaign," *Western Political Quarterly* 37 (December 1984): 628.
12. Although partisan sources were equally harsh on the candidates of the other major party, they were not as harsh on Perot, reflecting, perhaps the Republican and Democratic strategies not to criticize him in public. Nonpartisan sources, people who might be considered experts or just plain voters, were more positive about Clinton than Bush. Among both partisan and nonpartisan sources, Perot received the best press. "Clinton's the One," pp. 3–4.
13. Kiku Adatto, "The Incredible Shrinking Sound Bite," *New Republic* (May 28, 1990): 22.
14. Quoted in David R. Runkel, ed. *Campaign for President: The Managers Look at '88.* (Dover, Mass.: Auburn House, 1989), p. 136.
15. Quoted in Adatto, "Sound Bite," p. 22.
16. "Clinton's the One," p. 2.
17. Thomas E. Patterson, *Out of Order,* p. 106.
18. Ibid., pp. 119–120.
19. Ibid., p. 121.
20. Ibid., pp. 118–119.
21. Paul Lazarsfeld, Bernard Berelson, and Hazel Goudet, *The People's Choice* (New York: Columbia University Press, 1948); Bernard Berelson, Paul Lazarsfeld, and William McPhee, *Voting: A Study of Opinion Formation in a Presidential Campaign* (Chicago: University of Chicago Press, 1954).
22. Harold W. Stanley and Richard G. Niemi, *Vital Statistics on American Politics* (Washington, D.C.: Congressional Quarterly, 1994), pp. 72–74.
23. Michael J. Robinson, "Mass Media and the Margins of Democratic Politics: Non-Transformations in the USA," (Unpublished Paper, March 1993), pp. 81–83.
24. Edwin Diamond, Martha McKay, and Robert Silverman, "Pop Goes Politics," *American Behavioral Scientist,* 37 (November 1993): 258.

25. Robert V. Friedenberg, "The 1992 Presidential Debates, " in *The 1992 Presidential Campaign: A Communication Perspective*, ed. Robert E. Denton, Jr. (Westport, Conn.: Praeger, 1994), p. 90.

26. Peter Goldman, Thomas M. DeFrank, Mary Miller, et al., *Quest for the Presidency: 1992* (College Station, Texas: Texas A & M Press, 1994), p. 535.

27. In 1992, however, one network, CBS, decided to air an American League championship baseball game rather than the first presidential debate. It carried the other debates.

28. Elihu Katz and Jacob J. Feldman, "The Debates in the Light of Research: A Survey of Surveys," in *The Great Debates*, ed. Sidney Kraus (Bloomington, Ind.: Indiana University Press, 1962), p. 190.

29. John Carmody, "Glued to the Debates," *Washington Post* (October 17, 1992), pp. D1, 3; ———," The TV Column: 91 million Viewers Flock to Final Debate," *Washington Post* (October 21, 1992), pp. B 1, 6.

30. Part of the issue was who should ask the questions, journalists, average citizens, or both; a second point of contention was whether the debate should have a single moderator or be in a "meet-the-press" format. Bush preferred a panel of journalists like he had encountered in previous debates; Clinton wanted a town meeting and a single moderator. The compromise was to have both: a panel, a town meeting, and a single-journalist–panel combination.

31. In 1980, this elaborate preparation took a bizarre twist. The Reagan campaign obtained one of Carter's three debate briefing books. The book contained key lines, Reagan quotes, and pat answers. Knowing the quotes Carter would use, the questions he anticipated, and the answers he was advised to give helped Reagan's strategists prepare their responses to use in rebuttal.

32. Goldman, et al., *Quest for the Presidency: 1992*, pp. 555–556.

33. Ibid., pp. 560–562.

34. Nixon had closeted himself alone in a hotel before his first debate with Kennedy. He received only a ten-minute briefing.

35. Theodore H. White, *The Making of the President, 1960* (New York:Atheneum, 1988), p. 285; Peter Goldman, et. al. *Quest for the Presidency: The 1988 Campaign* (New York: Simon and Schuster, 1989), p. 387; Goldman, et al., *Quest for the Presidency: 1992*, pp. 557–558.

36. Quoted in the *New York Times*, "Transcript of the Presidential Debate" (October 14, 1988), p. A 14.

37. Quoted in "Campaign '92: Transcript of the First Presidential Debate," *New York Times* (October 12, 1992), p. A 16.

38. Quoted in *Campaign for President: The Managers Look at '92*, ed. Charles T. Royer (Hollis, N.H.: Hollis Publishing Co., 1994), p. 250.

39. Surveys taken at the conclusion of the debate indicated that a majority of people believed Ford had won. After the media played up the Eastern Europe comment and the public had a chance to digest it, the reaction was almost the opposite. By more than two to one Carter was perceived to be the winner.

40. Quoted in Royer, *Campaign for President*, p. 265.

41. L. Patrick Devlin, "Contrasts in Presidential Campaign Commercials of 1992," *American Behavioral Scientist*, 37 (November 1993): 272–273.

42. Edwin Diamond and Stephen Bates, "The Ads," *Public Opinion* 8 (December 1984/January 1985): 55–57, 64.

43. Another objective of this particular presidential advertisement was to contrast the younger, more vigorous president with his older, less energetic opponent, who, it was alleged, was not accustomed to working long hours.

44. One 1972 ad showed a profile of Democrat George McGovern, with an announcer stating a position that McGovern had taken and later changed. When the change in position was explained, another profile of McGovern, but one looking in the opposite direction, was flashed on the screen. This tactic of position change and profile rotation was repeated several times. Finally, when the announcer asked, "What about next year?" McGovern's face spun rapidly before viewers.

    These ads, however, did not appear to have much of an independent effect on the voters. Perceptions of McGovern were negative even before the ads were aired. Thus, the ads seemed to reenforce these perceptions not change or alter them.
45. People-in-the-street ads seem almost like news stories. That the people interviewed are not actors gives the ads credibility. Today, most candidates employ some variation of the ordinary people interviews in their advertisements.
46. Lynda Lee Kaid and Anne Johnston, "Negative versus Positive Television Advertising in U.S. Presidential Campaigns, 1960–1988," *Journal of Communications* 41 (Summer 1991): 54.
47. M. Hailey, "Crime Victims Condemn Dukakis," *Austin-American Statesman* (October 11, 1988), p. B 3.
48. The most potent of these Bush ads, called "Revolving Door," saw inmates walking through a revolving door of a prison with the announcer warning:

    As governor, Michael Dukakis vetoed mandatory sentences for drug dealers. He vetoed the death penalty. His revolving-door policy gave weekend furloughs to first-degree murderers not eligible for parole. While out, many committed other crimes like kidnapping and rape. And many are still at large. Now Michael Dukakis says he wants to do for America what he's done for Massachusetts. America can't afford that risk!

    L. Patrick Devlin, "Contrasts in Presidential Campaign Commercials of 1988," *American Behavioral Scientist* 32 (March/April 1989): 389.
49. Edwin Diamond and Adrian Marin, "Spots," *American Behavioral Scientist* 32 (March/April 1989): 386.
50. Devlin, "Contrasts in Presidential Campaign Commercials of 1992,"p. 288.
51. Darrell M. West, "Television Advertising in Election Campaigns," *Political Science Quarterly* 109 (Winter 1994–1995): 789–809.
52. Howard Kurtz, "In Advertising Give and Take, Clinton Camp Took and Responded," *Washington Post* (November 6, 1992), p. A 10.
53. His first infomercial received a Nielson rating of 12.2 which indicates that almost 12 million people watched at least part of the program.

SELECTED READINGS

Adatto, Kiku. "The Incredible Shrinking Sound Bite." *New Republic* (May 28, 1990): 20–33.

Crouse, Timothy. *The Boys on the Bus: Riding with the Campaign Press Corps.* New York: Random House, 1973.

Dennis, Jack and Diana Owen, "Perot and the Media." Paper presented at the annual meeting of the Midwest Political Science Association, Chicago, Ill., April 14–16, 1994.

Denton, Robert E. Jr., ed. *The 1992 Presidential Campaign: A Communication Perspective.* Westport, Conn.: Praeger, 1994.

Devlin, L. Patrick. "Contrasts in Presidential Campaign Commercials of 1992." *American Behavioral Scientist* 37 (November 1993): 272–290.

Diamond, Edwin and Stephen Bates. *The Spot,* 3rd ed. Cambridge, Mass.: MIT Press, 1992.

Friedenberg, Robert V., ed. *Rhetorical Studies of National Political Debates, 1960–1992,* 2nd ed. Westport, Conn.: Praeger, 1994.

Iyengar, Shanto and Donald Kinder. *News That Matters: Television and American Opinion.* Chicago: University of Chicago Press, 1987.

Jamieson, Kathleen Hall. *Packaging the Presidency: A History and Criticism of Presidential Campaign Advertising.* Oxford: Oxford University Press, 1992.

———. *Dirty Politics: Deception, Distraction, Democracy.* Oxford: Oxford University Press, 1992.

——— and David S. Birdsell. *Presidential Debates.* New York: Oxford University Press, 1988.

Kaid, Lynda Lee and Anne Johnston, "Negative versus Positive Television Advertising in U.S. Presidential Campaigns, 1960–1988," *Journal of Communications* 41 (Summer 1991): 53–64.

Lichter, S. Robert, Daniel Amundson, and Richard Noyes. *The Video Campaign: Network Coverage of the 1988 Primaries.* Washington, D.C.: American Enterprise Institute, 1988.

Owen, Diana. *Media Messages in American Presidential Elections.* New York: Greenwood Press, 1991.

Page, Benjamin I. *Choices and Echoes in Presidential Elections.* Chicago: University of Chicago Press, 1978.

Patterson, Thomas E. *Out of Order.* New York: Alfred A. Knopf, 1993.

Robinson, Michael J., and Margaret A. Sheehan. *Over the Wire and on TV: CBS and UPI in Campaign '80.* New York: Russell Sage Foundation, 1983.

Schudson, Michael. *Discovering the News.* New York: Basic Books, 1978.

PART IV

The Election

Celebrated cartoonist Thomas Nast created the symbol of the Democratic party—the donkey—in 1870. Nast also was the first to draw the elephant, which represented the Republican party, in 1874.

Chapter 8

The Vote and Its Meaning

INTRODUCTION

Predicting the results of an election is a favorite American practice. Politicians do it; the news media do it; even the public tries to anticipate the outcome far in advance of the event. It is a form of entertainment—somewhat akin to forecasting the winner of a sporting event.

Presidential elections are particularly prone to such predictions. National surveys report on the opinions of the American public at frequent intervals during the campaign. On election night television news commentators project a winner before most of the votes are counted. Election day surveys of voters exiting from the polls assess the mood of the electorate and present the first systematic analysis of the results. Subsequently, more in-depth studies reveal shifts in opinions and attitudes.

Most predictions and analyses of the electorate based on survey data are not conducted solely for their entertainment or news value, although many are. They also provide important information to candidates running for office and to those who have been elected. For the nominees, surveys of public opinion indicate the issues that can be effectively raised and those that should be avoided. They also suggest which audience might be most receptive to specific policy positions. For the successful candidates, analyses of voter preferences, opinions, and attitudes provide an interpretation of the vote, indicate the range and depth of public concern on the key issues, and signal the amount of support newly elected presidents are likely to receive as they begin their administration.

This chapter examines the presidential vote from three perspectives.

The first section deals with snapshots of the public at different points during the campaign. It discusses national polls, describes their methodology, and evaluates their effect. The news media's election eve predictions and analyses are also described.

The next section turns to an examination of the vote itself. After alluding to the election day surveys, it reports on the National Election Studies, which have been conducted since 1952. These studies, which are surveys of the national electorate, provide the basic data that scholars have used to analyze elections and understand voting behavior. The principal findings of these analyses are summarized for each presidential election since 1952.

The final section of the chapter discusses the relationship between campaigning and governing, between issue debates and public policy making, between candidate evaluations and presidential style. Do the campaign issues determine the form of agenda building? Does the projected or perceived image of the candidates affect the tone of the presidency or the actions of the one who is elected? Can an electoral coalition be converted into a governing party? Does the selection process help or hinder the president in meeting the expectations it creates? These questions are explored in an effort to determine the impact of the election on the operation of the presidency, the behavior of the president, and the functioning of the political system.

PREDICTING PRESIDENTIAL ELECTIONS

Public Opinion Polls

The most popular question during a campaign is, who is going to win? The public is naturally interested in the answer, and the news media and candidates are obsessed with it, although for different reasons. In focusing on the campaigns, the news media feel compelled to report who is ahead, how the candidates are perceived, and what issues are dividing the voters. In forging a winning coalition, candidates and their organizations need to know how the electorate is reacting to them and their issue positions. Waiting for this information until after the election is obviously too late.

Many of these data can be obtained from surveys of the population. Since 1916 there have been nationwide assessments of public opinion during elections. The largest and most comprehensive of the early surveys were the straw polls conducted by the *Literary Digest*, a popular monthly magazine. The *Digest* mailed millions of ballots and questionnaires to people who appeared on lists of automobile owners and in telephone directories. In 1924, 1928, and 1932, the poll correctly predicted the winner of the presidential election. In 1936, it did not: a huge Alfred Landon victory was forecast, and a huge Franklin Roosevelt victory occurred.

What went wrong? The *Digest* mailed 10 million questionnaires over the course of the campaign and received 2 million back. As the ballots were returned, they were tabulated. This procedure, which provided a running count, blurred shifts in public opinion that may have been occurring over the course of the campaign. But that was not its major problem. The principal difficulty of the *Digest*'s survey was that the sample of people who responded were not representative of the voting public. Automobile owners and telephone subscribers were simply not typical voters in 1936, since most people did not own cars or have telephones. This distinction mattered more in 1936 than it had in previous years, because of the Great Depression. There was a socioeconomic cleavage within the electorate. The *Literary Digest* sample did not reflect this cleavage; thus its results were inaccurate.[1]

While the *Digest* was tabulating its 2 million responses and predicting that Landon would be the next president, a number of other pollsters were conducting more scientific surveys and correctly forecasting Roosevelt's reelection.[2] The polls of George Gallup, Elmo Roper, and Archibald Crossley differed from the *Digest*'s in two principal respects: they were considerably smaller, and their samples approximated the characteristics of the population as a whole, permitting more accurate generalizations of public opinion to be made.

The *Digest* went out of business, but Gallup, Roper, and Crossley continued to poll and to improve their sampling techniques. In 1940, Gallup predicted Roosevelt would receive 52 percent of the vote; he actually received 55 percent. In 1944, Gallup forecast a 51.5 percent Roosevelt vote, very close to his actual 53.2 percent. Other pollsters also made predictions that closely approximated the results. As a consequence, public confidence in election polling began to grow.

The confidence was short-lived, however. In 1948, all major pollsters forecast a victory by Republican Thomas Dewey. Their errors resulted from poor sampling techniques, from the premature termination of polling before the end of the campaign, and from incorrect assumptions about how the undecided would vote.

In attempting to estimate the population in their samples, the pollsters had resorted to filling quotas. They interviewed a certain number of people with different demographic characteristics until the percentage of these groups in the sample resembled that percentage in the population as a whole. Simply because the percentages were approximately equal, however, did not mean that the sample was representative of the population. For example, interviewers avoided certain areas in cities, and their results were consequently biased.

Moreover, the interviewing stopped several weeks before the election. In mid-October, the polls showed that Dewey was ahead by a substantial margin. Burns Roper, son of Elmo Roper, polling for *Fortune* magazine, saw the lead as sufficiently large to predict a Dewey victory without the need for further surveys. A relatively large number of people, however, were undecided. Three weeks before the election, Gallup concluded that 8 percent of the voters had still not made up their minds. In estimating the final vote, he and other pollsters assumed that the undecided would divide their votes in much the same manner as the electorate as a whole. This assumption turned out to be incorrect. Most of those who were wavering in the closing days of the campaign were Democrats. In the end, most voted for Truman or did not vote at all.

The results of the 1948 election once again cast doubt on the accuracy of public opinion polls. Truman's victory also reemphasized the fact that surveys reflect opinion at the time they are taken, not necessarily days or weeks later. Opinion and voter preferences may change.

To improve the monitoring of shifts within the electorate, pollsters changed their method of selecting people to be interviewed. They developed more effective means of anticipating who would actually vote.[3] They polled continuously to identify more precisely and quickly any shifts that occurred in public sentiment and reactions to campaign events. They also extended their surveys to the day before the election to get as close to the time people actually voted as they could. These changes, plus the continued refinement of the questions, have produced more accurate forecasts.

Between 1936 and 1950, the average error of the final Gallup Poll was 3.6 percent; between 1952 and 1992, it fell to 1.6 percent.[4] (See Table 8–1)

Very close elections in 1960, 1968, and 1976, however, resulted in several pollsters making wrong predictions. In 1980, the size of Reagan's victory was substantially underestimated in some nationwide polls, whereas in 1992, Clinton's margin was overestimated by some pollsters who failed to allocate properly the undecided vote among the three candidates.[5]

Some of the problems in 1980 were similar to those in 1948. Polling stopped too early. With partisan ties weakening, voting behavior has in recent years become more volatile. The electorate tends to make up its mind later in the campaign and seems more susceptible to influence by candidates, issues, and events. In 1980, there were a large number of undecided voters. The CBS News/*New York Times* Poll estimated that approximately 20 percent of the electorate made up its mind in the final week of the campaign; many voters did so on the final day. Since most of the public polls were completed four days before the election, they did not detect the large surge for Reagan.

The problem in 1992 stemmed from Perot's candidacy and the difficulty anticipating his vote based on the experience of other third and independent party candidates. Not only did Perot gain support *from* the major party candidates, but his campaign brought out a large number of first-time voters whose turnout was difficult to predict.

There were relatively large numbers of late-deciders in 1992; much more than usual. Typically, most voters decide before the final week. In

TABLE 8–1

Final Preelection Polls and Results, 1948–1992
(in percentages)

Year/Candidates	Gallup Poll	Roper (1948–1976) CBS/*NYT* Polls (1988 and 1992)	Harris Poll	Actual Results*
1948				
Truman	44.5	37.1		49.6
Dewey	49.5	52.2		45.1
Others	6.0	4.3		5.3
1952				
Eisenhower	51.0			55.1
Stevenson	49.0			44.4
1956				
Eisenhower	59.5	60.0		57.4
Stevenson	49.0	38.0		42.0
1960				
Kennedy	51.0	49.0		49.7
Nixon	49.0	51.0		49.5
1964				
Johnson	64.0		64.0	61.1
Goldwater	36.0		36.0	38.5
1968				
Nixon	43.0		41.0	43.4
Humphrey	42.0		45.0	42.7
Wallace	15.0		14.0	13.4
1972				
Nixon	62.0		61.0	60.7
McGovern	38.0		39.0	37.5
1976				
Carter	48.0	51.0	46.0	50.1
Ford	49.0	47.0	45.0	48.0
Others	3.0	2.0	3.0	1.9
Undecided			6.0	
1980				
Reagan	47.0		46.0	50.7
Carter	44.0		41.0	41.0
Anderson	8.0		10.0	6.6
Others				1.7
Undecided	1.0		3.0	
1984				
Reagan	59.0		56.0	59.0
Mondale	41.0		44.0	41.0
Others/Undecided			2.0	
1988				
Bush	53.0	48.0	51.0	53.4
Dukakis	42.0	40.0	47.0	45.6
Others/Undecided	5.0	12.0	2.0	1.0
1992				
Clinton	44.0	44.0	44.0	43.0
Bush	37.0	35.0	38.0	37.5
Perot	14.0	15.0	17.0	18.9
Others/Undecided	5.0	6.0	1.0	1.6

* Prior to 1976 (with the exception of 1948) the percentage of undecided voters in polls and votes for minor candidates is not noted.

Source: Final Gallup poll, "Record of Gallup Poll Accuracy," *Gallup Opinion Index* (December 1992).

fact, in a normal election, one-half to two-thirds of the electorate make their decision before or during the national nominating conventions. As a result, the polls conducted in September are likely to be close to the final election results. In "trial heats" conducted by the Gallup organization the candidate who was ahead in early September won in ten of twelve elections since 1948, and the person ahead at the end of September won eleven of twelve times, Truman being the only exception.[6]

The election of 1992 was different. There was more volatility among voters and more late-deciders. The National Election Studies found that 47 percent of the electorate determined how they would vote after the conventions, whereas a survey conducted by Fred Steeper for the Republican National Committee indicated that 12 percent decided a few days before the election and another 12 percent on election day itself.[7] Accurate forecasts under these circumstances are more difficult to make. (See Box 8–1, "Why Polls Tend to Be Accurate" and Box 8–2, "How Polls Are Conducted.")

Television Forecasts

Forecasts continue right to the end, until all the votes are tabulated. The final projections are presented by the major television networks during the night of the election. In broadcasting the results the news media have three objectives: to report the vote, to forecast the winners, and to analyze the returns.

Beginning in the 1980s, the major networks and news services established a consortium to pool their resources in reporting the vote count. Known as the News Election Service (NES), this consortium assigns thousands of people to precincts and county election boards around the country to communicate the presidential, congressional, and gubernatorial vote as soon as it is tallied. The results are telephoned to a center, which feeds them into a central computer. Each of the networks (ABC, CBS, NBC, and CNN) and news services (Associated Press and United Press International) that participate in the consortium have terminals indicating how the vote is progressing.

If all the news media wished to do were report the results, this would suffice. They wish to do more, however. They want to analyze the vote and explain its meaning. To do so they depend on a large exit poll in which thousands of people are surveyed after they have voted.

Here's how exit polls work. A large number of precincts across the country are randomly selected. The random selection is made within states in such a way that principal geographic units (cities, suburbs, and rural areas), size of precincts, and their past vote are taken into account. Representatives of the polling organization administer the poll to voters who are chosen in a systematic way (for example, every fourth or fifth person) as they leave the voting booths. Voters are asked to complete a

Box 8–1

Why Polls Tend to Be Accurate

The main reason polls have become increasingly accurate is the improvement in sampling procedures. Since the objective of surveying is to generalize from a small number, it is essential that the people interviewed be representative of the population. The odds of the sample's being representative can be estimated when it is randomly selected.

Random selection does not mean haphazard choice. Rather, it means that every element in the population (in this case, the eligible electorate) has a known and usually equal chance of being included in the sample, and the choice of any one element is independent of the choice of any other. The *Literary Digest* sample of 1936 and the quota sample of 1948 were not random. There was no way to determine whether the people interviewed were typical. As it turned out, they were not—at least not of those who voted on election day.

Random selection is thus the key to sampling. There are several ways of conducting it. One technique is to conduct a *stratified cluster random sample*. In such a sample, the population is divided into geographic units and then grouped (stratified) on the basis of the size of communities. Within each stratum, smaller and smaller units are then randomly selected until a block in a city or part of a township is isolated. Then, a number of interviews are conducted according to a carefully prescribed procedure at each of these sampling points. Interviewers have no choice whom they interview or where they conduct the interviews. In 1992 the Gallup organization randomly selected three hundred fifty sampling points and held about five interviews at each.

Since sampling is based on probability theory, the likelihood of being right or wrong can be calculated. In a random sample the odds of being right are determined primarily by the size of the sample. The larger the sample, the more likely it is to be accurate, and the more confidence can be placed in the results. For national surveys, a sample of approximately eleven hundred yields an error of plus or minus 3 percent in 95 percent of the polls conducted. In other words, the population as a whole will not differ by more than 3 percent in either direction from the results of the sample, 95 percent of the time.

The way to improve the accuracy of a sample is to enlarge it.

short questionnaire (thirty to forty items) that is designed to elicit information on voting choices, political attitudes, candidate evaluations and feelings, as well as demographic characteristics of those who voted. Several times over the course of the day, the questionnaires are collected, tabulated, and their results telephoned to a central computer bank. After

---

Box 8–2

How Polls Are Conducted

The typical media poll is conducted on the telephone. Numbers are randomly selected, are dialed, and random selection is also used to determine the voter in the household to be interviewed. The average length of such an interview is fifteen to twenty minutes, during which voters are asked to evaluate the candidates, the issues, the parties, and frequently, the campaign itself. Information on the demography of the voter (race, age, sex, religion, education, and income) is also solicited. These demographic data can be weighted to reflect the population in the country as a whole.

Interviews are conducted over a one- to three-day period. The number of respondents vary. The total surveyed range anywhere from six hundred to twenty-four hundred. The larger samples, although more costly, are also more accurate. They have the added benefit of allowing analysts to break down the sample into smaller demographic groupings for the purposes of analyzing the vote. However, enlarging it adds to its cost. At some point a law of diminishing returns sets in. For example, to increase the accuracy of a nationwide sample to plus or minus 2 percent, a total of approximately twenty-four hundred randomly selected respondents is needed, as opposed to about ninety-six hundred for plus or minus 1 percent and six hundred for plus or minus 4 percent.

The accuracy of a poll in measuring public opinion is also affected by the questionnaire and the relationship between the interviewer and the respondent. A survey is only as good as its questions: how they are worded and what order they are in. If they suggest a particular answer, then they force opinion, rather than reflect it.

---

most or all of the election polls in a state have been completed, the findings of the exit poll are broadcast.

The exit poll is usually very accurate. Because it is conducted over the course of the day, there is little time bias that would under- or overrepresent certain types of voters. Moreover, the large number of voters sampled reduces the error to much less than that of the national surveys conducted by national polling organizations such as the Gallup Poll. In addition, the exit poll provides a sample of sufficient size to enable analysts to discern the attitudes, opinions, and choices of smaller groups and subgroups (such as Jews, African-American males, and unmarried, college-educated women) within the electorate. In 1992, 15,490 people leaving 300 polling places around the country participated in the survey. (See Table 8–2.)[8]

The focus of the questions is normally dictated by the objectives of the study. Public polls, such as those conducted by independent research organizations like Gallup and Harris and syndicated to newspapers and magazines, usually focus on who is ahead and how different groups of people feel about the candidate. "If the election were held today, for whom would you vote?" is the key question.

In addition to random selection and sample size, the likelihood of those interviewed actually voting must also be considered. Pollsters regularly ask respondents a series of questions to differentiate potential voters from nonvoters. Those whose answers suggest that they probably will not vote are eliminated or separated from the others when analyzing the results.

Finally, pollsters and candidates alike are interested in the currency of their polls. A survey measures opinion not only during the time in which interviews are conducted. To monitor changes as rapidly as possible, a technique known as *tracking* is used. Instead of simply interviewing the entire sample in one or two days and then analyzing the results, interviews are conducted continuously. As new responses are added, old ones are dropped. This procedure produces a rolling sample. Continuous analyses of this sample can identify emerging issues, monitor a candidate's strength among various constituencies, and evaluate the impact of the candidate's media advertising.

Early projections of the winner on election night based on exit polling have generated considerable criticism, primarily on the grounds that they discourage turnout and affect voting in states in which the polls are still open. This controversy was heightened in 1980. When the early returns and private polls all indicated a Ronald Reagan landslide, the networks projected a Reagan victory early in the evening while polls were still open in most parts of the country. At 9:30 PM Eastern Standard Time, President Jimmy Carter appeared before his supporters and acknowledged defeat. His concession speech was carried live on each of the major networks. Almost immediately Carter's early announcement incurred angry protests, particularly from defeated West Coast Democrats, who alleged that the president's remarks discouraged many Democrats from voting. It is difficult to substantiate their claim, however.[9]

TABLE 8–2

Portrait of the American Electorate, 1984–1992 (in percentages)

Percentage of 1992 Total		1984 Reagan	Mondale	1988 Bush	Dukakis	1992 Clinton	Bush	Perot
	Total vote	59%	40%	53%	45%	43%	38%	19%
46	Men	62	37	57	41	41	38	21
54	Women	56	44	50	49	46	37	17
87	Whites	64	35	59	40	39	41	20
8	Blacks	9	90	12	86	82	11	7
3	Hispanics	37	62	30	69	62	25	14
1	Asians	—	—	—	—	29	55	16
65	Married	62	38	57	42	40	40	20
35	Unmarried	52	47	46	53	49	33	18
22	18–29 years old	59	40	52	47	44	34	22
38	30–44 years old	57	42	54	45	42	38	20
24	45–59 years old	60	40	57	42	41	40	19
16	60 and older	60	40	50	49	50	38	12
6	Not high school graduate	50	50	43	56	55	28	17
25	High school graduate	60	39	50	49	43	36	20
29	Some college education	61	38	57	42	42	37	21
40	College graduate or more	58	41	56	43	44	39	18
24	College graduate	—	—	62	37	40	41	19
16	Postgraduate education	—	—	50	48	49	36	15
49	White Protestant	72	27	66	33	33	46	21
27	Catholic	54	45	52	47	44	36	20
4	Jewish	31	67	35	64	78	12	10
17	White born-again Christian	78	22	81	18	23	61	15
19	Union household	46	53	42	57	55	24	21

Family income under $15,000	14	45	55	37	62	59	23	18
$15,000–$29,999	24	57	42	49	50	45	35	20
$30,000–$49,999	30	59	40	56	44	41	38	21
$50,000–$74,999	20	66	33	56	42	40	42	18
$75,00 and over	13	69	30	62	37	36	48	16
Family's financial situation is								
Better today	25	86	14	—	—	24	62	14
Same today	41	50	50	—	—	41	41	18
Worse today	34	15	85	—	—	61	14	25
From the East	24	53	47	50	49	47	35	18
From the Midwest	27	58	41	52	47	42	37	21
From the South	20	64	36	58	41	42	43	16
From the West	20	61	38	52	46	44	34	22
Republicans	35	92	7	91	8	10	73	17
Independents	27	63	36	55	43	38	32	30
Democrats	38	25	74	17	82	77	10	13
Liberals	21	28	70	18	81	68	14	18
Moderates	49	53	47	49	50	48	31	21
Conservatives	29	82	17	80	19	18	65	17
Employed	68	60	39	56	43	42	38	20
Full-time student	5	52	47	44	54	50	35	15
Unemployed	6	32	67	37	62	56	24	20
Homemaker	8	62	38	58	41	36	45	19
Retired	13	60	40	50	49	51	36	13
First-time voters	11	61	38	51	47	48	30	22

Notes: 1992 data were collected by Voter Research and Surveys based on questionnaires completed by 15,490 voters leaving 300 polling places around the nation on election day. Data based on surveys of voters conducted by the *New York Times* and CBS News: 9,174 in 1984; and 11,645 in 1988. Those who gave no answer are not shown. Dashes indicate that a question was not asked or a category was not provided in a particular year. Family income categories in 1984: under $12,500, $12,500–$24,999, $25,000–$34,999, $35,000–$50,000, and over $50,000. In 1988: under $12,500, $12,500–$24,999, $25,000–$34,999, $35,000–$49,999, $50,000, and over. "Born-again Christian" was labeled "born-again Christian/fundamentalist" in 1992 and "fundamentalist and evangelical Christian" in 1988. Male and female college graduates include those with postgraduate degrees in 1976 and 1980; "occupation" refers to head of the household. Family financial situation is compared with four years ago in 1984 and 1988; 1984 numbers from NBC News.

Source: Voter Research and Surveys printed in the *New York Times*, November 5, 1992, p. B 9. Copyright © 1992 the New York Times Company. Reprinted by permission.

A number of researchers have studied the impact of the 1980 television projections on voting at all levels. They have found a small reduction in turnout in the West, which they associated with the election night predictions.[10] They did not, however, find evidence of vote switching as a result of the early projections of who was likely to win.[11]

The minimal effect of the election reporting on the outcome of the election seems to be related to the fact that relatively few people watch the broadcasts and then vote. Most people vote first and watch the returns later in the evening. Perhaps this pattern of voting and then watching or listening to the returns explains why George Bush's projected victory on the networks in 1988 before the polls closed on the West Coast did little to change the results in three out of four Pacific states (Washington, Oregon, and Hawaii) that went for Michael Dukakis. Nonetheless, sensitivity to the criticism that early returns affect turnout and voting behavior led the networks to agree prior to the 1992 election not to project winners in any election within a state until its polls had closed. Thus, it was Ross Perot, not the networks, who in 1992 first called Bill Clinton a winner at 10:30 PM EST. The networks followed suit about 15 minutes later. By 11:30 PM EST both Perot and Bush had given their concession speeches.

INTERPRETING THE ELECTION

In addition to predicting the results, the television networks also provide an instant analysis of them on election night. This analysis, based primarily on exit polls, relates voting decisions to the issue positions, ideological perspectives, and partisan preferences of the electorate. Patterns among demographic groups, issue stands, and electoral perceptions and choices are noted and used to explain why people voted for particular candidates.

Exit polls present a detailed picture of the electorate on election day. (See Table 8–2.) They do not, however, provide a longitudinal perspective. To understand changes in public attitudes and opinions, it is necessary to survey people over the course of the campaign, asking the same questions and, if possible, reinterviewing the same people before and after they vote. The nationwide polls conducted by Gallup and Harris often repeat questions, but they do not repeat respondents. The National Election Studies do. They reinterview respondents and ask them some of the same questions they posed to them earlier. This interview-reinterview technique has enabled social scientists to discern opinion changes and the factors that have contributed to those changes over the course of the campaign. The wealth of data that these studies have produced has served as a basis for political scientists to construct theories of why people vote as they do.

Models of Voting Behavior

There are two basic models of voting behavior: the *prospective*, which emphasizes the issues and looks to the future; and the *retrospective*, which emphasizes the candidates and looks to the past.

In the prospective voting model, voters compare their beliefs and policy preferences with those of the parties and their nominees. They make a determination of which party and which candidate espouse positions that are closer to their own and thus would more likely pursue those positions if elected. In other words, voters make a judgment on the prospects of obtaining future policy they desire based on the current positions of the candidates and the policies they promise to pursue.

In the retrospective voting model, voters also make a judgment about the future but do so primarily on the basis of the parties and their candidates' performance in the past. How they evaluate that performance is critical to the voting choice they will make on election day. In other words, history serves as a prologue for the future in the retrospective voting model.

Although a variety of factors are considered in performance evaluations, external conditions—how good or bad things seem to be—are almost always a major part of that analysis. If the economy is strong, society harmonious, and the nation perceived as secure, people assume that their leaders, particularly the president, must be doing a good job. If conditions are not good, then the president gets much of the blame. Thus, the key question that voters ask themselves when making a retrospective evaluation is: Am I better off now than I was before the party now in power and its candidates won control of the White House?

If an incumbent president or even vice-president is running, then this retrospective judgment should be closely related to the voting decision. If, however, there is no incumbent seeking reelection, then the retrospective judgment is less relevant for individuals seeking election but their partisan affiliation remains relevant.

Another component to a retrospective voting decision involves a comparison between the principal contenders. Which of them is more likely to do well in the future?[12] It is not sufficient to assess only the current administration, even if the president is seeking reelection, if the candidate for the opposition is thought to be markedly better or worse. Thus, in any one voting decision, voters weigh the parties and candidates' past performance as well as the promise offered by the challengers and their party.

In both models, partisanship is apt to be an important influence on the evaluations people make to arrive at their voting decision. As noted in Chapter 3, a partisan orientation provides voters with a lens through which the campaign is filtered, the candidates and issues are evaluated, and electoral judgments are made.

In the retrospective model, partisanship itself is the consequence of evaluations of the past performance of parties. It therefore functions as a summary judgment of how the parties and the candidates have performed, and as a basis for anticipating how they will perform in the future. Partisans who make a retrospective evaluation are more apt to rate presidents of their party more favorably and those of the other party less favorably. Similarly, partisans tend to be closer to their candidate's positions on the issues than to their opponent's, although most people do not necessarily arrive at their position by virtue of their partisanship alone.

Since the identification people have with political parties is the most stable and resilient factor affecting the voting decision, it is considered to be the single most important long-term influence on voting. Orientations voters have toward the candidates and issues are short-term factors that fluctuate from election to election. If strong enough, they can, of course, cause people to vote against their partisan inclinations or, over time, change those inclinations as the continuing dealignment of partisan allegiances suggest. For those who resist these changes, who adhere to their partisan identities, these identities serve as an inducement and a rationalization for supporting the party and its candidates.

Since a majority of the electorate continues to identify with a political party or leans in a partisan direction, the candidate of the dominant party should have the advantage—all things being equal. But all things are never equal. Candidates change, issues change, the public mood changes, and even the partisan identity of voters can shift. Thus, it is important to understand how the electorate evaluates these changes, how they feel about the candidates, how they perceive and evaluate them and their issue stands, and how their perceptions and evaluations affect their voting decisions and the election outcomes.[13] The next sections discuss the interplay of these components in presidential elections since 1952.

1952–1956: The Impact of Personality

In 1952, the Democrats were the dominant party, but the Republicans won the presidential election and gained a majority in both houses of Congress. The issues of that election—the fear of communism at home and abroad, the presence of corruption in high levels of government, and United States involvement in the Korean War—benefited the GOP, as did the popularity of its presidential candidate, former General Dwight D. Eisenhower. These short-term factors offset the Democrat's longer-term, partisan advantage and enabled the Republicans to win.[14] The electorate saw the Republicans as better able to deal with the problems of fighting communism, promoting efficiency in government, and ending the war. Eisenhower was also perceived in a more favorable light than his opponent, Adlai Stevenson. Although the public still regarded Democrats as more capable of handling domestic problems, the appeal of Eisenhower, combined with the more favorable attitude toward the Republican party in the areas of foreign affairs and government management, resulted in the victory of the minority party's candidate.

President Eisenhower's reelection four year later was also a consequence of his personal popularity, not his party's. Eisenhower was positively evaluated by voters. His opponent, Adlai Stevenson, was not. The Republicans did not win control of Congress, however, as they had in 1952. Their failure to do so in 1956 testified to the continuing partisan advantage that the Democrats enjoyed among the American electorate during this period.

1960–1972: The Increasing Importance of Issues

Beginning in 1960, the issues of the campaign seemed to play a more important role in the election's outcome than they had since the New Deal realignment. Noneconomic policy issues undercut the impact of a partisanship forged since the 1930s on economic ties. In general, these issues contributed to the defection of Democrats from their party's presidential candidates in 1960, 1968, and 1972 and to defections by Republicans (and southern Democrats) in 1964.

John Kennedy's Catholicism was a primary concern to many voters in 1960 and helps explain the closeness of the election. Despite the Democrats' dominance within the electorate, Kennedy received only 115,000 more votes than Richard Nixon, 0.3 percent more of the total vote.

Kennedy's Catholicism cost him votes. He lost about 2.2 percent of the popular vote, or approximately 1.5 million votes, because he was a Catholic.[15] The decline in Democratic voting was particularly evident in the heavily Protestant South. Outside the South, however, Kennedy picked up Democratic votes because of the massive support he received from Catholics. Almost 80 percent of the Catholic vote, 17 percent more than the Democrats normally obtained, went to Kennedy. In fact, the concentration of Catholics in the large industrial states may have contributed to the size of his Electoral College majority.[16]

Although Kennedy barely won in 1960, Lyndon Johnson won by a landslide four years later. Short-term factors also explain the magnitude of the Johnson victory.[17] Barry Goldwater was perceived as a minority candidate within a minority party, ideologically to the right of most Republicans. Moreover, he did not enjoy a favorable public image, as Johnson did. Policy attitudes also favored the Democrats, even in foreign affairs. Goldwater's militant anticommunism scared many voters. They saw Johnson as the peace candidate.

Goldwater's strong ideological convictions, coupled with his attempt to differentiate his policy positions from Johnson's, undoubtedly contributed to a greater issue awareness. Although most policy-conscious voters had their views on the issues reinforced by their partisan attitudes, two groups within the electorate did not. White southern Democrats, fearful of their party's civil rights initiatives, cast a majority of their votes for Goldwater, and northern Republicans, who disagreed with their candidate's policy positions, voted for Johnson. For the first time since the New Deal realignment, five states in the solid Democratic South (plus Goldwater's home state of Arizona) went Republican, auguring the major regional realignment that was to occur.

The impact of a new set of foreign policy and social issues that divided the Democrats began to be evident in 1968. With the Vietnam War, urban riots, campus unrest, and civil rights dividing the nation and splitting the Democratic party, partisan desertions increased. The Democratic share of the vote declined 19 percent, while the Republican proportion increased 4 percent. The third party candidacy of George Wallace accounted for much of the difference.

Wallace's support was much more issue based than support for Hubert Humphrey or Richard Nixon. The Alabama governor did not have as much personal appeal for those who voted for him as did his policy positions.[18] Unhappy with the Democratic party's handling of a wide range of social issues, white Democratic partisans, particularly in the South but to a limited degree in the urban North as well, turned from their party's presidential candidate, Hubert Humphrey, to vote for Wallace, who received 13.5 percent of the vote. Had Wallace not run, the Republican presidential vote undoubtedly would have been larger, since Nixon was the second choice of most Wallace voters.

The results of the 1968 presidential election thus deviated from the partisan alignment of the electorate. The voters made a retrospective judgment. A significant number of them had grievances against the Democratic party and against Lyndon Johnson's conduct of the presidency. This included many Democrats who voted for Wallace and, to a much lesser extent, for Nixon. A decline in the intensity of partisanship and a growth in the number of independents contributed to the amount of issue voting that occurred in 1968. Had it not been for the Democrats' large partisan advantage and the almost unanimous African American vote that Humphrey received, the presidential election would not have been nearly so close.[19]

The trend away from partisan presidential voting for the Democratic candidate continued in 1972. With a nominee who was ideologically and personally unpopular, the Democrats suffered their worst presidential defeat since 1920. Richard Nixon enjoyed a better public image than George McGovern. He was seen as the stronger presidential candidate. The electorate reacted to him personally in a positive manner, although less so than in 1960.[20] McGovern, on the other hand, was viewed negatively by non-Democrats and neutrally by Democrats. These perceptions, positive for Nixon and negative for McGovern, contributed to Nixon's victory, as did his stands on most of the issues. Most of the electorate saw the Republican standard-bearer as closer to their own positions than the Democratic candidate. McGovern was perceived as liberal on all issues and ideologically to the left of his own party. Thus, Democrats defected in considerable numbers, but Republicans did not.[21]

1976–1992: The Evaluation of Performance

1976. Issue differences narrowed in 1976. Neither Gerald Ford nor Jimmy Carter emphasized the social and cultural concerns that played a large role in the previous presidential contest. Both focused their attention on trust in government and on domestic economic matters. In the wake of Watergate and a recession that occurred during the Ford presidency, it is not surprising that these issues worked to the Democrats' advantage.

Carter was also helped by a slightly more favorable personal assessment than that given to Ford.[22] The latter's association with the Nixon administration, highlighted in the public mind by his pardon of the former president, his difficult struggle to win his own party's nomination, and his seeming inability to find a solution to the country's economic woes adversely affected his image as president.

Nonetheless, Ford was probably helped more than hurt by being the incumbent. He gained in recognition, reputation, and stature. He benefited from having a podium with a presidential seal on it. His style and manner in the office contrasted sharply with his predecessor's—much to Ford's advantage. As the campaign progressed, his presidential image improved.[23] It just did not improve quickly enough to allow him to hold on to the office.

With sociocultural issues muted and the Vietnam War over, economic matters divided the electorate along partisan lines. This shift put the candidate of the dominant party back into the driver's seat. Democrats had more faith in their party's ability to improve the economy. Carter won primarily because he was a Democrat and secondarily because his personal evaluation was more favorable than Ford's.

Carter was also helped by being a southerner. He received the electoral votes of every southern state except Virginia. In an otherwise divided Electoral College, this support proved to be decisive.

1980. When Carter sought reelection in 1980, being a Democrat, an incumbent, and a southerner was not sufficient. Poor performance ratings overcame the advantage partisanship and incumbency normally bring to a president of the dominant party. In 1976, Carter was judged on the basis of his potential *for* office. In 1980, he was judged on the basis of his performance *in* office. As the results of the election indicate, that judgment was very harsh. Carter's vote fell behind his 1976 percentages in every single state, and in approximately half the states it dropped at least 10 percent. Why did he lose so badly?

Personal evaluations of Carter and assessments of his policies were not nearly so favorable as they had been four years earlier. Starting the campaign with the lowest approval rating of any president since the ratings were first begun in 1952, Carter saw his performance in office approved by only 21 percent of the adult population in July 1980. Personal assessments of Ronald Reagan were also low, although, in contrast to Carter's ratings, they became more favorable as the campaign unfolded.

Economic conditions also seemed to benefit Reagan. Concerns about the economy, persistently high inflation, large-scale unemployment, and the decreasing competitiveness and productivity of American industry all worked to the advantage of the party out of power. For the first time in many years, the Republicans were seen as the party better able to invigorate the economy, return prosperity, and lower inflation. The Democrats, and particularly Carter, were blamed for the problems.

Dissatisfaction with the conduct of foreign affairs, culminating in frustration over the Soviet Union's invasion of Afghanistan and especially the failure of the United States to obtain the release of American hostages held in Iran contributed to Carter's negative evaluation and to changing public attitudes toward defense spending and foreign affairs. In 1980, most Americans supported increased military expenditures, a position with which Reagan was closely identified, combined with a less conciliatory approach and a tougher, more militant posture in dealing with problems abroad.

These issues, together with the negative assessment of Carter as president, explain why he lost. Twenty-seven percent of the Democrats who had supported Carter in 1976 deserted him four years later. Approximately 80 percent of these deserters voted for Reagan. They represented all ideological groups, not just conservatives. And Carter's share of the independent vote declined substantially.

Independent John Anderson benefited from the disaffected voters. He was a protest candidate who drew equally from Democrats and Republicans. Anderson was unable, however, to attract a solid core of supporters. Nor was he able to differentiate his policy positions sufficiently from Carter's and Reagan's to generate an issue-oriented vote. In the end, his failure to win any electoral votes and only 6.5 percent of the popular vote demonstrated the resiliency of the major parties and the legitimacy that their labels provided candidates for office, at least in 1980.

In summary, Carter was repudiated by the voters because of how they retrospectively evaluated his presidency. In 1980, it was Reagan who appeared to offer greater potential. He won primarily because he was the option that had become acceptable. He did not win because of his ideology or his specific policy positions. Although there was a desire for change, there was little direct ideological or issue voting.[24] Nor did Reagan's personal appeal in 1980 contribute significantly to his victory.[25]

1984. Four years later, Reagan's personal appeal did contribute to his victory. In 1984, voters rewarded President Reagan for what they considered to be a job well done with a landslide victory. What factors contributed to Reagan's impressive victory? Was his landslide primarily a product of his ideology, his issue stands, or his performance in office?

Ideology did not work to Reagan's advantage in 1984 any more than it did in the previous election. In 1984, the average voter considered himself or herself to be a moderate, holding issue positions slightly closer to the liberal Mondale than to the conservative Reagan.[26] This moderate perspective, however, did not easily translate into presidential voting. As a consequence, it did not adversely affect Reagan; nor did it help Mondale.

There was a potential for issue voting in 1984. The electorate did perceive a choice between the two candidates on a range of domestic matters. But it was conditions more than positions that seemed to influence the electorate's judgment. A resurgent economy, strengthened military, and renewed feelings of national pride brought the president broad support. Although voters agreed with Mondale more than with Reagan on many of the specific problems confronting the nation, they viewed Reagan as the person better able to deal with them.

Leadership was a dominant concern. Voters evaluated Reagan much more highly than Mondale in this regard. Reagan was seen as the stronger and more independent of the two candidates, less beholden to special and parochial interests. When leadership was combined with the ability to deal with the most pressing problems and a very favorable personal evaluation of Reagan, the president won hands down.

It was a retrospective vote. The electorate supported Reagan primarily for his performance in office. In other words, they voted *for* him in 1984 just as they had voted *against* Carter four years earlier.

1988. The trend of retrospective voting continued in 1988. George Bush won because the electorate evaluated the Reagan administration positively, associated Bush with that administration, and concluded that he, not Michael Dukakis, would be better able and more likely to maintain the good times and the policies that produced them.[27] That Bush was not as favorably evaluated as Reagan had been four years earlier partially accounts for his narrower victory.[28] Bush received 53 percent of the popular vote and 426 electoral votes, compared with Reagan's 59 percent and 535 electoral votes.

Partisanship affected voting behavior more in 1988 than it had in any election since 1960.[29] In the past a high correlation between partisan identities and voting behavior had worked to the Democrats' advantage. In 1988, it did not. An increase in Republican allegiances and a decline in Democratic ones produced an almost evenly divided electorate. There were slightly more Democrats but greater turnout and less defection among Republicans. In the end neither candidate was appreciably advantaged by partisan voting. Among independents, Bush enjoyed a solid lead of 12 percent. (See Table 8–2.)

Ideological orientations worked to reinforce partisan voting patterns in 1988, with the Republican candidate, Bush, winning overwhelmingly among Republicans and conservatives and the Democratic candidate, Dukakis, doing almost as well among Democrats and liberals. The problem for Dukakis, however, and any liberal for that matter, is that the proportion of the electorate that considers itself liberal has declined substantially. In 1988, almost twice as many people who voted considered themselves conservative rather than liberal.

In addition to ideology and party, issues affected voting behavior in 1988; however, they did not work to the advantage of either candidate. With neither partisanship nor issues producing a clear advantage for either candidate, the retrospective evaluation of the Reagan presidency seemed to be the deciding factor, the one that best explains the election outcome.[30] Sixty percent of the electorate approved of how Reagan had handled his job, and of them, almost 80 percent voted for Bush.[31] Thus, it is only a slight exaggeration to say that Reagan won the 1988 election. He won it for George Bush. In the light of this conclusion, Bush's decision to tie his fate inextricably and unalterably to the Reagan administration during the campaign proved to be a wise choice.

1992. Four years later, however, Bush was judged on his own performance in office, and that judgment was negative. Bush received only 37.4 percent of the popular vote in a three-person contest and 168 electoral votes (only 31 percent of the total). His 1992 vote declined among every population group.

With the economy in recession, budget and trade deficits rising, and layoffs of white-collar managers and blue-collar workers dominating the news, people were fearful about their economic future. Blaming the president for these unsatisfactory economic conditions, voters turned to the challengers and their promises for change.

Clinton was clearly helped by his partisan affiliation. With slightly more Democrats in the electorate than Republicans, Clinton received the vote of three out of four Democrats. For the first time since 1964, Republican defections actually exceeded those of Democrats and turnout, which traditionally benefits Republicans, was neutralized in 1992. Democratic turnout was up and Republican turnout was down.[32]

Still, Clinton's partisan advantage could have been offset by a lopsided vote of independents who constitute more than one-quarter of the electorate. In the 1980s, that vote had strongly favored the Republicans. In 1992, it did not. Independents divided their support among the three candidates, with Clinton the plurality victor at 38 percent and Perot and Bush splitting the rest. (See Table 8–2 .) In four years Bush had lost one-third of the independent vote, thereby dooming his reelection effort.

Nor did ideology work to the president's advantage as it had in previous elections. Although liberals and conservatives continued to support Democratic and Republican candidates respectively, Perot cut into both votes, dropping Bush's support among conservatives 15 percent from his 1988 level. Moreover, Clinton did comparably better among moderates than previous Democratic candidates had done, substantially leading Bush and Perot among this group.

Although Bush was credited with a successful foreign policy, the lower salience of foreign policy issues undercut Bush's achievements in this policy realm and even served to highlight his inattention to domestic matters. The economy was the principal issue and Clinton its principal beneficiary.

Among the traditional support groups Clinton continued to enjoy an advantage among women, Jews, African Americans and Hispanics, and lower-income, less-educated voters. The generational cleavages evident in past presidential elections were muted in 1992 with the youngest cohort of voters, those 18 to 29 years old, voting for Clinton at about the national average. Clinton also received a plurality of the male vote, the first time a Democratic candidate had done so since 1976. The only demographic groups that continued to vote for Bush were the wealthy; white Protestants, especially, born-again Christians; and those voters who identified themselves as homemakers. Perot's numbers were fairly steady among demographic groups. He did comparatively better among men than women, among the young than the old, and with independents than partisans.

Clinton won a solid victory. Even though he received only 43 percent of the vote, his popular vote margin over the president was 5.6 percent. In the Electoral College he won 32 states and the District of Columbia for a total of 370 votes, demonstrating once again how the Electoral College tends to enlarge the margin of victory for the winning candidate.

Had Perot not run, it is unlikely that the results of the election would have been any different. Exit polls of Perot voters indicate that they would have divided their votes fairly evenly between Clinton and Bush had Perot not run although the number voting would undoubtedly have declined. Among nonvoters surveyed, Clinton received at least as much support as he did among voters. In a two-person contest, however, Clinton would have received a larger mandate for governing.

CONVERTING ELECTORAL CHOICE INTO PUBLIC POLICY

The President's Imprecise Mandate

It is not unusual for the meaning of the election to be ambiguous. The reasons that people vote for presidents vary. Some do so because of their party affiliation, some because of issue stands, some because of their assessment of the candidates' potential or their past performance. For most, a combination of factors contributes to their voting decision. This combination makes it difficult to discern exactly what the electorate means, desires, or envisions by its electoral choice.

The president is rarely given a clear mandate for governing. For a mandate to exist the party's candidates must take discernible and compatible policy positions, and the electorate must vote for them because of those positions. Moreover, the results of the national election must be consistent. If one party wins the White House and another the Congress, it is difficult for a president to claim a mandate for governing.

Few elections meet these criteria for a mandate. Presidential candidates usually take a range of policy positions, often waffle on a few highly divisive and emotionally charged issues, may differ from their party and its other candidates for national office in their priorities and their stands, and rarely have coattails long enough to sweep others in with them. In fact, they may run behind their congressional candidates, as Bush did in 1988 and Clinton in 1992.

Mandates may not exist, but presidents have been successful in claiming them. They need to do so. They need to be sensitive to public desires and needs when fashioning their policy programs, and they need to obtain public support to get others in government, including members of Congress and federal executives, to back their initiatives.

For these reasons elections are important. They help an administration define its initial goals, but they do not dictate priorities or long-term policy decisions. Presidents must adjust to changing times. Their refusal to do so can result in an embarrassing defeat that weakens them politically. A case in point was the Clinton administration's resistance to dropping its principal campaign promise to stimulate the economy even though the economy was improving. Similarly Clinton clung to his comprehensive program to reform the health care system even though public support for it was waning. In both cases, he was out of touch with the public mood that had changed since the election.

Assuming that party is an influence on voting behavior, what cues can presidents cull from their partisan connection in defining their programmatic mandate? Party platforms normally contain a large number of positions and proposals, but there are problems in using the platform as a guide for a new administration. First and foremost, presidential candidates may not have exercised a major influence on the platform's formulation. Or, second, they may have had to accept certain compromises in the interests of party unity. It is not unusual for a nominee to disagree with one or several of the platform's positions or priorities. Carter personally opposed his party's abortion stand in 1980 and had major reservations about a $12-billion jobs program that the Democratic platform endorsed.

In addition to containing items the president-elect may oppose, the platform may omit some that he favors, particularly if they are controversial. There was no mention of granting amnesty to Vietnam draft dodgers and war resisters in the 1976 Democratic platform, although Carter had publicly stated his intention to do so if he was elected.[33]

On the other hand, presidential nominees usually do exercise influence over the contents of the platform, as Clinton did in 1992 and Bush and Dukakis had done in 1988. Surprisingly, Bush did not put as much of his imprint on the 1992 Republican platform even though his delegates controlled the platform committee.

There is a correlation between party platforms and presidential performance. Political scientist Jeff Fishel found that from 1960 to 1984 presidents "submitted legislation or signed executive orders that are broadly consistent with about two-thirds of their campaign pledges." Of these, a substantial percentage were enacted into law, ranging from a high of 89 percent of those proposed during the Johnson administration to a low of 61 percent during the Nixon years.[34] Although these figures do not reveal the importance of the promise, its scope, or its impact, they do suggest that, in general, campaign platforms and candidate pledges are important. They provide a foundation from which an administration's early policy initiatives emanate.[35]

Expectations and Performance

When campaigning, candidates also try to create an aura of leadership, conveying such attributes as assertiveness, decisiveness, compassion, and integrity. Kennedy promised to get the country moving, Johnson to continue the New Frontier-Great Society program, Nixon to "bring us together," Bush to maintain the Reagan policies that produced peace and prosperity for the eight previous years. In 1992, Clinton pledged policy change in a moderate direction and an end to gridlock between Congress and the presidency.

These promises created expectations of performance. In the 1976 election, Jimmy Carter heightened these expectations by his constant reference to the strong, decisive leadership he intended to exercise as president. His decline in popularity stemmed in large part from his failure to meet these leadership expectations as did Bush and Clinton's drop in public approval. In contrast, Reagan's high approval before, during, and after his reelection indicate that most of the public believed that he had provided the strong leadership he had promised in his 1980 and 1984 campaigns.

All new administrations, and to some extent most reelected ones, face diverse and often contradictory desires. By their ambiguity, candidates encourage voters to see what they want to see and to believe what they want to believe. Disillusionment naturally sets in once a new president begins to make decisions. Some supporters feel deceived, while others may be satisfied.

One political scientist, John E. Mueller, has referred to the disappointment groups may experience with an administration as "the coalitions of minorities variable." In explaining declines in popularity, Mueller notes that presidents' decisions inevitably alienate parts of the coalition that elected them. This alienation, greatest among independents and supporters who identify with the other party, produces a drop in popularity over time.[36]

The campaign's emphasis on personal and institutional leadership also inflates expectations. By creating the aura of assertiveness, decisiveness, and potency, candidates help shape public expectations of their performance in office. Most presidents contribute to the decline in their own popularity by promising more than they can deliver. The question is can the promise of leadership be conveyed during the campaign without creating unrealistic and unattainable expectations of the candidate's performance as president? For most candidates the answer seems to be "No."

The Electoral Coalition and Governing

Not only does the selection process inflate performance expectations and create a set of diverse policy goals, it also decreases the president's power to achieve them. The political muscle of the White House has been weakened by the decline in the power of party leaders and the growth of autonomous state and congressional electoral systems.

Today, presidential candidates are largely on their own. They essentially designate themselves to run. They create their own organizations, mount their own campaigns, win their own delegates, and set their own convention plans. They pay a price for this independence, however. By winning their party's nomination candidates gain a label and some organizational support. But in the general election, they must supplement that support with their own campaign organization as well as expand their prenomination electoral coalition. If elected, they must broaden their appeal and expand the coalition still further. One of Clinton's worst political mistakes was the emphasis he placed on homosexual rights on the second day of his administration, thereby fulfilling a campaign promise but alienating a portion of his electoral constituency in the process. With only 43 percent of the electorate voting for him, Clinton could not afford to antagonize some of his supporters.

The personalization of the presidential electoral process has serious implications for governing. To put it simply, it makes coalition building more difficult. The electoral process provides newly elected presidents with fewer political allies in the states and in Congress. It makes their partisan appeal less effective. It fractionalizes the bases of their support.

Personality politics has created a fertile environment for interest group pressures. Without strong party leaders to act as brokers and referees, groups vie for the nominee's attention and favor during the campaign and for the president's after the election is over. This group struggle provides a natural source of opposition and support for almost any presidential action or proposal. It enlarges the arena of policy making and contributes to the multiplicity of forces that converge on most presidential decisions.

Finally, the democratization of the selection process has also resulted in the separation of state, congressional, and presidential elections. The anti-Washington, anti-government mood of the electorate has given outsiders an electoral advantage. Carter and Clinton made much of the fact that they did not owe their nomination to the power brokers within their own party nor did they owe their election to members of Congress. Their electoral advantage, however, became a governing disadvantage. Almost as soon as they took office, they had difficulty getting Congress to follow their lead.

Personality Politics and Presidential Leadership

What are presidents to do under these circumstances? How can they lead, achieve their goals, and satisfy pluralistic interests at the same time?

Obviously, there is no set formula for success. Forces beyond the president's control may affect the course of events. Nonetheless, presidents would be wise to follow certain maxims in their struggle to convert promises into performance and perhaps also to get reelected.

1. They must define and limit their own priorities rather than have them defined and expanded for them. The priorities should be consistent and well focused.
2. They must build and rebuild their own issue coalitions rather than depend solely or even mostly on existing partisan or ideological divisions to support their goals.
3. They must be flexible enough to adjust to changing conditions and public moods yet consistent enough to provide direction and stability in their policy orientation.
4. They must take an assertive posture rather than let words and actions speak for themselves, being sensitive to public opinion but try to mold it at the same time.
5. Finally, they must grow in office utilizing the status of their position to enhance their personal esteem in the eyes of the public. To counter the increasingly negative media coverage, the White House must be a source of good news and good pictures.

Priority setting is a necessary presidential task. Without it, an administration appears to lack direction and leadership. People question what presidents are doing and have difficulty remembering what they have done. The absence of clear, achievable priorities at the beginning of the Carter administration, combined with the president's perceived inconsistency in some of his economic and foreign policy decisions affected Carter's approval ratings in the public opinion polls and contributed to his defeat four years later.

The Reagan administration understood the lesson of the Carter experience, but the Clinton administration did not. Reagan limited the issues, controlled the agenda, and, most important, focused the media on his principal policy objectives during his first term in office. Clinton did none of these. He had too many diverse goals, too diffusive a public appeal, and exercised too little control over news media coverage of his administration. All of these factors adversely affected his leadership image and his opportunities to achieve his policy objectives.

Presidents have discretion in deciding on their priorities. Reagan used this discretion at the beginning of his first term when he jettisoned his conservative social agenda in favor of major economic reforms. Bush chose to emphasize foreign policy and deemphasize domestic issues in the first three years of his administration, despite his campaign's emphasis on domestic concerns and his own promise to build a kinder and gentler America. Clinton stuck with his principal priority of stimulating the economy (even though the economy was recovering) but added a host of other policies from deficit reduction to child immunization to ending discrimination against homosexuals in the military to comprehensive health care and welfare reform. By doing so, he overwhelmed Congress and dissipated much of its energy and his public support.

Beyond establishing priorities and positions, presidents have to get them adopted. Their electoral coalition does not remain a cohesive entity within the governing system. The inevitable shifting of that coalition forces them to build and rebuild their own alliances around their policy objectives. Constructing these alliances requires organizing skills different from those used in winning an election.

Public appeals are often necessary to maintain a high level of support on potentially divisive national issues and to use that support to influence public officials to back the president's initiatives. The Reagan administration effectively marshaled public support in 1981 and 1982. The president took to the airwaves to explain his program to the American people and rally them behind it, particularly his budget and tax proposals. The White House then orchestrated the public's favorable response, directing it toward members of Congress. Bush and Clinton were much less successful in convincing the public to support controversial domestic policies.

In addition to mobilizing external forces, presidents need to employ other inducements and tactics to convince public officials, who have their own constituencies and must be responsive to them, to back presidential policy. This effort requires time, energy, and help. The president cannot do it alone.

As campaign organizations are necessary to win elections, so, too, are governing organizations necessary to gain support for presidential policies. Several offices within the White House have been established to provide liaison and backing for the president on Capitol Hill, in the bureaucracy, and with outside interest groups. By building and mending bridges, presidents can improve their chances for success. They can commit, convince, cajole, and otherwise gain cooperation despite the constitutional and political separation of institutions and powers.

Unlike winning the general election, making and implementing public policy are not all-or-nothing propositions. Assessments of performance are based on expectations, somewhat as they were in the elections. Part of the image problem all presidents face is the contrast between an idealized public conception of the institution's powers with the president's actual ability to get things done. The gap between expectations and performance explains why presidents need a public relations staff and why some grandstanding is inevitable.

If presidents cannot achieve their goals, they can at least look good trying, and perhaps they can even claim partial success. And finally, they can always change their public priorities to improve their batting average. Public appeals may or may not generate support within the governing coalition, but they can boost support outside it, and within the electoral coalition the next time around.

SUMMARY

Americans are fascinated by presidential elections. They want to know who will win, why the successful candidate has won, and what the election augurs for the next four years. Their fascination stems from four interrelated factors: elections are dramatic; they are decisive; they are participatory; and they affect future policy and leadership.

These factors suggest why so much attention has been devoted to predicting and analyzing presidential elections. Public opinion polls constantly monitor the attitudes and views of the electorate. They reflect and, to some extent, contribute to public interest through the hypothetical elections they continuously conduct and the news media report. Private surveys also record shifts in popular sentiment, helping the candidates who pay for them know what to say, to whom to say it, when and even how to say it, and whether the words have achieved their desired effect.

Polls have become fairly accurate measures of opinion at the time they are taken. They provide data that can be employed to help explain the meaning of the election: the issues that were most salient, the positions that were most popular, and the hopes and expectations that are initially directed toward the elected leaders of government.

The personality of the candidates, the issues of the campaign, and the retrospective evaluation of the administration and the party that has controlled it have dominated recent elections and the voting decisions of the electorate. Singularly and together, these factors, along with partisanship, explain the outcome of the vote. In 1960, it was Kennedy's religion that seemed to account for the closeness of the popular vote despite the large Democratic majority in the electorate. In 1964, it was Goldwater's uncompromising ideological and issue positions that helped provide Johnson with an overwhelming victory in all areas but the deep South. In 1968, it was the accumulation of grievances against the Democrats that spurred the Wallace candidacy and resulted in Nixon's triumph. In 1972, ideology, issues, and the perception of McGovern as incompetent split the Democratic party and culminated in Nixon's landslide. In 1976, however, partisanship was reinforced by issue, ideological, and personal evaluations to the benefit of the dominant party's nominee. In the next two elections, it was not. Dissatisfaction with Carter's performance in 1980 and satisfaction with Reagan's in 1984 overcame the Democrats' decreasing numerical advantage within the electorate, causing voters to cast their ballots for Reagan as the person they thought would be best qualified to lead. By 1988, the Democrats had lost their partisan advantage. The issues in that election, although important, did not favor one candidate at the expense of the other. This left the retrospective evaluation of the Reagan years as the critical factor. A majority of voters evaluated these years favorably and believed that Bush, not Dukakis, would be better able and more likely to continue them.

In a certain sense, the 1992 election was a rerun of 1980. The incumbent was rejected on the grounds that his performance in dealing with the nation's most pressing issue, the economy, was unsatisfactory and were he to be reelected, that performance would not markedly improve. Almost two-thirds of the electorate voted against the incumbent president. Of the other two candidates, Clinton was elected primarily because of his partisan affiliation and his perception as a moderate. That he came from the South, chose Gore as his running mate, and ran an excellent, highly focused campaign all contributed to his victory. Perot ran a strong race for an independent candidate, but independent candidates are disadvantaged within the electorate because they lack a solid base of support and within the Electoral College because of the winner-take-all system used by most of the states. These disadvantages, combined with Perot's early withdrawal and later reentry and his lack of experience in the public sector, were just too great to overcome.

The public has a diverse and inflated set of expectations after the election. That they may be conflicting, unrealistic, or in other ways unattainable matters little for a new president. They are expected to lead, to achieve, and to satisfy the interests of a heterogeneous coalition. Their failure or success will depend in large part on their ability to fulfill these expectations.

The election provides them with an open-ended mandate that means different things to different people, including the presidents themselves but does not provide them with the political clout to get things done. In the past, the electoral and governing coalitions were more closely connected by partisan ties than they seem to be today.

This situation has presented serious governing problems for recent presidents. To overcome them they must establish their own priorities, construct their own governing alliances, provide a sense of direction while flexibly moving among policy options, mold but be sensitive to public opinion, and use their office to enhance their image and their programs' chances for being enacted into law. It is not an easy task, and, unfortunately, disappointment in a president's performance has become the rule not the exception.

NOTES

1. Michael Wheeler, *Lies, Damn Lies, and Statistics* (New York: Dell, 1976), p. 84. Moreover, the 2 million people who returned the questionnaire were not necessarily even typical of those who received it. By virtue of responding, they displayed more interest and concern than the others who did not return the survey.
2. Archibald Crossley predicted that Roosevelt would receive 53.8 percent of the vote; George Gallup estimated that he would receive 55.7 percent; Elmo Roper forecast 61.7 percent. Roosevelt actually received 62.5 percent.
3. Unusually large turnout by certain groups may skew the predictions, however. The sizable turnout of Perot voters in 1992, for example, was not anticipated by some pollsters, causing them to underestimate the vote Perot actually received.
4. *The Gallup Poll Monthly* (November 1922), back cover page.
5. When the final Gallup survey did not allocate any of the undecided vote to Perot, the poll estimated Clinton's percentage at 49; when it did allocate it, it estimated it at 44. Clinton actually received 43 percent of the vote.
6. James E. Campbell and Kenneth A. Wink, "Trial-Heat Forecasts of the Presidential Vote," *American Politics Quarterly* 18 (July 1990): 257. Updated by the author.
7. According to Steeper, "Election day deciders divided equally among the three candidates. Those who decided in the few days before went slightly to Clinton over Bush, 39% to 34%, with Perot taking 19%." Fred Steeper, "1992 Post Election Summary," (Prepared for the Republican National Committee) January 10, 1993, p. 2. See also Paul R. Abramson, John H. Aldrich, and David W. Rohde, *Change and Continuity in the 1992 Elections* (Washington, D.C.: Congressional Quarterly, 1994), p. 64.
8. In the midterm election of 1994 two exit polls were conducted: one focusing on demographic data and voting patterns for members of Congress and the other on issue positions of the electorate, including an evaluation of government performance.
9. In general, turnout declined more in the East and Midwest than it did in the Far West in 1980. Even if there was a decline after Carter's concession, there is little evidence to suggest that Democrats behaved any differently from Republicans and independents. Hawaii, the last state to close its polls, voted for Carter.
10. Raymond Wolfinger and Peter Linquiti, "Tuning In and Turning Out," *Public Opinion* 4 (February/March 1981): 57–59.

11. Harold Mendelsohn and Irving Crespi, *Polls, Television, and the New Politics* (Scranton, Pa.: Chandler, 1970), pp. 234–236.

12. This view of retrospective voting was advanced by Anthony Downs, *An Economic Theory of Democracy* (New York: Harper and Row, 1957). Downs suggests that people evaluate the past performance of parties and elected officials in order to anticipate how they will perform in the future compared with their opponents.

13. For a very interesting, albeit sophisticated, article on the impact of emotions on learning, perceptions, and voting see George E. Marcus and Michael B. Mackuen, "Anxiety, Enthusiasm, and the Vote: The Emotional Underpinnings of Learning and Involvement During Presidential Campaigns," *American Political Science Review* 87 (September 1993): 672–685.

14. For an analysis of the components of the 1952 presidential election, see Angus Campbell, Philip E. Converse, Warren E. Miller, and Donald Stokes, *The American Voter* (New York: Wiley, 1960), pp. 524–527.

15. Philip E. Converse, Angus Campbell, Warren E. Miller, and Donald E. Stokes, "Stability and Change in 1960: A Reinstating Election," in *Elections and the Political Order*, ed. Angus Campbell, Philip E. Converse, Warren E. Miller, and Donald E. Stokes (New York: Wiley, 1966), p. 92.

16. Kennedy's Catholicism may have enlarged his Electoral College total by 22 votes. See Ithiel de Sola Pool, Robert P. Abelson, and Samuel Popkin, *Candidates, Issues, and Strategies* (Cambridge, Mass.: MIT Press, 1965), pp. 115–118.

17. For a discussion of the 1964 presidential election, see Philip E. Converse, Aage R. Clausen, and Warren E. Miller, "Election Myth and Reality: The 1964 Election, " *American Political Science Review* 59 (June 1965): 321–336.

18. Philip E. Converse, Warren E. Miller, Jerrold G. Rusk, and Arthur C. Wolfe, "Continuity and Change in American Politics: Parties and Issues in the 1968 Election," *American Political Science Review* 63 (December 1969): 1097. Wallace claimed that there was not "a dime's worth of difference" between the Republican and Democratic candidates and their parties. He took great care in making his own positions distinctive. The clarity with which he presented his views undoubtedly contributed to the issue orientation of his vote. People knew where Wallace stood.

19. Converse, et al., "Continuity and Change," p. 1085.

20. Warren E. Miller and Teresa E. Levitin, *Leadership and Change* (Cambridge, Mass.: Winthrop, 1976), p. 164.

21. Arthur H. Miller, Warren E. Miller, Alden S. Raine, and Thad A. Brown, "A Majority Party in Disarray: Policy Polarization in the 1972 Election," *American Political Science Review* 70 (1976): 753–778.

22. Arthur H. Miller and Warren E. Miller, "Partisanship and Performance: Rational Choice in the 1976 Presidential Elections," (Paper presented at the annual meeting of the American Political Science Association, Washington, D.C., September 1–4, 1977).

23. Ibid., p. 99.

24. Ibid., p. 7; Warren E. Miller, "Policy Directions and Presidential Leadership: Alternative Interpretations of the 1980 Presidential Election," (Paper presented at the annual meeting of the American Political Science Association, New York: September 3–6, 1981.)

25. According to Arthur H. Miller and Martin P. Wattenberg, "Reagan was the least positively evaluated candidate elected to the presidency in the history of the National Election Studies, which date back to 1952." "Policy and

Performance Voting in the 1980 Election," (Paper presented at the annual meeting of the American Political Science Association, New York, September 3–6, 1981), p. 15.

26. Paul R. Abramson, John H. Aldrich, and David W. Rohde, *Change and Continuity in the 1984 Elections* (Washington, D.C.: Congressional Quarterly, 1986), pp. 171–180.

27. J. Merrill Shanks and Warren E. Miller, "Alternative Interpretations of the 1988 Election," (Paper presented at the annual meeting of the American Political Science Association, Atlanta, Georgia, August 31–September 3, 1989), p. 58.

28. Paul R. Abramson, John H. Aldrich, and David W. Rohde, *Change and Continuity in the 1988 Elections* (Washington, D.C.: Congressional Quarterly, 1990), p. 195.

29. Ibid., p. 212.

30. J. Merrill Shanks and Warren E. Miller, "Partisanship, Policy and Performance: The Reagan Legacy in the 1988 Election," *British Journal of Political Science* 21 (April 1991): 129–197.

31. Abramson, et al., *Change and Continuity in the 1988 Elections*, pp. 193, 195, and 198.

32. This pattern reversed itself in the midterm elections of 1994 when Republican turnout was up and that of Democrats was down.

33. Another limitation to using a platform as a guide to the partisan attitudes and opinions of the public is that many people, including party rank and file, are unfamiliar with most of its contents. The platform per se is not the reason people vote for their party's candidates on election day.

34. Jeff Fishel, *Presidents and Promises* (Washington, D.C.: Congressional Quarterly, 1994), pp. 38, 42–43.

35. One reason campaign promises are important is that they are part of the public record; candidates and parties can be held accountable for them. Another is that they represent the interests of a significant portion of the population. To gain public approval, presidents must respond to these interests. In addition, organized groups, to whom promises have been made, have clout in Congress and in the bureaucracy. Presidents can either mobilize these groups to help them achieve their campaign promises or be thwarted by them if they fail to do so. George Bush ran into this problem in 1990 when he recanted on his pledge not to raise taxes. Conservative Republican members of Congress, who opposed tax increases in their own campaigns for office, voted against the budget compromise that contained a tax increase, a compromise that the president supported.

36. John E. Mueller, *War, Presidents, and Public Opinion* (New York: Wiley, 1973), pp. 205–208; 247–249.

SELECTED READINGS

Abramson, Paul R., John H. Aldrich, and David W. Rohde. *Change and Continuity in the 1992 Elections.* Washington, D.C.: Congressional Quarterly, 1994.

Bolce, Louis, Gerald DeMaio, and Douglas Muzzio, "The 1992 Republican 'Tent': No Blacks Walked In," *Political Science Quarterly,* 108 (Summer 1993): 255–270.

Dahl, Robert A. "Myth of the Presidential Mandate." *Political Science Quarterly* 105 (Fall 1990): 355–372.

Fiorina, Morris. *Retrospective Voting in American National Elections.* New Haven, Conn.: Yale University Press, 1981.

Fishel, Jeff. *Presidents and Promises.* Washington, D.C.: Congressional Quarterly, 1985.

Kelley, Stanley. *Interpreting Elections.* Princeton, N.J.: Princeton University Press, 1983.

Ladd, Everett Carll. "The 1992 Vote for President Clinton: Another Brittle Mandate?" *Political Science Quarterly* 108 (Spring 1993): 1–28.

Miller, Arthur H. and Martin P. Wattenberg. "Throwing the Rascals Out: Policy and Performance Evaluations of Presidential Candidates, 1952–1980." *American Political Science Review* 79 (1985): 359–372.

Pomper, Gerald M., F. Christopher Arterton, Ross K. Baker, et al. *The Election of 1992.* Chatham, N.J.: Chatham House, 1993.

Popkin, Samuel L. *The Reasoning Voter.* Chicago: University of Chicago Press, 1991.

Shanks, J. Merrill, and Warren E. Miller. "Partisanship, Policy and Performance: The Reagan Legacy in the 1988 Election," *British Journal of Political Science* 21 (1991): 129–197.

Wattenberg, Martin P. *The Rise of Candidate-Centered Politics.* Cambridge, Mass.: Harvard University Press, 1991.

This campaign poster was used in the 1816 campaign of Democrat James Monroe, who ran against Rufus King.

Chapter 9

Reforming the Electoral System

INTRODUCTION

The American political system has evolved significantly in recent years. Party rules, finance laws, and media coverage are very different from what they were thirty years ago. The composition of the electorate has changed as well, with the expansion of suffrage to all citizens eighteen years of age or older and the reduction of legal obstacles to voting, particularly in the South in the 1960s. In addition the Electoral College certainly does not function in the manner in which it was originally designed to do so. Have these changes been beneficial? Has the system been improved? Are further structural or operational adjustments desirable? These questions have elicited a continuing, and sometimes spirited, debate.

Critics have alleged that the electoral process is too long, too costly, and too burdensome, that it wears down candidates and numbs voters, resulting in too many personal accusations and too little substantive discussion, too much rhetoric and too little real debate. They have said that many qualified people are discouraged from running for office and much of the electorate is discouraged from participating in the election. Other criticisms are that the system benefits the rich, encourages factionalism, weakens parties, overemphasizes personality and underemphasizes policy, and that it is unduly influenced by the news media. It has also been contended that voters do not receive the information they need to make informed, rational decisions on election day.

In contrast, proponents argue that the political system is more democratic than ever. More, not fewer, people are involved, especially at the nomination stage. Candidates, even lesser-known ones, now have an opportunity to demonstrate their competence, endurance, motivation, and leadership capabilities. Parties remain important as vehicles through which the system operates and by which governing is accomplished. Those who defend the process believe voters do receive as much information as they desire and that most people can and do make informed and rational judgments.

The old adage "where you stand influences what you see" is applicable to the debate about electoral reform. No political process is completely neutral. There are always winners and losers. To a large extent the advantages that some enjoy are made possible by the disadvantages that others encounter. Rationalizations aside, much of the debate about the system, about equity, representation, and responsiveness, revolves around a very practical, political question: Who gains and who loses?

Proposals to change the system need to be assessed in the light of this question. They should also be judged on the basis of how such changes would affect the operation of the political system and influence governance. This chapter discusses some of these proposals and the effect they could have on the road to the White House. The chapter is organized into two sections: one dealing with the more recent developments in party rules, campaign finance, and media coverage; and the other examining the long-term, democratic issues of participation and voting.

MODIFYING RECENT CHANGES

Party Rules

Of all the changes that have recently occurred in the nomination process, none has caused more persistent controversy than the reforms governing the selection of delegates. Designed to encourage grass roots participation and broaden the base of representation, these reforms have also lengthened the nominating period, made the campaign more expensive, generated candidate-based organizations, weakened the influence of state and local party leaders, converted conventions into coronations, and loosened the ties between the parties and their nominees. As a consequence, governing has been made more difficult.

Since 1968, when the Democrats began to rewrite their rules for delegate selection, the parties have suffered from these unintended repercussions. Each succeeding presidential election has seen adjustments to the Democratic party's rules, changes that have attempted to reconcile expanded participation and representation with the traditional need to unify the party and have it play a consequential role in the national campaign. Although less reform conscious than the Democrats, the

Republicans have also tried to steer a middle course between greater rank-and-file involvement and more equitable representation on the one hand and the maintenance of successful electoral and governing coalitions on the other.

How to balance these often-competing goals has been a critical concern. Those who desire greater public participation have lauded the trend toward having more primaries and a larger percentage of delegates selected in them. Believing that the reforms have opened up the process and made it more democratic, they favor the continued selection of pledged delegates based on the proportion of the popular vote their candidate receives. In contrast, those who believe that greater control by state and national party leaders is desirable argue that the reforms have gone too far. They would prefer fewer primaries, a smaller percentage of delegates selected in them, and more unpledged delegates participating in the nominating conventions. They would also favor a larger involvement by the state and national party organizations in the presidential campaign. Giving all federal funds to the national party committees, and not to the candidate, has been proposed as one way to achieve the latter objective; continuing to solicit and spend soft money is another.

Strong party advocates appear to be in the ascendancy, although the Democrats did agree in 1992 to allocating elected delegates only by straight proportional voting. Proportional voting can have the effect of extending the nominating campaign, thereby delaying a consensus on the party's nominee. Although Democrats Michael Dukakis and Bill Clinton had amassed large leads early and seemed headed toward easy nominations, opponents Jesse Jackson and Jerry Brown were able to contest primaries and caucuses through June. In the process they garnered headlines, criticized the front runners, and appealed to their constituencies. Although they eventually agreed to support the national ticket, their extended campaign had the effect of weakening their party's nominees, effectively undercutting the impact of their own endorsements, and in the case of African Americans who supported Jackson in 1988, reducing turnout in the general election.

There has been widespread public support for shortening the nomination campaign, which Professor Thomas E. Patterson has argued, "... disrupts the policy process, discourages the candidacies of responsible officeholders, and wears out the voters."[1] It also diverts public attention from issues of government to campaign-related controversies. Moreover, Patterson notes that the long campaign generates more negative news about the candidates as it progresses, thereby souring voters on the choices they have on primary day.[2]

Several proposals have been made for addressing this issue. Some have even been introduced in the form of legislation in Congress. One would limit the period during which primaries or caucuses could be held; a second would cluster primaries and caucuses geographically, forcing states in designated regions to hold their elections on the same day; a third would create a national primary.

Having an official period during the spring of the election year for primaries and caucuses has been suggested as a way to reduce the impact the early contests have had on the nomination. A second but equally important objective has been to reduce the news media's influence on public opinion during these initial stages of the process.

The Democratic party has attempted to achieve these goals since 1984 by imposing its own window period during which primaries and caucuses could be held. Opposition from several states, however, including Iowa and New Hampshire, has forced the party to grant them exceptions to the imposed time frame. The exceptions, in turn, continue to produce the problem that generated the proposal in the first place—the holding of early contests that receive extensive media coverage and for that reason are disproportionally important to the candidates. This problem in turn has encouraged other states to move their primaries toward the beginning of the window period, thereby compressing the nomination process and starting the campaign earlier in the election cycle.

Compression has positive and negative effects. On the plus side, a compressed period requires candidates to organize more thoroughly, focus voter attention for a shorter period, and give advantage to nationally recognized candidates. A front-loaded nomination process, however, forces candidates to depend even more on the mass media to reach voters simultaneously in the states that hold their elections on the same days.

Reformers have suggested a regional primary system that extends over several months or even a national primary, held on a single day, to remedy the problem of some states continually exercising disproportionate influence. Of the two proposals, regional primaries have evolved from the desire of states to have a greater voice in the selection process.

Southern Democrats, in particular, unhappy over their party's standard-bearers in 1972 and 1984, over their party's national image, and over the contents of its recent platforms, regarded regional primaries as an opportunity to stamp the ticket with a southern imprint. These leaders convinced their state legislatures, all incidentally controlled by the Democrats in 1988, to hold primaries on the first Tuesday in which primaries could be held in March, and caucuses the following weekend. Some of the southern states have continued to hold their nomination contests during the same week at the beginning of the nomination process.

The movement toward regional primaries has accelerated. A series of primaries in the northeast are to be held during the first week of March in 1996, many of the southern states will hold their primaries during the second week, four large midwestern states plus Pennsylvania are likely to hold theirs the third week, with the California primary to follow them on the last Tuesday of March. Thus, without act of Congress or a rule imposed by the national party, regional primaries have been implemented because the states in a region have perceived it to be in their interest to do so.

Whether regional primaries give an advantage to the national party and its nominees in the general election is another issue. One fear is that regional primaries might exacerbate sectional rivalries, encourage local or area candidates, and produce more organizations to rival those of the state and national parties. Moreover, like straight proportional voting, they could impede the emergence of a consensus candidate, thereby extending the process to the convention and increasing, not decreasing, costs, time, and media attention.

Moreover, regional primaries help the best-organized and best-financed candidates, such as Bill Clinton and George Bush in 1992. They make it more difficult for candidates who lack a national reputation and a huge war chest to compete in regions outside their own.

The other option, and the one that represents the most sweeping change, is to institute a national primary. Although party leaders, including members of the reform commissions, have opposed such a proposal and Congress has been cool to the idea, the general public seems to be more favorably disposed. Gallup Polls taken over the last two decades indicate that about two-thirds of the electorate prefers such an election to the present system.[3]

Most proposals for a national primary call for a summer election followed by party conventions. Candidates who wished to enter their party's primary would be required to obtain a certain number of signatures. Any aspirant who won a majority would automatically receive the nomination. In some plans a plurality would be sufficient, provided it was at least 40 percent. In the event that no one received 40 percent, a runoff election would be held several weeks later between the top two finishers. Nominating conventions would continue to select the vice-presidential candidates and to decide on the platforms. A national primary would be consistent with the "one person, one vote" principle that guides most aspects of the U.S. electoral system. All participants would have an equal voice in the selection. No longer would those in the early, small primary and caucus states exercise disproportionate influence.

It is likely that a national primary would stimulate turnout. The attention given to such an election would provide greater incentive for voting than currently exists, particularly in those states that hold their nomination contests after the apparent winner has emerged. A national primary would probably result in nomination by a more representative electorate than is currently the case.

A single primary for each party would accelerate a nationalizing trend. Issues that affect the entire country would be the primary focus of attention. Thus, candidates for the nation's highest office would be forced to discuss the problems they would most likely address during the general election campaign and would most likely confront as president.

Moreover, the results of the election would be clear-cut. The media could no longer interpret primaries and caucus returns as they saw fit. An incumbent's ability to garner support through the timely release of grants, contracts, and other spoils of government might be more limited in a national contest. On the other hand, such an election would undoubtedly discourage challengers who lacked national reputations. No longer would an early victory catapult a relatively unknown aspirant into the position of serious contender and jeopardize a president's chances for renomination. In fact, lesser-known candidates, such as George McGovern, Jimmy Carter, Michael Dukakis, and even Bill Clinton, might find it extremely difficult to raise money, build an organization, and mount a national campaign. These difficulties would improve the chances that competent, experienced political leaders would be selected as their party's standard-bearers, or, depending on one's perspective, that older, tired, Washington-based politicians would be chosen.

From the standpoint of the major parties, a national primary would further weaken the ability of their leaders to influence the selection of the nominee. Successful candidates would probably not owe their victory to party officials. Moreover, a postprimary convention could not be expected to tie the nominee to the party, although it might tie the party to the nominee at least through the election. The trend toward personalizing politics would probably continue.

Such nominees, if elected, might also find governing much more difficult. They could not count on the support of party leaders if those leaders play little or no role in the candidate's nomination. Party leaders and members of Congress who have no stake in the election of the president would be hard to mobilize and quick to jump ship should the president get into political difficulty.

Whether a national primary winner would be the party's strongest candidate is also open to question. With a large field of contenders, those with the most devoted or ideological supporters might do best. On the other hand, candidates who do not arouse the passions of the diehards but who are more acceptable to the party's mainstream might not do as well. Everybody's second choice might not even finish second, unless a system of approval voting, which allows the electorate to list their top two or three choices in order, were used. But such a system would complicate the election, confuse the result, undercut its legitimacy, and perhaps add to its costs.

In addition to weakening the party, a national primary could lessen the ability of states to determine when and how their citizens would participate in the presidential nomination process, thereby undercutting the federal system of nominations. The ability of state party leaders and elected officials to affect the process and influence the outcome would suffer. These likely consequences have made it difficult to mobilize wide support for such a plan despite the general appeal of the idea to the general public.

Finance Laws

Closely related to the delegate selection process are the laws governing campaign finance. Enacted in the 1970s in reaction to secret and sometimes large, illegal bequests to candidates, to the disparity in contributions and spending among the candidates, and to the spiraling costs of modern campaigns, particularly television advertising, these laws were designed to improve accountability, reduce spending, subsidize nominations, and fund the general election. Some of these objectives have been achieved, but in the process other problems have been created.

The laws have taken campaign finance out of the back rooms and put much of it into the public spotlight. They have also, however, generated a nightmare of compliance procedures and reporting requirements. Detailed records of practically all contributions and expenditures of the presidential campaign organizations must now be kept and periodically reported to the Federal Election Commission.[4] Good accountants and attorneys, specializing in election law, are now as necessary as pollsters, image makers, and grass roots organizers.

The amount wealthy individuals can donate to the candidates for their party's nomination is limited by law, but not the amount they can contribute to their party's soft money account nor the amount they can spend independently (or on themselves were they to run and not accept federal funds). This situation has created incentives for candidates to obtain broad-based public support for their campaign, but it has not decreased their need for frequent appeals for funds as they seek the nomination and even after they effectively wrap it up. It has also created severe budget constraints, particularly during the early stages of the nomination process.

These constraints have encouraged candidates to circumvent the law as a matter of course. After its audit of 1992 campaign expenditures, the Federal Election Commission accused the Clinton and Bush campaigns of a large amount of illegal expenses and required them to repay the money to the U.S. Treasury.[5] One use of taxpayers' money was particularly troublesome—the expenditure of $37,500 by the Clinton campaign to settle a sexual harassment complaint against one of its officials.[6]

Nor have federal funds equalized the financial status of the candidates. Nationally known aspirants for the party's nomination still have an advantage. Conversely, the ease with which lesser-known, even fringe candidates can obtain matching grants encourages those who seek a platform to espouse their views or pursue their political ambitions to do so through the presidential election process partially *at public expense*. One way to deal with the dual problems of inequity and what some regard as the imprudent use of taxpayers' funds is to stiffen the eligibility requirements by increasing the amount that many candidates must raise to obtain government support but also increasing the size of the federal grant if they do meet the new and tougher requirements. Such a change would still permit those with some recognition and support to enter the race but would make more money available to them as they obtained private donations.

The financial discrepancy between the major party candidates is apt to be less in the general election. Although the Republicans had enjoyed an advantage over the years by virtue of their party's superior organizational and financial base at the national, state, and local levels, that advantage has declined in recent presidential elections. Whether it will continue to do so, however, is unclear.

The law has also not reduced or controlled candidate spending. On the contrary, the need to supplement increasing expenditures for fund-raising, media, polling, and other important campaign activities has actually increased the amount of money that the campaign organizations must raise and spend. This need combined with the failure to raise the contribution limits for individuals and groups has forced candidates to spend more time fund-raising and has encouraged them to circumvent the spending limits, particularly in those states that hold the earliest primaries and caucuses; it has also increased their dependence on party and non-party groups to supplement their campaign activities. This has meant that candidates have become more dependent on others in the conduct of their campaign. All of these consequences have worked to undermine public support for the electoral process and public financing. One illustration of this trend is the declining percentage of taxpayers who allocate their taxes to the campaign election fund.

Several changes have been proposed to alleviate these problems. Compliance procedures could be eased for the presidential campaigns. For example, the size of the contribution that must be reported could be increased, and the number of reports might be reduced. State spending limits in the nomination phase might be eliminated entirely. These changes would relieve campaign organizations of some of the burdens of record keeping but would also mean that less detailed information would be available less promptly to the public, thus compromising the public disclosure aspects of the law.

The soft money amendment, which has now been tightened, could be modified to limit the amount of contributions or could even be repealed. If it were repealed, revenues of the parties would be dramatically reduced. On the other hand, their expenditures and those of their nominees would be equal. Overall campaign spending would also be decreased. The absence of soft money, however, would damage party-building efforts in the states. It could also adversely affect turnout, the raison d'etre for the amendment. Turnout remains lower today than it was when the amendment was enacted into law.

Independent spending, though declining, is still another source of unequal expenditures. These expenses cannot be prevented, but there are ways in which their impact could be moderated. Congress could require television stations to allow candidates free time to respond to advertising paid for by PACs. Had such a requirement been in effect in 1988, Dukakis would have been permitted to reply without cost to the Willie Horton ad that was sponsored by a pro-Bush PAC.

A law, however, that forced the media to provide free time might be counterproductive, reducing rather than increasing the amount of public communications during the campaign. Television and radio stations would undoubtedly be discouraged from selling time to nonparty groups and individuals if they were under obligation to provide it free to the person or party who was the object of the commercial. A decrease in media advertising would reduce the information available to the public and increase the electorate's dependence on the candidates and the media for it.

The appearance of candidates on the late evening talk shows in 1992 has, however, given major candidates more "free" time to respond to questions about their policy positions and personal character and to do so in a way that allows them to give a complete answer rather than just a sound bite. But it has also given the producers and hosts of these shows subtle ways of influencing the electorate through the wording and sequencing of their questions to the candidates.

PAC contributions and electoral activities constitute another problem, at least from the perception of the public. One way to decrease the influence of PACs is to prohibit or reduce the amount of money that they could contribute to federal elections, and increase the contribution limits for individual donors to candidates and to parties. The purchasing power of contributions has declined by almost two-thirds since the limits were initially established in 1974. The problem with increasing the amount individuals could give or providing more income tax deductions for contributions, however, is that the wealthy would gain greater influence, as they have with the soft money provision, grass roots solicitation might suffer, and public perceptions of the fairness of the election might be adversely affected.

Another option would be to increase the amount of individual contributions that could be matched by federal grants. Such a provision would shift the burden of costs from those who were more willing and able to pay to the American taxpayers. Not only might such a shift be seen as politically undesirable, but it might also be unfeasible given the limited amount of money generated by the income tax check-off provision. In fact, even under the current arrangements for matching funds, the Federal Election Commission anticipates a possible shortfall in the early months of the 1996 campaign because the fund has not built up adequate reserves, requests for matching grants are expected to be large, and Treasury Department regulations require that money for the general election and the national nominating conventions be set aside *before* matching fund disbursements can be made.[7]

Although many lawmakers see problems with the finance laws, they cannot agree on solutions. The difficulty with amending the law lies in ensuring that no one political party benefits or suffers at the expense of the other. Maintaining this objective, however, decreases the partisan motive for passing the legislation.

In addition to the question of political equity, there is an even more fundamental issue for a democratic society. Competing needs have created contradictory goals. Freedom of speech implies the right to advance beliefs by contributing to the candidates and party of one's choice and spending independently on their behalf. In a democratic political system, however, a system in which the vote and presumably the voice of all citizens should be equal, the wealthy should not have an advantage. Yet appeals to a large segment of the electorate are very expensive. The difficulty of ensuring sufficient funds, protecting freedom of speech, and promoting political equality—all without partisan advantage—has generated considerable debate in the halls of Congress in recent years, but no easy or quick solutions.

News Media Coverage

A third significant change in the electoral process concerns the way in which information about the campaign is communicated to the voters. Beginning in the 1950s, television became the principal medium through which candidates made their appeals and by which voters obtained information. Since then, television's emphasis on the contest, the drama, and the style of candidates has affected every nook and cranny of the campaign from public perceptions of the candidates and the parties to the judgment of the electorate on election day.

Changes in party rules and finance laws have also contributed to the media's impact. The increasing number and complexity of preconvention contests have provided the news media with greater inducements to cover these events and interpret their results. The desire of the party to obtain maximum exposure for its nominating convention has resulted in two simultaneous conventions, the "official" one at the podium, carefully orchestrated by the party to benefit its nominees, and the unofficial one, mediated by the news media, designed to interest and entertain viewers and readers with behind-the-scenes reporting and analysis. The limited money available to presidential candidates who accept federal funding has also increased the importance of news about the election and may have contributed to its impact on the voters. Today candidates do not leave their coverage to chance. They attempt to influence it by carefully releasing favorable information, by staging events, and by paying for many commercial messages.

Is the coverage adequate? Do voters receive sufficient information from the news media to make an intelligent decision? Many believe they do not. Academics, especially, have urged that greater attention be paid to policy issues and less to the game format of who is ahead, most likely to win, and why. One proposal would have the networks and wire services assign special correspondents to cover the issues of the campaign, much as they assign people to report on its color, drama, and personal aspects. Another would be to place greater emphasis on campaign coverage itself and assess the accuracy of the statements and advertising claims of the candidates as some newspapers, such as the *Washington Post* and the *New York Times,* and major television networks have begun to do already.

In addition to criticizing the news media's treatment of the issues and its watchdog function in the campaign, academics and others have frequently called into question the amount and accuracy of election reporting. The law states that if the networks provide free time to some candidates, they must provide equal time to all running for the same position, including those of fringe parties. This "equal time" provision has in fact resulted in no or little free time, although coverage of debates between candidates for their party's nomination and later, between candidates of the major parties in the general election, is permitted. Networks are also required to be impartial in their coverage. Station licenses can be challenged and even revoked if biases are consistently evident in the presentation of the news.

Other than requiring fairness, preventing obscenity, and ensuring that public service commitments are met, there is little the government can do to ensure adequate coverage without impinging on the freedom of the press. The news media are free to choose which elections and candidates to emphasize, what kind and how much coverage to provide, how to interpret the results of primaries and caucuses, and even to predict who will win before the election is concluded.

There is much that candidates can do, however, to affect the coverage they receive. If their words are unreported or not reported correctly, or if their ideas are misinterpreted or their motives suspected by the national news, they can seek other mass media formats for reaching the general public as they did in 1992 by using the entertainment and talk shows. They can also employ satellite technology to reach local and regional audiences directly and thereby circumvent the national press. And they can agree to other "competitive" formats that will get national coverage because they fit into the game motif that the news media use.

Another media-related issue is the election-night projections based on exit polling data that the networks air before all voting has been completed. Since 1964, when a Lyndon Johnson landslide was predicted before the polls on the West Coast had closed, proposals have been advanced to limit or prohibit these glimpses into the immediate future. Beginning in 1984, the networks promised not to predict the outcome in any one state until a majority of its polls had closed. This voluntary restriction, however, did not rectify the problem of having different time zones in the United

States. This was addressed in 1992 when the networks and wire services voluntarily refrained from making any national forecast until voting across the continental U.S. was completed.

Other proposals to deal with the election-night projection issue include one that would establish a uniform hour at which voting ends or another to terminate the current process entirely and replace it with a national system of mail ballots.[8] These proposals have also encountered criticism. Could the networks be expected to wait until voting ended across the nation, given the competitive character of news reporting? Even if there was a uniform closing hour for the entire country, there still would be no guarantee that early forecasts, based on exit polls, could be eliminated. Moreover, a law, such as the one the House of Representatives passed in 1989 that would have forced thirty-nine states to change their voting hours, reduces their constitutional prerogative to conduct elections for federal officials. Eight states, including California, would have had to reduce the hours during which people could vote, conceivably contributing to lower turnout. Other states, which would have had to increase their hours, would face additional costs. And the proposal for a mail ballot would be expensive, time-consuming, and potentially more subject to fraud.

In addition to the obvious First Amendment problems that would be generated by restriction on what and when the news could report about the election, there is another more general media-related issue. People enjoy the election night broadcasts. After a lengthy campaign, workers and sympathizers are eager to learn the results and to celebrate or commiserate, whereas the public desires the ritualistic conclusion that the reporting and analysis of the results on election night provide. Moreover, exit polls have considerable value in the information they provide about the beliefs, attitudes, and motivations of the voters. In a democracy, it is essential to get as clear a reading of the pulse of the electorate as possible.

ENHANCING ELECTORAL CHOICE

Turnout

Although suffrage has expanded, a gap remains between those eligible to vote and those who actually do so. This gap, which will always exist in a system that does not compel voting, widened during the period from 1960 to 1988. It narrowed in 1992, but still only 55 percent of those eligible voted in that year's election.

The decline in the intensity of partisan allegiances, the shift from party-centered to candidate-centered campaigns, the growing levels of mistrust and lower confidence in public officials, and the weakening sense of efficacy on the part of many people have all contributed to lower turnout and produced a "disconnect" between American citizens and their political system. That disconnect threatens to undermine the legitimacy of American electoral institutions.

Low turnout in a free and open electoral process has been a source of embarrassment to the United States and of concern to its political leaders. How can a president legitimately claim a public mandate with the electoral support of so few of those who are eligible to vote? In his *substantial* electoral victory in 1988 George Bush received the votes of only 27 percent of the eligible adult population; in 1992, Bill Clinton's winning percentage was even lower, a little less than 24 percent of the eligible voters. Can a government still claim to be representative if almost half the electorate chooses not to participate in elections for public officials?

A variety of legal, institutional, and political obstacles must be overcome if turnout is to increase. Congress addressed one of the problem areas in 1993. It enacted legislation to ease registration procedures. The motor-voter law requires all states to permit registration by mail or at the time a person obtains or renews a driver's license.[9] Registration materials are supposed to be made available at many state offices. The new law has, however, met with resistance in several states, which have openly challenged it on the grounds that it constitutes an unfunded mandate by the federal government. In this view Congress has imposed an additional and costly requirement without providing the funds to the states to pay for it. To compel implementation, however, the attorney general has filed suit against the recalcitrant states. In the absence of legislation that rescinds the law or appropriates money for it, it is likely that the courts will decide this highly contentious issue.

Other proposals to make registration automatic, as it is in many European countries, or extending it to election day itself, as is already permitted in a few states, have been advanced. Countries or states, which have facilitated registration in these ways, have considerably higher levels of turnout than those that do not. These proposals have not been enacted into national law because of fears that they may increase the potential for voting fraud, decrease the ability of states to monitor federal elections, and generally lessen the responsibilities of citizenry.

Additionally, there has been an underlying partisan registration issue. The Republicans believe that easing registration would benefit the Democrats because a larger proportion of those who are not registered are at the lower end of the socioeconomic scale. It is not coincidence that the states that have resisted implementation are those headed by Republican governors.

Another proposal to enhance turnout would make election day a national holiday. Presumably this change would prevent work-related activities from interfering with voting for the bulk of the population. Many countries follow this practice or hold their elections on Sunday. The problem here is that an additional national holiday would cost employers millions of dollars in lost revenue and productivity, with no guarantee that turnout would increase. For workers in certain service areas the holiday might be a workday anyway.

Perhaps the most radical proposal would be simply to compel people to vote: to force them to go to the polls and cast a ballot. Penalties would be imposed on those who refused to do so. Australia, Belgium, and Italy require voting, and their turnout is very high.

One obvious problem with forcing people to vote is the compulsion itself. Some may be physically or mentally incapable of voting. Others may not care, have little interest, and have very limited information. They might not even know the names of the candidates. Would the selection of the best-qualified person be enhanced by the participation of these uninformed, uninterested, uncaring voters? Might demagogy be encouraged, or even slicker and more simplistic advertising develop? Would government be more responsive and more popular, or would it be more prone to what British philosopher John Stuart Mill referred to as "the tyranny of the majority"? Finally, is it democratic to force people to vote? If the right to vote is an essential component of a democratic society, then what about the right not to vote? Should it be protected as well?

In addition to easing or removing legal obstacles or creating a legal requirement to vote, there have been other kinds of suggestions for encouraging more people to participate. One is to change the electoral system itself to provide more incentives for those in the minority to vote by increasing the likelihood that their vote would produce tangible results for them. Instituting proportional representation for Congress or in the apportionment of electoral votes could produce this effect; directly electing the president might also do so. In these cases those in the minority would have greater incentive to vote than they do under the current system. Winner-take-all voting, which occurs in single-member legislative districts and in most states in the Electoral College, discourages turnout in noncompetitive elections.

Systemic changes, however, are difficult to accomplish. They upset the established political order and are likely to generate opposition from those who fear change, are used to the current arrangement, or benefit the most from it. Moreover, reforming the electoral system in this manner would require a constitutional amendment, which is always more difficult than enacting legislation. As a consequence, these proposals are not likely to be implemented in the short run nor in the absence of other changes.

Creating a more hospitable and engaging electoral climate is another way to increase turnout. If parties were strengthened, if their organizations were more broad-based, if they encouraged more participatory politics by providing more information to voters and more grass roots activities, turnout would likely be enhanced. But revitalizing the parties has proved extremely difficult, particularly in the current antiparty era.

Moreover, changes in the nomination process have weakened, not strengthened party structures, although organizational control over money and other campaign resources has begun to reverse that effect.

We have already referred to another potential arena of change—the communications industry. If candidates had greater access to the media, if they were given free time in addition to the time they purchased, if there were more debates during prime time, if candidates appeared on more interactive programs and more general entertainment formats, then more of the public might be turned on and thus would turn out. Greater exposure, however, might also numb the electorate; entertainment formats often emphasize style over substance and might trivialize the campaign.

Educating the people on the merits of participating and the responsibilities of citizenry might also generate greater involvement. If the public better understood what difference it makes who wins, if they had greater confidence that elected officials would keep their promises and that government would address salient issues, then voter turnout would likely be enhanced. But invigorating the electoral environment and encouraging more people to participate is not an easy task. If it were, it would have already occurred. It is difficult to convince nonvoters to spend the time and effort it takes to educate themselves about the candidates and the issues, to get involved in the campaign, and to vote on election day.

If, however, more people did vote, the parties and candidates would have to broaden their appeal. They would have to address the needs and desires of all the people and not concentrate on those who were most likely to vote. Those who have not participated as frequently in the current voluntary system of voting—the poorer, less educated, less fortunate—would receive more attention not only from candidates for office but from elected officials in office. More equitable policies might result.

The Electoral College

In addition to the problem of who votes, another source of contention is how the votes should be aggregated. Theoretically, the Constitution allows electors chosen by the states to vote as they please. In practice, all votes are cast for the popular vote winner in the state. The reason for this outcome is simple. The vote for president and vice-president is actually a vote for competing slates of electors selected in all but two states on a statewide basis. The slate that wins is the slate proposed by the winning candidate's party. Naturally the electors are expected to vote for their party's nominees.

This de facto system has been criticized as undemocratic, as unrepresentative of minority views within states, and as potentially unreflective of the nation's popular choice. Over the years, there have been numerous proposals to alter it. The first was introduced in Congress in 1797. Since then, there have been more than five hundred others.

In urging changes, critics have pointed to the Electoral College's archaic design, its electoral biases, and the undemocratic results it can produce. (See Chapter 1.) In recent years, four major plans—automatic, proportional, district, and direct election—have been proposed as constitutional amendments to alleviate some or all of these problems. The following sections will examine these proposals and the impact they could have on the way in which the president is selected.

The automatic plan. The electors in the Electoral College have been an anachronism since the development of the party system. Their role as partisan agents is not and has not been consistent with their exercising an independent judgment. In fact, sixteen states plus the District of Columbia prohibit such a judgment by requiring electors to cast their ballots for the winner of the state's popular vote. Although probably unenforceable because they seem to clash with the Constitution, these laws strongly indicate how electors should vote.

The so-called automatic plan would do away with the danger that electors may exercise their personal preferences. First proposed in 1826, it has received substantial support since that time, including the backing of Presidents John Kennedy and Lyndon Johnson. The plan simply keeps the Electoral College intact but eliminates the electors. Electoral votes are automatically credited to the candidate who has received the most popular votes within the state.

Other than removing the potential problem of faithless or unpledged electors, the plan would do little to change the system. It has not been enacted because Congress has not felt this particular problem to be of sufficient magnitude to justify a constitutional amendment to fix it. There have in fact been only eight faithless electors, who failed to vote for their party's nominees—six since 1948.[10] Additionally, one Democratic West Virginia elector in 1988 reversed the order of the nominees, voting for Lloyd Bentsen for president and Michael Dukakis for vice-president.

The proportional plan. Electing the entire slate of presidential electors has also been the focus of considerable attention. If the winner of the state's popular vote takes all the electoral votes, the impact of the dominant party is increased within that state and the larger, more competitive states, where voters tend to be more evenly divided, are benefited.

From the perspective of the other major party and minor parties within the state as well as independent candidates such as Ross Perot, this winner-take-all system is not desirable. In effect, it disenfranchises people who do not vote for the winning candidate. And it does more than that: it discourages a strong campaign effort by a party that has little chance of winning the presidential election in that state. Naturally the success of other candidates of that party is affected as well. The winner-take-all system also works to reduce voter turnout.

One way to rectify this problem would be to have proportional voting. Such a plan has been introduced on a number of occasions. Under a proportional system, the electors would be abolished, the winner-take-all principle would be eliminated, and a state's electoral vote would be divided in proportion to the popular vote the candidates received within the state. A majority of electoral votes would still be required for election. If no candidate obtained a majority in the Electoral College, most proportional plans call for a joint session of Congress to choose the president from among the top two or three candidates.

The proportional proposal would have a number of major consequences. It would decrease the influence of the most competitive states and increase the importance of the least competitive ones, where voters are likely to be more homogeneous. Under such a system, the *size* of the victory would count.

By rewarding large victories in relatively homogeneous states, the system would seem to encourage competition within those states. Having the electoral vote proportional to the popular vote provides an incentive to all the parties, not simply the dominant one, to mount a more vigorous campaign and to establish a more effective organization. This incentive could strengthen the other major party within the state, but it might also help third parties as well, thereby weakening the two-party system. Ross Perot, who received no electoral votes under the present winner-take-all system, would have received approximately 102 under the proportional plan. More importantly, Bill Clinton would not have received a majority if electoral votes were distributed according to the proportion of the vote candidates received in individual states. Under these circumstances, third party candidates such as Perot might have the power to decide the election between the major party candidates by instructing their delegates to support one of them.

If no candidate receives a majority of the electoral votes as would have occurred in 1992 had Perot's electors voted for him, the House of Representatives would probably have chosen Bill Clinton that year because the Democrats controlled a majority of the state delegations in the House at that time. Selection by the House, however, weakens a president's national mandate, might make the president more dependent on the House or might require promises or favors to legislators whose support was critical for victory, and in general, could decrease presidential influence in the initial period of an administration.

Operating under a proportional plan would in all likelihood make the Electoral College vote much closer, thereby reducing the claim most presidents wish to make that they have received broad public backing for themselves, their new administration, and the policy proposals they have advocated during their campaign. George Bush would have defeated Michael Dukakis by only 43.1 electoral votes in 1988, Jimmy Carter would have defeated Gerald Ford by only 11.7 in 1976, and Richard Nixon would have won by only 6.1 in 1968. (See Table 9–1.) And in at least one recent instance, a proportional electoral vote in the states might have changed the election results. Had this plan been in effect in 1960, Richard Nixon would probably have defeated John Kennedy by 266.1 to 265.6.[11]

The district plan. The district electoral system is another proposal aimed at reducing the effect of winner-take-all voting. This plan has had several variations, but its basic thrust would be to keep the Electoral College but to change the manner in which the electoral votes within the state are determined. Instead of selecting the entire slate on the basis of the statewide vote for president, only two electoral votes would be decided in this manner. The remaining votes would be allocated on the basis of the popular vote within individual districts (probably congressional districts). A majority of the electoral votes would still be necessary for election. If the vote in the Electoral College were not decisive, then most district plans call for a joint session of Congress to make the final selection.

For the very smallest states, those with three electoral votes, all three electors would have to be chosen by the state as a whole. For others, however, the combination of district and at-large selection would probably result in a split electoral vote. On a national level, this change would make the Electoral College more reflective of the partisan division of the newly elected Congress rather than of the popular division of the national electorate.

The losers under such an arrangement would be the large, competitive states and, most particularly, the cohesive, geographically concentrated groups within those states. The winners would include small states. Third and minor parties, especially those that are regionally based, might also be aided to the extent that they were capable of winning specific legislative districts. It is difficult to project whether Republicans or Democrats would benefit more from such an arrangement, since much would depend on how the legislative districts within the states were apportioned. If the 1960 presidential vote were aggregated on the basis of one electoral vote to the popular vote winner of each congressional district and two to the popular vote winner of each state, Nixon would have defeated Kennedy 278 to 245, with 14 unpledged electors. In 1976, the district system would have produced a tie, with Carter and Ford each receiving 269 votes. In 1992, Clinton would have beat Bush 324 to 214. (See Table 9–1.) The states of Maine and Nebraska are the only ones that presently choose their electors in this manner.

The direct election plan. Of all the plans to alter or replace the Electoral College, the direct popular vote has received the most attention and support. Designed to eliminate the College entirely and count the votes on a nationwide basis, it would elect the popular vote winner provided the winning candidate received a certain percentage of the total vote. In most plans,

TABLE 9–1

Voting for President, 1952–1992:
Four Methods for Aggregating the Votes

Year	Electoral College	Proportional Plan	District Plan	Direct Election (percentage of total votes)
1952				
Eisenhower	442	288.5	375	55.1
Stevenson	89	239.8	156	44.4
Others	0	2.7	0	0.5
1956				
Eisenhower	457	296.7	411	57.4
Stevenson	73	227.2	120	42.0
Others	1	7.1	0	0.6
1960				
Nixon	219	266.1	278	49.5
Kennedy	303	265.6	245	49.8
Others (Byrd)	15	5.3	14	0.7
1964				
Goldwater	52	213.6	72	38.5
Johnson	486	320.0	466	61.0
Others	0	3.9	0	0.5
1968				
Nixon	301	231.5	289	43.2
Humphrey	191	225.4	192	42.7
Wallace	46	78.8	57	13.5
Others	0	2.3	0	0.6
1972				
Nixon	520	330.3	474	60.7
McGovern	17	197.5	64	37.5
Others	1	10.0	0	1.8
1976				
Ford	240	258.0	269	48.0
Carter	297	269.7	269	50.1
Others	1	10.2	0	1.9
1980				
Reagan	489	272.9	396	50.7
Carter	49	220.9	142	41.0
Anderson	0	35.3	0	6.6
Others	0	8.9	0	1.7
1984				
Reagan	525	317.6	468	58.8
Mondale	13	216.6	70	40.6
Others	0	3.8	0	0
1988				
Bush	426	287.8	379	53.4
Dukakis	111	244.7	159	45.6
Others	1	5.5	0	1.0
1992				
Bush	168	203.3	214	37.5
Clinton	370	231.6	324	43.0
Perot	0	101.8	0	18.9
Others	0	1.3	0	0.6

Source: Figures on proportional and district vote for 1952–1980 were supplied to the author by Joseph B. Gorman of the Congressional Research Service, Library of Congress. Calculations for subsequent elections were made on the basis of data reported in the *Almanac of American Politics* (Washington, D.C.: National Journal. annual) and Federal Election Commission.

40 percent of the total vote would be necessary. In some, 50 percent would be required.[12] In the event that no one got the required percentage, a runoff between the top two candidates would be held to determine the winner.[13]

A direct popular vote would, of course, remedy a major problem of the present system—the possibility of electing a nonplurality president. It would better equalize voting power both among and within the states. The large, competitive states would lose some of their electoral clout by the elimination of the winner-take-all system. Party competition within the states and perhaps even nationwide would be increased. Turnout should also improve. Every vote would count in a direct election.

A direct election, however, might also encourage minor parties, which would weaken the two-party system. The possibility of denying a major party candidate 40 percent of the popular vote might be sufficient to entice a proliferation of candidates and produce a series of bargains and deals in which support was traded for favors with a new administration. Moreover, it is possible that the plurality winner might not be geographically representative of the entire country. A very large sectional vote might elect a candidate who trailed in other areas of the country. This result would upset the representational balance that has been achieved between the president's and Congress's electoral constituencies.

The organized groups that are geographically concentrated in the large industrial states would have their votes diluted by a direct election. Take Jewish voters, for example. Highly supportive of the Democratic party since World War II, they constitute approximately 3 percent of the total population but 14 percent in New York, one of the largest states. Thus, the impact of the New York Jewish vote is magnified under the present Electoral College arrangement as is that of Hispanic voters in Florida, Texas, and California.[14]

The Republican party has also been reluctant to lend its support to direct election. Republicans perceive that they benefit from the current arrangement, which provides more safe Republican states than Democratic ones. Although Republican Benjamin Harrison was the last nonplurality president to be elected, Gerald Ford came remarkably close in 1976. On the other hand, Richard Nixon's Electoral College victory in 1968 could conceivably have been upset by a stronger Wallace campaign in the southern border states.

A very close popular vote could also cause problems in a direct election. The winner might not be evident for days, even months. Voter fraud could have national consequences. Under such circumstances, large-scale challenges by the losing candidate would be more likely and would necessitate national recounts rather than confining such recounts to individual states, as the current Electoral College system does.

The provision for the situation in which no one received the required percentage of the popular vote has its drawbacks as well. A runoff election would extend the length of the campaign and add to its cost.

Considering that some aspirants begin their quest for the presidency a year or more before the election, a further protraction of the process might unduly tax the patience of the voters and produce an even greater numbing effect than currently exists. Moreover, it would also cut an already short transition period for a newly elected president and would further drain the time and energy of an incumbent seeking reelection.

There is still another difficulty with a contingency election. It could reverse the order in which the candidates originally finished. This result might undermine the ability of the eventual winner to govern successfully. It might also encourage spoiler candidacies. Third parties and independents seeking the presidency could exercise considerable power in the event of a close contest between the major parties. Imagine what Perot's influence would have been in a runoff between Clinton and Bush in 1992.

Nonetheless, the direct election plan is supported by public opinion and has been ritualistically praised by contemporary presidents. Gallup Polls conducted over the last three decades have consistently found the public favoring a direct election over the present electoral system by substantial margins.[15] Former presidents Carter and Ford have both urged the abolition of the Electoral College and its replacement by a popular vote.

In 1969, the House of Representatives actually voted for a constitutional amendment to establish direct election for president and vice-president, but the Senate refused to go along. Despite public opinion, it seems unlikely that sufficient impetus for such a change that requires a constitutional amendment will occur until the issue becomes salient to more people. It may take the election of a nonplurality president or some other electoral crisis to produce the outcry and generate the momentum needed to change the Electoral College system.

Despite the complaints that are ritualistically voiced during the election period that the candidates are no good, that there is very little difference between them, and that the campaigns are negative, superficial, and irrelevant, the electorate has not demanded that its congressional representatives change the system beyond extending suffrage to all citizens. Similarly, the reforms in finance laws and party rules have been designed to achieve the democratic goals of encouraging more people to support the candidates and to participate in their campaigns. The electoral system may not be perfect, but it has functioned with public support for over 200 years, a significant achievement in itself. This achievement is cited by those who oppose changing it on the grounds that "if it ain't broke, it don't need fixing."

SUMMARY

There have been changes and continuities in the way we select a president. In general the changes have made the system more democratic. The continuities link the system to its republican past.

The nomination process has been affected more than the general election. Significant modifications have occurred in the rules for choosing delegates, in the laws regulating contributions and expenditures, and in the news media through which appeals are made and voters obtain most of their information about the campaign. The composition of the electorate has been altered as well. In contrast, the Electoral College has continued to function in much the same way for the last century and a half, although certainly not as the framers intended it to.

Have these changes been beneficial or harmful? Have they functioned to make the system more efficient, more responsive, and more likely to result in the choice of a well-qualified candidate? Politicians, journalists, and political scientists disagree in their answers.

Much of the current controversy over campaign reform has focused on party rules. Designed to encourage greater rank-and-file participation in the selection of delegates, the new rules have helped democratize presidential nominations. In the process, however, they have also fractionalized and personalized the parties, weakened the position of their leadership, and in the case of the Democrats in the 1980s, disadvantaged their presidential candidates in the general election. These unintended consequences have stimulated a debate over the merits of the reforms.

A consensus seems to be emerging that some of them have gone too far and that stronger party control over the nomination process is needed. The Democrats have tried to move in this direction, modifying some of their rules. Their imposition of straight proportional voting in 1992, however, has the potential of producing the opposite effect, factionalizing the party still further and thereby preventing or delaying agreement on the nominee until later in the process. The Republicans continue to allow their state parties to determine the rules by which their caucuses and primaries are conducted.

Despite the inclinations of Democratic leaders to retrench to control the undesirable effects of the nomination process, a majority of the electorate would go even further—but in the other direction. They would have more participatory democracy, not less. They would abolish the present patchwork of state caucuses and primaries and replace them with a single, national primary.

Campaign finance legislation has also been designed to improve accountability, equalize contributions, control spending, and provide public disclosure. This legislation has enhanced public information, but it has done so only by increasing the burden on candidate organizations to keep detailed records and submit frequent reports. The law has reduced the direct influence of large donors on the presidential campaign but has not eliminated their indirect influence through the soft money contributions and independent expenditures. It has also contributed to the factionalizing of parties, encouraging multiple candidacies for the nomination. By giving the bulk of federal funds directly to the candidates, it has encouraged the development of separate candidate organizations and provided incentives for political action committees. Whether the end result has been to lessen the advantage of wealth and effectively open the process to a much larger group of aspirants is debatable. No consensus on how to improve the law is apparent.

News media coverage has also been the subject of considerable controversy. Television has made more people aware of presidential candidates than in the past, but that awareness has also tended to be indirect and much more passive than interactive. The reporting of information about personalities and campaign events exceeds that of substantive policy issues. Television news, in particular, is often blamed for the average voter's low level of interest and knowledge and for exercising undue influence on the electorate.

Whether or not this accusation is accurate, it is widespread and has generated persistent criticism of the news media. Few changes are likely, however, in the short run because the public is less concerned about media coverage than are the candidates, and any nonvoluntary attempt to affect coverage is apt to run up against the protections of the First Amendment.

Who votes and how the votes should be aggregated continue to prompt debate and elicit concern. The expansion of suffrage has made the election process more democratic in theory, but the decline in turnout and lower rates of participation have called this theoretical improvement into question. Although the failure of almost one-half of the electorate to exercise the franchise has been a source of embarrassment and dismay, there is little agreement on how to deal with this problem in a federal system that values individual initiative and civic responsibility.

Finally, the equity of the Electoral College has also been challenged, but none of the proposals to alter or abolish it, except by the direct election of the president, has received much public support. With no outcry for change, Congress has been reluctant to alter the system by initiating an amendment to the Constitution and seems unlikely to do so until an electoral crisis or unpopular result forces its hand.

Does the electoral process work? Yes. Can it be improved? Of course. Will it be changed? Probably, but if the past is any indication, there is no guarantee that legally imposed changes will produce only, or even, the desired effect. If politics is the art of the possible, then success is achieved by those who can adjust most quickly to the legal and political environment and turn it to their advantage.

NOTES

1. Thomas E. Patterson, *Out of Order* (New York: Alfred A. Knopf, 1993), p. 210.
2. Ibid.
3. *Gallup Poll*, No. 226 (July 1984): 23.
4. It normally takes the Federal Election Commission more than two years to

complete an audit of the expenses and determine which of them may not have been in compliance of the law.

5. Federal Election Commission, "Record," February 1995, pp. 3–5.
6. Jeff Gerth, "Clinton Campaign Ordered to Repay U.S. More Than $1 Million." *New York Times* (December 16, 1994), p. A 34.
7. Federal Election Commission, p. 2.
8. To provide as long a voting day as possible in the West, one plan would extend Daylight-Savings Time in Pacific states until the Sunday following each presidential election but revert to Standard Time in the rest of the country. Under such a system, the polls would then remain open until 7:00 PM Pacific Daylight Time and 9:00 PM Eastern Standard Time.
9. The Federal Election Commission has designed a national form that can be used for mail registration by the states.
10. There is some controversy whether three other electors in 1796 might also have gone against their party when voting for president. They supported John Adams although they were selected in states controlled by the Democratic Republicans. However, the fluidity of the party system in those days, combined with the weakness of party identification, makes their affiliation (if any) hard to establish.
11. It is difficult to calculate the 1960 vote precisely because the names of the Democratic presidential and vice-presidential candidates were not on the ballot in Alabama and because an unpledged slate of electors was chosen in Mississippi.
12. Abraham Lincoln was the only plurality president who failed to attain the 40 percent figure. He received 39.82 percent in 1860, although he probably would have received more had his name been on the ballot in nine southern states.
13. Other direct election proposals have recommended that a joint session of Congress decided the winner. The runoff provision was contained in the resolution that passed the House of Representatives in 1969. A direct election plan with a runoff provision failed to win the two-thirds Senate vote required to initiate a constitutional amendment in 1979.
14. John Kennedy carried New York by approximately 384,000 votes. He received a plurality of more than 800,000 from precincts that were primarily Jewish. Similarly, in Illinois, a state he carried by less than 9,000, Kennedy had a plurality of 55,000 from the so-called Jewish precincts. Mark R. Levy and Michael S. Kramer, *The Ethnic Factor* (New York: Simon and Schuster, 1972), p. 104.
15. A 1980 Gallup Poll found 67 percent favoring direct election over the present system, with only 19 percent opposed and the rest undecided. In Gallup surveys dating back to 1966, similar majorities have supported direct election and the elimination of the Electoral College. George H. Gallup, *The Gallup Poll* (Wilmington, Del.: Scholarly Resources, 1981), pp. 258–260.

SELECTED READINGS

Alexander, Herbert E. and Anthony Corrado, *Financing the 1992 Election.* Armonk, N.Y.: M.E. Sharpe, 1995.

Best, Judith. *The Case Against Direct Election of the President: A Defense of the Electoral College.* Ithaca, N.Y.: Cornell University Press, 1975.

Caeser, James W. and Andrew Busch. *Upside Down and Inside Out: The 1992 Elections and American Politics.* Lanham, MD.: Rowman and Littlefield, 1993.

Heard, Alexander. *Made in America: The Nomination and Election of Presidents.* New York: Harper Collins, 1991.

Longley, Lawrence D., and Alan G. Braun. *The Politics of Electoral College Reform.* New Haven, Conn.: Yale University Press, 1975.

Peirce, Neal R., and Lawrence D. Longley. *The People's President.* New Haven, Conn.: Yale University Press, 1981.

Polsby, Nelson W. *Consequences of Party Reform.* New York: Oxford University Press, 1983.

Sundquist, James L. *Constitutional Reform.* Washington, D.C.: Brookings Institution, 1986.

PART V

Appendixes

Appendix A

Results of Presidential Elections, 1860–1992

| Year | Candidates | | Electoral Vote | | Popular Vote | |
	Democrat	Republican	Democrat	Republican	Democrat	Republican
1860*	Stephen A. Douglas Herschel V. Johnson	Abraham Lincoln Hannibal Hamlin	12 4%	180 59%	1,380,202 29.5%	1,865,908 39.8%
1864†	George B. McClellan George H. Pendleton	Abraham Lincoln Andrew Johnson	21 9%	212 91%	1,812,807 45.0%	2,218,388 55.0%
1868‡	Horatio Seymour Francis P. Blair Jr.	Ulysses S. Grant Schuyler Colfax	80 27%	214 73%	2,708,744 47.3%	3,013,650 52.7%
1872§	Horace Greeley Benjamin Gratz Brown	Ulysses S. Grant Henry Wilson		286 78%	2,834,761 43.8%	3,598,235 55.6%
1876	Samuel J. Tilden Thomas A. Hendricks	Rutherford B. Hayes William A. Wheeler	184 50%	185 50%	4,288,546 51.0%	4,034,311 47.9%
1880	Winfield S. Hancock William H. English	James A. Garfield Chester A. Arthur	155 42%	214 58%	4,444,260 48.2%	4,446,158 48.3%
1884	Grover Cleveland Thomas A. Hendricks	James G. Blaine John A. Logan	219 55%	182 45%	4,874,621 48.5%	4,848,936 48.2%
1888	Grover Cleveland Allen G. Thurman	Benjamin Harrison Levi P. Morton	168 42%	233 58%	5,534,488 48.6%	5,443,892 47.8%
1892¶	Grover Cleveland Adlai E. Stevenson	Benjamin Harrison Whitelaw Reid	277 62%	145 33%	5,551,883 46.1%	5,179,244 43.0%

Year	Candidate / Running mate	Candidate / Running mate	Electoral	Electoral	Popular	Popular
1896	William J. Bryan / Arthur Sewall	William McKinley / Garret A. Hobart	176 39%	271 61%	6,511,495 46.7%	7,108,480 51.0%
1900	William J. Bryan / Adlai E. Stevenson	William McKinley / Theodore Roosevelt	155 35%	292 65%	6,358,345 45.5%	7,218,039 51.7%
1904	Alton B. Parker / Henry G. Davis	Theodore Roosevelt / Charles W. Fairbanks	140 29%	336 71%	5,028,898 37.6%	7,626,593 56.4%
1908	William J. Bryan / John W. Kern	William H. Taft / James S. Sherman	162 34%	321 66%	6,406,801 43.0%	7,676,258 51.6%
1912**	Woodrow Wilson / Thomas R. Marshall	William H. Taft / James S. Sherman	435 82%	8 2%	6,293,152 41.8%	3,486,333 23.2%
1916	Woodrow Wilson / Thomas R. Marshall	Charles E. Hughes / Charles W. Fairbanks	277 52%	254 48%	9,126,300 49.2%	8,546,789 46.1%
1920	James M. Cox / Franklin D. Roosevelt	Warren G. Harding / Calvin Coolidge	127 24%	404 76%	9,140,884 34.2%	16,133,314 60.3%
1924††	John W. Davis / Charles W. Bryant	Calvin Coolidge / Charles G. Dawes	136 26%	382 72%	8,386,169 28.8%	15,717,553 54.1%
1928	Alfred E. Smith / Joseph T. Robinson	Herbert C. Hoover / Charles Curtis	87 16%	444 84%	15,000,185 40.8%	21,411,991 58.2%
1932	Franklin D. Roosevelt / John N. Garner	Herbert C. Hoover / Charles Curtis	472 89%	59 11%	22,825,016 57.4%	15,758,397 39.6%
1936	Franklin D. Roosevelt / John N. Garner	Alfred M. Landon / Frank Knox	523 98%	8 2%	27,747,636 60.8%	16,679,543 36.5%

Appendix A *(continued)*

Results of Presidential Elections, 1860–1992

Year	Candidates Democrat	Candidates Republican	Electoral Vote Democrat	Electoral Vote Republican	Popular Vote Democrat	Popular Vote Republican
1940	Franklin D. Roosevelt Henry A. Wallace	Wendell L. Wilkie Charles L. McNary	449 85%	82 15%	27,263,448 54.7%	22,336,260 44.8%
1944	Franklin D. Roosevelt Harry S Truman	Thomas E. Dewey John W. Bricker	432 81%	99 19%	25,611,936 53.4%	22,013,372 45.9%
1948‡‡	Harry S Truman Alben W. Barkley	Thomas E. Dewey Earl Warren	303 57%	189 36%	24,105,587 49.5%	21,970,017 45.1%
1952	Adlai E. Stevenson John J. Sparkman	Dwight D. Eisenhower Richard M. Nixon	89 17%	442 83%	27,314,649 44.4%	33,936,137 55.1%
1956§§	Adlai E. Stevenson Estes Kefauver	Dwight D. Eisenhower Richard M. Nixon	73 14%	457 86%	26,030,172 42.0%	35,585,245 57.4%
1960¶¶	John F. Kennedy Lyndon B. Johnson	Richard M. Nixon Henry Cabot Lodge	303 56%	219 41%	34,221,344 49.8%	34,106,671 49.5%
1964	Lyndon B. Johnson Hubert H. Humphrey	Barry Goldwater William E. Miller	486 90%	52 10%	43,126,584 61.0%	27,177,838 38.5%
1968***	Hubert H. Humphrey Edmund S. Muskie	Richard M. Nixon Spiro T. Agnew	191 36%	301 56%	31,274,503 42.7%	31,785,148 43.2%
1972†††	George McGovern Sargent Shriver	Richard M. Nixon Spiro T. Agnew	17 3%	520 97%	29,171,791 37.5%	47,170,179 60.7%

Year	Candidates	Electoral Vote	%	Popular Vote	%
1976##	Jimmy Carter / Walter F. Mondale	297	55%	40,828,657	50.1%
	Gerald R. Ford / Robert Dole	240	45%	39,145,520	48.0%
1980	Jimmy Carter / Walter F. Mondale	49	10%	35,483,820	41.0%
	Ronald Reagan / George Bush	489	90%	43,901,812	50.7%
1984	Walter F. Mondale / Geraldine Ferraro	13	2%	37,577,137	40.6%
	Ronald Reagan / George Bush	525	98%	54,455,074	58.8%
1988§§§	Michael S. Dukakis / Lloyd Bentsen	111	21%	41,809,074	45.6%
	George Bush / Dan Quayle	426	79%	48,886,097	53.4%
1992¶¶¶	Bill Clinton / Al Gore	370	69%	44,909,889	43.0%
	George Bush / Dan Quayle	168	31%	39,104,545	37.5%

* 1860; John C. Breckinridge, Southern Democrat, polled 72 electoral votes; John Bell, Constitutional Union, polled 39 electoral votes.

† 1864; 81 electoral votes were not cast.

‡ 1868; 23 electoral votes were not cast.

§ 1872; Horace Greeley died after election, 63 Democratic electoral votes were scattered. 17 were not voted.

¶ 1892; James B. Weaver, People's party, polled 22 electoral votes.

** 1912; Theodore Roosevelt, Progressive party, polled 88 electoral votes.

†† 1924; Robert M. LaFollette, Progressive party, polled 13 electoral votes.

‡‡ 1948; J. Strom Thurmond, States' Rights party, polled 39 electoral votes.

§§ 1956; Walter B. Jones, Democrat, polled 1 electoral vote.

¶¶ 1960; Harry Flood Byrd, Democrat, polled 15 electoral votes.

*** 1968; George C. Wallace, American independent, polled 46 electoral votes.

††† 1972; John Hospers, Libertarian party, polled 1 electoral vote.

‡‡ 1976; Ronald Reagan, Republican, polled 1 electoral vote.

§§§ 1988; Lloyd Bentsen, the Democratic vice-presidential nominee, polled 1 electoral vote for president.

¶¶¶ 1992; H. Ross Perot received 19,742,267 popular votes (18.9%) but no electoral votes.

Source: Congress and the Nation (Washington D.C.: *The Congressional Quarterly*, 1985), Vol. VI, pp. 1090–1091, updated by the author. Copyrighted material reprinted with permission of Congressional Quarterly Inc.

Appendix B

1992 Electoral and Popular Vote Summary

State	Electoral Vote Bush	Electoral Vote Clinton	Bush	%*	Clinton	%	Perot	%	Total Popular Vote
AL	9		804,283	47.6	690,080	40.9	183,109	10.9	1,688,060
AK	3		102,000	39.5	78,294	30.2	73,481	28.4	258,506
AZ	8		572,086	38.5	543,050	36.5	353,741	23.8	1,486,975
AR		6	337,324	35.5	505,823	53.2	99,132	10.4	950,653
CA		54	3,630,574	32.6	5,121,325	46.0	2,296,006	20.6	11,131,721
CO		8	562,850	35.9	629,681	40.1	366,010	23.3	1,569,180
CT		8	578,313	35.8	682,318	42.2	348,771	21.6	1,616,332
DC		3	20,698	09.1	192,619	84.6	9,681	04.3	227,572
DE		3	102,313	35.3	126,055	43.5	59,213	20.4	289,735
FL	25		2,173,310	40.9	2,072,798	39.0	1,053,067	19.8	5,314,492
GA		13	995,252	42.9	1,008,966	43.5	309,657	13.3	2,321,125
HI		4	136,822	36.7	179,310	48.1	53,003	14.2	372,842
ID	4		202,645	42.0	137,013	28.4	130,395	27.0	482,142
IL		22	1,734,096	34.3	2,453,350	48.6	840,515	16.6	5,050,157
IN	12		989,375	42.9	848,420	36.8	455,934	19.8	2,305,871
IA		7	504,891	37.2	586,353	43.3	253,468	18.7	1,354,607
KS	6		449,951	38.9	390,434	33.7	312,358	27.0	1,157,236
KY		8	617,178	41.3	665,104	44.6	203,944	13.7	1,492,900
LA		9	733,386	41.0	815,971	45.6	211,478	11.8	1,790,017
ME		4	206,504	30.4	263,420	38.8	206,820	30.4	679,499
MD		10	707,094	35.6	988,571	49.8	281,414	14.2	1,985,046
MA		12	805,039	29.0	1,318,639	47.5	630,731	22.7	2,773,664
MI		18	1,554,940	36.4	1,871,182	43.8	824,813	19.3	4,274,673
MN		10	747,841	31.9	1,020,997	43.5	562,506	24.0	2,347,947
MS	7		487,793	49.7	400,258	40.8	85,626	08.7	981,793
MO		11	811,159	33.9	1,053,873	44.1	518,741	21.7	2,391,565

State	Electoral Vote		%	Vote	%	Vote	%	Vote	Total
MT		3	35.1	144,207	37.6	154,507	26.1	107,225	410,611
NE	5		46.6	344,346	29.4	217,344	23.6	174,687	739,283
NV		4	34.7	175,828	37.4	189,148	26.2	132,580	506,318
NH		4	37.6	202,484	38.9	209,040	22.6	121,337	537,945
NJ		15	40.6	1,356,865	43.0	1,436,206	15.6	521,829	3,343,594
NM		5	37.3	212,824	45.9	261,617	16.1	91,895	569,968
NY		33	33.9	2,346,649	49.7	3,444,450	15.8	1,090,721	6,926,933
NC	14		43.4	1,134,661	42.7	1,114,042	13.7	357,864	2,611,850
ND	3		44.2	136,244	32.2	99,168	23.1	71,084	308,133
OH		21	38.4	1,894,310	40.2	1,984,942	21.0	1,036,426	4,939,964
OK	8		42.6	592,929	34.0	473,066	23.0	319,878	1,390,359
OR		7	32.5	475,757	42.5	621,314	24.2	534,091	1,462,643
PA		23	36.1	1,791,841	45.2	2,239,164	18.2	902,667	4,959,810
RI		4	29.0	131,605	47.0	213,302	23.2	105,051	453,478
SC	8		48.0	577,507	39.9	479,514	11.6	138,872	1,202,527
SD	3		40.7	136,718	37.1	124,888	21.8	73,295	336,254
TN		11	42.4	841,300	47.1	933,521	10.1	199,968	1,982,638
TX	32		40.6	2,496,071	37.1	2,281,815	22.0	1,354,781	6,154,018
UT	5		43.4	322,632	24.7	183,429	27.3	203,400	743,999
VT		3	30.4	88,122	46.1	133,592	22.8	65,991	289,701
VA	13		45.0	1,150,517	41.0	1,038,650	13.6	348,639	2,558,665
WA		11	32.0	731,235	43.4	993,039	23.7	541,801	2,288,228
WV		5	35.4	241,974	48.4	331,001	15.9	108,829	683,711
WI		11	36.8	930,855	41.1	1,041,066	21.5	544,479	2,531,114
WY	3		39.6	79,347	34.0	68,160	25.6	51,263	200,587
Total:	168	370		39,104,545		44,909,889		19,742,267	104,426,659

Note: The total electoral vote was 538. The total electoral vote needed to win was 270.

*Remaining percentages to other ballot candidates or write-in vote.

Source: Federal Election Commission, *Federal Elections 1992* (Washingtion D.C.: Federal Election Commission, 1993), pp. 9–32.

Appendix C

1992 Electoral Vote Distribution

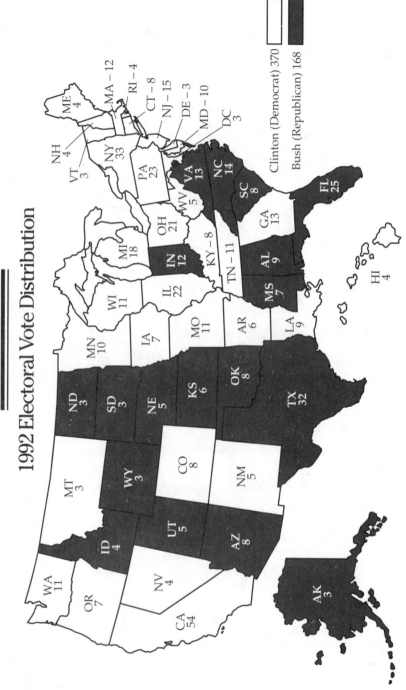

Clinton (Democrat) 370

Bush (Republican) 168

MA – 12
RI – 4
CT – 8
NJ – 15
DE – 3
MD – 10
DC
3

ME
4

NH
4

VT
3

NY
33

PA
23

VA
13

WV
5

NC
14

SC
8

FL
25

OH
21

KY – 8

TN – 11

GA
13

AL
9

MS
7

HI
4

MI
18

IN
12

IL
22

WI
11

MO
11

AR
6

LA
9

MN
10

IA
7

ND
3

SD
3

NE
5

KS
6

OK
8

TX
32

MT
3

WY
3

CO
8

NM
5

UT
5

ID
4

AZ
8

WA
11

OR
7

NV
4

CA
54

AK
3

Appendix D

Tentative 1996 Primary and Caucus Schedule*

Republicans	Date	State	Democrats
25 Caucus	2/12	Iowa	48 Caucus
16 Primary	2/20	New Hampshire	20 Primary
12 Primary	2/24	Delaware	14 Primary
39 Primary	2/27	Arizona	
18 Primary		North Dakota	
18 Primary		South Dakota	15 Primary
37 Primary	3/2	South Carolina	
	3/5	American Samoa	3 Caucus
26 Caucus /Primary		Colorado	49 Primary
27 Primary		Connecticut	53 Primary
42 Primary		Georgia	76 Primary
		Idaho	18 Caucus
32 Primary		Maryland	68 Primary
33 Caucus		Minnesota	76 Caucus
12 Primary		Vermont	
		Washington	74 Caucus
	3/7	Missouri	76 Caucus
102 Primary		New York	244 Primary
	3/7–3/21	North Dakota	14 Caucus
	3/9	Arizona	44 Caucus
		South Carolina	43 Primary
	3/9–3/11	Democrats Abroad	7 Caucus
	3/10	Nevada	18 Caucus
98 Primary	3/12	Florida	152 Primary
		Hawaii	20 Caucus
27 Primary		Louisiana	59 Caucus
		Maine	23 Primary
37 Primary		Massachusetts	93 Primary
32 Primary		Mississippi	38 Primary
38 Primary		Oklahoma	44 Primary
16 Primary		Rhode Island	22 Primary
37 Primary		Tennessee	68 Primary
123 Primary		Texas	194 Primary /Caucus
14 Primary	3/17	Puerto Rico	
69 Primary	3/19	Illinois	164 Primary
57 Primary		Michigan	128 Primary
67 Primary		Ohio	147 Primary
36 Primary		Wisconsin	79 Primary
	3/23	Wyoming	13 Caucus
	3/25	Utah	24 Caucus
163 Primary	3/26	California	363 Primary
		Vermont	15 Caucus
	3/30	US Virgin Islands	3 Caucus
31 Primary	4/2	Kansas	36 Caucus

Appendix D *(continued)*

Tentative 1996 Primary and Caucus Schedule[*]

Republicans	Date	State	Democrats
	4/4	Alaska	13 Caucus
	4/7	Puerto Rico	51 Primary
	4/13	Virginia	79 Caucus
73 Primary	4/23	Pennsylvania	167 Primary
19 Convention	4/26	Alaska	
14 Caucus	5/2	Nevada	
15 Caucus	5/3	Maine	
20 Caucus	5/4	Wyoming	
	5/5	Guam	3 Caucus
14 Primary	5/7	District of Columbia	17 Primary
52 Primary		Indiana	74 Primary
58 Primary		North Carolina	84 Primary
24 Primary	5/14	Nebraska	25 Primary
18 Primary		West Virginia	30 Primary
20 Primary	5/21	Arkansas	
23 Primary		Oregon	47 Primary
	5/28	Arkansas	36 Primary
23 Primary		Idaho	
26 Primary		Kentucky	51 Primary
36 Primary		Washington	
39 Primary	6/4	Alabama	54 Primary
14 Primary		Montana	16 Primary
48 Primary		New Jersey	104 Primary
18 Primary		New Mexico	25 Primary

Dates not yet determined.

4		American Samoa	
4		Guam	
14 Caucus		Hawaii (March)	
35 Caucus		Missouri	
14 Caucus		Nevada	
4 Caucus		US Virgin Islands	
28 Convention		Utah (May)	
53 Caucus		Virginia (March/April)	

[*]Changes are anticipated in this preliminary schedule. Louisiana is challenging Iowa with plans to hold the first Republican caucus on February 6, 1996. Since Iowa's law designates that its caucuses will be held a week before any others, Iowa is likely to move its caucus to the end of January if Louisiana goes ahead with its plan for an early February date. Similarly, Delaware continues to vie New Hampshire for an early primary date. New Hampshire law requires that a contest be held on a Tuesday, at least one week before any other primary. Thus, if Delaware stays with its February 24th date, New Hampshire will move its primary one week earlier to February 13th.

There is a good chance that the New England states of Maine, Massachusetts, Rhode Island and Connecticut will each agree to move their primaries to March 5th, thereby joining Vermont for a northeast regional primary. Similarly Pennsylvania seems likely to join four midwestern states who plan to hold their contests on March 19th. Others that may move their contests forward include Minnesota, Washington, and possibly Oregon.

Source: Jamers A. Barnes, "Campaign Overload," *National Journal,* (May 13, 1995), p. 1159.

Acknowledgments *(continued from p. iv)*

Table 2–4: "Estimated Soft Money Expenditures, 1980–1992" from Herbert E. Alexander and Anthony Corrado, *Financing the 1992 Election* (Armond, New York: M. E. Sharpe, 1995), table 5–1. Copyright © 1995 by M. E. Sharpe, Inc. Reprinted with the permission of the publishers.

Table 2–6: "Campaign Costs Then and Now," *New York Times,* (March 3, 1992): A20. Copyright © 1992 by The New York Times Company. Reprinted with the permission of the *New York Times.*

Table 3–4: "Vote by Groups in Presidential Elections , 1952–1992 (in percentages) from Gallup Poll Index (November 1992): 9. Reprinted with the permission of The Gallup Organization.

Table 4–3: "The Democratic Primary Electorate," *New York Times,* (July 12, 1992): 18. Copyright © 1992 by The New York Times Company. Reprinted with the permission of the *New York Times.*

Page 115: Herblock cartoon. Copyright © 1988 by Herblock in the *Washington Post.*

Page 116: George Bush letter. Reprinted with the permission of George Bush.

Page 117: Various quotes from Charles R. Royer, ed., *Campaign for President: The Managers Look at '92* (Hollis, NH: Hollis Publishing Company, 1994). Copyright © 1994 by the Institute of Politics, Harvard University. Reprinted with permission.

Figure 4–1: "Amount of Coverage 1988 vs. 1992" from "The Parties Pick Their Candidates," *Media Monitor* VI (March 1992): 2. *Media Monitor* is published by the Center for Media and Public Affairs, a nonpartisan and nonprofit research organization. Reprinted with the permission of Center for Media and Public Affairs.

Box 4–3: "Pre-New Hampshire Television Advertisement" (1) Elizabeth Kolbert, "Kerry: Promoting Vision and Courage" (page A22) (2) Karen De Witt, "Brown: Capitalizing on 'Outsider' Role" (page A20), (3) "Tsongas: Disdain for Rivals' Plans" (page A21), and (4) Gwen Ifill, "Clinton: The Personal Approach" (page A22) all from the *New York Times* (February 11, 1992). Copyright © 1992 by the New York Times Company. Reprinted with the permission of the *New York Times.*

Box 4–4: "Negative Democratic Advertising" (1) Bruce Weber, "Brown: Countering the Image of 'Flakiness'" (page A15) and (2) Elizabeth Kolbert, "Clinton: Taking Aim at Brown" (page A16), both from the *New York Times* (March 29,1992). Copyright © 1992 by The New York Times Company. Reprinted with the permission of the *New York Times.*

Box 4–5: "Negative Republican Advertising" from "30-Second Politics," the *Washington Post* (March 14, 1992): A12. Copyright © 1992 by The Washington Post. Reprinted with the permission of the publishers.

Table 5–1: "Delegate Votes at Nominating Conventions, 1940–1996" from Richard C. Bain and Judith H. Parris, *Convention Decisions and Voting Records, Second Edition* (Washington D.C.: Brookings Institution, 1973), Appendix C, updated by author. Copyright © 1973 by The Brookings Institution. Reprinted with the permission of the publishers.

Box 5–2: "Contrasts in the Party Platforms." Republican Party Platform as printed in the *New York Times* (August 18, 1992): A10. Copyright © 1992 by The New York Times Company. Reprinted with the permission of the *New York Times.* Democratic Party Platform as printed in *Congressional Quarterly* (July 4, 1992): 59–67. Copyright © 1992 by Congressional Quarterly, Inc. Reprinted with the permission of the publishers.

Table 5–2: "Republican Party Conventions and Nominees, 1900–1996." Updated from *National Party Conventions, 1831–72,* p. 8–9. Copyright © 1976 by Congressional Quarterly, Inc. Reprinted with the permission of the publishers.

Table 5–3: "Democratic Party Conventions and Nominees, 1900–1996." Updated from *National Party Conventions, 1831–72,* p. 8–9. Copyright © 1976 by Congressional Quarterly, Inc. Reprinted with the permission of the publishers.

Figure 5–1: "Combined Average Ratings for ABC, CBS, and NBC for Convention Coverage" as it appears in Wendy Zeligson Adler, "The Conventions on Prime Times" in *The Homestretch: New Politics, New Media, New Voters?* (New York: Freedom Forum Media

Studies Center, 1992). Reprinted with the permission of Freedom Forum Media Studies Center at Columbia University in New York.

Page 176: Quotes from Howard Kurtz, "Brush Fires in the Forest of Newsmakers," the *Washington Post* (July 14, 1992): A18. Copyright © 1992 by The Washington Post. Reprinted with the permission of the publishers.

Table 5–4: "Impact of Conventions on Candidate Popularity, 1992," *The Gallup Poll Monthly* (August 1992): 25. Reprinted with the permission of The Gallup Organization.

Page 198: Fred Steeper quotes. Reprinted with the permission of the Republican National Committee.

Table 7–1: "Election Topics on the News" from "Clinton's the One," *Media Monitor* (November 1992): 3. *Media Monitor* is published by the Center for Media and Public Affairs, a nonpartisan and nonprofit research organization. Reprinted with the permission of Center for Media and Public Affairs.

Box 7–1: Excerpts from *Quest for the Presidency: 1992*, edited by Peter Goldman, et al. (College Station, Texas: Texas A & M University Press, 1994). Copyright © 1994 by Newsweek, Inc., and Texas A & M University Press. Reprinted with permission. "Debate Questions and Answers Memorandum to Clinton" from "Memorandum to Governor Clinton" from Paul Begala and Mike Donilon. Reprinted from *Quest for the Presidency: 1992*, edited by Peter Goldman, et al. (College Station, Texas: Texas A & M University Press, 1994). Copyright © 1994 by Newsweek, Inc., and Texas A & M University Press. Reprinted with permission.

Box 7–2: "The Willie Horton Ad: ''Weekend Passes'" from the *New York Times*, "A 30-Second Ad on Crime" (November 3, 1988): B20. Copyright © 1988 by The New York Times Company. Reprinted with the permission of the *New York Times*.

Table 7–2: "Public Use of Media to Follow Presidential Campaigns, 1952–1992" from Harold W. Stanley and Richard G. Niemi, *Vital Statistics on American Politics*, p. 72–73. Copyright © 1994 by Congressional Quarterly, Inc. Reprinted with the permission of the publishers.

Table 7–4: "Public Support Before, During, and After the 1992 Debates" based on *The Gallup Poll Monthly* (September and October 1992). Reprinted with the permission of The Gallup Organization.

Figure 7–1: "Percent of Negative Televised Presidential Advertisements—1960–1992" from Lynda Lee Kaid and Anne Johnston, "Negative versus Positive Television Advertising in U.S. Presidential Campaigns, 1960–1988," *Journal of Communication* 43, no. 3 (Summer 1991): 57. Copyright © 1991 by The Annenberg School of Communication. Reprinted with the permission of Oxford University Press Journals. Updated by author from data provided in L. Patrick Devlin, "Contrasts in Presidential Campaign Commercials of 1992," *American Behavioral Scientist* 37 (November 1993): 288. Copyright © 1993 by Sage Publications, Inc. Reprinted with the permission of the publishers.

Box 7–3: "Attack and Response: Bush and Clinton Ads in 1992" from Richard L. Berke, "Bush: TV Spot Harshly Denounces Clinton's Record" and "Clinton: Issuing a Quick Response" both from the *New York Times* (October 30, 1992): A19. Copyright © 1992 by The New York Times Company. Reprinted with the permission of the *New York Times*.

Table 8–1: "Final Preelection Polls and Results, 1948–1992 (in percentages)" from Final Gallup Poll, "Record of Gallup Poll Accuracy," *Gallup Poll Index* (December 1992). Reprinted with the permission of The Gallup Organization.

Table 8–2: "Portrait of the American Electorate, 1984–1992" including surveys from the *New York Times* (November 5, 1992): B9. Copyright © 1992 by The New York Times Company. Reprinted with the permission of the *New York Times*.

Appendix A: "Results of Presidential Elections, 1860–1992." Updated from *Congress and the Nation, Vol VI*, pp. 1090–1091. Copyright © 1985 by Congressional Quarterly, Inc. Reprinted with the permission of the publishers.

Index